T0332461

The Psychology of Cyber Crime:

Concepts and Principles

Gráinne Kirwan
Dun Laoghaire Institute of Art, Design and Technology, Ireland

Andrew Power
Dun Laoghaire Institute of Art, Design and Technology, Ireland

A volume in the Advances in Digital Crime, Forensics, and Cyber Terrorism (ADCFCT) Book Series

Information Science
REFERENCE

Managing Director:	Lindsay Johnston
Senior Editorial Director:	Heather Probst
Book Production Manager:	Sean Woznicki
Development Manager:	Joel Gamon
Development Editor:	Michael Killian
Acquisitions Editor:	Erika Gallagher
Typesetters:	Milan Vracarich Jr.
Print Coordinator:	Jamie Snavely
Cover Design:	Nick Newcomer

Published in the United States of America by
Information Science Reference (an imprint of IGI Global)
701 E. Chocolate Avenue
Hershey PA 17033
Tel: 717-533-8845
Fax: 717-533-8661
E-mail: cust@igi-global.com
Web site: http://www.igi-global.com

Library of Congress Cataloging-in-Publication Data

Kirwan, Grainne, 1978-
  The psychology of cyber crime: concepts and principles / by Grainne Kirwan
and Andrew Power.
       p. cm.
  Includes bibliographical references and index.
  Summary: "This book examines the psychology of cybercrime, considering many aspects of cybercrime, including research on offenders, legal issues, the impact of cybercrime on victims, punishment, and preventative measures"--
Provided by publisher.
  ISBN 978-1-61350-350-8 (hbk.) -- ISBN 978-1-61350-351-5 (ebook) -- ISBN 978-1-61350-352-2 (print & perpetual access) 1. Computer crimes--Psychological aspects. I. Power, Andrew, 1965- II. Title.
  HV6773.K57 2012
  364.3--dc23
                                    2011031997

This book is published in the IGI Global book series Advances in Digital Crime, Forensics, and Cyber Terrorism (ADCF-CT) Book Series (ISSN: 2327-0381; eISSN: 2327-0373)

British Cataloguing in Publication Data
A Cataloguing in Publication record for this book is available from the British Library.

Advances in Digital Crime, Forensics, and Cyber Terrorism (ADCFCT) Book Series

ISSN: 2327-0381
EISSN: 2327-0373

MISSION

The digital revolution has allowed for greater global connectivity and has improved the way we share and present information. With this new ease of communication and access also come many new challenges and threats as cyber crime and digital perpetrators are constantly developing new ways to attack systems and gain access to private information.

The **Advances in Digital Crime, Forensics, and Cyber Terrorism (ADCFCT) Book Series** seeks to publish the latest research in diverse fields pertaining to crime, warfare, terrorism and forensics in the digital sphere. By advancing research available in these fields, the **ADCFCT** aims to present researchers, academicians, and students with the most current available knowledge and assist security and law enforcement professionals with a better understanding of the current tools, applications, and methodologies being implemented and discussed in the field.

COVERAGE

- Computer Virology
- Cryptography
- Cyber Warfare
- Database Forensics
- Digital Crime
- Encryption
- Identity Theft
- Malware
- Telecommunications Fraud
- Watermarking

IGI Global is currently accepting manuscripts for publication within this series. To submit a proposal for a volume in this series, please contact our Acquisition Editors at Acquisitions@igi-global.com or visit: http://www.igi-global.com/publish/.

Titles in this Series

For a list of additional titles in this series, please visit: www.igi-global.com

The Psychology of Cyber Crime Concepts and Principles
Gráinne Kirwan (Dun Laoghaire Institute of Art, Design and Technology, Ireland) and Andrew Power (Dun Laoghaire Institute of Art, Design and Technology, Ireland)
Information Science Reference • copyright 2012 • 372pp • H/C (ISBN: 9781613503508) • US $195.00 (our price)

Cyber Crime and the Victimization of Women Laws, Rights and Regulations
Debarati Halder (Centre for Cyber Victim Counselling (CCVC), India) and K. Jaishankar (Manonmaniam Sundaranar University, India)
Information Science Reference • copyright 2012 • 264pp • H/C (ISBN: 9781609608309) • US $195.00 (our price)

Digital Forensics for the Health Sciences Applications in Practice and Research
Andriani Daskalaki (Max Planck Institute for Molecular Genetics, Germany)
Medical Information Science Reference • copyright 2011 • 418pp • H/C (ISBN: 9781609604837) • US $245.00 (our price)

Cyber Security, Cyber Crime and Cyber Forensics Applications and Perspectives
Raghu Santanam (Arizona State University, USA) M. Sethumadhavan (Amrita University, India) and Mohit Virendra (Brocade Communications Systems, USA)
Information Science Reference • copyright 2011 • 296pp • H/C (ISBN: 9781609601232) • US $180.00 (our price)

Handbook of Research on Computational Forensics, Digital Crime, and Investigation Methods and Solutions
Chang-Tsun Li (University of Warwick, UK)
Information Science Reference • copyright 2010 • 620pp • H/C (ISBN: 9781605668369) • US $295.00 (our price)

Homeland Security Preparedness and Information Systems Strategies for Managing Public Policy
Christopher G. Reddick (University of Texas at San Antonio, USA)
Information Science Reference • copyright 2010 • 274pp • H/C (ISBN: 9781605668345) • US $180.00 (our price)

DISSEMINATOR of KNOWLEDGE

www.igi-global.com

701 E. Chocolate Ave., Hershey, PA 17033
Order online at www.igi-global.com or call 717-533-8845 x100
To place a standing order for titles released in this series, contact: cust@igi-global.com
Mon-Fri 8:00 am - 5:00 pm (est) or fax 24 hours a day 717-533-8661

Table of Contents

Section 2
Internet-Specific Crimes

Section 3
Online Variations of Offline Crimes

Section 4
Crimes in Virtual Worlds

Detailed Table of Contents

Section 1
Introduction

Chapter 1

The objective of this chapter is to set the scene for the remainder of the book. The core of this book seeks to address both the theory of crime and the question of forensic psychology's contribution to the understanding of cybercrime. Specific examples of online crime such as hacking, malware, identity theft, child pornography and cyberbullying are dealt with in some detail in later chapters. Before exploring these subjects it is necessary to set out some context. The first section of this chapter seeks to define the nature of online crime or cybercrime and look at the ways in which society is responding to it. The nature of the response is multi-faceted. Governments attempt to respond with law, corporations with policies and procedures, suppliers with terms and conditions, users with peer pressure, technologists with code. The second section looks at how international laws have evolved through what are referred to as 'soft law' and seeks to draw lessons for the evolution of laws for the internet. The final section looks at the more general area of governance and also looks at how ideas of governance have evolved and how some of the theoretical work in this field may offer guidance for the governance of the internet.

Chapter 2

Considering the severity of the problem of cybercrime, it must next be deliberated whether forensic psychology can aid in the detection, prevention and governance of these crimes or not. While forensic psychology to date has generally focused on violent, sexual and juvenile offences, most of its theory and practice can also be applied to other offences, such as cybercrime. This chapter aims to investigate if forensic psychology can be useful in solving the problem of cybercrime, and briefly considers to what extent it has been applied to these crimes so far. Initially, definitions of forensic psychology will be discussed, and the primary responsibilities and activities of forensic psychologists will be described.

Following this the authors will examine how each of these responsibilities and activities may be applied to cybercrime cases, before determining to what extent forensic psychology has been involved in cyber-crime cases to date. Suggestions will be made for how to promote the benefits of forensic psychology in cybercrime cases, and finally proposals for future research and potential trends will be highlighted. In order to provide background to the reader who is not familiar with forensic psychology, a very brief overview of some of the key research in the field is provided in the appropriate sections below. However, the reader is encouraged to consult a textbook on the area in order to gain a more thorough appreciation of the breadth and depth of research in this field to date (see for example Davies, Hollin & Bull, 2008; Howitt, 2009 or Huss, 2009).

Chapter 3

Theories of crime have been an important part of criminological literature for many years. Different theories address the issue of crime at various levels, ranging from societal, through community and socialisation influence theories, to the most specific level, individual theories. The aim of most of the theories of crime is to explain why crime occurs and who is most likely to engage in criminal acts, and as such they are an important element of developing a thorough understanding of the psychology of cybercrime. Many of the high level theories of crime are mainly sociological, geographical or political in scope, whereas theories of crime that consider socialisation and individual differences are those which are most suited to psychological discussion. Because of this, the current chapter will primarily focus on these types of theories of crime, although reference will be made to higher level theories as appropriate. Some of the theories of crime considered in this chapter include biological theories, labelling theories, geographical and routine activity theories, trait theories learning theories, psychoanalytic theories, ad-diction and arousal theories and neutralization theories, as well as examining the complex theory of crime proposed by Eysenck and the complicated issue of defining crime due to its existence as a social construct. While it must be remembered that there has been little empirical examination of how these theories specifically relate to cybercrime, some theories show potential for explaining the nature of the phenomenon. This chapter aims to determine which theories are most suitable for further investigation and applicability to cybercriminal cases.

Section 2
Internet-Specific Crimes

Chapter 4
Is the Research to Date on Hackers Sufficient to Gain a Complete Understanding

Of all the types of cybercrime that exist, hackers are the cybercriminals who have probably engaged both the imagination of the general public and the interest of the entertainment industry the most. They are also those who have elicited the greatest quantity of psychological academic literature. It seems that we have an unsatisfied desire to comprehend why any individual would be drawn to this type of activity, which seems in some cases to have little immediate benefit for the cybercriminal. This chapter aims to determine if we have discovered all that we need to about the psychology and motivations of hackers. Despite the vast quantities of literature in this area, it seems that we still do not have a thorough grasp on the mentality of the hacker. The chapter will commence with some background information regarding the methods used by hackers, a description of the history of hacking behaviour and terminology, and the legal dimensions of hacking. Following this, the chapter will consider the very diverse motives of hackers, as determined by psychological and criminological research. The personalities of computer hackers will then be examined, with special consideration of how psychological profiling could be used to help in solving hacking cases. Issues regarding punishment and prevention of hacking attacks will then be examined, and finally the difficulties in carrying out hacker research and potential directions for future research in this area will be explored.

Chapter 5

Most computer users are likely to have some exposure to malware (malicious software), in the form of spyware, computer viruses, worms or Trojans. This chapter aims to determine if malware developers, and in particular virus writers, can be psychologically profiled. Initially, the chapter will clarify the distinctions between different types of malware, and provide a brief history of some of the most famous malware programs which have been developed. It is important to remember that malware producers and hackers are not necessarily the same individuals, although there is no doubt that at least some individuals engage in both behaviours and the terms are sometimes used interchangeably in the media. A key researcher in the psychology of virus writers, Sarah Gordon, distinguishes between hackers and virus writers "In general, hackers frown upon virus writers. After all, hacking requires system knowledge and skill and is somewhat "sexy" in today's counterculture, while virus writing is still looked down upon, mostly for its indiscriminate damage and lack of required skill" (PBS Frontline, n.d., no pagination). The psychology of hackers and the skills required to engage in hacking activities have previously been described in Chapter 4, and while there is some overlap, it is certain that there are differences between the methods, motives and skills of the two groups. Malware is prolific, and the known prevalence rates for infection, as well as the quantity of known malware programs, will be identified. A brief overview of how malware applications are developed and distributed will be considered, especially in light of the use of social psychology in encouraging individuals to download and distribute the programs. However there is a lack of empirical psychological study relating to virus writers, and much of the literature is based on case studies and individual interviews. Nevertheless, some tentative explanations for the motives of virus writers can be put forward, and there is some limited information available regarding the psychological profile and personality characteristics of virus writers. In particular, similarities with the psychology of vandalism will be explored, in order to determine if similar theories might explain both phenomena. The chapter will also explore methods of reducing and preventing damage done by malware, and it will explore the psychological mechanisms that can predict if a computer user is likely to engage in safe online behaviour. Finally consideration will be given to future trends in malware development, such as the increasing threat of malware on portable devices, and suggestions for important future research in the area.

Probably the type of online crime with which most people have direct experience involves attempts at identity theft and fraud. Most individuals have received an email involving an attempt to get them to part with their money. This chapter aims to describe some of the common types of identity theft and fraud which can occur online, as well as attempting to determine what makes us vulnerable to such attacks. To do this, the chapter will examine some aspects of human decision making, as well as identifying the social engineering tactics used by prospective fraudsters. The chapter will describe the known prevalence rates and costs of online identity theft and fraud, and will compare these types of offences to offline fraud schemes. The methods of attack will be described, including phishing, keyloggers, social engineering, advance fee frauds, and other techniques. An attempt will be made to determine what the psychology of the identity thief and fraudster is, based on comparisons to similar offline offenders. In addition to this, the effects on the victim will be considered, including the phenomenon of victim blaming, where others place partial blame on the victim for the criminal event. Possible methods of preventing identity theft and online fraud will be considered, along with potential future trends and research.

Internet child pornography is a topic which is eliciting greater attention from society and the media, as parents and caregivers become more aware of the risks to their children and law enforcement agencies become more aware of the techniques and strategies used by offenders. Sheldon and Howitt (2007) indicate that at least in terms of convictions, internet child pornography is the major activity that constitutes Internet related sex crimes. However, the distribution of child pornography in itself is not a new offence, but rather one which has been facilitated by the introduction of new technologies such as digital photography and the internet. Before the popularity of the internet, public concern and academic interest in child pornography was quite low as it was considered to be a small and specialist issue. However, the proliferation of images of child sexual abuse online has altered public opinion considerably. This chapter considers how online distribution of child pornography is different to offline distribution. It also considers the psychology of the online child pornography offender and considers the difference between these individuals and contact offenders, attempting to determine if online offenders later progress to offend offline as well. The chapter will then examine what psychological effects child pornography can have on the victims involved, and finally examines the rehabilitation techniques that have been used on these offenders.

There has been significant media interest in the possible dangers of child predation on the internet, but it is not necessarily a new type of offence (Wolak, Finkelhor, Mitchell & Ybarra, 2008). Indeed, in many cases it seems to bear more resemblance to statutory rape than paedophilia. Nevertheless, the Internet does seem to provide an easier route for child predators to encounter and engage with children and teenagers, and the question as to if it enables child predators in their acts should be considered. This chapter will attempt to address this question. Initially paedophilia will be defined, and problems with its diagnosis will be considered. An attempt will be made to quantify the problem of online child predation, and the techniques used by online child predators will be described. The psychology of child predators will be considered, including an overview of some of the main theories of paedophilic behaviour. The psychology of victims will also be considered, with an overview of the risk factors of online predation, along with the psychological effects on victims. Potential solutions will then be reviewed, including rehabilitation efforts and prevention methods. Finally, future trends in online predation will be considered.

Chapter 9
Cyberbullying and Cyberstalking: Are They as Serious as Their Offline Counterparts?

This chapter considers two of the most personal forms of online attack – cyberbullying and cyberstalking. While not always technically criminal events, in some jurisdictions cyberbullying acts are offences, especially when they include direct threats or physical assault. Indeed Jewkes (2010) indicates that cyberbullying occupies "a grey area between social harms and illegal acts, depending on their severity and the legal jurisdiction in which they take place" (p. 526). Cyberstalking may also be included in the stalking laws of many jurisdictions. This chapter aims to determine if cyberbullying and cyberstalking are as severe as their offline counterparts, particularly from a psychological perspective. Case studies of both cyberbullying and cyberstalking are provided, along with definitions of both activities. Known prevalence rates of the phenomena are provided, although as with most types of criminal events, the true prevalence rates of these activities is unknown. Descriptions are provided of some of the techniques used during cyberbullying and cyberstalking attacks, and differences between online and traditional stalking and bullying are considered. The demographic and psychological traits of cyberstalkers and cyberbullies are described, along with the traits of their victims, and the psychological effects of victimisation. Possible solutions for these problems are considered, including both preventative measures and suitable responses. Finally, potential future trends in the area are considered, including the possible use of online gaming and social networking sites for harassment, as well as the underexamined phenomenon of workplace cyberbullying.

Chapter 10
Music, Video and Software Piracy: Do Offenders see Them as Criminal Activities?

Of all the types of cybercrime considered in this book, piracy, illegal file sharing and/or other types of copyright infringement are probably the offences that members of the general public are most likely to have committed. Yar (2007) indicates that piracy activity seems to be very widespread, including individuals from various social classes, although there seems to be a disproportionate number of young people engaging in the activity. This chapter aims to determine if those involved in piracy and online copyright infringement activities see themselves as criminals. It also aims to examine how such offenders justify their actions and how they can be dissuaded from such acts. Definitions of key terms in the area will be presented, along with some examples of real events relating to illegal file sharing. A description of some of the methods used during illegal file sharing and piracy will be provided, along with a historical view of how copyright infringement has developed over time. The known current prevalence rates and costs of offending will be considered, along with arguments presented from industry and academia regarding the effects of file sharing on legitimate sales. Similarly, the problem of trying to estimate the true cost of piracy and illegal file sharing will be highlighted. The psychology of offenders will be considered, and in particular, the phenomenon of the lack of insight of offenders into their own criminality will be investigated. In particular, the roles of self-control, social learning and justifications in illegal file sharing will be analysed. Some potential solutions for these crimes will be considered, including the determination of appropriate punishments and the development of suitable educational campaigns. Finally, potential future trends and research will be described.

Chapter 11
Cyberterrorism: Can Terrorist Goals be Achieved using the Internet?

Cyberterrorism is a subject which has gained considerable interest from both researchers and media, particularly since the attacks on the United States of America on September 11th 2001. Nevertheless, there is a considerable lack of empirical research in the area, with most writings based on theoretical or anecdotal accounts, despite many calls by leaders in the field for more empirically sound methods. This is further complicated by the difficulty in even finding consensus as to what does and does not constitute cyberterrorism. This chapter aims to determine if cyberterrorism is a likely strategy to be used by terrorists, and if so, how it might be used to strike terror into the hearts of citizens. Following some illustrative scenarios of terrorist activity online, some of the conflicting definitions of the subject will be considered. The methods used by terrorists online will then be outlined, including both an examination of the possibility of using the internet for a large scale attack, and using the internet for more conventional activities such as recruitment and fundraising. The psychology of terrorism will then be examined, including investigations of the personalities and psychiatric health of terrorists, and it will be examined as to whether or not the findings relating to 'traditional' terrorists can also be applied to online terrorist activity. The potential effects of an attack on victims will also be considered. Consideration will be given as to how terrorist activity online could be prevented, while also recognising that the increasing online presence of terrorist organisations may be a double-edged sword, enabling counter-terrorism agencies to employ new strategies in their work.

Section 4
Crimes in Virtual Worlds

Chapter 12
Crime in Virtual Worlds: Should Victims Feel Distressed?

The final type of cybercrime to be considered involves crimes that occur in online virtual worlds. While there is considerable literature available on other cybercrimes, as outlined in the previous chapters of this book, relatively little academic literature has been published concerning crime in online virtual worlds (Wall & Williams, 2007). Nevertheless, several cases have come to light concerning specific crimes in these environments, including both property offences (such as theft) and crimes against the person (such as sexual assault). It should be noted that while the term 'crime' will be used in this chapter to describe these events, they may not necessarily be illegal or criminal events, at least so far as the offline world would consider them to be. This chapter aims to describe these types of virtual crimes, and to determine if they could and should be considered criminal events. The effects of the crimes on the victims will also be considered, and the necessity for policing virtual worlds will be discussed. In addition, the online community needs to consider how to deal with virtual offenders – if their offence has real-world consequences, should they be punished offline, or only in the virtual world?

Traditional government is being hollowed out as power dissipates upwards to supranational institutions and downwards to sub national agencies. Governments are also losing influence with their citizens as power is lost to interest groups, influential individuals and media organizations. Citizens are disengaging with the political process as they perceive their ability to effect change is diminishing. As individuals spend more time online, form relationships and interest groups in virtual worlds, the polis is becoming virtual. This chapter looks at how technology, which has already begun to transform service delivery in the public sector, can also transform consultation and participation. If power and influence has been dissipated from the government, can it be regained by finding new ways to engage online with the citizens on whose behalf it exists to serve?

Preface

INTRODUCTION

As more individuals own and operate Internet enabled devices, and more critical governmental and industrial systems rely on advanced technologies, the issue of cybercrime has become a crucial concern for both the general public and professionals alike. There have been several recent news stories relating to cybercrime. These include relatively low level irritations, such as links to malware on social networking sites (BBC News, 2010), as well as the much more worrying fear that a complex computer worm which is capable of causing disruption to major systems such as transport, emergency and power systems, may have reached the black market and become available to terrorists (Kiley, 2010).

To illustrate the importance of the psychology of cybercrime, a recent case study can be explored. A very high profile cybercrime case occurred in April and May of 2011, where millions of users of the Sony Playstation Network and Sony Online Entertainment had personal details stolen by hackers (BBC News, 2011a). Users of the services had a great deal of personal information taken, including dates of birth, credit card details, names and home addresses. These attacks had a significant effect on Sony itself, with calls for the CEO to resign and a drop in share prices. At the time of writing, it is still unclear as to exactly who completed the attack and why, but this is one area where a deeper understanding of the motives and psychology of hackers, a topic outlined in Chapter 4, could be of assistance to cybercrime investigators as they attempt to identify the culprits. The attacks also led to strong psychological reactions in users. Many considered switching to alternative gaming consoles and networks as their trust in Sony and the Playstation Network had been adversely affected (GamePolitics.com, 2011). Internet users who are the victims of cybercrime can experience strong psychological reactions, even if the crimes occur purely in the virtual world, and these reactions are explored in Chapter 12. It is crucial that these psychological reactions of victims are understood, and not belittled by companies and organisations online, as to do so could result in significant losses as consumers turn to more 'caring' or considerate rivals. Those customers who did remain with Sony found themselves facing additional worries, as an exploit was found on the website which was set up to allow users to reset their passwords, which would allow hackers to impersonate users (BBC News, 2011b). Chapter 6 considers why online users are at such high risk of identity theft, and the methods by which such risks can be reduced. As with many types of offline crime, it is preferable to prevent cybercrime whenever possible, as to do so avoids unnecessary financial losses and psychological stresses. In this regard, many chapters of this book explore how cybercrimes can be prevented, particularly in relation to information campaigns targeted at internet users. How these campaigns are presented and implemented influences how effective they can be, and an understanding of psychological principles can help to develop influential and successful campaigns that reduce the risk of victimisation.

While there have been several books on cybercrime published over the past decade (from the early works by Wall, 2001 and Thomas & Loader, 2000 to the more recent works, such as that of Jewkes & Yar, 2010), these primarily focus on technological, sociological or criminological aspects of cybercrime, with limited psychological analysis. Similarly, while several journal articles and book chapters have begun to examine psychological aspects of cybercrime, and some books have been written about the psychology of particular cybercrimes (see for example Chiesa, Ducci & Ciappi, 2009 regarding hackers; Taylor & Quayle, 2003 regarding child pornography; Sheldon & Howitt, 2007 regarding sex offenders) no single central resource was available which would provide the reader with both an overview of the main types of cybercrime, and how forensic psychology could provide insights into the phenomena. The *Psychology of Cybercrime: Concepts and Principles* attempts to address a gap in the literature for a book that primarily focuses on how principles of forensic psychology could be applied to cybercrime cases.

This book draws on the expertise of the authors in cyberpsychology and online governance. As with the study of cybercrime, cyberpsychology is also a growing area – it has developed from early texts, such as Wallace's (1999) "The Psychology of the Internet" to the more recent "*Oxford Handbook of Internet Psychology*" (Joinson, McKenna, Postmes, & Reips, 2007) and "*Psychological Aspects of Cyberspace*" (Barak, 2008). There are also a number of peer-reviewed journals in the area, including *Cyberpsychology, Behaviour and Social Networking* (formerly *Cyberpsychology and Behaviour*), *Computers in Human Behaviour* and *The Journal of Computer Mediated Communication*, along with an increasing number of specialist international conferences. While some of the theories, models and research in conventional psychology can be directly applied to cyberpsychology, this is not always the case, and as such this provides a basis for the argument that cyberpsychology could be considered to be a qualitatively new area within psychology (Kirwan, 2010). Human behaviour online cannot be explained simply by examining offline behaviour and extrapolating from this to predict how people will behave on the Internet. Similarly, the study of forensic cyberpsychology requires particular focus in order to determine how similar online crime is to its offline counterpart.

This *Psychology of Cybercrime* is designed as a source for researchers and practitioners in the disciplines of criminology, cyberpsychology and forensic psychology, though it is also likely to be of significant interest to many who work in the field of information technology and other related disciplines. The *Psychology of Cybercrime* applies the theories of forensic psychology directly to cybercrime. Where research has been completed about a specific cybercrime, the key findings are presented with appropriate critical analysis. If there is limited psychological research about the specific cybercrime, the literature from similar offline crimes (such as in the case of terrorism) is examined and an exploration of how this literature can be applied to the online world is presented.

The *Psychology of Cybercrime* is not limited to documenting offenders and their behaviours. Consideration is given to the effects on victims, legal and governance issues, punishment and preventative measures. The chapters are organised to address specific categories of cybercrime and include case studies that provide examples to which the theory can be applied. Key definitions are provided and, as might be expected in a field as dynamic as cybercrime, suggestions for further research and areas for further development are proposed. In many cases, practical suggestions for methods of tackling the problems are discussed.

The text is divided into four sections. The first section provides the reader with a foundational review of the key disciplines. Chapter 1 sets the scene for remainder of the book by providing the contextual background to cybercrime. The nature of online crime or cybercrime and the ways in which society is responding to it is explored. The legal response to cybercrime is reviewed as is the field of online governance. Chapter 2 considers how forensic psychology can aid in the examination of cybercrime. The role of a forensic psychologist is discussed as is their current involvement in cybercrime, and how this involvement might be further expanded. Chapter 3 discusses the various theories of crime which form an important part of criminological literature. Different theories address the issue of crime at various levels, ranging from societal, through community and socialisation influence theories, to the most specific level, individual theories. The goal is to determine which theories are most suitable for further investigation and apply best to cybercriminal cases.

The second section identifies internet specific crimes, or offences that could not exist without the use of computers. Chapter 4 looks at the subject of hacking; the motivations of hackers, the value of psychological profiling in hacking cases, the punishment of hackers and the prevention of hacking attacks. Chapter 5 examines the phenomenon of 'malware', or malicious software. The distinctions between hackers and virus writers are considered as are the differing approaches to dealing with these distinct problems.

The third section discusses crimes that can occur without computers, but have become more prevalent or easier because of technology – crimes such as music, video and software piracy, child pornography and paedophilia, terrorism, identity theft and fraud. These chapters include a section identifying the similarities and differences between online and offline offenders in these categories. Chapter 6 deals with one of the most commonly experienced types of cybercrime; identity theft and fraud. Common types of online identity theft and fraud are examined as are the reasons why systems and individuals find themselves vulnerable to such attacks. Internet child pornography is considered in Chapter 7. This difficult and sensitive topic is gaining greater attention from society and the media, as parents and caregivers become more aware of the risks to their children and law enforcement agencies become more aware of the techniques and strategies used by offenders. Chapter 8 continues with the related area of child predation on the internet. The psychology of child predators is considered, including an overview of some of the main theories of paedophilic behaviour and an overview of the risk factors of online predation. Chapter 9 looks at cyberbullying and cyberstalking. Case studies are provided, along with definitions of both activities. Prevalence rates of the phenomena are provided, as are descriptions of some of the techniques used during cyberbullying and cyberstalking attacks. Chapter 10 deals with piracy, illegal file sharing and copyright infringement. Consideration is given to the whether those involved in piracy and online copyright infringement activities see themselves as criminals, as well as examining how offenders justify their actions and how they can be dissuaded from such acts. Chapter 11 deals with the subject of cyberterrorism. This is a subject that has gained considerable interest from both researchers and media. The psychology of terrorism is examined, including investigations of the personalities and psychiatric health of terrorists, and it will be examined as to whether or not the findings relating to 'traditional' terrorists can also be applied to online terrorist activity.

The final section of the book considers crimes that take place within virtual worlds, such as the theft of virtual property, or an assault on a person's avatar. These chapters question the nature of these offences, and the suitability of 'real-life' punishments for online offences. Chapter 12 deals with crimes that occur in online virtual worlds. Several cases are described and an attempt made to establish if these 'virtual crimes' could or should be considered criminal events. The effects of the crimes on the victims will also be considered, and the necessity for policing virtual worlds will be discussed. Chapter 13 attempts to look at how governments and law makers are dealing with the question of cybercrime. As technology provides new ways for us to interact as citizens as well as consumers how will technology transform service delivery, governance and civic participation. If citizens as well as criminals are moving online how will the institutions of government move online?

SECTION 1: INTRODUCTION

This introductory section provides the reader with a foundational review of the key disciplines involved in the study of the psychology of cybercrime. These include definitions of cybercrime, descriptions of the discipline of forensic psychology and explanations of theories of crime as they relate to cybercrime.

Chapter 1: Creating the Ground Rules: How can Cybercrimes be Defined and Governed?

The objective of this chapter is to set the scene for remainder of the book. The core of the *Psychology of Cybercrime* seeks to address both the theory of crime and the question of forensic psychology's contribution to the understanding of cybercrime. Specific examples of online crime such as hacking, malware, identity theft, child pornography and cyberbullying are dealt with in some detail in later chapters. This chapter seeks to first define the nature of online crime or cybercrime and look at the ways in which society is responding to it. The nature of the response is multi-faceted. Governments attempt to respond with law, corporations with policies and procedures, suppliers with terms and conditions, users with peer pressure, technologists with code. The chapter then looks at how international laws have evolved through what are referred to a 'soft law' and seeks to draw lessons for the evolution of laws for the internet. The question of how ideas of governance have evolved and how some of the theoretical work in this field may offer guidance for the governance of the internet is also considered.

Chapter 2: Can Forensic Psychology Contribute to Solving the Problem of Cybercrime?

This chapter considers if forensic psychology can aid in the detection, prevention and governance of online crimes. Forensic psychology to date has generally focused on violent, sexual and juvenile offences, but most of its theory and practice can also be applied to other offences, such as cybercrime. Chapter Two aims to investigate if forensic psychology can be useful in solving the problem of cybercrime, and briefly considers to what extent it has been applied to these crimes so far. Definitions of forensic psychology are discussed, and the primary responsibilities and activities of forensic psychologists are described. How each of these responsibilities and activities may be applied to cybercrime cases is examined and a determination made as to what extent forensic psychology has been involved in cybercrime cases to date. Suggestions are made for how to promote the benefits of forensic psychology in cybercrime cases, and finally proposals for future research and potential trends are discussed.

Chapter 3: Can Theories of Crime be Applied to Cybercriminal Acts?

Theories of crime are an important part of criminological literature. Different theories address the issue of crime at various levels, ranging from societal, through community and socialisation influence theories, to the most specific level, individual theories. The aim of most of the theories of crime is to explain why crime occurs and who is most likely to engage in criminal acts, and as such they are an important element of developing a thorough understanding of the psychology of cybercrime. Many of the high level theories of crime are mainly sociological, geographical or political in scope, whereas theories of crime that consider socialisation and individual differences are those which are most suited to psychological discussion. While it must be remembered that there has been little empirical examination of how these theories specifically relate to cybercrime, some theories show potential for explaining the nature of the phenomenon. This chapter aims to determine which theories are most suitable for further investigation and applicability to cybercriminal cases.

SECTION 2: INTERNET-SPECIFIC CRIMES

This section identifies internet specific crimes, or offences that could not exist without the use of computers. These include hacking and malware development.

Chapter 4: Is the Research to Date on Hackers Sufficient to Gain a Complete Understanding of the Psychology Involved?

This chapter aims to determine if we have discovered all that we need to about the psychology and motivations of hackers. Hackers are the cybercriminals who have engaged the imagination of the general public the most. They are also those who have elicited the greatest quantity of psychological academic literature. Despite the vast quantities of literature in this area, it seems that we still do not have a thorough grasp on the mentality of the hacker. The chapter commences with some background information regarding the methods used by hackers, a description of the history of hacking behaviour and terminology, and the legal dimensions of hacking. The chapter goes on to consider the very diverse motives of hackers, as determined by psychological and criminological research. The personalities of computer hackers are examined, with special consideration of how psychological profiling could be used to help in hacking cases. Issues regarding punishment and prevention of hacking attacks are examined, finally the difficulties in carrying out hacker research and potential directions for future research in this area is explored.

Chapter 5: Malware: Can Virus Writers be Psychologically Profiled?

Most computer users are likely to have some exposure to malicious software or malware. This can take the form of spyware, computer viruses, worms or Trojan horses. This chapter looks at how malware developers, and in particular virus writers, can be psychologically profiled. The chapter clarifies the distinctions between different types of malware, and provides a brief history of some of the most famous malware programs which have been developed. Malware producers and hackers are not necessarily the same individuals, although some individuals engage in both behaviours and the terms are sometimes used interchangeably in the media. Malware is prolific, and the known prevalence rates for infection, as well as the quantity of known malware programs are identified. A brief overview of how malware applications are developed and distributed is considered, in light of the use of social psychology in encouraging individuals to download and distribute the programs. Some tentative explanations for the motives of virus writers are put forward, similarities with the psychology of vandalism are explored, in order to determine if similar theories might explain both phenomena. The chapter also explores methods of reducing and preventing damage done by malware, and the psychological mechanisms that can predict if a computer user is likely to engage in safe online behaviour.

SECTION 3: ONLINE VARIATIONS OF OFFLINE CRIMES

The third section of the book discusses crimes that can occur without computers, but have become more prevalent or easier because of technology. There are several examples of this, including copyright infringement, identity theft, fraud, terrorism, child pornography and the use of the Internet to groom children by sexual predators. This section also examines cyberbullying and cyberstalking, which are considered to be criminal offences by some jurisdictions, or which may include elements of criminal activity, such as threats of physical violence.

Chapter 6: Identity Theft and Online Fraud: What Makes us Vulnerable to Scam Artists Online?

Most individuals have received an email involving some kind of attempt at getting them to part with their money. This chapter describes some of the common types of identity theft and fraud which can occur online, as well as attempting to determine what makes us vulnerable to such attacks. To do this, the chapter examines some aspects of human decision making, as well as identifying the social engineering tactics used by prospective fraudsters. The chapter describes the known prevalence rates and costs of online identity theft and fraud, and compares these types of offences to offline fraud schemes. The methods of attack are described, including phishing, keyloggers, social engineering, advance fee frauds, and other techniques. The psychology of the identity thief and fraudster is examined, based on comparisons to similar offline offenders. The effects on the victim are also considered, including the phenomenon of victim blaming, where others place partial blame on the victim for the criminal event. Possible methods of preventing identity theft and online fraud are considered, along with potential future trends and research.

Chapter 7: Internet Child Pornography: A Stepping Stone to Contact Offences?

Child pornography is a topic which is getting greater attention from society and the media, as parents and caregivers become more aware of the risks to their children and law enforcement agencies become more aware of the techniques and strategies used by offenders. The distribution of child pornography is not a new offence, but rather one which has been facilitated by the introduction of new technologies such as digital photography and the internet. Before the popularity of the internet, public concern and academic interest in child pornography was quite low as it was considered to be a small and specialist issue. However, the proliferation of images of child sexual abuse online has altered public opinion considerably. This chapter considers how online distribution of child pornography is different to offline distribution. It also considers the psychology of the online child pornography offender and considers the difference between these individuals and contact offenders, attempting to determine if online offenders later progress to offend offline as well.

Chapter 8: Online Child Predators: Does Internet Society make Predation Easy?

The internet seems to provide an easier route for child predators to encounter and engage with children and teenagers. This chapter addresses the question of how the internet may facilitate this process. Initially paedophilia is defined, and problems with its diagnosis considered. An attempt is made to quantify the problem of online child predation, and the techniques used by online child predators are described. The psychology of child predators is considered, including an overview of some of the main theories of paedophilic behaviour. The psychology of victims is also considered, with an overview of the risk factors of online predation, along with the psychological effects on victims. Potential solutions are reviewed, including rehabilitation efforts and prevention methods.

Chapter 9: Cyberbullying and Cyberstalking: Are They as Serious as Their Offline Counterparts?

Two of the most personal forms of online attack are cyberbullying and cyberstalking. While this activity is not always considered criminal, some jurisdictions treat cyberbullying acts as offences. This is especially the case when they include direct threats or physical assault. Cyberstalking may also be included in the stalking laws of many jurisdictions. This chapter examines cyberbullying and cyberstalking and questions if they are as severe as their offline counterparts, particularly from a psychological perspective. Case studies of both cyberbullying and cyberstalking are provided, along with definitions of both activities. Known prevalence rates of the phenomena are provided, although as with most types of criminal events, the true prevalence rates of these activities is unknown. Descriptions are provided of some of the techniques used during cyberbullying and cyberstalking attacks, and differences between online and traditional stalking and bullying are considered. The demographic and psychological traits of cyberstalkers and cyberbullies are described, along with the traits of their victims, and the psychological effects of victimisation. Possible solutions for these problems are considered, including both preventative measures and suitable responses. Finally, potential future trends in the area are considered, including the possible use of online gaming and social networking sites for harassment, as well as the underexamined phenomenon of workplace cyberbullying.

Chapter 10: Music, Video and Software Piracy: Do Offenders See Them as Criminal Activities?

Chapter 10 considers the issue of piracy, illegal file sharing and other types of copyright infringement and if those involved in piracy and online copyright infringement activities see themselves as criminals. It also examines how such offenders justify their actions and how they can be dissuaded from such acts. Definitions of key terms in the area are presented, along with some examples of real events relating to illegal file sharing. A description of some of the methods used during illegal file sharing and piracy are provided, along with a historical view of how copyright infringement has developed over time. The known current prevalence rates and costs of offending, and the arguments presented from industry and academia regarding the effects of file sharing on legitimate sales are considered. Similarly, the problem of trying to estimate the true cost of piracy and illegal file sharing is highlighted. The psychology of offenders is considered, and in particular, the phenomenon of the lack of insight of offenders into their own criminality will be investigated. In particular, the roles of self-control, social learning and justifications in illegal file sharing are analysed. Some potential solutions for these crimes are considered, including the determination of appropriate punishments and the development of suitable educational campaigns.

Chapter 11: Cyberterrorism: Can Terrorist Goals be Achieved using the Internet?

Cyberterrorism has gained considerable interest from both researchers and media, in particular since the attacks on the United States of America on September 11th 2001. Nevertheless, there is a considerable lack of empirical research in the area, with most writings based on theoretical or anecdotal accounts, despite many calls by leaders in the field for more empirically sound methods. This is further complicated by the difficulty in even finding consensus as to what does and does not constitute cyberterrorism. This chapter aims to determine if cyberterrorism is a likely strategy to be used by terrorists, and if so, how it might be used to strike terror into the hearts of citizens. Following some illustrative scenarios of terrorist activity online, some of the conflicting definitions of the subject are considered. The methods used by terrorists online will be outlined, including both an examination of the possibility of using the internet for a large scale attack, and using the internet for more conventional activities such as recruitment and fundraising. The psychology of terrorism is examined, including investigations of the personalities and psychiatric health of terrorists, and it will be examined as to whether or not the findings relating to 'traditional' terrorists can also be applied to online terrorist activity. The potential effects of an attack on victims is also considered as is how terrorist activity online can be prevented.

SECTION 4: CRIMES IN VIRTUAL WORLDS

This final section of the book considers crimes that take place within virtual worlds. While not necessarily considered criminal events in the offline world, these 'crimes' can still have very serious consequences for the individuals involved.

Chapter 12: Crime in Virtual Worlds: Should Victims Feel Distressed?

The final type of cybercrime to be considered involves crimes that occur in online virtual worlds. While there is considerable literature available on other cybercrimes, as outlined in the previous chapters of this book, relatively little academic literature has been published concerning crime in online virtual worlds. Several cases have come to light concerning specific crimes in these environments, including both property offences (such as theft) and crimes against the person (such as sexual assault). It should be noted that while the term 'crime' is used in this chapter to describe these events, they may not necessarily be illegal or criminal events, at least so far as the offline world would consider them to be. This chapter describes these types of virtual crimes, and determines if they could and should be considered criminal events. The effect of the crimes on the victims is also considered, and the necessity for policing virtual worlds discussed. In addition, the online community needs to consider how to deal with virtual offenders – if their offence has real-world consequences, should they be punished offline, or only in the virtual world?

Chapter 13: On-Line Governance

Power is dissipating from traditional government; upwards to supranational institutions and downwards to sub national agencies. Governments are also losing influence with their citizens as power is lost to interest groups, influential individuals and media organizations. Citizens are disengaging with the political process as they perceive their ability to effect change is diminishing. As individuals spend more time online, form relationships and interest groups in virtual worlds, the polis is becoming virtual. This chapter looks at how technology, which has already begun to transform service delivery in the public sector, can also transform consultation and participation. If power and influence has been dissipated from the government, can it be regained by finding new ways to engage online with the citizens on whose behalf it exists to serve?

CONCLUSION

The objective of this book has been to draw together on one place the recent psychological thinking and research on a range of crimes and antisocial behaviours which are becoming more common in our increasingly interconnected lives. There is a case to be made that the very suffix of cyber has been outgrown by the degree to which humanity has been wired. When we made a conscious decision to 'go online' or to 'log in' to our online lives it made sense to distinguish between the 'world' and the 'cyberworld' between 'crime and 'cybercrime', between 'laws' and 'cyberlaws'. The day is surely coming when such distinctions are no longer useful and we have simply integrated into every aspect of our lives a degree of interconnectedness, group work, or networking. As the technology becomes ubiquitous in our lives and social networking assumes no more novelty than water cooler conversation the use of the prefix cyber will seem quaint.

Until cyber assumes the status of, fax, telegraph, or computer room, it remains a useful way to hold up our online behaviours to the norms and learning of a decade or more of study into the disciplines of psychology, forensics, sociology and law and ask is this different. Do we need new approaches or can we adapt our knowledge to fit this new medium. This book seeks to take the knowledge established in an offline world and measure it for fit against the needs of the online world and offer suggestions where the fit is not exact. Much cybercrime is committed for much the same motives and by much the same people as have always been tempted to criminal activity, although there are some exceptions. Many of the differences relate to the opportunity, access, impact, and range of activities that can be engaged in, although factors such as the anonymity and disinhibition that the Internet affords are also important psychological differences. Psychological study has much to offer in the study of cybercrime, as is evident in the following chapters, and it is important that these insights are evaluated and employed as useful weapons in developing anti-cybercrime strategies.

REFERENCES

Barak, A. (2008). *Psychological aspects of cyberspace: Theory, research, applications*. New York: Cambridge University Press.

BBC News (2010, November 24). *Facebook news feeds beset with malware*. Retrieved November 25, 2010 from http://www.bbc.co.uk/news/technology-11827856

BBC News (2011a, May 3). *Sony warns of almost 25 million extra user detail theft*. Retrieved May 23, 2011 from http://www.bbc.co.uk/news/technology-13256817

BBC News (2011b, May 19). *Sony faces further security woes*. Retrieved May 23, 2011 from http://www.bbc.co.uk/news/technology-13454201

Chiesa, R., Ducci, S., & Ciappi, S. (2009). *Profiling hackers: The science of criminal profiling as applied to the world of hacking*. Boca Raton, FL: Auerbach Publications.

GamePolitics.com. (2011, April 28). *Survey: A fifth of PS3 owners considering move to Xbox 360*. Retrieved May 23, 2011 from http://gamepolitics.com/2011/04/28/survey-fifth-ps3-owners-considering-move-xbox-360

Jewkes, Y., & Yar, M. (2010). *Handbook of Internet Crime*. Cullompton, England: Willan Publishing.

Joinson, A., McKenna, K., Postmes, T., & Reips, U. D. (2007). *The Oxford handbook of Internet psychology*. Oxford: Oxford University Press.

Kiley, S. (2010, November 25). Super Virus a Target for Cyber Terrorists. *Sky News*. Retrieved November 25, 2010 from http://news.sky.com/skynews/ Home/World-News/Stuxnet-Worm-Virus-Targeted-At-Irans-Nuclear-Plant-Is-In-Hands-Of-Bad-Guys-Sky-News-Sources-Say/Article/201011415827544?lpos=World_News_Carousel_Region_1&lid=ARTICLE_ 15827544_Stuxnet_Worm%3A_Virus_Targeted_ At_Irans_Nuclear_Plant_Is_In_Hands_Of_ Bad_Guys%2C_Sky_News_Sources_Say

Kirwan, G. (2010). Cyberpsychology: An overview of emerging research in emerging environments. *The Irish Journal of Psychology, 31*, 157–172.

Sheldon, K., & Howitt, D. (2007). *Sex offenders and the Internet*. Chichester, England: John Wiley & Sons Ltd.

Taylor, M., & Quayle, E. (2003). *Child Pornography: An Internet Crime*. New York: Brunner-Routledge.

Thomas, D., & Loader, B. D. (2000). *Cybercrime: Law enforcement, security and surveillance in the information age*. London: Routledge.

Wall, D. S. (2001). *Crime and the Internet*. London: Routledge.

Wallace, P. (1999). *The psychology of the Internet*. Cambridge: Cambridge University Press.

ADDITIONAL READING

Barak, A. (2008). *Psychological aspects of cyberspace: Theory, research, applications*. New York: Cambridge University Press.

Joinson, A., McKenna, K., Postmes, T., & Reips, U. D. (2007). *The Oxford handbook of Internet psychology*. Oxford: Oxford University Press.

Kirwan, G. (2010). Cyberpsychology: An overview of emerging research in emerging environments. *The Irish Journal of Psychology, 31*, 157–172.

Acknowledgment

Writing a book is a long and far from solitary process, and involves the advice, support and help of many more individuals than the list of authors suggests. As such, we would like to acknowledge the help of all who were involved during the writing and publication process.

Firstly, we would like to thank the staff and students of the Institute of Art, Design and Technology, Dun Laoghaire Ireland. Their support, encouragement and inspiration were integral to the successful completion of this book. In particular, we would like to thank Dr. Irene Connolly, who helpfully advised on appropriate literature for inclusion in the sections on cyberbullying.

Special thanks also go to the publishing team at IGI Global, whose contributions throughout the whole process from inception of the initial idea to final publication have been invaluable. In particular we would like to thank Kristin Klinger, Erika Carter and Jan Travers, who guided us through the early stages of proposal reviews and who saw the potential of book before it was even written. Special thanks to Michael Killian whose friendly emails and responses to our queries assisted us in keeping this project on schedule.

It's difficult when writing such a long document to see the commas for the semi-colons, and we are grateful to Siobhán and Paul Dolan for proof-reading an early version of this book.

The preparation of a manuscript also requires the patience and support of family members, who tolerated our lack of sociability and absence at family events. So thank you to both our families for their interest and encouragement over the past two years, and particular thanks to Glen and Eleanor for their support and understanding.

Finally, we would like to thank all those who encouraged us in this project throughout its development. If it was a detailed discussion regarding a particular concept, or just a coffee to help to clear our heads, we're grateful.

This book is dedicated to the memories of our fathers, David Power and Liam Kirwan.

Grainne Kirwan
Dun Laoghaire Institute of Art, Design and Technology, Ireland

Andrew Power
Dun Laoghaire Institute of Art, Design and Technology, Ireland

Section 1
Introduction

Chapter 1
Creating the Ground Rules:
How can Cybercrimes be Defined and Governed?

ABSTRACT

The objective of this chapter is to set the scene for the remainder of the book. The core of this book seeks to address both the theory of crime and the question of forensic psychology's contribution to the understanding of cybercrime. Specific examples of online crime such as hacking, malware, identity theft, child pornography and cyberbullying are dealt with in some detail in later chapters. Before exploring these subjects it is necessary to set out some context.

The first section of this chapter seeks to define the nature of online crime or cybercrime and look at the ways in which society is responding to it. The nature of the response is multi-faceted. Governments attempt to respond with law, corporations with policies and procedures, suppliers with terms and conditions, users with peer pressure, technologists with code.

The second section looks at how international laws have evolved through what are referred to as 'soft law' and seeks to draw lessons for the evolution of laws for the internet. The final section looks at the more general area of governance and also looks at how ideas of governance have evolved and how some of the theoretical work in this field may offer guidance for the governance of the internet.

BACKGROUND

Definitions

Online crime takes many forms and a distinction should be made between activities such as; the theft of goods online which is clearly a crime, private law issues such as disputes between buyers and sellers of online goods, and issues of anti social behavior or harassment. Certain activities, such as spamming, hacking and cracking can, depending on severity, target and context, fit into any one of the three categories listed.

The variety of activities and intents has meant that the term cybercrime has come to encompass a range of activities and has not yet achieved a single agreed definition. Definitions include, *"crime committed using a computer and the internet to*

DOI: 10.4018/978-1-61350-350-8.ch001

steal a person's identity or sell contraband or stalk victims or disrupt operations with malevolent programs", which is used by Princeton University (n.d.). It has also been defined in the New World Encyclopedia (n.d.) as *"a term used broadly to describe activity in which computers or computer networks are the tool, target, or place of criminal activity. Cybercrime takes a number of forms including identity theft, internet fraud, violation of copyright laws through file sharing, hacking, computer viruses, denial of service attacks, and spam"*. The IT security company Symantec (n.d.) defines two categories of cybercrime, *"Type I, examples of this type of cybercrime include but are not limited to phishing, theft or manipulation of data or services via hacking or viruses, identity theft, and bank or e-commerce fraud. Type II cybercrime includes, but is not limited to activities such as cyberstalking and harassment, child predation, extortion, blackmail, stock market manipulation, complex corporate espionage, and planning or carrying out terrorist activities"*. More succinct definitions include, *"crimes perpetrated over the internet, typically having to do with online fraud"* (PC Mag Encyclopedia, n.d.) or *"crime committed using the Internet, for example stealing someone's personal information or introducing harmful programs into someone's computer"*. (Macmillan Dictionary, n.d.)

Some of these definitions are clearly more specific than others and thus more useful in the framing of any legal position on the subject. However the more common understanding of cybercrime as being any activity occurring online which has intended negative consequences for others is more suitable to our purpose of an exploration of the field. This chapter takes a broad definition of the term cybercrime and assumes it to cover a wide range of activities which may vary from those which are clearly breaches of criminal law to those which could more accurately be described as private law issues. Types of crime can be categorized as internet enabled crimes, internet specific crimes and new crimes committed in a virtual world.

Types of Crime

Technology and crime have a long association, each advance in technology that provides an opportunity to be exploited for gain is matched by advances in the technology of detection. The Internet simply provides a new medium. Two categories of online crime have been observed for many years and a third, with the advent of online virtual environments, is a more recent development. The first category is composed of those crimes which existed offline but are now greatly facilitated by the Internet. These include misuse of credit cards, information theft, defamation, blackmail, obscenity, hate sites, money laundering, and copyright infringement. In the main, comprehensive national laws exist to deal with these issues in offline environments. With the exception of the cross border nature of the online version of these activities enabled by the internet existing legal frameworks are capable of dealing with them.

The second category is made up of crimes that had not existed before the arrival of networked computing and more specifically the proliferation of the internet. These include, hacking, cyber vandalism, dissemination of viruses, denial of service attacks, and domain name hijacking. National laws have been introduced in many jurisdictions in an attempt to combat these crimes (for example, an overview of the UK law in this area is available at JISC Legal www.jisclegal.ac.uk).

A third category comes into play when individuals are acting through their online avatars (representations of the user in the form of a three-dimensional model, from the Sanskrit 'avatara' meaning incarnation) or alternate personas. Do these individuals or their avatars constitute a new public, and present new issues of governance, both in cyberspace and of cyberspace? Harassing another individual through their online representation may be criminal or at the very least antisocial. There is, however, no doubt that these activities have lead to very real crimes offline.

An example is when activities online 'spill out' into the real world, such as when the theft of online virtual goods leads to a serious crime offline. In June 2005, Qiu Chengwei, a Chinese national, won a virtual sword in the online game *Legend of Mir 3*. Qiu lent the sword to a fellow gamer Zhu Caoyuan who subsequently sold it. When Qiu reported the incident to the police he was told a virtual sword was not real property and was not protected by law. Qiu went to the home of Zhu and stabbed him to death in a very real crime for which he is now serving a life sentence (Reuters, 2005). In 2008 a Russian member of the Platanium clan of an MMORPG (Massively Multiplayer Online Role-Playing Game) was assaulted in the Russian city of Ufa by a member of the rival Coo-clocks clan in retaliation for a virtual assault in a role playing game (probably Lineage II). The man died of his injuries en route to hospital (Truta, 2008). As a result of incidents like these some countries, such as South Korea, have set up a section within the police force specifically to deal with 'in-game' crime (BBC News, 2005).

Even if the activity does not spill over into the real world but remains online it is clear that crime can occur. In August 2005 a Japanese man was arrested for using software 'bots' (web robots, or 'bots' are software applications that run automated tasks over the Internet) to 'virtually' assault online characters in the computer game *Lineage II* and steal their virtual possessions. He was then able to sell these items through a Japanese auction website for real money (Knight, 2005). In October 2008, a Dutch court sentenced two teenagers to 360 hours of community service for 'virtually' beating up a classmate and stealing his digital goods ("Woman faces jail", 2008). Also in 2008, a 43 year old Japanese piano teacher who was 'virtually' married to a man in the online role playing game *Maple Story*, was so upset when he 'virtually' divorced her that she hacked his PC and deleted him from the game, thus committing a sort of 'virtual murder'(Associated Press, 2008). This resulted in her arrest for illegally accessing his computer but and may yet result in a civil suit for damages (Emigh, 2008). In 2007, a Dutch teenager was arrested for stealing virtual furniture from 'rooms' in *Habbo Hotel*, a 3D social networking website; this virtual furniture was valued at €4,000 (BBC News, 2007). In Britain a couple are divorcing after the wife discovered her husband's online alter-ego was having an affair online with another, virtual, woman (Morris, 2008).

Offensive activities such as online assault, or the virtual rape of an individual's avatar, have had very real effects with reports of depression and suicide resulting. This cyber bullying can occur as people become more closely associated with their online persona to the extent that it is viewed, both by themselves and others, as an extension of themselves. These issues and the psychology behind this form of online behavior is covered in more detail in Chapter 12, *Crime in Virtual Worlds – are they really criminal offences?*

RESPONDING TO CYBERCRIME

A number of approaches to dealing with the issue of cybercrime have been tried. Governments, corporations, individuals and service providers all have an interest in dealing effectively with cybercrime. Whilst to date much of their activities and initiatives have been independent of each other their combined effect is largely positive and mutually reinforcing. This section will look at how these four groups have approached the problem of cybercrime.

Government Response, the Law of the Land

There are a number of views about the need for 'cyberlaws'. One argument is that rules for online activities in cyberspace need to come from territorial states (Goldsmith 1998). Another view is that there is a case for considering cyberspace as a different place where we can and should make new rules. Johnson and Post (1997) were among the first to argue that cyberspace constitutes a new and different space where different rules must apply. Their argument was that, in the off-line world there is generally a correspondence between borders drawn in physical space, between nation states, and borders in legal space. The point at which one set of laws stops and another starts is normally at the physical border of a country. This correspondence results from four interrelated considerations. First, the *power* to control a space; law making requires an ability to enforce the law and impose sanctions; this is done by national governments. Second, the *effect* of a law given the proximity of the law maker to those affected. A third consideration is the *legitimacy* of the law, or the degree to which the law is implemented with the consent of the governed. Finally, the *notice* given to those affected by the law, or the warnings provided to those affected to abide by a given law. The advent of the Internet has broken the link between geography and these four principles. How does an individual know where the other individuals, services or institutions might be located or what rules, if any, apply?

Is there a virtual space or cyberspace where traditional legal systems have no jurisdiction, where a new order can be built by the inhabitants of that space? The idea of cyberspace as a place you can go to where new laws might apply is supported by the fact that you must make a decision to go there, normally by deciding to access a computer and enter a password. In this sense there is a boundary you cross to get 'there'. David Post (1996) suggested that it may be that cyberspace could signal the *"final days of a governance system relying on individual sovereign states as [the] primary law-making authority, a system that has served us, often for better and sometimes for worse, for the last half millennium"*.

The governance of this new virtual space could take a number of forms. A centralized system of control, would involve coordination amongst the existing sovereign powers and some form of multi lateral agreement or 'Grand Internet Treaty'. The establishment of international governing bodies similar to the World Trade Organization would also be needed. An alternative option would be the decentralization of law making and the development of processes which do not seek to impose a framework of law but which allow one to emerge. In this case individual service providers would develop their own systems of governance and standards of behavior. The law would come from the bottom up as users select the services, products and environment that match their own standards of behavior and ethics. In this scenario our understanding of justice may change as we see what emerges from un-coerced individual choice (Post 1996).

It should be noted at this point that the growing familiarity of the online world and the growing proportion of the population that are spending time online has undermined this view of the internet as a separate space. This is particularly true amongst younger users who have never known a world without an online component. Shirky (2009, p196) argues that *"the internet augments real world social life rather than providing an alternative to it. Instead of becoming a separate cyberspace, our electronic networks are becoming embedded in real life."*

Different approaches to cybercrime have been tried, for example the Council of Europe developed a *Convention on Cybercrime* (Council of Europe, 2001) whereas in the US there is a *National Strategy to Secure Cyberspace* (U.S. Department of Homeland Security, 2003). Europe's convention was created to *"pursue a common criminal policy aimed at the protection of society against cybercrime, especially by adopting appropriate legislation and fostering international co-operation."* It deals particularly with infringements of copyright, computer-related fraud, child pornography and violations of network security. America's national strategy is part of the greater 'Homeland Security' project and is focused on preventing the use of the internet for the facilitation of a terrorist attack.

Private or Corporate Response, the Rules of the Game

Cannataci and Mifsud-Bonnici (2007, p.60), make the case that *'there is developing a mesh of private and state rules and remedies which are independent and complementary'*. This language is echoed by Eckersley (2007, p.81) who talks of the *'mutual enmeshment'* of law and politics and the *'constitutive tensions'* between the regulative ideals of treaty law and the actual production of treaty law. In terms of the law as users of the internet community experience it, they often adopt rules and remedies based on their fitness for purpose. State regulation may be appropriate to control certain activities, technical standards may be more appropriate in other situations, and private regulation may be appropriate where access to State courts or processes are impossible. The intertwining of state and private regulation is both inevitable and necessary to provide real-time solutions to millions of online customers and consumers. This should lead to greater collaboration between private groups and states in the development and administration of rules. The mesh of regulation, just like the mesh of a fishing net, is more effective in catching larger participants than smaller ones. Corporate organizations are more likely to comply with regulations than individuals, thus the task of governance is to reduce the gaps in the mesh. Swire (2005, p.1975) uses the metaphor of elephants and mice to explain this situation:

In short elephants are organizations that will be subject to the law, while mice can hope to ignore it. Elephants are large companies or other organizations that have major operations in a country. Elephants are powerful and have a thick skin, but are impossible to hide. They are undoubtedly subject to a counties jurisdiction. Once laws are enacted, they likely, will have to comply. By contrast mice are small and mobile actors, such as pornography sites or copyright violators, who can reopen immediately after being kicked off a

server or can move offshore. Mice breed annoyingly quickly – new sites can open at any time. Where harm over the Internet is caused by mice, hidden in crannies in the network, traditional legal enforcement is more difficult.

This kind of thinking is not unique to governance of the internet. Other areas of the law require cross border, multi-state and non-state involvement. Morison and Livingstone (1995, p.180) cite environmental law as a field in which an international approach is required and one which is enabled by technology when he states,

Acid rain and river pollution means that preventing pollution in one country may require action in another. Since television and radio signals can cross frontiers, regulatory action which stays within one set of boundaries is likely to prove of limited effectiveness.

Writing in 1995 Morison could see the impact of television and radio signals crossing borders, the arrival of the internet has only served to increase this issue.

Technical Response, the Law as Code

The technical component of the mesh is as important as the private/public regulation components. As Boyle (1997, p.201) colorfully puts it,

...information wants to be free and the thick fingers of Leviathan are too clumsy to hold it back, [but] the position is less clear if the information is guarded by digital fences backed by state power maintained through private systems of surveillance and control.

Much of what can or cannot be done online is in the hands of the technologists who have built the network, and infrastructure. Sitting on top of this is the software used to create the environments of social networks which are themselves limited by their technical specifications. The computers used to access the internet have further limitations, some by design and others through various security software installed by; the user, their employer, parent or in some cases the state. The internet is a web of firewalls, antivirus software and restricted domains. It is a web of security that on the one hand offers a system of protection or control and on the other hand presents a challenge to those hackers inclined to see such measures as anathema to the spirit of the internet.

The choices that are made about what is or is not appropriate behavior can be made by technologists and designers rather than public representatives or the judiciary. These are normative choices which have far reaching impacts. For example, the design of Facebook made certain normative assumptions about privacy which may be consistent with the thinking of young, liberal, Californian IT professionals, but may not align with other sections of society. Some aspects of what can and cannot be done, or even what may be considered right or wrong, will be determined by software engineers. They will find ways to prevent file sharing or illegal downloading or many other elements of our online activities. Blocking or filtering software has largely removed the need for states to struggle with issues of censorship as they did in the late 1990s. These issues are well discussed by Lessig (2000) in his book, *Code and Other Laws of Cyberspace*. If individuals can control the flow of information to their (or their child's) computer there is less need for the state to try the impossible and eliminate it from the web. The challenge for these 'technical governors' of behavior is their ability to recognize the possibilities of their role.

Whether at national, corporate, or end-user level, the option of responding to inappropriate or illegal behavior through technology rather than regulation offers a lower cost 'soft law' approach which is expanded on later in this chapter. However unless the technical solutions to, for example, distributing a malicious virus are backed up by some form of legal impediment with clear consequences it will be viewed as no more than a technical challenge by some.

User Response, Negotiated Law

Private regulations exist in the realm of codes of behavior agreed amongst groups of users or laid down by commercial organizations that provide a service or social networking environment. One method of establishing standards of behavior is online dispute resolution. The growth of Online Dispute Resolution (ODR) was *'not intended to challenge or displace an existing legal regime but to fill a vacuum where the authority of law was absent'* (Katsh 2007, p.99). Katsh describes a number of experiments with ODR: a Virtual Magistrate to aid in disputes between ISPs and users, an Online Ombudsman Office to offer a general dispute resolution service (run by the University of Massachusetts) and an ODR to resolve family disputes (proposed by the University of Maryland).

The online auction site eBay is an example of a company whose ability to be successful is dependent on the trust of its customers that goods and services will exchange at agreed prices and that buyers and sellers will act in good faith. The feedback rating system goes someway to providing this assurance but when disputes arose there needed to be an effective process for dispute resolution. eBay engaged an internet start up, SquareTrade. com to provide this service. By automating the process and using web pages with forms and options to choose from, rather than an open ended email system, SquareTrade is able to handle many million individual disputes each year.

Another example of effective dispute resolution is the World Intellectual Property Organization (WIPO) a specialized agency of the United Nations. It is dedicated to developing a balanced and accessible international intellectual property system. One function is the domain name dispute resolution process which provides an inexpensive way of dealing with cybersquatting and bypasses the cumbersome use of national law. The case goes to arbitration on the basis of certain rules determining the right to a domain name, if the arbitrator rules that the cybersquatting is taking place an order is issued to the relevant domain name registrar who simply re-assigns the domain name. This is a good example of a new regime emerging to address a vacuum in national law.

Social networking sites are also self governing either by the collective will of the users or by the use of moderators. Behavior on such sites which is considered inappropriate by other users causes a reaction and can lead to exclusion. The choice of moderation style is important in influencing the nature of the online conversations and the ethos of the environment. Wright (2006) outlined two broad types of moderation that are used in British and European government-run online discussion forums. These are content moderation, which can be either automated or manual, and interactive moderation, which has a broader remit. Interactive moderation requires a range of roles for the moderator such as replying to messages, encouraging people to join the debate and providing summaries. Interactive moderation is similar to Edwards' (2002) description of the moderator as a democratic intermediary.

The current situation seems to be that the response is dependent on the degree of perceived 'seriousness' of the activity. Criminal activity continues to be addressed by national laws and greater cooperation between states is the best route to all forms of crime that cross-national borders. Civil wrongs, where possible, are addressed through the service provider and in some cases via the civil courts. Other anti-social activity, of the hacking or spamming variety, is tackled by technical solutions where possible and the cat and mouse game between hackers and the software security industry continues. However the more we are living and interacting online the more examples we see of attempts to provide online solutions to online problems. At the moment this is largely at the lower end of a scale of cost, or level of serious wrong doing but perhaps it gives clues to future

solutions. This intertwining of state, private, and technical solutions is likely to continue to develop as the de-facto model of Internet governance.

LESSONS FROM INTERNATIONAL LAW

The notion of law as the commands of the king backed by force seemed sufficient, and survived up to the time of Austin's (1882/2000) work. By the time Hart (1961) was writing his *Concept of Law* the world was a changed place and the interdependence of States on each other had been driven home to the politicians and peoples of Europe by a half century of world conflict. Hart conceived of law as a set of rules. These primary and secondary rules provided a framework not just for the administration of justice but as a way for States to interact. When Dworkin (1986) moved the definition of law further from the embodiment of the State, and defined law as interpretation, he put the law in the hands of the judiciary and thus included non-State or supra-State law making bodies.

In considering a framework of law for the internet, there are lessons which can be taken from these writers on international law. There is a move away from systems of command and control. Individual states have less autonomy. It is increasingly important to include non-state actors. Governance is improved by peer review. There is a risk of loss of legitimacy as power moves further from the individual citizen. A further lesson is the danger of such a framework being perceived as an instrument of the West. Just as international law can be perceived in, for example the Middle East, '*not as a shield but as a sword*', (Allain 2004, p.392) so too the governance of the internet, with its roots in the US, must avoid the trap of being seen as another colonial weapon of the West. If this perception takes hold then developing systems of law online will be fraught with issues of legitimacy.

Another lesson from international law is the emergence of soft law as a more effective solution than hard law in many multi state situations. Hard law is defined as the rules and regulations that make up legal systems in the traditional sense and soft laws those which consist of informal rules which are non-binding but due to cultural norms or standards of conduct, have practical effect. Senden (2004) similarly defines soft law as,

Rules of conduct that are laid down in instruments which have not been attributed legally binding force as such, but nevertheless may have certain (indirect) legal effects, and that are aimed at and may produce practical effects.

Hard law in this context can provide a basis for enforcement by setting standards for acceptable behavior with reputational consequences if breached. A system of centralized enforcement though the United Nations Security Council or the International Monetary Fund is also possible. Hard law can also been seen in situations where international commitments are incorporated into domestic law. States may chose the hard law route when (a) the benefits of cooperation are high and the cost of breach also high; (b) when noncompliance may be difficult to detect; (c) when States wish to form alliances such as the EU or NATO; (d) when domestic agencies are given power to make agreements with little control from the executive; and (e) when a State is seeking to enhance its international credibility (Abbott & Snidal 2000, p.429). However hard law does entail significant costs and can restrict countries behavior and sovereignty. In the context of hard versus soft law, cost refers to the potential for inferior outcomes, loss of authority and reduction in sovereignty.

In the early days of the internet the instinct of governments was to solve the perceived problems of control by hard law. For example in the US the Clinton administration tried on many occasions to pass laws to control pornography online. The Communications Decency Act (1996) was fol-

lowed by the Child Online Protection Act (1998) which was followed by the Children's Internet Protection Act (1999). All were passed into law and all were challenged in the courts under freedom of speech issues. Only the Children's Internet Protection Act survived the challenges but as it was limited to controlling usage in public libraries, and with libraries given the option to opt in or out, it is effectively defunct also. Boyle (1997, p.189) asserted,

Federal judges had come a long way towards recognizing both the technological resistance of the Internet to censorship and the fact that a global net could never be effectively regulated by a single national jurisdiction

Soft law reduces the cost by limiting one or more of the dimensions of obligation, precision or delegation. Escape clauses can be added, commitments can be imprecise, or delegation to sub-state bodies to facilitate future political change can be added. Rather than seeing these elements as undermining the law they can be seen as allowing States to enter agreements without threat to sovereignty, allowing for future uncertainty, and lowering the barriers to future, harder legalization. In choosing between hard and soft law solutions States face a trade-off between the advantages and disadvantages of both. Soft law can lessen sovereignty cost by offering a range of institutional agreements from which States can choose. Soft law offers an effective way to deal with uncertainty, especially when it initiates processes that allow actors to learn about the impact of agreements over time. Uncertainty presents a major challenge for institutions of international governance and is considered below in the context of Cooney and Lang's (2007) writing on adaptive governance.

Soft law offers techniques for compromise and cooperation between States and private actors. Non-state organizations will normally press for hard law solutions to raise the cost of violation by other parties, however soft law may be both more achievable, as private actors may lack the ability to enter binding treaties, and it is also more flexible to changing circumstances.

States and non-state actors can achieve many of their goals through soft legalization that is more easily attained or even preferable........ Soft law is valuable on its own, not just as a steppingstone to hard law. Soft law provides a basis for efficient international 'contracts,' and it helps create normative 'covenants' and discourses that can reshape international politics. (Abbott & Snidal 2000, p.456).

States will often opt for a soft law solution if substantive agreements are impossible to attain. Soft law can provide opportunities for deliberation, systematic comparisons, and learning (Schäfer, 2006). It may not commit a government to a policy but it may achieve the desired result by moral persuasion and peer pressure. It may also allow a state to engage with an issue otherwise impossible for domestic reasons and open the possibility for more substantive agreements in the future.

The relative legitimacy of hard versus soft laws can depend on the society they are seeking to govern. In the context of online social networks soft laws have a power and system of enforcement more effective than the hard laws that might attempt to assert legitimacy.

In considering the appropriate legal framework for the international realm of the internet the nature both of the activities taking place and the individuals and organizations using it need to be considered. The legitimacy or appropriateness of hard versus soft laws depends on the society they are seeking to legalize. In the context of online social networks soft laws have a power and potential for support which may make them more effective than the hard laws that might attempt to assert legitimacy. The confluence of States, individuals, businesses, and other non-state actors that make up the legal, regulatory and technical web

of behaviors that constitute the internet make it somewhat unique. As Eckersley (2007, p. 80) said,

treaty making is shaped and constrained, on the one hand by the deeper constitutional structure and associated norms of international society, and on the other hand, by the particular roles, interests and identities of those State and non-State actors involved in the rule making process.

A second part of the framework for considering law on the internet can be taken from the writing of Cooney and Lang (2007). They describe a need to develop flexible and adaptive international institutions, to respond to rapidly changing global conditions, as well as to changes in our knowledge of the causes of global problems. They also describe the recent development of learning-centered alternatives to traditional command-and-control regulatory frameworks, variously described as 'experimentalist' governance, 'reflexive' governance, or 'new' governance. Elements of these approaches contribute to what Cooney and Lang call adaptive governance.

The key elements of this adaptive governance are firstly, its focus on facilitating continuous learning as a response to uncertainty and systemic unpredictability, redefining the problem and revisiting the question of what constitutes relevant 'knowledge' about a particular problem. Secondly, adaptive governance sees policy making as experimentation. It is a process of 'learning by doing', and treating policy interventions as quasi-experiments. Finally adaptive governance is an iterative process of review and revision. Monitoring and feedback mechanisms help facilitate learning, not only by fine tuning the particular policy instruments chosen, but also by drawing attention to relevant knowledge gaps. Policy making is less about the attainment of a single optimal solution and more about providing a forum for the ongoing creation of consensual knowledge and agreed processes to guide policy.

Adaptive governance accepts and responds to uncertainty through promoting learning, avoiding irreversible interventions and impacts, encouraging constant monitoring of outcomes, facilitating broad participation in policy-making processes, encouraging transparency, and reflexively highlighting the limitations of the knowledge on which policy choices are based. (Cooney & Lang, 2007, p.1)

In common with the thinking demonstrated above when discussing soft law, adaptive governance allows for a wider participation in the formulation of policy and law. Secondly it allows for an iterative or progressive approach to policy making and law making. The solution needs to come from State, citizen, and corporation and the solution will develop over time as knowledge, systems, and technologies develop.

The identities and interests of States can be shaped by both domestic and transnational discursive practices, and NGOs are increasingly significant to any understanding of the discursive processes and legitimacy of multilateral agreements. Eckersley (2007, p.105)

An example of soft law in the area of cyber-law is the Council of Europe's *Convention on Cybercrime* (Council of Europe, 2001). In fact what Slaughter (2004, p.264) describes as the *'vibrant laboratory'* of the EU provides many lessons on how to establish the necessary degree of collective cooperation amongst a diverse group of states and yet maintain the locus of political power at national level. The UN General Assembly initiated a World Summit on the Information Society (WSIS) to offer a further platform for the development of principles and guidelines. The first phase took place in Geneva in 2003 and the second in Tunis in 2005 (World Summit on the Information Society, 2010).

Other areas where a soft law approach has worked in an international context are outlined by

Sindico (2006) and include forestry, labor rights and sustainable development. Sindico goes on to describe soft law as a 'pioneer' of hard law. Soft law and voluntary standards in particular are a stage in the creation of legal norms. They are necessitated by the challenge of sustainable global governance. However in the case of the law of the internet it is unclear if soft law can be seen as a route to hard law. The particular prevalence of non-state actors in the creation and management of virtual space and the uniquely strong position of technical standards and rules in the governing of that space, make the route to a hard law solution non-linear at best and opaque at worst.

Perhaps the main soft laws, if they can be called that, are the very technical standards that underpin the net itself. These are set out in the requests for comments (RFCs) run by the Internet Engineering Task Force (IETF) but have largely emerged as technical standards from discussions between various parties, rather than being decreed in the form of hard law. This is quite a peculiar situation given that under present law the definition of nearly every product is formally set down in hard law regulation.

These ideas of soft law and adaptive governance offer further lessons to the notion of a structure of laws for the internet. Systems of informal rules which may not be binding but have effect through a shared understanding of their benefits. Adaptable law which is flexible and open to change as knowledge develops. Agreements which include States and non-state actors, and which involve both the citizen and business. Finally, soft law offers lessons on continuous learning in a changing environment, resulting in an evolving system of laws.

GOVERNANCE ISSUES

One approach to managing the growth of cyber-crime is to look at how, or if, the internet and its virtual worlds are, or could be, governed. A centralized system of control involving coordination amongst the existing sovereign powers is one governance option. However the structure of international society is anarchic, in the sense that there is no world government to enforce international legal norms (Eckersley, 2007, p.81). Or as Slaughter (2004, p.8) said,

'..world government is both infeasible and undesirable. We need more government on a global and a regional scale, but we don't want the centralization of decision making power and coercive authority so far from the people actually governed'

The likelihood of some 'Grand Internet Treaty' being agreed between states seems less and less likely. At the 2005 International Summit on the Information Society in Tunis, Internet Governance was defined as, "...*the development and application by governments, the private sector, and civil society, in their respective roles, of shared principles, norms, rules, decision making procedures and programmes, that shape the evolution and utilization of the Internet.*" (Working Group on Internet Governance, 2005, p.4)

The decentralization of law making and the development of processes which do not seek to impose a framework of law but which allows one to emerge is one way in which governance may evolve. Service providers would develop their own systems of governance and standards of behavior. The law would come from the bottom up as users select the services, products and environment that match their own standards of behavior and ethics. In the example cited above of the stolen sword in the game *Legend of Mir 3*, strong internal governance either through user agreed ethics or technical restrictions could have provided the 'victim' of theft with some opportunity for redress. It could also have provided some form of punishment, perhaps through exclusion, to the perpetrator of the theft. This may have been sufficient to address the sense of loss and helplessness that presumably led to the subsequent

offline crime. Our understanding of justice may change as we see what emerges from un-coerced individual choice (Post, 1996). The appropriate legal or ethical framework in one context or virtual environment may be quite different in another. MacSíthigh (2008) argues that the increased availability of user-generated content is influencing the development of cyberlaw. As individuals and businesses develop more content, services and applications the ability of the State to keep up with appropriate legislation or even guidelines is limited. MacSíthigh lists several examples of self regulation and co-regulation of activities online. For example a joint government/industry group like the Broadband Strategy Group in the UK has established guidelines for British media producers. In other cases governments have drafted codes of behavior for industry groups which are observed on a voluntary basis (MacSíthigh 2008, p.86).

Foucault, who was writing before the advent of the internet provided some guidance in his analysis of power. His notions of power as surveillance and control predicted some of the thinking about behavior being influenced by the knowledge that all of our actions online can be recorded, monitored or directed. In this sense technical solutions offer part of the solution to governance of the internet.

'Power is not ensured by right but by technique, not by law but by normalization, not by punishment but by control,' (Foucault 1978, p.138). He also asserted *'Government is a function of technology'* (Foucault, as cited in Rabinow, 1984, p. 295). This technical control may be exercised by the State but is often in the hands of the commercial organizations that design and develop the technologies we use.

It is important, when thinking about how the online citizen may be governed, to consider the relationship between governments and technology. The first serious attempt by governments to embrace new technologies as a method for improving governance was as part of the New Public Management (NPM) agenda of the late 1980s and early 1990s. NPM was about breaking up monopolistic public-service structures and using incentives to influence activities and adopting private-sector management techniques. This appealed to the Thatcher and Reagan administrations in the 1980s who blamed 'Big Government' for the global economic downturn of that time (Evans, 2009, p.38). NPM administrative reform was market and competence based, and with an emphasis on deregulation and governance. These four categories of changes came from the view that a public organization could be analyzed in the same manner as a firm.

New Public Management led to the first steps being taken by governments towards using technology under the term eGovernment. This was driven by the desire to improve efficiency and to replicate private sector management practices. Inevitably the starting point in the use of technology was in service delivery. Existing processes were replicated in new and more efficient ways mostly by putting repetitive tasks, like form filling and information provision, online. Few however were making use of the additional functionality of the technology to do new things. Morison and Newman (2001, p1) put this well when they stated, *"It may be that any efficiency gains that are made by reinventing government and viewing it as just another provider are at the expense of an opportunity to use technology to more fundamentally reinvent democracy and re-work the relationship between citizen and state".*

Communications technologies available through the internet offer the state new ways of engaging the public. A fuller discussion on the use of technology by the state can be found in Chapter 13 – Governing a Virtual World. For now it is sufficient to note that as technology becomes more prevalent in the lives of more of the electorate, barriers to entry will fall. The expansion of the use of communications technologies has led governments to move beyond the efficiency mantra of NPM as alternative ways of thinking about governance have emerged. These included network governance, Public Value Management

(PVM) and Digital-Era Governance (DEG). These perspectives offer some guidance to the governance of online worlds and are briefly described below.

Network Governance

In the latter half of the twentieth century there was an important shift, from the welfare state to the neo-liberal state, and a further shift towards a third way (Loughlin 2004). This third way envisaged a form of networked governance where the state played a facilitating role in partnership with civil society. Giddens (1998), who popularized the term 'the third way', wrote about democratizing democracy. It was not that people had tired of the democratic state but rather that they felt it was insufficiently democratic. Writing at the beginning of the New Labour period of public service reform, he believed it symbolized a rhetorical break both with Old Labour command and control and the New Right's minimal state. This *'reflexive citizenry'* called for more input into the process of government, driven in part by a growing distrust of politicians. This new way of thinking about the state's relationship with the citizen coincided with the move from what Kamarck (2007) described as the *'Bureaucratic Century'* to the *'Information Age'*.

Networked governance refers to the increasing way in which public services are delivered through collaborative networks involving state and non-state actors. Evans' view (2009) is the NPM focuses on the role of the public servant; takes the politics out of public policy deliberation; and its market orientation is at odds with the concept of public service. The success of public service reform rests on the development of representative as well as technocratic networks which can meet the demands of both representative democracy and the efficient delivery of public goods. Evans (2009, p.35) goes on to say that NPM is unable to manage this new networked environment because its very nature is at odds with the concept of public service, preferring the language of the customer to that of the citizen.

The effectiveness of networks can be evaluated in a number of ways; achieving win-win situations, activating actors and resources, limiting interaction cost, procuring commitment, political-administrative management, the quality and transparency of the interaction, and the prudent use of network structuring (Kickert, Klijn, & Koppenjan 1997, p.175).

Public Value Management

Public Value Management (PVM) emerged as a response to the development of networked governance and the limits of NPM. Whilst network governance sought to mitigate some of these by the greater involvement of a range of stake holders some problems remained. Evans (2009, p.44) identifies a number of obstacles to representative and responsive networked governance. The problem of steering clusters of state and NGOs outside traditional organizational boundaries and the absence of operational rules. The absence of policy instruments for managing network performance (monitoring and evaluation). The dangers of networks being subject to interest capture and resource dependency, problems of democratic control and accountability, and the ability of networks to resist and/or dilute government aims.

PVM argues that these shortcomings can be overcome through reforming network norms, values and operational rules aimed at achieving public value. Public value should be determined collectively through inclusive deliberation involving elected and appointed government officials, key stakeholders and the public. This deliberation can be 'bottom-up' through consultation or 'top-down/government knows best'. The closer to the 'bottom up', consultative end of the continuum, the greater the ability of the citizen to affect policy outcomes.

Public value governance demands a commitment to broader goals than those envisaged under traditional management regimes. Evans (2009, p.46) offers some suggestions.

Public managers need to understand the network environment through scoping the field of action, identifying all potential partners and their resources. Public managers need to develop 'smart partnerships' through policy community-building. To ensure public value, public managers should establish clear deliberative rules and intelligent performance indicators linked directly to negotiated policy objectives. Monitoring systems should be designed to identify movements towards or away from achieving these objectives. Work plans should be subject to annual audits and evaluations with effective reporting systems both to politicians and to the public. Oppositionist networks should be allowed to form to ensure that all interests are given voice.

Digital-Era Governance

New Public Management was described earlier as being based on the principles of disaggregation, competition, and incentivisation. Dunleavy, Margetts, Bastow and Tinkler (2006) make that case that a range of information technology centered changes are leading to reintegration, needs based holism, and digitization in a move they call Digital-Era Governance (DEG). The reintegration of functions into government, the building of holistic needs oriented structures and progressing the digitalization of administrative process, combines to reverse some of the changes introduced by NPM.

The first wave of e-government was focused on the back office: systems were automated, tasks were simplified, some processes were put online but essentially the system remained unchanged. In Ireland the oft quoted examples of the Revenue Online Service (ROS) and Motor Tax Online are typical of this first wave of activity. The growth of the internet and the capabilities of Web 2.0 in terms of social networking technologies, mobile computing and the general pervasiveness of the online life of the nation, represents opportunities for structural changes in the way public services are understood, accessed and delivered. Large scale switchovers to the use of email and the evolution of websites from 'shop windows' to the core of the service are examples of this. Two trigger points in this evolution may be: firstly, the point at which the electronic version of every file is considered the authoritative version and a hard copy only printed as needed, and secondly, the point at which a government agency no longer 'has' a website but rather 'is' a web site.

Technology allows for the reintegration of services so that to the citizen, a single point of engagement is possible with state services. This holistic approach should allow reduction in the duplication of information and form filling as the citizen can enter information once, and go to a single source to be directed to the service needed. In the 1980's Hood (1983 cited in Dunleavy et al 2005) argued that it was not sufficient for governments just to deliver services but that they needed to actively do *information seeking* to establish needs. The two-way dialogue, made possible by changes in the digital era, brings this concept of a connected citizenry ever closer.

For these digitization changes to be effective and truly cost saving both in time and resources they need to run in place of conventional administrative process and not in parallel. This movement to Digital Era Governance would thus need to be driven by a combination of incentive and removal of traditional channels. Governments will have to actively manage the displacement of service users to the new electronic channels (Dunleavy et al., 2005, p.487).

This concept of governance is both in its early stages of development and yet at a tipping point in terms of public demand/readiness to accept these kinds of changes to the way they engage with the state. The level of citizen engagement is higher and the combining of services in a more holistic approach to service delivery will result

in an outcomes approach rather than an input or outputs approach. The reliance on electronic engagement will provide a wealth of comprehensive data on the level of citizen/state engagement and the evaluation of performance may be limited by the quantity of data rather than the lack of it. In parallel with the development of service delivery technologies advances in data mining and data gathering technologies may address this evaluative issue. Much work has been done on user surveys, customer forums, and online dispute resolution in the private sector from which evaluators in the public sector can benefit.

What all three of these alternative views of governance have in common is an attempt to broaden out the governance structure to a range of government and non government actors. The technologies available through Web 2.0 innovations allow for new ways for the state to communicate with citizens. It is clear that many parts of both traditional government and the general population are not yet quite ready for this leap of faith but it is equally clear that this is the direction in which governance is moving.

FUTURE TRENDS AND RESEARCH

In the area of cyberlaw further research is needed in codifying the types of crime and selecting the appropriate response for each category. Research into compiling the various codes of conduct on Social Networking sites and establishing a base set of standards which users and service providers can agree on is also desirable. Online dispute resolution is a further area ready for research and expanding the range of activities that can be addressed in this manner.

Future research in the field of governance is needed in eConsultation and also in eBudgeting (the process of allowing the citizens input into the spending priorities of the state). Also, the distinction between governing the behavior of online participants and the use of social networks as a tool of governance would be fruitful.

CONCLUSION

The internet continues to grow both in terms of functionality and number of participants. The amount of time spent by participants online also continues to grow. As we spend an increasing proportion of our day online and perform an increasing number of tasks the concept of a cybercitizen is a real and meaningful one. As cybercitizens we need a frame-work of laws, rules, or guidelines to maintain a sense of order online. Some of this frame-work is growing organically and some will be imposed. As governments increasingly see the opportunities to engage with us online the emphasis may be on the latter. It is important to maintain this understanding of the way our actions will be monitored and restricted as we proceed with the remaining chapters in this book.

REFERENCES

Abbott, K. W., & Snidal, D. (2000). Hard and Soft Law in International Governance. *International Organization*, *54*, 421–456. doi:10.1162/002081800551280

Allain, J. (2004). Orientalism and International Law: The Middle East as the Underclass of the International Legal Order. *Leiden Journal of International Law*, *17*, 391–404. doi:10.1017/S0922156504001864

Associated Press. (2008, October 24). Japanese woman faces jail over online murder. *The Guardian*. Retrieved from http://www.guardian.co.uk/world/2008 /oct/24/japan-games

Austin, J. (2000). *The Province of Jurisprudence Determined*. New York: Prometheus Books. (originally London 1832)

BBC News (2005, March 31). Game theft led to fatal attack. *Technology*. Retrieved from http://news.bbc.co.uk/1/hi/technology /4397159.stm

BBC News (2007, November 14). 'Virtual theft' leads to arrest. *Technology*. Retrieved from http://news.bbc.co.uk/2/hi/technology /7094764.stm

Boyle, J. (1997). Foucault in cyberspace: surveillance, sovereignty, and hardwired censors. *University of Cincinnati Law Review*, *66*, 177–205.

Cannataci, J., & Mifsud-Bonnici, J. (2007). Weaving the Mesh: Finding Remedies in Cyberspace. *International Review of Law Computers & Technology*, *21*, 59–78. doi:10.1080/13600860701281705

Cooney, R., & Lang, A. (2007). Taking Uncertainty Seriously: Adaptive Governance and International Trade. *European Journal of International Law*, *18*, 523. doi:10.1093/ejil/chm030

Council of Europe. (2001). *Convention on Cybercrime*. Retrieved from http://conventions.coe.int/Treaty/ en/Treaties/Html/185.htm

Cybercrime (n.d.). In *Macmillan Dictionary*. Retrieved from http://www.macmillandictionary.com /dictionary/british/cybercrime

Cybercrime (n.d.). In *New World Encyclopedia*. Retrieved from http://www.newworldencyclopedia.org /entry/Cyber_crime

Cybercrime (n.d.) in *PC Magazine Encyclopedia*. Retrieved from http://www.pcmag.com/encyclopedia_term/ 0,2542,t=cybercrime&i=40628,00.asp

Cybercrime (n.d.) in *Princeton WordNet*. Retrieved from http://wordnetweb.princeton.edu/perl/webwn?s=cybercrime

Dunleavy, P., Margetts, H., Bastow, S., & Tinkler, J. (2006). New Public Management is Dead – Long Live Digital-Era Governance. *Journal of Public Administration: Research and Theory*, *16*, 467–494. doi:10.1093/jopart/mui057

Dworkin, R. (1986). *Law's Empire*. Oregon: Hart Publishing.

Eckersley, R. (2007). Soft law, hard politics, and the Climate Change Treaty. In Reus-Smit, C. (Ed.), *The Politics of International Law* (pp. 80–105). Cambridge: Cambridge University Press.

Edwards, A. (2002). The Moderator as an Emerging Democratic Intermediary: The Role of the Moderator in Internet Discussions about Public Issues. *Information Polity, 7*, 3–20.

Emigh, J. (2008, October 24). Online gamer arrested for 'virtual murder' in Japan. *Betanews*. Retrieved from http://www.betanews.com/article/Online-gamer-arrested-for-virtual-murder-in-Japan/1224888499

Evans, M. (2009). Gordon Brown and public management reform – a project in search of a 'big idea'? *Policy Studies, 30*, 33–51. doi:10.1080/01442870802576181

Foucault, M. (1978). The history of sexuality: *Vol. 1. An introduction*. New York: Pantheon.

Giddens, A. (1998). *The Third Way: The Renewal of Social Democracy*. Cambridge, UK: Polity.

Goldsmith, J. L. (1998). Against Cyberanarchy. *The University of Chicago Law Review. University of Chicago. Law School, 65*, 1199–1250. doi:10.2307/1600262

Hart, H. L. A. (1994). *The Concept of Law* (2nd ed.). Oxford, UK: Oxford University Press.

Hood, C. (1983). *The Tools of Government*. Basingstoke, UK: Macmillan.

Johnson, D., & Post, D. (1996). Law and Borders – The Rise of Law in Cyberspace. *Stanford Law Review, 48*, 1367–1402. doi:10.2307/1229390

Kamarch, E. (2007). *The End of Government as we know it: Making public policy work*. Lynne Rienner Publishers.

Katsh, E. (2007). Online Dispute Resolution: Some Implications for the Emergence of Law in Cyberspace. *International Review of Law Computers & Technology, 21*, 97–107. doi:10.1080/13600860701492096

Kickert, W. J. M., Klijn, E. H., & Koppenjan, J. F. M. (1997). *Managing Networks in the Public Sector. Managing Complex Networks*. London: Sage.

Knight, W. (2005, August 18). Computer characters mugged in virtual crime spree. *New Scientist*. Retrieved from http://www.newscientist.com/article/dn7865

Lessig, L. (2000). *Code and Other Laws of Cyberspace*. Princeton, NJ: Princeton University Press.

Loughlan, J. (2004). The Transformation of Governance: New Directions in Policy and Politics. *The Australian Journal of Politics and History, 50*, 8–22. doi:10.1111/j.1467-8497.2004.00317.x

MacSíthigh, D. (2008). The mass age of internet law. *Information & Communications Technology Law, 17*, 79–94. doi:10.1080/13600830802204187

Morison, J., & Livingstone, S. (1995). *Reshaping Public Power*. London: Sweet & Maxwell.

Morison, J., & Newman, D. (2001). On-line Citizenship: Consultation and Participation in New Labour's Britain and Beyond. *International Review of Law Computers & Technology, 15*, 171–194. doi:10.1080/13600860120070501

Morris, S. (2008, November 14). Internet affair leads to couple's real life divorce. *The Guardian*. Retrieved from http://www.guardian.co.uk/technology/2008 /nov/14/second-life-virtual-worlds-divorce

Post, D. (1996). Governing Cyberspace. *Wayne Law Review, 43*, 155–171.

Rabinow, P. (1984). *The Foucault Reader*. London: Penguin.

Reuters (2005, March 30). Gamer gets life for murder over virtual sword. *CNET.* Retrieved from http://news.cnet.co.uk/gamesgear/ 0,39029682,39189904,00.htm

Schäfer, A. (2006). Resolving Deadlock: Why International Organisations Introduce Soft Law. *European Law Journal, 12,* 194–208. doi:10.1111/ j.1468-0386.2006.00315.x

Senden, L. (2004). *Soft Law in European Community Law.* Portland, OR: Hart Publishing.

Shirky, C. (2009). *Here Comes Everybody.* London: Penguin.

Sindico, F. (2006). Soft Law and the Elusive Quest for Sustainable Global Governance. *Leiden Journal of International Law, 19,* 829–846. doi:10.1017/S0922156506003608

Slaughter, A. (2004). *A New World Order.* Princeton University Press.

Swire, P. (2005). Elephants and mice revisited: law and choice of law on the Internet. *University of Pennsylvania Law Review, 153,* 1975–2001. doi:10.2307/4150654

Symantec (n.d.) *What is Cybercrime?* Retrieved from http://www.symantec.com/norton/ cyber-crime/definition.jsp

Truta, F. (2008, January 18). Russia - Gamer Kills Gamer over Gamer Killing Gamer... Er, In-Game! *Softpedia.* Retrieved from http://news.softpedia. com/news/Russia-Gamer-Kills-Gamer-over-Gamer-Killing-Gamer-Er-In-Game-76619.shtml

U.S. Department of Homeland Security. (2003). *National Strategy to Secure Cyberspace.* Retrieved from http://www.dhs.gov/files/publications /editorial_0329.shtm

Woman faces jail for hacking her virtual husband to death (2008, October 10). *The Irish Times.* Retrieved from http://www.irishtimes.com/newspaper/ frontpage/2008/1025/1224838828960.html

Working Group on Internet Governance. (2005) *Report of the Working Group on Internet Governance.* Retrieved from http://www.wgig.org/docs/ WGIGREPORT.doc

World Summit on the Information Society. (2010). *Home.* Retrieved from http://www.itu.int/wsis/ index.html

Wright, S. (2006). Government-run Online Discussion Forums: Moderation, Censorship and the Shadow of Control. *British Journal of Politics and International Relations, 8,* 550–568. doi:10.1111/j.1467-856X.2006.00247.x

ADDITIONAL READING

Dunleavy, P., Margetts, H., Bastow, S., & Tinkler, J. (2006). *Digital Era Governance: IT Corporations, the State, and E-Government.* Oxford: Oxford University Press.

Kamarch, E. (2007). *The End of Government as we know it: Making public policy work.* Lynne Rienner Publishers.

Lessig, L. (2000). *Code and Other Laws of Cyberspace.* Princeton, N.J.: Princeton University Press.

Senden, L. (2004). *Soft Law in European Community Law.* Portland, OR: Hart Publishing.

Shirky, C. (2009). *Here comes everybody.* London: Penguin.

Slaughter, A. (2004). *A New World Order.* Princeton University Press.

Chapter 2
Can Forensic Psychology Contribute to Solving the Problem of Cybercrime?

ABSTRACT

Considering the severity of the problem of cybercrime, it must next be deliberated whether forensic psychology can aid in the detection, prevention and governance of these crimes or not. While forensic psychology to date has generally focused on violent, sexual and juvenile offences, most of its theory and practice can also be applied to other offences, such as cybercrime. This chapter aims to investigate if forensic psychology can be useful in solving the problem of cybercrime, and briefly considers to what extent it has been applied to these crimes so far. Initially, definitions of forensic psychology will be discussed, and the primary responsibilities and activities of forensic psychologists will be described. Following this the authors will examine how each of these responsibilities and activities may be applied to cybercrime cases, before determining to what extent forensic psychology has been involved in cybercrime cases to date. Suggestions will be made for how to promote the benefits of forensic psychology in cybercrime cases, and finally proposals for future research and potential trends will be highlighted. In order to provide background to the reader who is not familiar with forensic psychology, a very brief overview of some of the key research in the field is provided in the appropriate sections below. However, the reader is encouraged to consult a textbook on the area in order to gain a more thorough appreciation of the breadth and depth of research in this field to date (see for example Davies, Hollin & Bull, 2008; Howitt, 2009 or Huss, 2009).

BACKGROUND

Forensic psychology is one of the fields of psychology of which the general public is most widely aware, thanks in part to the numerous television programmes and films that have portrayed the topic, such as *Cracker, Criminal Minds* and *Silence of the Lambs*. However, the area of offender profiling which is the most commonly portrayed activity of forensic psychologists in the media, is actually an area in which very few forensic psychologists engage, with the majority actually working in prison settings (British Psychological Society, 2010), and with only about

DOI: 10.4018/978-1-61350-350-8.ch002

10% of forensic psychologists and psychiatrists ever having engaged in criminal profiling (Torres, Boccaccini & Miller, 2006). So, if the majority of forensic psychologists are not involved in offender profiling, it must be clarified what exactly forensic psychology is, and in what other activities its practitioners engage.

What is Forensic Psychology?

There have been numerous definitions offered for forensic psychology over the history of its existence. Howitt (2009) specifies that while "forensic psychology literally is psychology to do with courts of law" (p. 1), the actual use of the term is much broader. Howitt indicates that the term 'criminal psychology', referring to "the activities of all psychologists whose work is related to the criminal justice system" (p.1) can also be used. Between them, these two definitions cover the vast majority of the work of forensic psychologists. In truth, while most forensic psychologists work directly with offenders, often completing assessments or directing rehabilitation programmes, forensic psychology does involve almost every aspect of the criminal justice system. This includes everyone from the victim and eyewitnesses of the crime (perhaps offering counselling, support, or assisting in gathering witness statements), to the police (developing profiles, but also aiding in suspect interviewing and advising in staff recruitment, training and morale), to judges and lawyers (advising on how to select jury members, how to instruct juries when presenting evidence, and providing advice on human decision making strategies) and sometimes even extending their help to the general public in advising on how to persuade people to engage in crime reduction strategies.

Some definitions of forensic psychology can be quite broad, such as that of Wrightsman (2001) who indicates forensic psychology is "any application of psychological knowledge or methods to a task faced by the legal system" (p.2), whereas others have a considerably narrower focus, such as that of Blackburn (1996) who specifies that forensic psychology is "the provision of psychological information for the purpose of facilitating a legal decision" (p. 7). Howitt (2009) highlights that such narrow definitions are problematic, as they exclude the work of many psychologists who work in criminological settings such as prisons but do not work directly in courts. Such definitions also exclude the work of those who teach or research in topics related to psychology and crime. Davies, Hollin and Bull (2008) indicate that forensic psychology is a combination of both *"legal psychology* covering the application of psychological knowledge and methods to the process of law and *criminological psychology* dealing with the application of psychological theory and method to the understanding (and reduction) of criminal behaviour" (p. xiii), but they do note that the use of the term 'forensic psychology' to encompass both has been contentious. Nevertheless, it is the term that has generally been accepted by the profession, supported by the British Psychological Society's decision to change the name of their 'Division of Criminological and Legal Psychology' to the 'Division of Forensic Psychology' in 1999.

For the purposes of this book, the broadest definition of forensic psychology will be used, and it will be considered to include any way by which psychology can be of assistance at any stage in the criminal justice process. With this in mind, an overview will be provided of some of the main roles of forensic psychologists, and how they can be applied specifically to cybercrime.

Principal Roles of Forensic Psychologists and Their Application to Cybercrime

As outlined above, few forensic psychologists are engaged in offender profiling, despite its popularity in the media. Nevertheless, it is an area where some work has been completed in cybercrime cases, and as such is of interest for this book. In addition, there are a wide variety of other activities that are encompassed within forensic psychology and which may be of assistance in cybercrime cases to varying extents. Some of the most common activities which practicing forensic psychologists engage in include offender rehabilitation and offender assessment. Based on this, and other factors, some psychologists often provide expert testimony in courts, particularly where the psychological health of the offender may be in question. Psychology can also be of assistance in aiding investigators to obtain reliable information from witnesses and victims, as well as successful methods of interviewing suspects and detecting deception. Police psychology, considering the recruitment, stress levels and training of police officers is another area of interest, as is the behaviour of juries. From a more societal perspective, forensic psychology also concerns itself with the wellbeing of victims and crime prevention methods.

Offender Profiling

Offender profiling can be defined as "a technique for identifying the major personality and behavioural characteristics of an individual based upon an analysis of the crimes he or she has committed" (Douglas, Ressler, Burgess & Hartman, 1986, p. 405). In truth, there are several techniques which can be used to develop a profile (Ainsworth, 2001), including the *Crime Scene Analysis* technique used as the basis for the United States Federal Bureau of Investigation technique, *Diagnostic Evaluation* which relies on clinical judgements of a profiler, and *Investigative Psychology* which utilises a statistical approach to profiling (though it should be noted that investigative psychology is generally considered to have a broader remit than profiling alone, with Canter & Youngs, 2009 suggesting that it "provides a framework for the integration of many aspects of psychology into all areas of police and other investigations", p. 5).

Offender profiles have been used in many criminal investigations, and profiles have even been developed of historical offenders, such as Jack the Ripper (Ogan & Allison, 2005; Canter & Youngs, 2009, pp. 54-57). One of the most famous early profiles was James Brussel's 1956 profile of George Metesky, the New York Bomber, although since then many profilers have published descriptions of the cases they have worked on and the profiles they have developed (see for example Britton, 1997, 2000; Canter, 1994; 2003; Cook, 2001; Douglas & Olshaker, 1995, 1999, 2000). While offender profiling is most commonly associated with high-profile homicide, child abduction and sexual assault cases, it can also be used for many other types of offence, such as property crime, organised crime, and terrorism (Canter & Youngs, 2009).

Alison and Kebbell (2006) indicate that there are two key assumptions that underlie profiling methods – the 'consistency assumption' and the 'homology assumption'. The consistency assumption states that the behaviour of an offender will remain fairly consistent across their offences – that they will exhibit similar behaviours throughout all their crimes. So for example, if an offender brings a weapon to the crime scene on one occasion, the consistency assumption dictates that they will bring weapons to most of their crime scenes. There are problems with this assumption – the offender may not have a weapon available every time they plan to commit an offence, or the offender may not have initially brought weapons to the crime scene, but has learned from prior experience that a weapon would be useful.

The homology assumption "is that similar offence styles have to be associated with similar offender background characteristics" (p. 153). This suggests that if, for example, an offender is generally an anxious person, then this anxiety will also be evident in how they complete their crimes (so they may avoid situations where it is more likely that they will be apprehended, they may be careful in their choice of victim to ensure that they will be less likely to report the crime, and so on). Again, there are problems with this assumption – people portray different characteristics in different situations. While a person may be very outgoing and chatty with their friends, they may be considerably quieter and introverted while among family members.

The effectiveness and utility of offender profiling is difficult to prove, in part because it is difficult to obtain a representative sample of profiles (Alison & Kebbell, 2006). In an attempt to verify the effectiveness of profiling empirically, Alison, Smith, Eastman and Rainbow (2003) assessed 3,090 statements that made up twenty-one offender profiles. They found that three-quarters of these were repetition of the details of police data. Of the remaining statements, 92% were unsubstantiated, with over half of the statements being unverifiable. However, Alison and Kebbell (2006) indicate that there are some methods by which the utility of offender profiles can be improved to the extent that they would be a useful and more reliable tool for investigations.

Regarding the use of offender profiling in cybercrime, there are several examples of studies and papers which have examined this field. As early as 1998, Gudaitis outlined the need for a multidimensional profiling method to specifically assess cybercriminals. Nykodym, Taylor and Vilela (2005) indicate that the use of offender profiling to investigate cybercrime, particularly where the offender is potentially an insider in a victimised company, could be very useful. Jahankhani and Al-Nemrat (2010) indicate that, as technology rapidly changes, then there may also be rapid changes in the behaviour of cybercriminals. As such, one of the key assumptions of offender profiling, the consistency assumption, cannot be relied on when creating profiles of cybercriminals. However, this is disputed by Preuß, Furnell and Papadaki (2007) who report the analysis of twelve hacking incidents in Germany. They found that the methods used by hackers years ago were still the preferred methods, with hackers using the method which required the least effort. Rogers (2003) indicates that offender profiling could be useful

in a variety of ways for cybercriminal investigation, including helping the investigators to search hard drives more effectively, narrowing the pool of potential suspects, identifying a motive, and determining the characteristics of victims which make them more appealing to offenders.

The Hackers Profiling Project (Chiesa, Ducci & Ciappi, 2009) took place between 2003 and 2009, and produced a large quantity of information regarding the profile of existing hackers, including demographics, socioeconomic background, social relationships, psychological traits and hacking activities. The results of this study are considered in more detail in Chapter 4. However, it should be noted that this project aimed to create a profile of hackers based on completion of a self-report questionnaire, rather than any attempts to develop a profile of a hacker from their activities and offences alone. Nevertheless, the scale and scope of the Hackers Profiling Project is an important initial step in developing the database of information required to make accurate profiles of offenders in the future.

One particular aspect of offender profiling which is likely not to be applicable to cybercrime is the technique of geographical profiling. This activity seeks to identify an offender's base through examining the locations of their crime scenes (Canter, 2003; Canter & Youngs, 2009). Similarly to other profiling techniques, geographical profiling is also subject to weaknesses, and predictions are not always accurate (see for example Paulsen, 2006; Snook, Zito, Bennell & Taylor, 2005). Because of the international nature of the internet, there may be little or no geographical links between the target of the offender and where they themselves live. Nevertheless, there may be some theories within criminal psychogeography that could be of assistance in investigating some cybercrime cases. For example, Routine Activity Theory (RAT), originally devised by Cohen and Felson (1979) proposes that crime develops "as a byproduct of other activities in which the criminal engages" (Canter & Youngs, 2009, p.172). For offline crimes, this might suggest to investigators that the burglar chose to target a house or business which they must pass on their way to a location that they regularly visit, such as their school, workplace or social welfare office. Online, it may mean that the offender targets companies whose websites they regularly visit. This seemed to be the case for Adrian Lamo, when he chose to hack the *New York Times*, whose website he regularly visited for news updates.

Psychological Disorders and Offender Assessment

Some forensic psychologists assess suspects and offenders for psychological disorders, later providing a report or expert testimony for use in court (Gudjonsson & Haward, 1998). This task is compounded by a lack of agreement between legal systems and psychology as to what constitutes a psychological disorder.

Defining abnormal behaviour, and hence psychological disorders, has proven difficult in psychology. Modern definitions of abnormal behaviour frequently use deviance, discomfort and/or dysfunction in order to determine what symptom or symptoms should be used in psychological diagnosis (Sue, Sue & Sue, 2005). *Deviance* refers to how frequent or rare a given behaviour is, but is insufficient in itself to define abnormality. For example, it is quite rare to experience hallucinations or delusions, but it is also rare for a person to climb Mount Everest, which would not be considered by most to necessarily be abnormal behaviour. *Discomfort* relates to how the behaviour or emotion impacts on the individual, either physically or psychologically. However, again it is insufficient to completely define abnormality – it is normal for a person to feel emotional discomfort following a traumatic experience such as bereavement, to the extent that if the individual doesn't demonstrate any discomfort we then consider them to be behaving in an abnormal fashion. Finally, *dysfunction* relates to how the individual

is managing their daily life – are their symptoms permitting them to continue to work, study and socialise to their full potential? A difficulty with this approach relates to the problems in assessing the person's full potential – it can be difficult to determine if a child's grades in school are related to poor aptitude, or to an emotional reaction to psychological difficulties.

A further complication for assessment in forensic psychology is that insanity is a legal term, rather than a psychological one (Huss, 2009). It does not correspond with the diagnoses provided in the American Psychological Association's Diagnostic and Statistical Manual (DSM), and it is possible for someone to suffer from psychological disorders without being insane. There have been many descriptions and definitions of insanity over time, which are outlined by Huss (2009), with many relating to comprehension of right and wrong or control of impulses.

A suspect may be diagnosed with any type of psychological disorder, and psychologists will normally assess for mood disorders, schizophrenia, anxiety disorders, personality disorders and dissociative disorders, amongst others. Assessment is completed using a variety of methods, including interview, psychometric tests, clinical history and observations. A particular psychological concept of interest in forensic psychology is that of psychopathy, a specific form of antisocial personality disorder. This disorder is characterised by the DSM-IV-TR as a failure to conform to social norms with respect to lawful behaviours, a tendency to lie frequently, impulsivity, irritability, irresponsibility, and a lack of remorse for their actions. While the term psychopath is most commonly associated with serial killers such as Ted Bundy, psychopaths are not necessarily criminal in nature (Babiak & Hare, 2006).

There has been relatively little work done investigating psychological disorders and cybercriminals. It has been suggested that there is a link between Asperger's Syndrome (AS) and hacking behaviours (Hunter, 2009) with hackers such as Gary McKinnon (whose case is discussed in Chapter 4) and Owen Walker (Gleeson, 2008) both being diagnosed with the disorder. Asperger's Syndrome is a disorder on the autistic spectrum, characterised by intact cognitive ability and no delays in early language milestones (Toth & King, 2008), but there is significant impairment in social interaction skills, lack of emotional reciprocity and repetitive and strong interests in limited numbers of activities (Sue et al, 2005). Hunter (2009) indicates that these characteristics could lead AS individuals to spend more time with computers indicating that "For a person with Asperger's Syndrome, computers can provide a perfect solitary pastime as well as a refuge from the unpredictability of people (p. 46). While there has yet to be an empirical study linking hacking with AS, it would appear that the symptoms of AS do lend themselves to developing an interest in such behaviours.

Punishment, Rehabilitation and Risk Assessment

In addition to the initial assessment of the suspect or offender, a forensic psychologist may also be asked to assess their risk of future offending, and to design and implement a rehabilitation programme for the individual. In law, punishments can take a variety of methods (such as fines, imprisonment, community service, and so on), and can also have a variety of aims, such as incapacitation, deterrence, restitution or rehabilitation. Incapacitation refers to reducing the offender's ability to commit further offences. This is often managed through electronic tagging or imprisonment. In the case of Kevin Mitnick, one of the most famous computer hackers, great measures were taken to reduce his ability to commit further offences. Littman (1996, as cited by MacKinnon, 1997) indicates that US Magistrate Venetta Tassopulos "took the unusual step of ordering the young Panorama City computer whiz held without bail, ruling that when armed with a keyboard he posed a danger to the

community" (p. 17). Mitnick's telephone access was also severely restricted.

Deterrence can be aimed either at the individual offender (in the hope that they personally will not reoffend) or at society in general (in the hope that the punishment of the individual will deter others from engaging in criminal behaviours). Smith (2004) cites the example of an apparently successful case of individual deterrence. Simon Vallor created computer viruses, and on conviction spent eight months in prison. He is quoted as saying "I would never try to create a virus again… Going to prison was terrible. It was the worst time of my life." (p. 6). Smith (2004) indicates that hackers generally know how their fellows have fared in the legal system, and that convictions are difficult to obtain. As such, hope for general deterrence seems low.

Restitution aims to compensate the victim for the damage done by the offender. The most obvious example of this in cybercrime cases relates to music, video and software piracy. In 2009, Jammie Thomas-Rasset was fined almost two million dollars for sharing songs over the internet. While her fine was later reduced to $54,000, it is an example of the music industry attempting to reclaim some of their perceived losses from online piracy (BBC News, 2010). As well as providing restitution, cases such as this are also hoped to contribute towards achieving general deterrence, although it is unclear if they are effective due to the large numbers of illegal file sharers and relatively few court cases to date. A potentially more effective deterrent is the controversial internet piracy bill in the United Kingdom, which proposes to limit broadband speeds of illegal file-sharers, effectively resulting in incapacitation as their internet connectivity slows to dial-up speeds.

Ideally, upon completion of the punishment, the offender would be rehabilitated and would no longer re-offend. The development of rehabilitation programmes can be quite difficult, and as Huss (2009) argues, it is important not to think of offenders as a homogenous group. The motives, psychology and backgrounds of different types of offenders can vary greatly, and a treatment programme needs to be specialised for the offender involved. Even within cybercrime, there is considerable variety in the types of offender – cyberterrorists will require very different treatment than child pornography distributers. Even within a specific group, different treatment approaches are suitable – for hackers with Asperger's Syndrome, treatment can encompass a variety of approaches, including Applied Behaviour Analysis (ABA), enhancing social competence and targeted intervention strategies (Toth & King, 2008), but it is unknown how many hackers do not suffer from Asperger's Syndrome, and alternative treatment programmes would need to be developed. A more thorough consideration of suitable punishment and treatment approaches for each type of cybercriminal are provided in the appropriate chapters throughout this book, although it should be noted that all rehabilitation programmes require considerable evaluation in order to determine their effectiveness.

Forensic psychologists are also often required to assess the risk that a particular offender presents to society. This is an extremely difficult task to accomplish, especially as it is problematical to determine the accuracy of an assessment, even with the benefit of hindsight. An offender who has been judged to be of low risk and is released, may still reoffend, and the error would not be noted unless the offender is apprehended. Similarly, an offender who is judged to be of high risk and who is detained may never have offended again, even if released. For some cybercriminals, such as hackers or identity thieves, the consequences of an inaccurate risk assessment are relatively low, as the offences tend to mostly involve just monetary losses. However, for other offenders such as child predators or child pornography distributers, inaccurate risk assessments can have very serious consequences for potential victims. As such great care must be taken by forensic psychologists to consider all the risk factors for the offence and offender, and to err on the side of caution whenever is appropriate.

Interviewing Suspects and Detecting Deception

Suspect interrogation is often one of the most exciting tasks carried out by media portrayals of forensic psychologists. The tension in the interrogation room heightens as the psychologist slowly 'pushes the suspect's buttons' until they eventually crack and confess to the crime. In practice, while the psychologist may advise the police on potentially effective strategies, it is unlikely that they would interrogate suspects directly.

Kebbell and Hurren (2006) summarise the research to date in this field. They describe how suspect confessions can be a key component of a prosecutions argument, as well as a number of police interviewing techniques. Some of the more effective strategies include appealing to the suspect's conscience, identifying inconsistencies in suspect's stories, using praise or flattery and offering moral justifications. Other techniques, such as hostility, insulting the suspect and being aggressive reduce the likelihood of obtaining a confession. To date, there is a lack of research evidence indicating the most suitable methods of suspect interviewing for cybercrime cases, but it seems unlikely that they would vary considerably from the techniques which have been found effective for other offences. Rogers (2003) indicates that criminal profiling could help investigators interrogate cybercrime suspects effectively, but there does not appear to be any documented cases of this occurring to date.

An important point to note is that suspects can be very agitated and distressed during arrest and detention (Gudjonsson, 2003), and this may be especially the case for vulnerable suspects, such as children or those with psychological difficulties (such as Asperger's Syndrome described above). It is therefore important that these individuals are accompanied by an appropriate adult during interrogation. Another issue of importance is the possibility of false confessions, which could be caused by a wide variety of reasons. Gudjonsson (2003) differentiates between three types of false confessions: Voluntary false confessions; Coerced-compliant false confessions and Coerced-internalised false confessions. Voluntary false confessions "are offered by individuals without any external pressure from the police" (Gudjonsson, 2003, p. 194) and can occur because the offender wishes to gain notoriety, to protect the criminal, or because they lack the ability to distinguish fact from fantasy (Kassin & Wrightsman, 1985). For example, an innocent person may confess to being a hacker as they believe that if they do so, they will be accepted as a hero within the hacking community, or they may be offered a position within IT security. Coerced-compliant false confessions occur when the interrogation process is coercive to the extent that the suspect eventually gives in to the demands of the interrogators to confess. This may be due to physical discomfort, such as sleep deprivation, or to obtain perceived instrumental gain, such as being allowed to go home. Finally, coerced-internalised false confessions occur when the suspect believes during questioning (and sometimes afterwards) that they are indeed guilty of the crime, despite being innocent, normally due to persuasiveness of the interrogators. As with all types of suspects, interviewers should be wary of inducing false confessions in suspected cybercriminals, especially those with known or suspected psychological difficulties.

While it is very difficult to assess how many false confessions occur (Gudjonsson, 2003), it seems likely that a greater number of suspects deny carrying out an offence that they actually have committed. Therefore another important element of forensic psychology involves the ability to detect deception accurately. Again, this is an element of the discipline which has been subject to media portrayal – most notably in the television series 'Lie to Me'. While the traditional method of lie detection has involved the polygraph machine, police officers today have a much broader array of techniques to investigate if a suspect is being deceptive. Vrij (2006) describes a number of these tools, including voice-stress analysers,

thermal imaging, and the traditional polygraph, and argues that these methods are unreliable, mainly because they depend on the assumption that liars are more physiologically and emotionally aroused than truth-tellers, which may not necessarily be the case. He suggests that other techniques such as the 'Guilty Knowledge Test', encouraging suspects to elaborate and the strategic use of evidence provide more reliable results. Other techniques, such as Statement Validity Analysis (Howitt, 2009), microexpression detection (Porter & ten Brinke, 2008), subtle expression detection (Warren, Schertler & Bull, 2009) and fMRI scans (Langleben, 2008) have also been used to detect deception, to varying degrees of accuracy. However, determining reliable methods of lie detection has been difficult and complete accuracy remains elusive, even with high levels of training and expensive equipment. It should also be noted that it is not always the offender who is suspected of lying – in some cases the accuracy of the statements of victims or witnesses may also be in question (see for example Edestein, Luten & Ekman, 2006).

Witness Evidence

There has been considerable research in forensic psychology in methods of improving the accuracy of eyewitness evidence. Notable early work by Elizabeth Loftus (see for example Loftus & Palmer, 1974 and Loftus, Miller & Burns, 1978) has been built on by more recent research, to the extent that considerable direction can now be given to police officers interviewing eyewitnesses to crimes in order to obtain the greatest possible quantity of reliable information. Blackwell-Young (2008) outlines some of the key principles relating to the accuracy of eyewitness memory, including weapon focus, witness credibility, eyewitness confidence, stress and post-incident influences, such as questioning. Research in cognitive and forensic psychology eventually led to the development of the 'cognitive interview' by Geiselman,

Fisher, MacKinnon and Holland (1986), a technique designed to improve eyewitness testimony through a number of strategies, such as mentally reinstating the witness and reporting events from alternative perspectives. The cognitive interview is often preferred by psychologists over forensic hypnosis as a memory retrieval technique (Howitt, 2009, p. 209-212).

There are rarely eyewitnesses in cybercrime cases, with the exception of crimes which occur within virtual worlds (as considered in Chapter 12) or child pornography or predation. Again, with those exceptions, victims of cybercrime are often corporations rather than individuals, and it is possible that many victims of cybercrimes such as hacking never realise that they have been victimised. Even those individuals who become aware of their victimisation, such as with identity theft, often have little information they can provide which is analogous to the eyewitness testimony of offline crimes. As such, this is an area for which forensic psychology has limited input in cybercrime, although the vast literature on the interviewing of child witnesses and victims should be consulted for cases of child pornography or child predation (see for example McCauley & Fisher, 1995; Lamb, Orlbach, Hershkowitz, Esplin & Horowitz, 2007).

Nonetheless, it should be noted that the investigation of offences and interviewing of suspects and witnesses are only some of the ways in which forensic psychologists can help police officers. Recruitment, training, and stress levels of police officers can also be improved through the influence of forensic psychology.

Police Psychology

Police psychology is generally considered to include the contributions that psychology can make to criminal investigations, such as offender profiling, eyewitness interviewing and suspect interrogation outlined above. However, it also refers to other elements of police life and work, such as the training provided, recruitment procedures and the stresses which police officers regularly find themselves under.

While a greater number of police forces are recognising the seriousness of cybercrime issues, until relatively recently many countries did not have specialised police departments specifically for investigating these offences. In the early days of cybercrime, police officers who were not given any formal training in the field would be required to work on these cases as they arose. These early pioneers of cybercrime investigation paved the way for the current situation where many modern police forces do have dedicated units for these offences and international collaborations are becoming more common.

Forensic psychologists, along with organisational psychologists, can aid police forces in the recruitment of suitable personnel. Policing is a very diverse job, and many countries have a central initial recruitment and training scheme, after which individuals can specialise for specific roles. However, the variety of tasks which police officers deal with on a daily basis can be very diverse, varying from armed combat to administrative work, and it can be difficult to specify the ideal personnel characteristics for a role which may eventually involve anything from managing minor traffic violations to controlling riots. Police psychology can help with this by analysing the tasks completed by police officers, and using this to determine the psychometric profile best suited to that work.

An increasing number of police forces are also training their personnel in matters relating to cybercrime, an activity which could be assisted by educational and forensic psychologists to ensure that the material is presented in the best possible manner. Unfortunately, most of this training relates only to the investigation of cybercrime while neglecting the psychological aspects. While many police forces also provide their recruits with some basic training in psychology, it is rarely specialised enough to provide officers with support for cybercrime cases.

Finally, police officers in many different roles can be subject to high levels of stress. In addition to the life stressors experienced by most individuals (such as financial problems or moving house), and the stressors caused by many jobs (such as dealing effectively with management and peers, unclear responsibilities, or administrative backlog), police officers can also be subject to unusual and extreme stressors, such as attending scenes of serious accidents or being in life-threatening situations (Ainsworth, 2002). These types of situations may result in the police officer developing Acute Stress Disorder (ASD) or Post Traumatic Stress Disorder (PTSD). These disorders involve the person having experienced an event involving fear, horror or helplessness, along with additional symptoms such as emotional numbing, heightened autonomic arousal (such as startle responses or sleep disturbances), flashbacks or intrusive memories (American Psychiatric Association, 2000). ASD and PTSD differ in onset and duration, and individuals with an initial diagnosis of ASD can receive a diagnosis of PTSD if their symptoms last longer than about four weeks. While more commonly associated with severe, potentially life-threatening events, such as violent or sexual assaults, both ASD and PTSD can also occur following relatively minor events. The likelihood of developing these disorders depends on both the nature of the event itself and the coping mechanisms of the police officer.

While dedicated cybercrime officers are unlikely to experience such life-threatening situations themselves, they can, nonetheless be affected by some of the material they work with, particularly if it relates to images of child pornography. Krause (2009) indicates that in some cases this repeated exposure to disturbing images has resulted in severe stress reactions and she outlines the symptoms experienced by some of these individuals, as well as safeguards designed to reduce the impact of the material on the law

enforcement personnel. Perez, Jones, Englert and Sachau (2010) carried out an empirical study to examine the psychological impact of internet child pornography on police officers, specifically examining Secondary Traumatic Stress Disorder (STSD) and burnout. They found that higher exposure to the disturbing images was related to higher levels of STSD and cynicism. Further, personnel with high levels of STSD and burnout showed higher protectiveness of their family, general distrust, and intent to leave or transfer from their position. On the other hand, their work also had some positive effect on them, as they scored high in professional efficacy, feeling that their work made a difference in society.

Cybercrime Juries

O'Ciardhuain (2004) presents an extended model of an 'ideal' procedure which should occur during cybercrime investigations and prosecutions. His model considers the difficulties inherent in obtaining usable data in cybercrime cases. However, it is not known if juries understand how important it is that these procedures are followed and that the data is not corrupted. It is important that juries are aware of the ambiguity of evidence obtained, particularly where multiple users have access to an individual computer where the evidence was obtained, or the evidence is not transported, stored and analysed appropriately.

The data collected in cybercrime cases can be very complex. In addition to understanding the legal terminology of the courtroom, a jury must also be (or become) familiar with the terminology and processes of the technology in question. With some types of crime this is more difficult than others. For example, a case relating to hacking behaviours could include phrases such as 'white-hat', 'distributed denial of service', 'packet sniffers', 'phishing', 'social engineering' and 'dumpster-diving', amongst many more (see Chapter 4 for definitions of each of these).

This specialist knowledge is not a new topic in jury research. There have been many arguments that a jury would be better off if it was made up of legal experts rather than lay people, and some countries have hybrid (or 'escabianto') juries for this reason (Acre, 1998). But no study has yet examined the effects of these requirements to comprehend extended terminology and complex information on the jury. There is no requirement that a court be satisfied that a juror "has the capacity to understand a legal case, to comprehend the evidence presented and the judge's instructions" (Kapardis, 2003, p. 147). Jurors have been shown to have poor recall of important trial information, especially in complex cases such as fraud (Nathanson, 1995). Walker (2001) also considers the "tension between efficiency and technical accuracy versus community involvement and the mediation of law through social standards" (p. 205).

It is considered by many that the evidence in cybercrime courts can leave a jury confused (Carney & Rogers, 2004; Carrier & Spafford, 2004; Rogers, 2003). Carney and Rogers (2004) argue that juries may find it easier to evaluate the evidence if they are provided with a degree of statistical probability, similar to that which is produced in DNA cases. Carney and Rogers also outline the effectiveness of the Trojan defence – that the defendant did not intentionally engage in the malicious behaviour but that a Trojan installed on their computer did so instead. While a good investigator may be able to accurately tell if the material on the computer was intentionally installed or not, Carney and Rogers indicate that a major problem is in convincing the judge and jury of this in a way that can be easily understood (Casey, 2002; Smith & Bace, 2003; Sommer, 1997). Expert testimony by those in computer forensics often leaves the jury confused (Smith & Bace, 2003).

A second factor of interest when considering cybercrime juries is to determine what affects their decision making. There are several models of jury decision making: the Bayesian probability theory model; the algebraic weighted average model; the stochastic Poisson process model; and the cognitive story model (Hastie, 1993). Of these, the story model is of the most interest for cybercrime cases. It suggests that jurors recreate a 'story' of the crime from the evidence presented, and compare this to a schema which they associate with a certain criminal activity. For example, in a kidnapping case, a jurors' schema might involve a stranger taking a child from their home. If the case involves a family member (such as a parent) illegally taking a child from their home instead, then the juror involved may not accept the act as criminal, as it does not fit into their schema, and would be less likely to convict. Jury members can have different schema, and so one person may be willing to convict while another, given exactly the same evidence, is more likely to acquit.

The story model is of particular interest when we consider hacking cases. 'White hat' hackers will often suggest prosocial motives for their offending behaviours – perhaps suggesting that they only hacked a system in order to highlight flaws and vulnerabilities in it. This is a defence which has been used by several high profile hackers, both inside and outside of the courtroom. It is possible that this 'white-hat' defence might interfere with the schema of jurors, making them more likely to acquit, even though criminal activity has probably occurred.

Victims of Cybercrime

An often forgotten participant in the criminal justice system is the victim, although the repercussions of the crime can be more severe for them than for any other individual in the process. There are a number of psychological reactions that are experienced by many victims of crime. These vary according to the type of crime experienced and the coping strategy and personality of the individual victim, but can include Acute Stress Disorder (ASD) or Post-Traumatic Stress Disorder

(PTSD), self-blaming for victimization, 'victim blaming' (where others put all or partial blame for the crime on the victim themselves), and a need for retribution.

For many negative life events, but particularly for sexual assault cases, the victim can engage in self-blaming activity (Miller, Markman & Handley, 2007). Here, the victim can blame themselves for voluntarily engaging in any behavior preceding the offence, even though this behavior may be only tangentially related to the offence taking place. For example, the victim may later blame themselves for walking home alone instead of accepting a lift from a friend, or smiling socially at the rapist prior to the assault. Similar self-blaming can occur for other offences, such as blaming the self for not watching personal belongings more carefully prior to a theft. In cybercrime cases, the victim may also experience self-blaming behaviours. For example, if the person was a victim of identity theft, they may feel that they should have taken more care of their personal information, or been less gullible of social engineering tactics.

Related to self-blame is victim blaming. Mendelsohn (1974, as cited in Walklate, 2006), suggested that there is a spectrum of shared responsibility between the victim and the offender. In some cases, the victim can be seen as playing no role in the facilitation of the offence (for example, innocent bystanders of a terrorist attack). Sometimes the 'victim' is actually the offender, and should take full responsibility for the crime (such as if the individual makes an insurance claim for a non-existent injury). However, in most cases, victims fall between these two criteria, and are seen in some way to facilitate the offence (for example, by not fitting an alarm to their property or by provoking a fight in which they subsequently become injured). In these cases, the victim can frequently be fully or partially blamed for their victimization by others, including family, friends, insurance companies and law enforcement officials, who may indicate that the incident was the victim's own fault due to their negligence or actions. There is a considerable amount of controversy regarding this model of shared responsibility and victim blaming, especially with regard to sexual assault cases. This victim-blaming can also occur in cybercrime cases, as friends, relations and colleagues of the victim indicate to them the errors they made. It should be noted that at least some victim-blaming is not intended to be malicious, and rather is meant to provide advice to the victim to prevent revictimisation. However, it can still have a negative effect on the victim, as they feel in some way responsible for the event. Particular care should be taken in cases of internet child grooming – it is important that the child learns how to protect themselves appropriately without feeling that they are being blamed for the predator's behaviours.

After victimization, some individuals can experience either ASD or PTSD (Scarpa, Haden & Hurley, 2006; Hoyle & Zedner, 2007), experiencing similar effects to those described in the police psychology section above. As most cybercrime is not life threatening, it is unlikely that most victims would experience these disorders. However, anecdotal evidence indicates that some victims of crimes in virtual worlds have experienced at least some of the symptoms of ASD, and this is described in more detail in Chapter 12.

Following victimization, many individuals experience a need for retribution. They feel that the person or group who has targeted them should be punished for their actions in some way. This has especially been noted in the families of homicide victims (Haines, 1996), but can also occur in the victims of other crimes. It has also been found that if the court does not provide retribution when the offender is known, the victim can experience this as a type of secondary victimization, where they feel that they have not been adequately protected by society and their rights have not been suitably maintained (Orth, 2000 as cited by Montada, 2003). Again, this need for retribution is clearly seen in some victims of crime in online virtual worlds, with limited evidence for it in other cybercrimes.

Crime Prevention

A final aspect of the work of forensic psychologists which will be considered here is their contribution to the prevention of crime. This can take several main forms. Welsh and Farrington (2006) make distinctions between attempts to reduce crime by focusing on children, offenders, victims and physical places (for example, by increasing street lighting, or the use of closed circuit television cameras).

Interventions with at-risk groups to reduce their risk of starting a criminal career are described by Welsh and Farrington (2004). These can target either the individual and their family, or peer groups, schools and communities. They vary from general parent education programmes, to pre-school programmes, to skills programmes, which can target behaviours such as social skills, critical thinking and creative problem solving. Welsh and Farrington (2004) indicate that there are many programmes that are effective in reducing delinquency, and that they can be very cost-effective to implement, when compared to the costs to the criminal justice system if they are not (p. 258).

Other authors have investigated how to educate and inform victims and potential victims in order to reduce their likelihood of victimisation or repeat victimisation. For example, it has been investigated how to reduce the likelihood of a residential property being repeatedly burgled (Farrell & Pease, 2006).

With regard to cybercrime, we currently have insufficient knowledge to predict accurately who is at most risk of becoming an offender. As such, crime prevention strategies to date have mostly focused on education of victims and potential victims, and the use of technology to improve safety. This has been most notable with regard to child safety online, with software available that will limit the websites children can visit and the amount of time spent online. There have also been a considerable number of web based resources developed to inform children and parents about

internet safety (such as www.netsmartz.org). Similarly, there are several options for people to protect their computers against virus attacks, hacking and other forms of malware and intrusion. However, many individuals do not engage in adequate protection of themselves or their family.

Forensic psychology can aim to address this by identifying ways in which individuals can be encouraged to take better care online. For example, it has been demonstrated that individuals' safety behaviours can be improved by emphasising their personal responsibility and by stressing the positive outcomes of safe online behaviour (LaRose, Rifon & Enbody, 2008). It is also important that parents find a good balance between protecting their children and allowing them to experience the educational and psychosocial benefits of the online world (Tynes, 2007), and that they target specific types of online behaviour to improve their child's safety (Ybarra, Mitchell, Finkelhor & Wolak, 2007). With these important findings in mind, it is essential that the practical benefits of forensic psychology for cybercrime be promoted adequately so that the research can benefit users and law enforcement personnel in the real world.

PROMOTING THE BENEFITS OF FORENSIC PSYCHOLOGY IN CYBERCRIME CASES

With forensic psychology being more widely accepted by law enforcement agencies and the general public in recent years, now is a key moment in time to emphasise how the investigation and handling of cybercrime can be improved by drawing on the research and experience of the field. Initially, it would seem prudent to target those law enforcement agencies that have specific cybercrime units, especially if the law enforcement agency has previous positive experience of working with forensic psychologists in non-cybercrime cases. If these law enforcement agencies then have positive experiences regarding the application of forensic psychology to cybercrime cases, agencies who are initially less open to the input of psychologists may be more likely to trial their own collaborations.

While it is useful to emphasise the positive examples of how forensic psychology can be of assistance in cybercrime cases to both law enforcement agencies and the general public, it is also vital that the limitations of the field are always made clear to all those involved. One of the negative effects of the proliferation of media portrayals of offender profiling is that it tends to promote it as more successful and exact than it is in real life. It is essential that forensic psychologists are clear and candid as to what they can and cannot add to help to solve the case or the situation, so that there are fewer unreasonable expectations and less disappointment if the psychologist cannot provide all the answers.

FUTURE TRENDS AND RESEARCH

This chapter has highlighted some of the contributions that forensic psychology has already provided in cybercrime cases, although many of these will be considered in more depth and detail in the chapters that follow. However, it also highlights some of the areas where forensic psychology needs to focus its study in order to allow us a greater insight into the world of the cybercriminal.

The link between psychological disorders and cybercriminals requires further investigation. A great deal of work is still to be done on offender profiling of cybercriminals – while there has been more interest in this area of research in recent years it is still significantly behind the level of data available for many other types of offenders.

The development of suitable rehabilitation techniques for cybercrime offenders is also an area of interest that would benefit from further research, as would investigation of appropriate methods of crime prevention. In particular, effective strategies to accomplish general deterrence would be of par-

ticular benefit, so as to discourage new offenders from starting careers in cybercrime. Similarly, it is important that psychologists determine the most effective ways of informing internet users about online safety and protection against all types of cybercrime. Finally, it is important that more is learned about the effects of cybercrime on victims. This topic will be returned to in Chapter 7.

CONCLUSION

Forensic psychology can add a great deal to our understanding of cybercrime, and could eventually be very useful in our efforts to solve the problem of online crime. However, research in the field is still in its infancy, and until there is a greater focus on the advantages that forensic psychology can add, the benefits remain limited. There is little doubt that forensic psychology has been of great assistance to law enforcement agencies to date, but specific focus on cybercrime has so far been quite limited. However, the potential for forensic psychological contribution is evident, in a wide variety of areas including offender profiling, offender rehabilitation and assessment, victimology, risk assessment and crime reduction strategies. The following chapter will further the investigation of the overlap between forensic psychology and cybercrime, and will consider how general theories of crime can be adapted to cybercrime.

REFERENCES

Acre, R. (1998). Empirical studies on jury size. *Expert Evidence*, 6, 227–241. doi:10.1023/A:1008886718211

Ainsworth, P. B. (2001). *Offender Profiling and Crime Analysis*. Cullompton, England: Willan Publishing.

Ainsworth, P. B. (2002). *Psychology and Policing*. Cullompton, England: Willan Publishing.

Alison, L., & Kebbell, M. R. (2006). Offender Profiling: Limits and Potential. In Kebbell, M. R., & Davies, G. M. (Eds.), *Practical Psychology for Forensic Investigations and Prosecutions* (pp. 152–163). Chichester, West Sussex: John Wiley & Sons, Ltd.

Alison, L. J., Smith, M. D., Eastoman, O., & Rainbow, L. (2003). Toulmin's philosophy of argument and its relevance to offender profiling. *Journal of Psychology. Crime and Law, 9,* 173–181. doi:10.1080/1068316031000116265

American Psychiatric Association. (2000). *Diagnostic and statistical manual of mental disorders* (4th ed., Text revision). Author.

Babiak, P., & Hare, R. D. (2006). *Snakes in suits: When psychopaths go to work.* New York: Regan Books.

BBC News (25th January 2010). *$2 million file sharing fine slashed to $54,000.* Retrieved 20th August 2010 from http://news.bbc.co.uk/2/hi / technology/8478305.stm

Blackburn, R. (1996). What is forensic psychology? *Legal and Criminological Psychology, 1,* 3–16. doi:10.1111/j.2044-8333.1996.tb00304.x

Blackwell-Young, J. (2008). Witness evidence (pp. 209-233). In G. Davies, C. Hollin & R. Bull (eds) *Forensic Psychology.* Chichester, West Susex: Wiley.

British Psychological Society. (2010). *Forensic Psychology.* Retrieved 18th August 2010 from http://www.bps.org.uk/careers/what-do-psychologists-do/areas/forensic.cfm

Britton, P. (1997). *The Jigsaw Man.* London: Corgi.

Britton, P. (2000). *Picking up the Pieces.* London: Corgi.

Canter, D. (1994). *Criminal Shadows: Inside the Mind of the Serial Killer.* London: HarperCollins Publishers.

Canter, D. (2003). *Mapping Murder: Walking in Killers' Footsteps.* London: Virgin Books.

Canter, D., & Youngs, D. (2009). *Investigative Psychology: Offender Profiling and the Analysis of Criminal Action.* Chichester, England: Wiley.

Carney, M., & Rogers, M. (2004). The Trojan Made Me Do It: A First Step in Statistical Based Computer Forensics Event Reconstruction. *International Journal of Digital Evidence, 2 (4).* Retrieved 28th April 2008 from http://cs.ua.edu/691Dixon/Forensics/trojan.pdf

Carrier, B., & Spafford, E. (2003). Getting physical with digital forensics investigation. *International Journal of Digital Evidence (Fall 2003).*

Casey, E. (2002). *Handbook of computer crime investigation: forensic tools and technology.* San Diego, Calif.: Academic Press.

Chiesa, R., Ducci, S., & Ciappi, S. (2009). *Profiling Hackers: The Science of Criminal Profiling as Applied to the World of Hacking.* Boca Raton, FL: CRC press.

Cohen, L. E., & Felson, M. (1979). Social change and crime rate change: a routine activity approach. *American Sociological Review, 4,* 588–609. doi:10.2307/2094589

Cook, S. (2001). *The Real Cracker: Investigating the Criminal Mind.* London: Channel 4 books.

Davies, G., Hollin, C., & Bull, R. (2008). *Forensic Psychology.* Chichester, England: Wiley.

Douglas, J., & Olshaker, M. (1995). *Mind Hunter: Inside the FBI's Elite Serial Crime Unit.* New York: Pocket Books.

Douglas, J., & Olshaker, M. (1999). *The Anatomy of Motive.* London: Simon & Schuster.

Douglas, J., & Olshaker, M. (2000). *The Cases that Haunt Us.* London: Pocket Books.

Douglas, J. E., Ressler, R., Burgess, A., & Hartman, C. (1986). Criminal profiling from crime scene analysis. *Behavioral Sciences & the Law*, *4*, 401–421. doi:10.1002/bsl.2370040405

Edestein, R. S., Luten, T. L., & Ekman, P. (2006). Detecting lies in children and adults. *Law and Human Behavior*, *30*, 1–10..doi:10.1007/s10979-006-9031-2

Farrell, G., & Pease, K. (2006). Preventing Repeat Residential Burglary Victimisation. In Welsh, B., & Farrington, D. (Eds.), *Preventing Crime: What works for children, offenders, victims and places* (pp. 161–177). Dordrecht, The Netherlands: Springer.

Geiselman, R. E., Fisher, R. P., MacKinnon, D. P., & Holland, H. L. (1986). Enhancement of eyewitness memory with the cognitive interview. *The American Journal of Psychology*, *99*, 385–401. doi:10.2307/1422492

Gleeson, S. (2008, July 16). Freed hacker could work for police. *The New Zealand Herald*. p. A3

Gudaitis, T. M. (1998). The missing link in information security: Three dimensional profiling. *Cyberpsychology & Behavior*, *1*, 321–340.. doi:10.1089/cpb.1998.1.321

Gudjonsson, G. H. (2003). *The psychology of interrogations and confessions: A handbook*. Chichester, West Sussex: Wiley.

Gudjonsson, G. H., & Haward, L. R. C. (1998). *Forensic Psychology: A guide to practice*. New York: Routledge.

Haines, H. H. (1996). *Against Capital Punishment: The Anti-Death Penalty Movement in America 1972-1994*. Oxford University Press.

Hastie, R. (1993). Introduction. In R. Hastie (ed.) *Inside the Juror: The Psychology of Juror Decision Making* (3-41). Cambridge: Cambridge University Press.

Howitt, D. (2009). *Introduction to Forensic & Criminal Psychology* (3rd ed.). Harlow, England: Pearson Education.

Hoyle, C., & Zedner, L. (2007). Victims, Victimization, and Criminal Justice. In Maguire, M., Morgan, R., & Reiner, R. (Eds.), *The Oxford Handbook of Criminology* (4th ed., pp. 461–495). Oxford University Press.

Hunter, A. (2009). High-Tech Rascality: Asperger's Syndrome, Hackers, Geeks, and Personality Types in the ICT Industry. *New Zealand Sociology*, *24*, 39–61.

Huss, M. T. (2009). *Forensic Psychology: Research, Clinical Practice, and Applications*. Chichester, England: Wiley-Blackwell.

Jahankhani, H., & Al-Nemrat, A. (2010). Examination of Cyber-criminal Behaviour. *International Journal of Information Science and Management, Special Issue*. January/June 2010. Retrieved 18th August 2010 from http://www.srlst.com/ijist/special% 20issue/ijism-special-issue2010_files/Special-Issue201041.pdf

Kapardis, A. (2003). *Psychology and Law: A Critical Introduction (2nd Edition)*. Port Melbourne: Cambridge University Press.

Kassin, S. M., & Wrightsman, L. S. (1985). Confession evidence. In Kassin, S. M., & Wrightsman, L. S. (Eds.), *The Psychology of evidence and trial procedures* (pp. 67–94). London: Sage.

Kebbell, M. R., & Hurren, E. (2006). Improving the Interviewing of Suspected Offenders. In Kebbell, M. R., & Davies, G. M. (Eds.), *Practical Psychology for Forensic Investigations and Prosecutions* (pp. 101–119). Chichester, West Sussex: John Wiley & Sons, Ltd.doi:10.1002/9780470713389

Krause, M. (2009). Identifying and Managing stress in child pornography and child exploitation investigators. *Journal of Police and Criminal Psychology*, *24*, 22–29..doi:10.1007/s11896-008-9033-8

Lamb, M. E., Orlbach, Y., Hershkowitz, I., Esplin, P. W., & Horowitz, D. (2007). Structured forensic interview protocols improve the quality and informativeness of investigative interviews with children: A review of research using the NICHD Investigative Interview Protocol. *Child Abuse & Neglect*, *31*, 1201–1231..doi:10.1016/j.chiabu.2007.03.021

Langleben, D. D. (2008). Detection of deception with fMRI: Are we there yet? *Legal and Criminological Psychology*, *13*, 1–9.. doi:10.1348/135532507X251641

LaRose. (2008, March). Rifon & Enbody, (2008). Promoting Personal Responsibility for Internet Safety. *Communications of the ACM*, *51*(3), 71–76..doi:10.1145/1325555.1325569

Loftus, E., Miller, D. G., & Burns, H. J. (1978). Semantic integration of verbal information into a visual memory. *Journal of Experimental Psychology. Human Learning and Memory*, *4*, 19–31. doi:10.1037/0278-7393.4.1.19

Loftus, E., & Palmer, J. C. (1974). Reconstructions of automobile destruction: an example of the interaction between language and memory. *Journal of Verbal Learning and Verbal Behavior*, *13*, 585–589. doi:10.1016/S0022-5371(74)80011-3

MacKinnon, R. C. (1997). Punishing the Persona: Correctional Strategies for the Virtual Offender. In Jones, S. (Ed.), *Virtual Culture: Identity and communication in cybersociety* (pp. 206–235). London: Sage.

McCauley, M. R., & Fisher, R. P. (1995). Facilitating children's eyewitness recall with the revised cognitive interview. *The Journal of Applied Psychology*, *80*, 510–516. doi:10.1037/0021-9010.80.4.510

Miller, A. K., Markman, K. D., & Handley, I. M. (2007). Self-blame among sexual assault victims prospectively predicts revictimisation: A perceived sociolegal context model of risk. *Basic and Applied Social Psychology*, *29*, 129–136. doi:10.1080/01973530701331585

Montada, L. (2003). Justice, Equality and Fairness in Human Relations. In Millan, T., Lerner, M. J., & Weiner, I. B. (Eds.), *Handbook of Psychology: Personality and Social Psychology* (pp. 537–568). Wiley.

Nathanson, H. S. (1995). Strengthening the criminal jury: long overdue. *Criminal Law Quarterly*, *38*, 217–248.

Nykodym, N., Taylor, R., & Vilela, J. (2005). Criminal profiling and insider cybercrime. *Computer Law & Security Report*, *21*, 408–414. doi:10.1016/j.clsr.2005.07.001

O'Ciardhuain, S. (2004). An Extended model of cybercrime investigations. *International Journal of Digital Evidence, 3 (1)*. Retrieved on 28th April 2008 from http://www.utica.edu/academic/institutes /ecii/publications/articles/A0B70121-FD6C-3DBA-0EA5C3E93CC575FA.pdf

Ogan, J., & Allison, L. (2005). Jack the Ripper and the Whitechapel murders: a very Victorian critical incident. In Allison, L. (Ed.), *The Forensic Psychologist's Casebook: Psychological Profiling and criminal investigation* (pp. 23–46). Cullompton, England: Willan Publishing.

Paulsen, D. J. (2006). Connecting the dots: assessing the accuracy of geographic profiling software. *Policing: An International Journal of Police Strategies and Management*, *29*, 306–334.. doi:10.1108/13639510610667682

Perez, L. M., Jones, J., Englert, D. R., & Sachau, D. (2010). Secondary Traumatic Stress and Burnout among law enforcement investigators exposed to disturbing media images. *Journal of Police and Criminal Psychology, 25*, 113–124..doi:10.1007/s11896-010-9066-7

Porter, S., & ten Brinke, L. (2008). Reading between the Lies: Identifying concealed and falsified emotions in universal facial expressions. *Psychological Science, 19*, 508–514..doi:10.1111/j.1467-9280.2008.02116.x

Preuß, J., Furnell, S. M., & Papadaki, M. (2007). Considering the potential of criminal profiling to combat hacking. *Journal in Computer Virology, 3*, 135–141..doi:10.1007/s11416-007-0042-4

Rogers, M. (2003). The role of criminal profiling in the computer forensic process. *Computers & Security, 22*, 292–298..doi:10.1016/S0167-4048(03)00405-X

Scarpa, A., Haden, S. C., & Hurley, J. (2006). Community Violence Victimization and Symptoms of Posttraumatic Stress Disorder. *Journal of Interpersonal Violence, 21*, 446–469. doi:10.1177/0886260505285726

Smith, F., & Bace, R. (2003). *A guide to forensic testimony: The art and practice of presenting testimony as an expert technical witness*. Boston, MA: Addison Wesley.

Smith, R. G. (2004). Cyber Crime Sentencing. The Effectiveness of Criminal Justice Responses. *Crime in Australia: International Connections.* Australian Institute of Criminology International Conference, Hilton on the Park, Melbourne, Australia. 29-30 November 2004.

Snook, B., Zito, M., Bennell, C., & Taylor, P. J. (2005). On the complexity and accuracy of geographic profiling strategies. *Journal of Quantitative Criminology, 21*(1)..doi:10.1007/s10940-004-1785-4

Sommer, P. (1997). Computer forensics: An introduction. Retrieved June 3, 2003, from http://www.virtualcity.co.uk/ vcaforensics.htm

Sue, D., Sue, D. W., & Sue, S. (2005). *Essentials of Understanding Abnormal Behaviour*. Boston: Houghton Mifflin.

Torres, A. N., Boccaccini, M. T., & Miller, H. A. (2006). Perceptions of the validity and utility of criminal profiling among forensic psychologists and psychiatrists. *Professional Psychology, Research and Practice, 37*, 51–58. doi:10.1037/0735-7028.37.1.51

Toth, K., & King, B. H. (2008). Asperger's Syndrome: Diagnosis and Treatment. *The American Journal of Psychiatry, 165*, 958–963. doi:10.1176/appi.ajp.2008.08020272

Tynes, B. M. (2007). Internet Safety Gone Wild? Sacrificing the Educational and Psychosocial benefits of online social environments. *Journal of Adolescent Research, 22*, 575–584. doi:10.1177/0743558407303979

Vrij, A. (2006). Detecting Deception. In Kebbell, M. R., & Davies, G. M. (Eds.), *Practical Psychology for Forensic Investigations and Prosecutions* (pp. 89–102). Chichester, West Sussex: John Wiley & Sons, Ltd.

Walker, C. (2001). The Criminal Courts Online. In Wall, D. S. (Ed.), *Crime and the Internet* (pp. 195–214). London: Routledge.

Walklate, S. (2006). *Imagining the Victim of Crime*. Open University Press. 2006.

Warren, G., Schertler, E., & Bull, P. (2009). Detecting Deception from Emotional and Unemotional Cues. *Journal of Nonverbal Behavior, 33*, 59–69.. doi:10.1007/s10919-008-0057-7

Welsh, B., & Farrington, D. (2006). *Preventing Crime: What works for children, offenders, victims and places*. Dordrecht, The Netherlands: Springer.

Welsh, B. C., & Farrington, D. P. (2004). Effective programmes to prevent delinquency. In Adler, J. (Ed.), *Forensic Psychology: Concepts, debates and practice. Cullompton, Devon: Willan Publishing* (pp. 245–265).

Wrightsman, L. S. (2001). *Forensic Psychology.* Stanford, CT: Wadsworth.

Ybarra, M. L., Mitchell, K. J., Finkelhor, D., & Wolak, J. (2007). Internet Prevention Messages: Targeting the Right Online Behaviours. *Archives of Pediatrics & Adolescent Medicine, 161*, 138–145. doi:10.1001/archpedi.161.2.138

ADDITIONAL READING

Canter, D., & Youngs, D. (2009). *Investigative Psychology: Offender Profiling and the Analysis of Criminal Action.* Chichester, England: Wiley.

Carney, M., & Rogers, M. (2004). The Trojan Made Me Do It: A First Step in Statistical Based Computer Forensics Event Reconstruction. *International Journal of Digital Evidence, 2 (4).* Retrieved 28th April 2008 from http://cs.ua.edu/691Dixon/Forensics /trojan.pdf

Davies, G., Hollin, C., & Bull, R. (2008). *Forensic Psychology.* Chichester, England: Wiley.

Howitt, D. (2009). *Introduction to Forensic & Criminal Psychology* (3rd ed.). Harlow, England: Pearson Education.

Huss, M. T. (2009). *Forensic Psychology: Research, Clinical Practice, and Applications.* Chichester, England: Wiley-Blackwell.

Jahankhani, H., & Al-Nemrat, A. (2010). Examination of Cyber-criminal Behaviour. *International Journal of Information Science and Management, Special Issue.* January/June 2010. Retrieved 18th August 2010 from http://www.srlst.com/ijist/special%20issue /ijism-special-issue2010_files/Special-Issue201041.pdf

MacKinnon, R. C. (1997). Punishing the Persona: Correctional Strategies for the Virtual Offender. In Jones, S. (Ed.), *Virtual Culture: Identity and communication in cybersociety* (pp. 206–235). London: Sage.

Nykodym, N., Taylor, R., & Vilela, J. (2005). Criminal profiling and insider cybercrime. *Computer Law & Security Report, 21*, 408–414. doi:10.1016/j.clsr.2005.07.001

Preuß, J., Furnell, S. M., & Papadaki, M. (2007). Considering the potential of criminal profiling to combat hacking. *Journal in Computer Virology, 3*, 135–141..doi:10.1007/s11416-007-0042-4

Rogers, M. (2003). The role of criminal profiling in the computer forensic process. *Computers & Security, 22*, 292–298..doi:10.1016/S0167-4048(03)00405-X

Smith, R. G. (2004). Cyber Crime Sentencing. The Effectiveness of Criminal Justice Responses. *Crime in Australia: International Connections.* Australian Institute of Criminology International Conference, Hilton on the Park, Melbourne, Australia. 29-30 November 2004.

Chapter 3
Can Theories of Crime be Applied to Cybercriminal Acts?

ABSTRACT

Theories of crime have been an important part of criminological literature for many years. Different theories address the issue of crime at various levels, ranging from societal, through community and socialisation influence theories, to the most specific level, individual theories. The aim of most of the theories of crime is to explain why crime occurs and who is most likely to engage in criminal acts, and as such they are an important element of developing a thorough understanding of the psychology of cybercrime. Many of the high level theories of crime are mainly sociological, geographical or political in scope, whereas theories of crime that consider socialisation and individual differences are those which are most suited to psychological discussion. Because of this, the current chapter will primarily focus on these types of theories of crime, although reference will be made to higher level theories as appropriate. Some of the theories of crime considered in this chapter include biological theories, labelling theories, geographical and routine activity theories, trait theories learning theories, psychoanalytic theories, addiction and arousal theories and neutralization theories, as well as examining the complex theory of crime proposed by Eysenck and the complicated issue of defining crime due to its existence as a social construct. While it must be remembered that there has been little empirical examination of how these theories specifically relate to cybercrime, some theories show potential for explaining the nature of the phenomenon. This chapter aims to determine which theories are most suitable for further investigation and applicability to cybercriminal cases.

DEFINITIONS AND KEY TERMS

Theoretical explanations of crime are important for several reasons. Not only do they help society to understand how and why crime occurs, but they can also be useful in helping to predict future criminal behaviour. Theories of crime are also of assistance in attempting to prepare successful rehabilitative interventions for offenders, as well as developing crime prevention strategies that have the best chance of success in a given society. There are many theories of crime, providing various levels of explanation of criminal events. It is important to note that many of these theories of crime are

DOI: 10.4018/978-1-61350-350-8.ch003

not seen as competing with each other. In contrast, most criminal events can best be explained by utilising facets from a number of the theories that follow, and so in many cases the theories can be seen as complementary in nature. When several theories of crime are contemplated in conjunction with each other, they are often stronger than any single theory can ever be. Nevertheless, some theories of crime have fallen out of favour with the academic and professional communities, while others are currently seen as integral to current criminological theory. Similarly, not all theories of crime are appropriate to cybercriminal acts, and in many cases there has been little or no research testing the applicability of theories to cybercrime.

Levels of Explanation of Crime

Howitt (2009) indicates that theories of crime can occur at various levels. High level explanations of crime can include societal (or macro) levels and community or local levels. Other theories consider crime at a more personal level, including socialisation influence theories and individual approaches. Most theories of crime can fit into one or more of these levels, although few theories consider all levels in explaining crime.

Societal Theories

Societal or macro-level theories are considered by Howitt (2009) to be the broadest theories, and suggest that crime can be considered at a societal level rather than as a result of individual differences. Howitt gives the example of strain theory, which describes how it is impossible for all members of society to achieve all of society's goals (such as wealth). The remaining members of society can only achieve these goals through criminal or detrimental means, such as theft. Other societal level theories include control theory (as described by McGuire, 2004), which attempts to examine the structures that maintain social order in society, such as governments and legal entities.

An application of these theories to cybercrime involves the social construction of crime, which is described below.

Community Theories

According to Howitt, crime and criminality is not randomly distributed within communities or cities, and so community or locality theories may need to be considered. Some areas of cities will have higher crime rates than others, often those areas that are economically deprived. The Internet does not have such geographical tendencies, although some international variations in cybercriminal activity have been noted and are discussed below.

Socialisation Influence Theories

Group and socialisation influence theories have more of a connection with psychology than community or societal theories do. There are several theories of this kind, but they generally relate to how people around the individual impact on their likelihood of becoming an offender. These can include family and friends, as well as other influences on their lives, such as teachers, and media. One of the key applications of this level of theory to cybercrime involves the concept of observational learning, where our behaviours are shaped by watching how other individuals behave in similar circumstances. This theory is described under the heading of 'learning theories' below.

Individual Theories

Individual theories consider how certain characteristics specific to the person may influence their likelihood of becoming an offender. For example, two children brought up with the same social group, in the same community, may still vary in whether they become criminals or not. Individual theories seek to identify personal characteristics which may help to differentiate between those who are at risk of offending and those who are not. These may include biological differences, such as neurological or genetic differences, or psychological differences, such as personality or cognitive differences. Several theories of this type are considered in this chapter.

THEORIES OF CRIME AND THEIR APPLICATION TO CYBERCRIME

Having considered the levels at which theories of crime can be placed, attention will now be focused on briefly describing some of the most relevant theories of crime in terms of psychological significance and application to cybercrime. It is beyond the scope of this chapter to consider all theories of crime, or to discuss the sometimes quite complex rationale behind some of the theories. Similarly, in many cases, original theories of crime have been expanded on and enhanced by academics and practitioners, and to describe all facets of each of the theories would require considerable detail while simultaneously being unnecessarily complex in achieving the aim of the chapter. The interested reader is advised to consult key handbooks in the field (such as Maguire, Morgan & Reiner, 2007), collections of classic texts (such as Muncie, McLaughlin & Langan, 1996) as well as relevant journals in criminology and forensic psychology.

Social Construction of Crime

Howitt (2009) explains that it is important to consider how crime "simply is not a static, universal thing that needs no explanation in itself" (p. 78). Society decides what constitutes a criminal act, and an event may be defined as criminal or otherwise depending on a particular set of circumstances. Howitt specifically gives the example of how it is not necessarily a criminal event for a person to take another individual's property without their wishes – a bailiff may legitimately do so in many countries. It is also important to realise that what constitutes a crime varies according to historical and cultural contexts. Certain recreational drugs are legally available in some countries, but not others. Similarly, the prohibition movement resulted in the curtailment of the distribution of alcoholic drinks at one point in the history of the United States of America, while current laws relating to alcohol distribution are considerably different. Howitt describes how the social construction of crime often falls to certain groups within society, often those with power or who hold specific professions.

Within the area of cybercrime, the social construction of crime has a particular importance. Certain cybercrimes, such as the ownership and distribution of child pornography, were already defined as criminal events due to their similarity to offline counterparts. Other topics were more of a grey area, such as the production and distribution of potentially malicious software. While such acts are intuitively recognised as not socially acceptable, specific laws had to be developed in order to define the action as illegal. Other online acts, such as a virtual assault on another person's avatar in an online virtual world, still require much clarification as to whether or not they constitute a criminal act. This is a topic which is difficult to address for many reasons, not least because acts which are illegal in most jurisdictions (such as theft or murder), are sometimes a legitimate part of gameplay in some virtual worlds. And so the social construction of cybercrime is still at an evolutionary stage, with a degree of uncertainty remaining as to the legality of some online acts.

Biological Theories of Crime

A "comparison of the criminal skull with the skulls of normal women reveals the fact that female criminals approximate more to males, both criminal and normal, than to normal women, especially in the superciliary arches in the seam of the sutures, in the lower jaw-bones, and in peculiarities of the occipital region" (Lombroso & Ferrero, 1895, p. 28).

The above quote may seem bizarre in the modern context, but at the time of writing it was a relatively common belief that criminals could be recognised by their physiological characteristics. A classic example of this theory was *phrenology*. This was a study of the shape of the human head, founded by a physician named Francis Gall with the assumption that the size and shape of the brain was reflected in the size and shape of the skull, and so variations in a person's skull might demonstrate individual differences in personality and other psychological constructs. For example, areas at the top of the head were thought to be associated with characteristics such as spirituality, hope and agreeableness. Other areas were associated with characteristics which may be connected with criminal tendencies, such as destructiveness (just above the left ear) and combativeness. Lombroso (1897, as cited by Jamel, 2008) furthered the study of phrenology and attempted to describe the shape of the criminal skull, feeling that criminal brains would differ in shape from those of non-offenders. He felt that the criminal brain would be less developed than non-offenders, and that criminals would be more likely to have a range of physiological characteristics, such as thick lips, a receding chin, a large jaw and asymmetrical faces, amongst other characteristics. Of course, these theories have long been refuted, and while many psychologists and physicians keep a 'Fowler's phrenology head', it is generally used for decorative purposes, rather than for any psychological merit.

Nevertheless, it is possible that neural abnormalities play a role in criminality. Injury to the brain may be linked with criminality, although it is sometimes difficult to determine a causal relationship (Jamel, 2008), as those who are engaged in more violent acts are more likely to experience trauma to the brain. Palmer (2008) outlines research which demonstrates how certain neural structures have been particularly associated with criminality, including damage to the frontal lobe (which may cause difficulty in the person's ability to plan appropriately, as well as causing personality changes), and the temporal lobe (specifically structures known as the amygdala and hippocampus). Palmer also describes how such results need to be interpreted with caution due to the difficulties in determining causality.

There is some evidence that neural activity levels may also have a role to play in criminality. Specifically, unusual levels of neural activity have been noted in individuals with Antisocial Personality Disorder, a disorder characterised by aggressiveness, irresponsibility and criminal activity (see the review by Davey, 2008, pp. 412-418). Specifically, these individuals seem to have low levels of activity as recorded by electroencephalographs (EEGs), as well as inactivity in areas of the brain associated with learning to avoid feared outcomes.

Setting aside the science of neural structures and physiology, other biological theories of criminality do exist. For example, there is some evidence of a genetic influence on criminality. Repeatedly, studies show that males commit more crimes than females do (Smith, 2005). There have been suggestions that this is due, at least in part, to the presence of the Y chromosome in males, and a longstanding theory of crime suggested that the additional Y chromosome in males with Klinefelter's syndrome might lead to higher levels of aggression and criminality, although Howitt (2009) argues that this theory is now generally discredited within forensic psychology. Other research, including studies of identical and fraternal twins, has provided some evidence for the contribution of genetics to criminality (as identical twins are more likely to be similar in their likelihood of being criminal than fraternal twins are), although as Howitt argues, this is still not necessarily indicative of a conclusive link between genetics and criminology. The link between gender and offending may also be partially explained by the increased level of testosterone and other biochemical agents in males. Testosterone has been linked to higher levels of aggression, violence and dominance, although there are some problems in determining cause and effect, as aggressive feelings may cause testosterone levels to rise (Jamel, 2008).

While there is some evidence that the majority of cybercriminals are male, with relatively few females noted in the academic literature, otherwise there is very little information regarding how biological theories may explain cybercrime. To date, there are no known studies examining the neural structures, genetics or hormonal levels of cybercriminals, and so it is extremely difficult to determine how useful these theories may be.

Learning Theories and their Application to Criminality

In psychology, learning refers to a relatively stable change in behaviour or knowledge. Learning theory can be applied to forensic psychology in two principal ways – through the development of interventions for offenders that will hopefully alter their behaviours, and through an attempt to explain how criminal behaviours are learned in the first place. Several methods of learning have been proposed, including classical conditioning, operant conditioning, and observational learning.

Classical conditioning occurs when an individual learns associations between stimuli, with early work in the area being completed by Ivan Pavlov. Pavlov (1904) taught dogs to salivate upon hearing a bell ring by ringing it just before the presentation of the dog's food. Specifically, Pavlov trained the dogs to engage in an automatic, reflexive behaviour to a *conditioned stimulus* (the bell), which would normally only occur with an *unconditioned stimulus* (the food). This salivation in response to the bell is known as a *conditioned response*. Classical conditioning can be utilised to prevent criminal behaviour through socialisation during childhood. If a child misbehaves, they may be punished by their guardian (an unconditioned stimulus). When the child considers misbehaving in the future (now a conditioned stimulus), they may be prevented from doing so as they experi-

ence a conditioned fear response associated with the punishment previously inflicted. It is possible that similar learning principles apply to individuals engaged in cybercrime. For example, it has been argued that some of those involved in cyberbullying would not engage in offline bullying because if they did so, they would see the upset they cause the victim and hence feel an emotional response, such as guilt. As the bullying occurs online, the bully is not exposed to the conditioned stimulus of their victim's reaction, and so does not experience the conditioned response of guilt.

While classical conditioning concerns itself with emotional and physiological responses, operant conditioning considers how individuals learn voluntary behaviours and actions due to the consequences of actions and events. Much of the initial work in this field was completed by B.F. Skinner. Skinner completed many experiments with laboratory animals, using different types of reinforcement and punishment to determine which schedules were the most effective in altering behaviour. From a criminal perspective, various crimes can have several reinforcing features, such as the property obtained from a burglary or the release of frustration following an aggressive act. But engaging in criminal behaviour also has a series of potential punishments, such as imprisonment, fines and potential loss of respect and support from friends and family members. Operant conditioning suggests that potential offenders will continue to engage in acts that are reinforced, while desisting from acts that are punished. As the chances of reinforcement following a burglary, for instance, is relatively high (the thief is quite likely to obtain some goods of value), this behaviour is likely to continue, even though the same behaviour also carries a smaller likelihood of being punished (if the offender is apprehended and penalised). Overall, the perceived benefits outweigh the perceived potential punishments. With some types of cybercrime, such as online identity theft, the perpetrator may perceive the chance of being punished as very small, especially given the relative anonymity provided by the Internet. Simultaneously, the potential benefits are very desirable, as the perpetrator may use another person's credit to purchase goods and obtain significant quantities of cash. The principles of operant conditioning apply to a popular criminological theory known as *rational choice theory,* which suggests that a potential offender weighs up the potential costs and benefits of engaging in the criminal activity.

Finally, observational learning relates to how learning can occur indirectly, through observing other people in similar situations, and then imitating it. Probably the most famous experiment demonstrating observational learning was conducted by Albert Bandura (1965) where young children were shown videos of adults attacking *Bobo* dolls – large, inflatable dolls which will return to standing positions in most circumstances. Children were separated into three groups, and each group saw a different ending to the video. Some children saw the adult rewarded for their behaviour, some saw the adult being punished for the behaviour, while others saw videos where there were no consequences for the adult who attacked the doll. The children were then allowed to play in a room with a Bobo doll, and those children who had viewed the adult be punished for their aggressive behaviour were less likely to imitate the aggressive behaviours than those who had viewed the other two videos. In forensic psychology, there has repeatedly been evidence to support this theory, as individuals are more likely to become criminals if their parents or siblings have engaged in criminal behaviour (see for example, Fergusson, Horwood & Nagin, 2000; West & Farrington, 1977; Robins, West & Herjanic, 1975; Farrington, Jolliffe, Loeber, Stouthamer-Loeber & Kalb, 2001). Similarly, an individual is more likely to be engaged in criminal behaviour if their peer group are offenders. Some evidence for this theory can also be seen in cybercriminal events. For example, social learning appears to have an important influence on whether or not an individual engages in illegal downloading of copyrighted material (see Chapter 10), and there appears to be a tendency among some computer virus developers to associate with others engaged in similar activities (see Chapter 5).

Eysenck's Theory of Crime

Eysenck developed a theory examining the impact of genetics on crime (see section on biological theories in this chapter), as well as personality traits which he has written on extensively (see for example Eysenck, 1977; Eysenck, 1987/1996; Eysenck & Eysenck, 1970; Eysenck & Eysenck, 1977). In brief, he proposed that heredity is mediated through personality, but that both play a part in determining whether or not an individual will engage in criminal behaviour. He also indicates that environmental variables also have an impact, and that interactions between these variables need to be considered.

The personality variables which Eysenck felt were important related to the three factors of extraversion, psychoticism and neuroticism. Different traits are associated with each of these factors. Those high in extraversion were considered to be sociable, sensation-seeking, dominant, venturesome and assertive. High levels of psychoticism are associated with being impersonal, cold, aggressive, impulsive and unempathic. Neurotic individuals were considered to be depressed, anxious, shy, emotional, irrational and to have low self-esteem. Eysenck applied the classical conditioning learning theory (see section on learning theories above) to his explanation of crime, and determined that individuals with high levels of extraversion, neuroticism and psychoticism would be most likely to be involved in criminal behaviour, although he notes that criminals are not homogenous and individual differences may occur. The influence of environmental factors involves the failure of socialisation to inhibit behaviours and tendencies associated with criminality, such as a failure to defer gratification, and is strongly linked to classical conditioning theory.

While Howitt (2009) praises Eysenck's theory for its scope, encompassing several levels of theorising, Howitt indicates that many practitioners and academics disagree with Eysenck's theory, criticising its lack of support by research findings and its attempt to reduce the complexity of criminal behaviour to gross individual differences. Due to the complex theory proposed by Eysenck, involving a combination of socialisation, genetic factors and personality traits, it is difficult to determine if it applies to cybercriminals. Nevertheless, given the level of critique of Eysenck's theory, it seems unlikely that it is of extensive use in furthering our understanding of cybercrime.

Other Trait Theories of Crime

Throughout the history of forensic psychology, attempts have been made to uncover any underlying personality traits that offenders may have. Eysenck's theory and research is one example of this, but examinations have also been made of many other traits, including moral development (see for example, Palmer & Hollin, 1998; Trevethan & Walker, 1989), empathy (see for example Broidy, Cauffman, Espelage, Mazerolle & Piquero, 2003; Jolliffe & Farrington, 2004), intelligence (for example, Lopez-Leon & Rosner, 2010; Levine, 2008; Langevin & Curnoe, 2008), self-control (see for example Piquero, Moffitt & Wright, 2007; Conner, Stein & Longshore, 2008; Holtfreter, Reisig, Piquero & Piquero, 2010; Baron, 2003) and impulsiveness (see for example Meier, Slutske, Arndt & Cadoret, 2008; Shuman & Gold, 2008), along with many other psychological traits.

The empirical support for each of these traits as a correlate or predictor of criminality is mixed, with some characteristics demonstrating more reliable results than others. Nevertheless, for several reasons, there is rarely unambiguous support for any characteristic as an explanation for criminal involvement. This is at least in part due to the difficulty in determining causality – it

is not always certain whether the individual has developed this personality trait as a result of their criminality, or if the criminality results from the personality trait. Similarly, it is possible that there are underlying reasons for both the personality trait and the criminality – for example, individuals may demonstrate lower levels of self-control and higher levels of criminality, but both of these factors may be as a result of another variable, such as criminality within the family of origin.

One of the key reasons why it is important not to generalise with relation to trait theory and criminality is due to the lack of homogeneity in criminals. For example, an individual who is engaged in fraud may have very different traits to an individual who commits a murder. Even within offences, a wide variety of personality traits can be expected. A sexually motivated serial killer may have a very different set of personality traits to the individual who kills their loved one due to jealousy at uncovering an extra-marital affair. Two white-collar offenders may have very different personality traits if one's motive is to benefit financially and the other's motive is to bring disrepute to a company name.

This difficulty also needs to be considered when discussing the traits of cybercriminals. It is almost certainly impossible to determine a set of psychological characteristics that will describe all cybercriminals, when such a group includes identity thieves, virus writers, cyberterrorists, cyberstalkers and distributors of child pornography. Again, even within a specific type of online crime, there may be a wide variety of personality traits held by perpetrators, depending on their specific circumstances. Nevertheless, some work has been done in this area. For example, there is some evidence that hackers have poor interpersonal relationships (see Chapter 4), and that those involved in illegal file downloading have low levels of self-control (see Chapter 10). Despite its shortcomings, trait theory can provide insight into the psychology of cybercriminals, and help to establish a more thorough understanding of the phenomenon. It is important, however, that findings from such studies are interpreted with caution.

Psychoanalytic Theories of Crime

Psychoanalytic theory offers several possible suggestions for criminal events. Freud's concept of the *id*, an unconscious construct which seeks pleasure and destruction, must be constantly monitored and curtailed by the *ego*, which is guided by the *superego* (an internalisation of the standards and morals of society). Therefore, according to psychoanalytic theory, inadequate superego formation and functioning may lead to criminal behaviour. As the superego is formed during childhood, the child's relationship with their parents is central to appropriate superego development, and an unsatisfactory relationship can therefore be a cause of later criminality. However, as Blackburn (1993) describes, psychoanalytic theory does not comprehensively account for criminal activity. In particular, it has been noted by Kline (1987) that some criminal activity, such as white collar crimes, involve rational thought and conscious planning, and so are not suitable for inclusion in a theory that mostly concerns itself with unconscious conflict. It would seem that many cybercriminal activities require such rational thought, and as such psychoanalytic theories do not seem to be the most suitable approach in order to explain such criminality. Nevertheless, psychoanalytic theory may be of use in further understanding certain types of online criminal, such as paedophiles who use the Internet to contact and groom children, and there have been extensive writings about how psychoanalytic theory may explain paedophilic behaviour (see for example De Masi, 2008; Socarides, 2004). Howitt (2009) suggests that while psychoanalytic theory has been useful in directing the attention of forensic psychology researchers towards early childhood development, in many cases psychoanalytic concepts are not supported by research. Therefore it seems unlikely that these theories will be of great assistance in furthering our understanding of the reasons for cybercrime.

Addiction and Arousal Theory

McQuade (2006) proposes that *arousal theory* may be an explanation for cybercrime. Arousal theory suggests that individuals like a certain level of arousal, and will engage in acts to maintain this level. Some individuals fill this need through some extreme sports or potentially risky behaviours, while others turn to criminal activity in order to maintain their desired levels of arousal. McQuade links arousal theory to excessive playing of computer games, and suggests that cybercriminals such as cyberstalkers and hackers may also experience a psychological thrill from their activities. He also discusses the much debated topic of internet addiction, which may also provide some insights into cybercriminal behaviour.

Howitt (2009) outlines the arguments for and against the theory that criminal behaviour may be an addiction. He describes how there is evidence that those involved in criminal behaviour tend to also have other addictions, such as substance or alcohol abuse. While this may suggest the existence of addiction prone personalities, it is also possible that the addictions are as a result of problems in earlier development. It should also be noted that often property offenders steal in order to pay for drugs or alcohol to feed their addictions, and as such, causality is difficult to determine. Howitt does suggest that successful treatments for criminality often have considerable overlap with successful treatments for addictions, with similar processes of change in therapy. He cites the research of Kilpatrick (1997) who found that joyriders demonstrated some characteristics of addiction, including tolerance (they needed to carry out more offences in order to get the same emotional effect), conflict (an awareness of the negative consequences of their actions), withdrawal following a length of time abstaining from the activity and relapse following decisions to stop the activity. Howitt also cites the research of McGuire (1997), who found similar evidence of 'addiction' to shoplifting.

Some cybercriminals have indicated in interviews that they get a thrill from their actions, for example, some hackers and virus developers have indicated that they derive pleasure from these activities. Howitt suggests that addiction theory may explain why some individuals persist in committing crimes throughout their lives, while most other offenders cease most criminal activity during late adolescence or early adulthood. Similar 'age-out' tendencies seem to be noted in virus-writers and hackers, and it may suggest that those cybercriminals who do not cease their offending by their early twenties may be addicted to the activity. Nevertheless, addiction to criminality does not explain why an individual would engage in criminal activity to begin with – it is possible that arousal theory would explain initial engagement in the criminal act, and addiction theory would explain why some individuals become persistent offenders. Overall, a relationship between addiction and cybercrime is at present pure speculation, and empirical evidence in the area is lacking. As such, it seems that while addiction to crime has the potential to explain some aspects of cybercrime, it is unlikely to be a major explanation for it.

Neutralization Theory

Neutralization theory refers to an approach initially developed by Sykes and Matza (1957). Prior to their research, it was felt that offenders generally held different sets of moral values to the rest of society, perhaps seeing offending behaviors as being morally acceptable (McGuire, 2004). Research findings challenged this position, however, as it was found that generally, offenders hold similar moral values to non-offenders. Sykes and Matza's theory attempts to resolve this problem, by describing how individuals might offer explanations for the occasions when they behave in ways that they may see as morally unacceptable.

Effectively, neutralizations permit the offender to offer excuses for their behavior. Such excuses may involve denying responsibility for their actions, perhaps by indicating that they were forced to engage in burglaries in order to provide for their families. Other neutralizations can include denial of injury to the victim. For example, the offender may steal the victim's car, but may indicate that the victim will be able to claim the cost back from their insurance company, and so they are not actually experiencing a loss at all. Several other theorists describe other types of neutralizations that offenders may use. A similar concept to neutralization involves cognitive distortions, faulty lines of thought where the offender may believe that they are not really causing harm.

There is some evidence for neutralization theory among cybercriminals. It may apply to individuals who are involved in copyright infringement, who indicate that they are actually helping to launch careers of music artists by illegally downloading their work. Cognitive distortions are common amongst those who engage in paedophilia or the collection of child pornography – perhaps suggesting that the child enjoys the sexual encounter, or that they are not causing any harm as long as they only collect the pornographic materials without creating any themselves. Similarly, those who complete criminal type acts in virtual worlds may also employ neutralizations and cognitive distortions by convincing themselves that as the act was not against offline criminal law, it was not an immoral behavior. Of course, the justifications provided by offenders do not really excuse the criminal behaviors in most cases, but they do provide a tool for the offender to allow them to carry out the crime without reducing their self-image.

Labelling Theory

Blackburn (1993) describes labelling theory, which considers how the labels that are applied to offenders may impact how they are treated by society, and how they behave. So for example, by labelling an adolescent as an 'offender' following a relatively minor infringement, it may then lead to the adolescent seeing themselves as an offender, and engaging in behaviours to fit in with this label, such as further offending. Classic studies such as the Stanford Prison Experiment (Haney, Banks & Zimbardo, 1973), demonstrate how quickly a given label can impact on an individual's behaviour. In the Stanford study, a sample of volunteer students were assigned the title of 'prisoner', while other students were assigned the role of 'guard'. Although neither group was given any specific training, the 'inmates' seemed to develop passivity, depression and dependence. The 'guards' became aggressive and experienced an increase in group identification and dehumanizing behaviour towards the 'prisoners'.

Labelling theory has some application to cybercrime. For example, as can be seen in Chapter 4, there has been a long history of the application of certain names to different types of hackers. Some individuals within the hacking community have assigned alternative names (such as 'crackers') to individuals engaged in harmful activities in order to differentiate themselves from those that they perceive to be involved in criminal activity. An alternative perspective to this includes those that illegally share or download music or video files (see Chapter 10). In many cases, although individuals will admit to engaging in this illegal activity, they will not classify themselves as offenders. In attempts to encourage individuals to see the criminality of these acts, some agencies have produced short video clips which attempt to highlight to viewers that copyright infringement is theft.

Geographical Theories of Crime

It is well known that, as a general rule, crime is higher in urban areas rather than rural ones (Bottoms, 2007). Bottoms (2007) describes the work of the Chicago School of Sociology which carried out large amounts of research in criminology, one aspect of which related to mapping of delinquent residences. The researchers of the Chicago School found that rates of juvenile delinquency residence had a specific geographical pattern within cities, which had considerable long-term stability. However, such geographical analysis of crime is not limited to lay outs of cities, nor to urban-rural comparisons, but it can also be carried out at local levels (for example, specific areas of housing estates that may be more prone to criminal events than others) and global levels, where certain countries are associated with higher crime rates than others. Internationally, some countries have high levels of some types of crime, while other countries are noted as having particularly low levels of criminal activity.

As far as cybercrime is concerned, geographical influences may have some impact. It is difficult to examine local levels of cybercrime, but some trends do seem to be notable at international levels. For example, the same countries regularly appear in Symantec's security reports (see Symantec, 2010) of the top ten countries with the highest amount of malicious activity. These lists often include countries such as the United States, Russia, Brazil and China. There are reasons why these countries would appear to be the highest developers of malware. In some cases, such as the United States, it is possibly due in part to the relative ease of access to private computer systems, but also due to the fact that Symantec's method of capturing the data is by analysing the IP addresses of the sending mail servers, many of which are based in the US (Whitney, 2010). However, there may be other societal reasons for the high levels of malware development in other countries. Greenberg (2007) quotes Bill Pennington of White Hat Security, who suggested that computer science graduates in Russia or China may have the choice of working for nothing, or to make money by using their abilities for disreputable reasons.

Routine Activity Theory

Routine activity theory was outlined by Clarke and Felson (1993) and attempts to define criminal events in terms of the common actions of offenders and victims. In the initial theory, Clarke and Felson suggested that a criminal event required three variables to occur simultaneously. These included a motivated offender, a suitable target and an absence of guardians. With regard to a property offence, such as a burglary, the theory suggests that if a suitably motivated offender (perhaps one seeking funding to buy drugs) finds a house which appears to have objects of value in it, which is unattended by its owners, then there is a heightened probability that an offence will take place. Routine activity theory has some overlap with geographical theories as criminal events are more likely to occur in geographical areas which are described by the factors in routine activity theory.

From a cybercriminological perspective, there may be some evidence for routine activity theory. Several types of cybercrime are more likely to be carried out by individuals with considerable, unsupervised access to technology. Certainly, it is difficult to surreptitiously carry out certain cybercrimes, such as the collection of child pornography, without a personal computer that other individuals do not have access to. Similarly, a complex computer virus is more easily developed if the individual has unlimited access to a privately held computer. Hackers who attempt to develop *botnets* (a network of controlled personal computers) are possibly the best example of a cybercriminal application of routine activity theory. They are motivated to enhance their computing power, perhaps to disable a specific website (what is known as a *distributed denial of service attack*). Suitable targets involve any Internet user's computer whose resources can be employed to complete the desired act. A lack of suitable guardians in this case would refer to a computer which has not been adequately protected through the use of anti-virus software

and a firewall. In a similar way, routine activity theory can be applied to almost all types of cybercrime and malicious online behaviour, and as such it is a useful addition to our understanding of cybercriminal events.

CONCLUSION

There have been many theories of crime proposed over the history of criminology and forensic psychology, and this chapter has attempted to focus on those theories which are both psychological in nature and have the most applicability to cybercrime cases. Despite a severe lack of empirical research examining the applicability of many of these theories to cybercrime, it is possible that several of the theories may still enhance our understanding of the issue. Specifically, those theories which attempt to explain crime at the socialisation influence and individual levels seem most appropriate to cybercrime. Even within these levels, some theories seem to be more appropriate for cybercriminal cases than others. Those which seem to have the most potential include neutralization theory, learning theory, trait theory, routine activity theory, and to a certain extent, arousal and addiction theory. Other theories, such as labelling theory and psychoanalytic theory may also provide some insights into the problem for specific groups of cybercriminals. As with crime of all types, it is unlikely that one theory of crime is sufficient to completely understand the nature of the phenomenon or the perpetrators – it is only through integrating theories that a fuller appreciation of the complexity of the issue can be attained. Having now provided a background to cybercrime, forensic psychology, and theories of crime, most of the remainder of this book will consider the practical application of theory and research relating to specific types of cybercrime. This will commence with an examination of crimes which are only possible since the advent of computing, specifically hacking (Chapter 4) and malware development (Chapter 5).

REFERENCES

Bandura, A. (1965). Influence of models' reinforcement contingencies on the acquisition of imitative behaviours. *Journal of Personality and Social Psychology*, *1*, 589–595. doi:10.1037/h0022070

Baron, S. W. (2003). Self-control, social consequences and criminal behavior: Street youth and the general theory of crime. *Journal of Research in Crime and Delinquency*, *40*, 403–425. doi:10.1177/0022427803256071

Blackburn, R. (1993). *The Psychology of Criminal Conduct: Theory, Research and Practice*. Chichester, England: John Wiley & Sons.

Bottoms, A. E. (2007). Place, space, crime, and disorder. In Maguire, M., Morgan, R., & Reiner, R. (Eds.), *The Oxford Handbook of Criminology* (4th ed., pp. 528–574). Oxford: Oxford University Press.

Broidy, L., Cauffman, E., Espelage, D. L., Mazerolle, P., & Piquero, A. (2003). Sex differences in empathy and its relation to juvenile offending. *Violence and Victims*, *18*, 503–516. doi:10.1891/vivi.2003.18.5.503

Clarke, R. V., & Felson, M. (1993). *Routine activity and rational choice*. New Brunswick, NJ: Transaction Publishers.

Conner, B. T., Stein, J. A., & Longshore, D. (2008). Examining self-control as a multidimensional predictor of crime and drug use in adolescents with criminal histories. *The Journal of Behavioral Health Services & Research*, *36*, 137–149. doi:10.1007/s11414-008-9121-7

Davey, G. (2008). *Psychopathology: Research, assessment and treatment in clinical psychology*. Chichester, England: John Wiley & Sons Ltd.

DeMasi, F. (2007). The paedophile and his inner world: Theoretical and clinical considerations on the analysis of a patient. *The International Journal of Psycho-Analysis*, *88*, 147–165. doi:10.1516/B5AJ-CG0B-E4HC-WB07

Eysenck, H. J. (1977). *Crime and Personality* (3rd ed.). London: Routledge.

Eysenck, H. J. (1996). Personality theory and the problem of criminality. In J. Muncie, E. McLaughlin & M. Langan (Eds.) *Criminological Perspectives: A reader* (pp. 81-98). London: Sage Publications Ltd. (Reprinted from *Applying psychology to Imprisonment*, pp. 30-46, by B. McGurk, D. Thornton and M. Williams, Eds., 1987, London: HMSO.

Eysenck, S. B. G., & Eysenck, H. J. (1970). Crime and personality: an empirical study of the three-factor theory. *The British Journal of Criminology*, *10*, 225–239.

Eysenck, S. B. G., & Eysenck, H. J. (1977). Personality differences between prisoners and controls. *Psychological Reports*, *40*, 1023–1028. doi:10.2466/pr0.1977.40.3c.1023

Farrington, D. P., Jolliffe, D., Loeber, R., Stouthamer-Loeber, M., & Kalb, L. M. (2001). The concentration of offenders in families, and family criminality in the prediction of boys' delinquency. *Journal of Adolescence*, *24*, 579–596. doi:10.1006/jado.2001.0424

Fergusson, D. M., Horwood, L. J., & Nagin, D. S. (2000). Offending trajectories in a New Zealand birth cohort. *Criminology*, *38*, 525–552. doi:10.1111/j.1745-9125.2000.tb00898.x

Greenberg, A. (2007, July 16). The top countries for cybercrime: China overtakes U.S. in hosting web pages that install malicious programs. *MSNBC*. Retrieved November 20, 2010 from http://www.msnbc.msn.com/id/19789995/ ns/technology_and_science-security

Haney, C., Banks, C., & Zimbardo, P. (1973). Interpersonal dynamics in a simulated prison. *International Journal of Criminology and Penology*, *1*, 69–97.

Holtfreter, K., Reisig, M. D., Piquero, N. L., & Piquero, A. R. (2010). Low self-control and fraud: Offending, victimization and their overlap. *Criminal Justice and Behavior*, *37*, 188–203. doi:10.1177/0093854809354977

Howitt, D. (2009). *Introduction to Forensic & Criminal Psychology* (3rd ed.). Harlow, England: Pearson Education Ltd.

Jamel, J. (2008). Crime and its causes. In Davies, G., Hollin, C., & Bull, R. (Eds.), *Forensic Psychology* (pp. 3–28). Chichester, England: John Wiley & Sons Ltd.

Jolliffe, D., & Farrington, D. P. (2004). Empathy and offending: A systematic review and meta-analysis. *Aggression and Violent Behavior*, *9*, 441–476. doi:10.1016/j.avb.2003.03.001

Kilpatrick, R. (1997). Joy-riding: an addictive behavior. In Hodge, J. E., McMurran, M., & Hollin, C. R. (Eds.), *Addicted to Crime?* (pp. 165–190). Chichester, England: Wiley.

Kline, P. (1987). Psychoanalysis and crime. In McGurk, B. J., Thornton, D. M., & Williams, M. (Eds.), *Applying Psychology to Imprisonment: Theory and practice*. London: HMSO.

Langevin, R., & Curnoe, S. (2008). Are the mentally retarded and learning disordered over-represented among sex offenders and paraphilics? *International Journal of Offender Therapy and Comparative Criminology*, *52*, 401–415. doi:10.1177/0306624X07305826

Levine, S. Z. (2008). Using intelligence to predict subsequent contacts with the criminal justice system for sex offences. *Personality and Individual Differences*, *44*, 453–463. doi:10.1016/j.paid.2007.09.010

Lombroso, C., & Ferrero, W. (1895). *The Female Offender*. London: Fisher Unwin.

Lopez-Leon, M., & Rosner, R. (2010). Intellectual quotient of juveniles evaluated in a forensic psychiatry clinic after committing a violent crime. *Journal of Forensic Sciences*, *55*, 229–231. doi:10.1111/j.1556-4029.2009.01225.x

Maguire, M., Morgan, R., & Reiner, R. (2007). *The Oxford Handbook of Criminology* (4th ed.). Oxford: Oxford University Press.

McGuire, J. (1997). 'Irrational' shoplifting and models of addiction. In Hodge, J. E., McMurran, M., & Hollin, C. R. (Eds.), *Addicted to Crime?* (pp. 207–231). Chichester, England: Wiley.

McGuire, J. (2004). *Understanding psychology and crime: perspectives on theory and action*. Maidenhead, England: Open University Press.

McQuade, S. C. (2006). *Understanding and managing cybercrime*. Boston, MA: Allyn & Bacon.

Meier, M. H., Slutske, W. S., Arndt, S., & Cadoret, R. J. (2008). Impulsive and callous traits are more strongly associated with delinquent behavior in higher risk neighborhoods among boys and girls. *Journal of Abnormal Psychology*, *117*, 377–385. doi:10.1037/0021-843X.117.2.377

Muncie, J., McLaughlin, E., & Langan, M. (1996). *Criminological Perspectives: A Reader*. London: Sage Publications Ltd.

Palmer, E. J., & Hollin, C. R. (1998). Comparison of patterns of moral development in young offenders and non-offenders. *Legal and Criminological Psychology*, *3*, 225–235. doi:10.1111/j.2044-8333.1998.tb00363.x

Pavlov, I. (1965). On conditioned reflexes. In Hernstein, R. J., & Boring, E. G. (Eds.), *A source book in the history of psychology*. Cambridge, MA: Harvard University Press. (Original work published 1904)

Piquero, A. R., Moffitt, T. E., & Wright, B. E. (2007). Self control and criminal career dimensions. *Journal of Contemporary Criminal Justice, 23*, 72–89. doi:10.1177/1043986206298949

Robins, L. N., West, P. A., & Herjanic, B. L. (1975). Arrests and delinquency in two generations: a study of black urban families and their children. *Journal of Child Psychology and Psychiatry, and Allied Disciplines, 16*, 125–140. doi:10.1111/j.1469-7610.1975.tb01262.x

Smith, C. (2005). Gender and crime. In Hale, C., Hayward, K., Wahidin, A., & Wincup, E. (Eds.), *Criminology* (pp. 345–365). Oxford: Oxford University Press.

Socarides, C. W. (2004). *The mind of the paedophile: psychoanalytic perspectives*. London: H. Karnac Ltd.

Sykes, G., & Matza, D. (1957). Techniques of neutralization; a theory of delinquency. *American Sociological Review, 22*, 664–670. doi:10.2307/2089195

Symantec (2010). Symantec Intelligence Quarterly: July-September 2010. Retrieved November 20, 2010 from http://www.symantec.com/content/en/us/ enterprise/white_papers/b-symc_intelligence_qtrly_ july_to_sept_WP_21157366.en-us.pdf

Trevethan, S. D., & Walker, L. J. (1989). Hypothetical versus real-life moral reasoning among psychopathic and delinquent youth. *Development and Psychopathology, 1*, 91–103. doi:10.1017/S0954579400000286

West, D. J., & Farrington, D. P. (1977). *The delinquent way of life*. London: Heinemann.

Whitney, L. (2010, March 26). Symantec finds China top source of malware. *CNET Security*. Retrieved November 20, 2010 from http://news.cnet.com/8301-1009_3-20001234-83.html

ADDITIONAL READING

Baron, S. W. (2003). Self-control, social consequences and criminal behavior: Street youth and the general theory of crime. *Journal of Research in Crime and Delinquency, 40*, 403–425. doi:10.1177/0022427803256071

Clarke, R. V., & Felson, M. (1993). *Routine activity and rational choice*. New Brunswick, NJ: Transaction Publishers.

Eysenck, H. J. (1977). *Crime and Personality* (3rd ed.). London: Routledge.

Eysenck, H. J. (1996). Personality theory and the problem of criminality. In J. Muncie, E. McLaughlin and M. Langan (Eds.) *Criminological Perspectives: A reader* (pp. 81-98). London: Sage Publications Ltd. (Reprinted from *Applying psychology to Imprisonment*, pp. 30-46, by B. McGurk, D. Thornton and M. Williams, Eds., 1987, London: HMSO.

Eysenck, S. B. G., & Eysenck, H. J. (1970). Crime and personality: an empirical study of the three-factor theory. *The British Journal of Criminology, 10*, 225–239.

Eysenck, S. B. G., & Eysenck, H. J. (1977). Personality differences between prisoners and controls. *Psychological Reports, 40*, 1023–1028. doi:10.2466/pr0.1977.40.3c.1023

Farrington, D. P., Jolliffe, D., Loeber, R., Stouthamer-Loeber, M., & Kalb, L. M. (2001). The concentration of offenders in families, and family criminality in the prediction of boys' delinquency. *Journal of Adolescence, 24*, 579–596. doi:10.1006/jado.2001.0424

Haney, C., Banks, C., & Zimbardo, P. (1973). Interpersonal dynamics in a simulated prison. *International Journal of Criminology and Penology, 1*, 69–97.

Howitt, D. (2009). *Introduction to Forensic & Criminal Psychology* (3rd ed.). Harlow, England: Pearson Education Ltd.

Jamel, J. (2008). Crime and its causes. In Davies, G., Hollin, C., & Bull, R. (Eds.), *Forensic Psychology* (pp. 3–28). Chichester, England: John Wiley & Sons Ltd.

Maguire, M., Morgan, R., & Reiner, R. (2007). *The Oxford Handbook of Criminology* (4th ed.). Oxford: Oxford University Press.

McQuade, S. C. (2006). *Understanding and managing cybercrime*. Boston, MA: Allyn & Bacon.

Pavlov, I. (1965). On conditioned reflexes. In Hernstein, R. J., & Boring, E. G. (Eds.), *A source book in the history of psychology*. Cambridge, MA: Harvard University Press. (Original work published 1904)

Piquero, A. R., Moffitt, T. E., & Wright, B. E. (2007). Self control and criminal career dimensions. *Journal of Contemporary Criminal Justice, 23*, 72–89. doi:10.1177/1043986206298949

Smith, C. (2005). Gender and crime. In Hale, C., Hayward, K., Wahidin, A., & Wincup, E. (Eds.), *Criminology* (pp. 345–365). Oxford: Oxford University Press.

Sykes, G., & Matza, D. (1957). Techniques of neutralization; a theory of delinquency. *American Sociological Review, 22*, 664–670. doi:10.2307/2089195

Trevethan, S. D., & Walker, L. J. (1989). Hypothetical versus real-life moral reasoning among psychopathic and delinquent youth. *Development and Psychopathology, 1*, 91–103. doi:10.1017/S0954579400000286

West, D. J., & Farrington, D. P. (1977). *The delinquent way of life*. London: Heinemann.

Section 2
Internet–Specific Crimes

Chapter 4

Is the Research to Date on Hackers Sufficient to Gain a Complete Understanding of the Psychology Involved?

ABSTRACT

Of all the types of cybercrime that exist, hackers are the cybercriminals who have probably engaged both the imagination of the general public and the interest of the entertainment industry the most. They are also those who have elicited the greatest quantity of psychological academic literature. It seems that we have an unsatisfied desire to comprehend why any individual would be drawn to this type of activity, which seems in some cases to have little immediate benefit for the cybercriminal.

This chapter aims to determine if we have discovered all that we need to about the psychology and motivations of hackers. Despite the vast quantities of literature in this area, it seems that we still do not have a thorough grasp on the mentality of the hacker. The chapter will commence with some background information regarding the methods used by hackers, a description of the history of hacking behaviour and terminology, and the legal dimensions of hacking. Following this, the chapter will consider the very diverse motives of hackers, as determined by psychological and criminological research. The personalities of computer hackers will then be examined, with special consideration of how psychological profiling could be used to help in solving hacking cases. Issues regarding punishment and prevention of hacking attacks will then be examined, and finally the difficulties in carrying out hacker research and potential directions for future research in this area will be explored.

BACKGROUND

There are numerous cases of famous hackers available in the literature. Former hacker Kevin Mitnick in particular has made a career from advising on computer security and has authored a number of

DOI: 10.4018/978-1-61350-350-8.ch004

books on hacking, with a particular focus on social engineering methods (see for example Mitnick & Simon, 2002 and Mitnick & Simon, 2005). Adrian Lamo has also experienced a lot of publicity due to his hacking activities. His 'white-hat' attempts to improve the security of firms led to mixed responses from the companies involved – some were highly appreciative of his efforts, while others filed lawsuits against him (see Mitnick & Simon, 2005). More recently, a hacker using the alias 'Neo' (the name of the main character from the 'Matrix' series of movies) has leaked data to a television station about pay details of managers of a Latvian bank that received financial support using Twitter (BBC News, 24th February 2010).

However, one of the most interesting hackers from a psychological perspective has to be Gary McKinnon, who hacked into 97 US government computers, including the US Navy and NASA, between 2001 and 2002, using the online name 'Solo'. His declared motive was "to prove US intelligence had found an alien craft run on clean fuel" (BBC News, 28th July 2009, para. 3). McKinnon's actions do not seem to be those that most individuals would take – his hacking became an obsession, and his real-life began to suffer the consequences – he lost his job and girlfriend, and eventually stopped eating properly and neglected his personal hygiene. In hindsight he indicated that he "almost wanted to be caught, because it was ruining me" (Boyd, 2008). McKinnon, a British citizen, fought extradition to the United States, despite admitting to the hacking charges, as it was feared that his mental health would be at risk if he was extradited. McKinnon has been diagnosed as having Asperger's Syndrome, an Autistic Spectrum Disorder, one of the symptoms of which can be the development of restricted, repetitive patterns of behavior, interests, and activities. McKinnon denies that his hacking was malicious in nature, or that it caused damage costing $800,000, although he faces up to 70 years in prison if convicted in the U.S., where prosecutors claim that he completed "the biggest military computer hack of all time" (BBC News, 31st July 2009). This case is of particular interest due to the diagnosed nature of McKinnon's psychological status, to which his defence say the authorities in the UK have not given proper consideration. They suggest that if he was to be extradited, McKinnon would suffer from "disastrous consequences" and that he should be tried on lesser charges in the

UK in order to protect his mental health (BBC News, 31st July 2009). They indicate that there is "clear, uncontradicted expert evidence" that the stress of extradition could result in psychosis and suicide (BBC News, 9th June 2009), and later they indicated that he was suffering from "very severe depression" (BBC News, 10th December 2009).

While Gary McKinnon may not be the most typical of hackers, his case is of particular interest due to the role that his psychological disorder may have played in the origin of his crimes, and the considerations that may need to be taken with regard to his punishment due to the psychological effects he may suffer.

Definitions and Key Terms

Levy (1984) suggests that hacking began in the late 1950s at a few US universities at a time when computers were rare. The original 'hackers' were motivated to use and improve computer technology, and it is arguable that without them computers would not be as widespread as they are today. Indeed, many hackers today still defend their actions in similar ways, suggesting that they only hack in order to illustrate to the public how governments and large organisations are 'corrupt'. However, by the early 1960s hacking had begun to result in financial abuses and as such was becoming a nuisance to other computer users

The term 'hacker' is a cause for confusion among those wishing to study the field. The media, and the vast majority of the general public use it primarily to denote a person who gains unauthorised access to computer systems. However, many online individuals define a 'hacker' as simply a person who is proficient at building and modifying computer systems. The term 'cracker' is often used instead to describe those involved in criminal activity. This term was supposedly coined by hackers ca. 1985 to distinguish themselves from the journalistic misuse of 'hacker'. 'Cracking' normally involves maliciously accessing a network (as per the common perception of 'hacking').

Sterling (1992) indicates that there is considerable lack of consistency in what 'cybercriminals' call themselves. He suggests that most of them choose to call themselves 'hacker'. "Nobody who hacks into systems willingly describes himself (rarely, herself) as a 'computer intruder', 'computer trespasser', 'cracker', 'wormer', 'darkside hacker' or 'high-tech street gangster'." (p. 56). Sterling indicates that despite numerous attempts to invent terms for the press and public to use in place of the original meaning of 'hacker', few people actually use them. Simpson (2006, as cited in Tavani, 2007) differentiates between the two by defining a hacker as anyone who "accesses a computer system or network without authorisation from the owner" and a cracker as a hacker who has "the intention of doing harm or destroying data".

Further confusion is added by the distinction between 'white-hat' and 'black-hat' 'hackers'. 'White-hats' are those who enjoy working with computers, and who may infiltrate the systems of other individuals or groups, but who do not cause malicious damage in the process. Some 'white-hat' hackers can also be termed 'ethical' hackers, and can be company employees or consultants who are specifically tasked with finding exploits in order to make the software more secure. 'Black-hats' are those who hack with the intent of carrying out some form of damaging action. However, it should be noted that some 'white-hat hackers' are involved in criminal activity of some kind, as many do attempt to gain unauthorised access to the computers or networks of other people or groups. They sometimes justify this action by contacting the individual or group afterwards in an attempt to warn them of the flaw in their security system. Despite the differences recognised in cybercultures between 'white-hat' and 'black-hat' hackers (or hackers and crackers), Tavani (2007) suggests that many governments and businesses would view non-malicious hacking as a form of trespass, a view which much legislation supports. A third group are the 'grey hat' hackers, a term used to describe hackers who search for exploits,

but only disclose these exploits to the system administrators under certain circumstances, often in the hopes of monetary reward. Grey-hat hackers are not affiliated with any specific company or organisation, and sometimes distinguish themselves from white-hat hackers on this basis.

Other members of the Internet underground include 'phreakers' and 'script-kiddies'. Phreakers are a specific type of hacker, those who participate in hacking telephone systems. Script-kiddies are individuals who are not proficient at hacking, and who download pre-written scripts and tools which are widely available on the Internet in order to carry out their hacking activities (Murphy, 2004). Many hackers start out as script-kiddies, and build their skills from there. They are generally viewed with little respect by the more experienced hackers, and many do not consider them to be true hackers at all.

In essence, 'hacking' can be seen not as a state of being, but a continuum. At one extreme of this continuum, there is only "an intellectual curiosity and fascination with the technology... a world of beauty and purity" (Bissett & Shipton, 1999, p 904). Further along, there emerges an obsession to make all information free and accessible to everyone, for there to be no secrets possible within this 'beautiful world of technology'. Following this, an anti-authority impulse begins to manifest itself in response to commercial or legal obstacles, and the illegal aspects of 'hacking' or 'cracking' begin to appear.

The nomenclature of hacking could be of the utmost importance for the individual involved. Bryant and Marshall (2008) suggest that labelling theory may have an application in the terms used by hackers. Labelling theory is one of the sociological theories of crime, suggesting that once a person is named or defined in a certain manner, consequences flow from this, including the possibility that the definition can become a means of defence or adjustment to the societal reaction to them (Rock, 2007). It is therefore possible that once an individual has been assigned the term 'hacker' (or 'cracker' or 'black-hat' or any of the other terms discussed above), then the individual begins to alter their behaviour accordingly in order to fit in with the label assigned to them. As such, the media usage of the term 'hacker' to include mainly those who hack for malicious reasons may have an impact on those who term themselves hackers, but whose hacking activities were primarily in the original definition of the term – it is possible that the media usage of the term may alter their behaviours.

Bearing all this in mind, for the purposes of conciseness, the high level term 'hacker' will be used throughout this chapter, though it should be remembered that the individuals involved in the research that follows may define themselves differently to this, or be described differently by their victims or law-enforcement personnel.

Classifications of Hackers

In addition to the high level distinctions between hackers and crackers, and white-hats and black-hates, several researchers have suggested further classifications of hackers. Rogers (2000) suggests seven categories of hacker, including 'newbies' (who have limited skills and experience, and are reliant on tools developed by others), 'cyber-punks' (who deliberately attack and vandalise), 'internals' (who are insiders with privileged access and who are often disgruntled employees), 'coders' (who have high skill levels), 'old guard hackers' (who have no criminal intent and high skill levels, and so would most likely equate to 'white-hat' hackers), 'professional criminals' and 'cyber-terrorists'.

Chiesa, Ducci and Ciappi (2009) suggested an alternative and more complex classification system, involving nine categories of hackers. These include 'Wannabe lamers', 'script-kiddies', '37337 K-rAd iRC #hack 0-day exploitz guy', 'crackers', 'ethical hackers', 'quiet, paranoid and skilled hacker', 'cyber-warriors', 'industrial spies' and 'government agent'. This classification

system shows some overlap with that suggested by Rogers (2000), for example, 'ethical hackers' are similar to 'old guard hackers' and 'wannabe lamers' would share many of the characteristics of 'newbies'. Most distinctions within many classification systems refer to the experience levels, methods and motives of each type of hacker.

Taylor (2001) suggests that as well as the original hackers, other variants include the 'hacker/cracker' (who breaks into computer systems), the 'Microserf' who was or still is associated with hacker groups but who now work within corporate structures, and 'hacktivists' whose actions are motivated by political drive. This hacktivism "draws on the creative use of computer technology for the purposes of facilitating online protests, performing civil disobedience in cyberspace and disrupting the flow of information by deliberately intervening in the networks of global capital" (Gunkel, 2005, p.595).

Warren and Leitch (2009) also identify the 'hacker-taggers' – hackers who leave a 'tag' on a website that they have hacked. They do not aim to interfere with the function of the website, or to steal data, they simply aim to leave their 'tag' on the website. For example, they may leave the website they have hacked as it was, but include a single line saying "This Website is owned by (name)". Warren and Leitch (2009) suggest that based on their research, hacker-taggers are very competitive, with a strong desire to succeed. They also exchange information amongst themselves regarding successful defacements but cause minimal or no damage to the websites. They could be individual hackers or groups, and they rely upon media reports to cause political damage or embarrassment. This type of behaviour could potentially be compared to 'tagging' in graffiti culture (see Halsey & Young, 2002 for a description of the importance of tagging in graffiti).

Types of Hacker Attack

There are several types of damage that a hacker can inflict on a computer system or website. These range from a straightforward *intrusion* of a system (which may involve accessing classified information or leaving behind malicious software) to *defacement* of a website or system (as occurred with the US House of Representatives website just before President Obama's State of the Union address in January 2010).

One of the most famous types of hacker attack is a Denial of Service (DoS) attack. This occurs where a hacker floods the system or website with requests, to the extent that the system cannot cope with the demands and is unable to handle legitimate requests from users. The *Central Applications Office* (CAO), which processes the vast majority of applications to third level courses by school leavers in Ireland was apparently the victim of such an attack in August 2010. The alleged attack was scheduled to coincide with the date that offers of college places were made, preventing thousands of hopeful students from accepting their offered place. A slight variation on the DoS is a Distributed Denial of Service (DDOS) attack, where the hacker uses a botnet (a remotely controlled collection of systems) to flood the system with the requests.

Bryant and Marshall (2008) suggest that the likelihood of a hacking attack being successful depends on six major elements. These are the hacker's experience and expertise, their freedom to move through the network, the nature of the attack, the victim's experience and expertise, the guardianship of the victim (such as firewalls) and the guardianship of the hacker (measures designed to stop them from acting beyond their home network). Bryant and Marshall suggest a formula which may illustrate the interaction between these factors. However, the high number of unknowns for this formula, combined with the relatively little information it provides about the hacker themselves, may mean that it provides little assistance to the investigators.

Known Prevalence Rates, and the 'Dark Figure' of Hacking

Rantala (for the US Dept of Justice, Bureau of Justice Statistics; 2008) in a survey of 7,818 businesses that responded to the National Computer Crime Survey in 2005, found that few businesses that detected an incident reported the cybercrime. The proportion of businesses that experienced a cyberattack (such as viruses, denial of service, vandalism or sabotage) or computer security incident (such as spyware, hacking, port scanning, and theft of information) seems to be few, at 6% and 12% respectively.

The Computer Security Institute (CSI) Computer Crime and Security Survey (2009) found that 29.2% of respondents had experienced denial-of-service attacks (up from 21% in 2008); with 17.3% had experienced password sniffing (compared to 9% in 2008). A further 13.5% had experienced website defacement (compared to 6% in 2008). However it is unknown how many companies who had been the target of such attacks did not respond to the survey or report their victimisation.

Overall, it is extremely difficult to determine how much hacking activity occurs, partially due to difficulties in completing a methodical survey of the extent of the problem, and partially due to some victims' preference not to admit to being victimised for the sake of avoiding negative publicity. It is also possible that some victims are never aware of the fact that they have been victimised, or if they are, they manage the problem privately (through the use of protection software or fixing/replacing their equipment) and do not report the event. As such, it can be expected that the true extent of hacking activity far exceeds what is recorded and reported by official agencies. The difference between these is termed the 'dark figure'.

In the UK, Garlik (2009) attempt to estimate the dark figure of cybercrime in their annual reports. They estimate that just under 50% of UK businesses experienced a security incident, with 25% experiencing a serious breach. Sixteen percent of businesses experienced an attack from an unauthorised outsider. It is not entirely clear how Garlik reached these figures, and, due to the company's interest in selling computer security products, these statistics need to be carefully interpreted.

METHODS OF HACKING

There are a number of different methods by which hackers infiltrate systems. The international 'Honeynet' project (www.honeynet.org) is designed to monitor hacking attempts by placing computers with limited or no security patches (honeypots) on the Internet and monitoring any hacking attempts on them. Honeynet Projects have been in use since June 2000, and since then they have provided considerable data concerning the methods and motivations of hackers.

Loper (2000) carried out an extended case-study of a hacker mailing list. He did not interact with the participants of the mailing list in any way. He sought to categorize common activities in the hacker culture, and found that consistent themes may be found in hacker communication. Some of these included 'identity' (e.g. if an individual impersonated a list user), subcultural activities (including the definition and ethics of hacking, corporate and government distrust, and the portrayal of hacking in the media, among others), 'hacktivism' ('hacking' combined with activism), and communication (discussion about the list itself, and its proper use).

There are four main methods that hackers use to infiltrate systems (outlined by a hacker named Dustin, in Mitnick & Simon, 2005, p. 126): 'technical entry into the network', 'social engineering', 'dumpster diving' and 'physical entry'.

The first, 'technical entry into the network', reflects the common perception held amongst the general public of what hacking is – the individual hacker sitting at their computer at a remote loca-

tion, gaining access to the network of the target. A hacker may use a variety of tools and techniques to do this, including (among many others) 'port-scanning' to obtain a list of all applications and services running on a computer, which will assist them in devising a strategy of attack. They may also engage in 'packet-sniffing', capturing network traffic and potentially intercepting unencrypted data or 'pinging', which allows a hacker to determine if a system is present on a network. Furnell (2010) also lists a number of technical tools that hackers can employ, including vulnerability scanners (that search for known security holes) and password crackers. While not specifically an instrument of most hackers, computer viruses and other malware can also be used to cause considerable damage to the systems of home users and organisations. These are considered in more detail in Chapter 5.

'Social engineering' is becoming increasingly popular – this involves using deception to persuade humans to assist in the penetration of the network. For example, a hacker may call a receptionist at a company, saying they are from an IT support company and need the administrator's password to try to correct a bug in the system. Social engineering could also include eavesdropping on conversations between employees of a company to find out useful information, or 'shoulder surfing' – covertly watching an employee enter their username and password with the intention of using that information in a hacking attempt later. Variations on social engineering include 'phishing' and 'pharming' (Sanders-Reach, 2005), which are discussed in more detail in Chapter 6 as they are frequently used for identity theft.

'Dumpster diving' refers to cybercriminals actually searching in the rubbish bins of a company for useful articles. This may include scraps of paper with user names and passwords, old computer hard drives which may still have sensitive information on them, or even confidential files that may have been discarded without being properly shredded.

Finally, 'physical entry' is just that – where the hacker manages to enter a building directly and carry out the hack from the inside. Sometimes, this could be as simple as getting through a lax security system, and finding a vacant computer terminal which has been left logged on.

These methods indicate that the hacker does not necessarily need to have advanced technical skills in order to complete a successful attack. Social engineering and physical entry tactics do not require any specific computer skills, and can be some of the most effective means of accomplishing a task. However, Calcutt (1999) suggests that the descriptions of the activities of malicious hackers are regularly over-hyped, fuelling fear and confusion. He indicates that "reports of the threat to society posed by Mitnick and others have been hyped out of all proportion" (p. 57).

MOTIVES FOR HACKING

Lafrance (2004) proposes that understanding cybercriminals' motivation can help to improve security measures. Unfortunately, Voiskounsky and Smyslova (2003) indicate that although there is a great deal of discussion regarding the psychology of hackers in the media, there has been little work carried out by psychologists in this area. Nevertheless, some theories have been put forward to suggest the reasons why hackers do what they do.

Zager (2002, as cited in Lafrance, 2004) indicates that there are three different types of hackers, depending on their motivations. These are 'casual hackers', 'political hackers', and 'organised crime hackers'. *'Casual hackers'* form the biggest group, and most are not very skilled. They are frequently motivated by curiosity, or by the thrill of success. They may hope to gain financially from their hacking. Many 'script-kiddies' would fall under this category, and their inexperience can make them relatively easy to track. They may also be motivated by the wish to be accepted by other

hackers, or to gain notoriety. *'Political hackers'* have specific targets, and are pursuing a specific cause. These may also be called 'cyber-activists', and their knowledge and skill-sets can vary greatly. Their activities can include website defacements and Denial of Service attacks. *'Organised crime hackers'* are primarily motivated by financial gain. This may include obtaining bank details, credit card numbers or confidential information. These hackers target their victims very carefully, and spend a lot of time gathering information before they attack. They commonly use social engineering in their approach, and are very careful to avoid detection.

Taylor (1999) discusses the motivations that hackers sometimes give for their actions. These include feelings of addiction, the urge of curiosity, boredom with the educational system, enjoyment of feelings of power, peer recognition in the hacking culture and political acts. Kabay (1998) indicates that there may be personality differences between American and European hackers, with European hackers being more politically motivated, although there appear to be no definitive studies in this area. Max Kilger (as cited in Spitzner, 2003) suggests that hackers have six main motivations, which he has compiled into the acronym MEECES – Money, Ego, Entertainment, Cause (basic ideology), Entrance to a social group and Status.

Lafrance (2004) describes the motivations that could underlie attacks by insiders in organisations. These include economical profit, revenge, personal interest in a specific file, and external pressure from people or organisations outside of the company (such as organised crime or a family member). Fötinger and Ziegler (2004) also propose that the hacker may be experiencing a deep sense of inferiority, and that the power they achieve through their hacking activities may increase their self-esteem. Schneier (2003) suggests that hackers do not break into systems for profit, but simply to satisfy their intellectual curiosity, for the thrill, and to 'see if they can'. He verifies that the common excuse of hackers, that they are simply testing the security of the system, is insufficient.

Despite these taxonomies and theories, Calcutt (1999) suggests that "there is no discernible motive force which drives their [crackers] existence" (p. 60). He suggests that their activities are relatively random. Similarly, Hayes (1989) suggests that teenage hackers are rarely politically motivated, with the exception of their contempt for 'bureaucracies' that impede on their exploits.

Fötinger and Ziegler (2004) suggest that hackers' main motivations are reputation, respect and acknowledgement. They suggest that the work of hackers fulfils a self-actualization need (involving personal growth and fulfillment) according to Maslow's (1970) hierarchy of needs. This would indicate that the hacker has already got their lower needs (biological, safety, belongingness and love, and esteem needs) already sufficiently catered for. If this is the case, it would suggest that the individual is neither hacking for financial needs to survive, nor for emotional attachments, nor to make them accepted among their peer group. This seems highly unlikely, given what we understand to date about hackers.

From a behavioral learning perspective, Rogers (as cited in Fötinger & Ziegler, 2004) suggests that there are several positive reinforcements to hacking behavior. These would include the increase in knowledge, prestige within the hacking community, celebrity status amongst the media, successful completion of a puzzle (e.g. how to infiltrate a particularly difficult system), or the possibility of employment by the computer security industry in the future.

Bryant and Marshall (2008) suggest that the motives of early hackers were to prove themselves against the authorities of the network, with very little malicious intent. Their rewards were self-esteem and peer recognition. However as the number of network users increased, other motives began to appear. When applied to Rogers (2000) taxonomy of hackers, different motives could be assigned to each (for example, cyberterrorists

were motivated by ideals, professional criminals were motivated by profit, whereas internals were disgruntled).

Taylor (2003) indicates that "psycho-sexual theories suggest that hacking provides men (and especially young, pubescent men) with a cathartic outlet for their frustrations and a biological urge to dominate" (p. 130). He continues to explore the psycho-sexual theory in depth, using quotes from hackers to support the suggestion that the final moments of a successful hack has some orgasmic qualities for the hacker, comparing the activity to a form of masturbation. However, Taylor also indicates that a more practical explanation for the higher proportion of male hackers is that the social conditions mean that it is less likely for females to be programmers, and that if they do choose to be involved, that it can be a 'hostile environment'.

Rennie and Shore (2007) reviewed the literature relating to the motives of hacking, and analysed them using Ajzen's (1985, 1991) 'Theory of Planned Behaviour' and Beveren's (2001) 'Flow Theory'. The 'Theory of Planned Behaviour' has been used in a variety of contexts to both explain and predict behaviours, as well as targeting strategies for changing behaviour. 'Flow theory' attempts to explain absorption in a particular activity, where the experience itself is desired, rather than any specific end goal, and is a common explanation for excessive internet activity. When experiencing flow, users feel concentration, curiosity, intrinsic interest and control (Shernoff, Csikszentmihalyi, Schneider & Shernoff, 2003). The emotions reported by hackers are similar to those reported by other people experiencing flow (Rennie & Shore, 2007), and some of the motives offered as explanations by hackers (such as intrinsic interest and curiosity) would also seem to be supported by flow theory. Rennie and Shore (2007) indicate that flow theory therefore explains the progression of the hacker career, but it on its own cannot provide a complete model for computer crime. As such, they propose an advanced model of hacker development, incorporating other factors, such as ideology, vandalism and career, to predict the eventual type of individual which emerges, such as penetration testers, hacktivists and cyberterrorists. They indicate that flow theory explains the development of hackers from script-kiddies or newbies to experienced and skilled hackers. They indicate that an important method of dealing with the problem is to address it early, and to reduce the likelihood that teenagers will start hacking behaviours in the first place.

Having considered so many different theoretical approaches, it is worth considering the empirical work in this area, although it is very sparse in comparison to the theoretical writings. In the BKA study cited by Fötinger and Ziegler (2004), it was found that the hackers claimed that they were motivated primarily by 'trial and error' - honing their skills (33.1% of respondents) or economic reasons (51.3% of respondents). Woo, Kim and Dominick (2004) carried out a content analysis of 462 defaced websites, and concluded that about 70% of the defacements could be classified as simple pranks, while the rest had a more political motive. Voiskounsky and Smyslova (2003) were unable to uncover reliable trends in hacker motivation in an on-line survey.

Bernhardt Lieberman (2003, as cited in Fötinger and Ziegler, 2004) interviewed a total of 42 hackers. He found that hackers considered the 'intellectual challenge' and a wish to 'learn about computers and computing' to be their primary motivations. 'Breaking the law' and 'to achieve notoriety' were listed as their lowest-rated motivations. These findings are contradictory to both the public perception, and the opinions listed in many articles and books on the subject.

Chiesa, Ducci and Ciappi (2009) describe several motives cited by hackers, including intellectual curiosity, love of technology, fun and games, making the PC world safer, fighting for freedom, conflict with authority, rebelliousness, spirit of adventure and ownership, boredom, fame-seeking, anger and frustration, political reasons, escape from family and/or society and professional

reasons. Kirwan (2006) found that the motivations of hackers were very wide-ranging, and little in the way of consistent patterns could be observed. There were no clear differences between the cited motivations of white-hats and black-hats, despite the fact that discrepancies were expected due to the presence of criminal intent in black-hat hackers. She found that the motivations cited in online interviews with hackers were often quite vague, with hackers often citing 'commendable' reasons for their actions (such as to protect their friends' systems, or because they were passionate about computers), whereas those motives indicated by a content analysis of hacker bulletin boards were much more specific, and included the 'darker' side of hacking related activities, such as unlawfully accessing another person's files.

Based on the literature to date, it appears that hackers have quite a wide range of motivations for their actions. It is unfortunate that we must rely solely on the stated responses of cybercriminals to questions regarding motivation – there is a strong possibility that they are replying in what they perceive to be a socially acceptable way, and as such the results may be quite biased.

PROFILE AND PERSONALITY CHARACTERISTICS OF OFFENDERS

Introduction to Psychological Profiling

Offender profiling is the topic which most non-psychologists associate with forensic psychology, due to its prevalence in the media in films such as *Silence of the Lambs* and television programmes such as *Cracker* and *Criminal Minds*. In truth, there is a great deal more to forensic psychology than offender profiling alone, as can be seen in the breadth of forensic psychology outlined in this book, and specifically in Chapter 2. However, researchers into the psychology of hackers have attempted to utilize the theory and practice of offender profiling in their work.

A number of very useful texts are available to the reader outlining the fundamentals of offender profiling (see for example Canter & Youngs, 2009; Ainsworth, 2001; and Alison, 2005). In brief, much offender profiling research has been completed in the FBI Behavioural Science Unit. Some psychologists engaged in offender profiling utilize a clinical approach, while others focus on the use of multivariate statistics in order to create the profile. Criminal profiling can be defined as "the process of using crime scene evidence to make inferences about potential suspects, including personality characteristics and psychopathy" (Torres, Boccaccini & Miller, 2006, p. 51). While mostly used for serious offences such as murder, sexual assault and child abduction, particularly where such offences are considered to be part of a series by a single offender, the principles of profiling can be applied to almost any criminal event (such as organized crime, terrorism, arson, burglaries, robberies and fraud – see Canter & Youngs, 2009). Variations on profiling can also be used to attempt to find the geographical location of offenders, a sub-topic known as 'criminal psychogeography' (Canter & Youngs, 2009).

It should be noted that profiling is not the solution to all criminal investigations. It is rarely capable of identifying a single guilty suspect, despite the media suggestions to the contrary. In most cases, the main goal of profiling is to narrow the pool of potential suspects (Douglas & Olshaker, 1995). In addition, when Torres et al (2006) surveyed forensic psychologists and psychiatrists, fewer than 25% believed that profiling "was scientifically reliable or valid" (p. 51), although respondents viewed it as useful, and generally supported research in the area.

Donato (2009) suggests that criminal profiling can be applied to computer hacking, aiding digital investigations. However, Donato's proposed methodology does not allow for much psychological insights into the hacker involved, focusing more on using clues to establish the technological prowess of the hacker based on the mistakes they make during the attack. Little attention is placed on social engineering techniques, or on determining the hacker's psychological makeup. Similarly, it does not invoke the 'ghosts of hackers past' – most methods of offender profiling are based at least in part on an analysis of what types of evidence were left behind by offenders with certain characteristics, and Donato generally overlooks this. It is likely that the first step in creating reliable offender profiles of hackers involves investigating the psychological and demographic characteristics of previous offenders, so that new clues can be matched up to previous scenes of cybercrimes. While Donato's idea that criminal profiling can be applied to hacking behaviours is sound in principle, it appears that a great deal more background work identifying the common characteristics of these offenders is needed before it can realistically be used as a tool to aid investigations.

Demographic Characteristics

Bissett and Shipton (1999) describe the common media stereotype of the computer hacker. He is "an evil genius, usually male, usually acting alone, and employing fiendish cunning at the computer terminal to outwit a faceless bureaucracy or establishment" (p. 905). Levy (1984) wrote that, at that time, there had never been a star quality female hacker, and that most of the males existed as bachelors. Bissett and Shipton state that at their time of writing, there was only one female member of the hacker group 'Cult of the Dead Cow', although there was also a female white-hat hacker (Meinel, 1998). Indeed, Bissett and Shipton suggest that the language and images used in the 'Cult of the Dead Cow' all suggest adolescent or young adult male activity. Kirwan (2006) found evidence to suggest that the vast majority of hackers were male and older than the stereotype suggested. Young, Zhang and Prybutok (2007) indicated that when they attended a DefCon conference, it did appear that most of the hackers were between the ages of 12 and 28 years old

Murphy (2004) suggests that the common perception of a malicious hacker "…is that of a gifted but socially inept teenager. Generally they are visualised as male, loners with poor self-esteem and a greater ability to interact with computers and technology than with other people." (p. 12). Then again, Murphy also suggests that the hackers may be more socially cognizant than previously thought, at least as far as the organised hacking groups on the Internet are concerned. He also suggests that hackers, in particular white-hats, are as likely to form romantic relationships and have children as the rest of society.

Woo (2003) found that hackers who strongly endorsed nationalism showed higher aggressiveness scores than hackers with lower levels of nationalism. Woo also found links between high levels of narcissism and high levels of aggression amongst hackers. Fötinger and Ziegler (2004) suggest that hackers are task-oriented rather than time-oriented. They suggest that hackers are more likely to hold nocturnal habits, because there are less distractions at night. This may also be because IT security personnel are less likely to be monitoring the systems of organisations at night, and so their hacking activities are less likely to be noticed.

Kabay (1998) indicates that while the participants in public hacker meetings are predominantly young people, that some computer criminals have been people in their thirties. He also points out the lack of knowledge concerning personality profiles of cybercriminals, and while he suggests that the writing in hacker publications seems 'uniformly immature' it cannot be verified if this trait is representative of the hacker population as a whole. Platt (1994) visited hacker conventions, and found that the delegates were much more trusting and mild-mannered than he had expected. He felt less threatened by them than by 'normal' teenage males, and even noted that they showed

"an amazing degree of naïve trust" (p.1), at least as far as other delegates were concerned.

Kabay (1998) indicates that although there are a considerable number of popular books published in this area, it is unknown whether the hackers profiled in these sources are representative of the rest of the hacker population. Loper (2000) also laments the lack of theory and empirical research in the area of hacking, although there have since been some more robust studies in the area.

Fötinger and Ziegler (2004) cite an example of such research. They describe a large scale study by the German Federal Bureau of Criminal Investigation (Bundeskriminalamt, BKA). Following a large scale hacking attack on an Internet provider in the area of Münster, Germany in 1999, the BKA issued questionnaires to the hackers involved. Overall, 663 questionnaires were returned to the BKA, although 64 of these carried virtually no information. Of the remaining sample of 599, only 35 were female. On average, the females were found to be consistently older than the males (male average was 22.2 years, female average was 34.7 years). The females also only used approximately half the number of hacked accounts as the males (average 6.8 for females, with 14.1 for males). Overall, 72.2% of the alleged criminals lived with their parents while the crimes were committed. The BKA suggests the following profile of the typical offenders:

- Male
- Between 16 and 21 years old
- Lives with parents
- Has a middle or higher education
- Has medium to high knowledge of computers
- Is a student or trainee
- Uses the computer in his spare time
- Often meets in cliques or busies himself with television, videos and music

The Home Office (2005) report the findings of the Offending, Crime and Justice Survey (OCJS) which was carried out in 2003, and asked participants to self-report their hacking behaviours. They found that 0.9% of Internet users said they had used the Internet to hack into other computers, with males more likely than females (1.3% vs. 0.5%), and younger people (aged 10-25) more likely then older people to admit to hacking behaviours.

While many hackers are suspected to be either in full-time education or unemployed at the time of their highest activity levels, there are numerous hackers who have later progressed to more reputable professions, often in the IT security field. However, companies are advised to think carefully about hiring a former hacker, both for security and for client confidence reasons (see Cushing, 2001 for further discussion of this phenomenon taken from the corporation's perspective).

Overall, it would appear that the evidence concerning the demographic characteristics of hackers is quite contradictory, with some studies finding that the vast majority of hackers conform to the common stereotype, with other studies refuting this.

Ethical Positions

Rogers (as cited in Fötinger & Ziegler, 2004) suggests that moral development theory could be useful in understanding at least some groups of hackers, as there have been many documented anecdotal accounts of the lack of concern by hackers over the systems they have infiltrated. Young et al (2007) also found that the hackers had a high level of moral disengagement, and disregard any negative consequences of hacking by blaming the victims.

Many hackers subscribe to a common code of ethics. This code has changed somewhat over time. In 1984, Levy suggested several key characteristics of the then 'hacker ethic'. These include the principles that access to computers, and anything which might teach a person something about the way the world works, should be unlimited and total; that all information should be free and available to the public, that authority should not

be trusted; that hackers should be judged only by their hacking prowess, that the creation of art and beauty using computer technology is possible and that computers can change one's life for the better.

Mizrach (n.d.) carried out a content analysis of twenty-nine online documents in order to determine how widely accepted the hacker ethic is, and if it had changed since Levy's description in 1984. He determined that there is a new hacker ethic, which more current hackers live by, which has some continuity from the previous one. Mizrach indicates that this new hacker ethic evolved like the old one, informally and by processes of mutual reinforcement. He indicates that the new hacker ethic contains some ambiguities and contradictions. The new hacker he identified has ten main principles, including that harm should not be done, privacy should be protected, all computer resources should be used and not wasted, attempts should be made to exceed the known limitations of technology, that free communication with peers should be permitted, that no traces of hacker activity should be left behind, that information should be shared, that hackers should defend themselves against governments and corporations, that it is right to fix security holes and that the integrity of systems should be perpetually tested.

Mizrach indicates that the hacker ethic changed for several reasons. Firstly, there is far more computing power available now than when the original hacker ethic was formed. Secondly, a belief amongst hackers has developed that society has changed for the worse. Thirdly, a belief that the computer industry has discarded the original hacker ethic, and so new hackers had to respond to this. And finally, that there has been a generational change – that young hackers today are qualitatively different to hackers of a previous generation. Mizrach suggests that breaking the hacker ethic results mostly in anathema or social ostracisation.

Tavani (2007) suggests that many hackers "have embraced, either explicitly or implicitly, the following three principles" (p. 176) – that firstly information should be free, that hackers provide society with a useful service, and that activities in cyberspace do not harm people in the real world. Tavani goes on to explain the problems with these three principles, at least in theory. For example, he suggests that in many cases, hackers are probably aware that there are limits to the appropriate freedom of information (if all information was free, then privacy would be compromised and the integrity and accuracy of information would be questionable). As such, Tavani seems to propose a third version of the hacker ethic.

Lieberman (2003, as cited in Fötinger & Ziegler, 2004) questioned hackers on their subscription to the hacker ethic (as outlined by Levy, 1984), and found that although many hackers agreed with most of the principles involved, only 7% indicated that privacy was not important to them. Richard Spinello (2000) indicates that even though many hackers maintain that hacking is for fun and not damaging, and that many of them consider even looking for personal information such as credit card numbers as immoral and unethical, any act of trespassing is unethical, even if there is no attempt to gain personal information. He indicates that "people should not go where they do not belong, either in real space or in cyberspace" (p. 179). He does not argue that searching for personal information is more 'wrong' than simply 'looking around', but that "this does not excuse the latter activity".

As the hacker ethic appears to be a very dynamic concept, it is difficult to determine exactly whether or not the modern hacker subscribes to it completely. However, most hackers (particularly white-hat hackers) do appear to hold their ethical principles in high regard. It must be remembered that there are several flaws in the logic of the arguments hackers use regarding their code of ethics, and a further understanding of their position regarding this is highly desirable.

Interpersonal Relationships

Interpersonal behaviour has been studied in various areas of criminal psychology for some time,

although there has been relatively little research to date regarding the interpersonal relationship skills of hackers. Lieberman (2003, as cited in Fötinger & Ziegler, 2004) gave hackers a questionnaire on social anxiety and social avoidance, and found that the answers given go against the stereotyped image of hackers as loners who are incapable of social interaction. Lieberman also found that many hackers had normal romantic relationships and sex lives. He did find that the male stereotype held true for his sample – although they varied in race and age, none were female. Similarly, Woo, Kim and Dominick's (2004) study indicated that hackers are not the lonely, isolated individuals sometimes portrayed in the media but are members of an extensive social network.

Contradicting these findings, Rogers (as cited in Fötinger & Ziegler, 2004) suggests that psychoanalytic explanations of crime (which focus primarily on unconscious factors) are inadequate at explaining criminal behaviour that is planned, such as hacking. He indicates that the success of control theory in explaining hacking is inconsistent – the majority of hackers who have responded to requests for research indicate that they are withdrawn, uncomfortable with other people, and are introverted. Similarly, Chesebro and Bonsall (1989) suggest that hackers eschew social contacts. Rogers also indicates that hackers tend to associate with other individuals who also engage in hacking behaviour, even holding conventions to share their abilities. This suggests that hackers may have relatively high respect for other hackers (otherwise, they would be unlikely to be communicating with them).

Turkle (1984, as cited in Chesebro & Bonsall, 1989) suggests that hackers regard the computer as an extension of the self and as a friend. She suggests that the computer is employed to create a self-contained reality and to substitute for direct face-to-face interactions with other human beings. She indicates that "The hacker culture appears to be made up of people who need to avoid complicated social situations, who for one reason or another got frightened off or hurt too badly by the risks and complexities of relationships" (p. 216).

Kirwan (2006) found that hackers were more likely to indicate weaker relationships with family members than a control group of non-hacker computer users. In addition, the control group demonstrated higher levels on a measure of interpersonal relationships than the hacking group. She found no clear differences between the interpersonal relationships of the 'white-hat' and 'black-hat' groups. These findings were given additional support by the findings of a content analysis of hacker bulletin boards, which suggested that, while hackers appear to be capable of forming close relationships, they also appear to be more likely to have difficulties in those relationships than 'normal' computer users. Nevertheless, it was also found that many of the case study hackers (both white-hat and black-hat) were involved in romantic relationships, supporting the findings of Lieberman (2003).

As such, the findings regarding the interpersonal skills of hackers are extremely varied. Based on the more empirical work, it would appear that hackers have interpersonal skills which might be slightly inferior, but are not too dissimilar from the population as a whole.

PUNISHMENT

Brenner (2006) indicates that according to Section 1030 of the US Code, depending on the type of hacking activity engaged in, offenders can be fined, imprisoned for up to ten years, or both. This imprisonment can be extended to up to 20 years for repeat offenders. Tavani (2007) suggests that most involved would "support legislation that would distinguish between the degrees of punishment handed to those who are found guilty of trespass in cyberspace" (p. 202). Tavani goes on to indicate that in real-world counterparts of these activities (such as breaking and entering), a distinction would normally be made between offenders who have engaged in different degrees of

criminal activity (so that the offender who picks a lock but does not enter a premises would normally receive a lesser sentence than the offender who enters the premises but does not steal or damage anything, but who in turn would receive a lesser sentence than the offender who commits burglary).

Brenner (2006) indicates that most US states do tend to use a "two-tiered approach" (p. 84), distinguishing 'simple hacking' (gaining unauthorized access to a computer) from 'aggravated hacking' (gaining unauthorized access to a computer that results in the commission of some further criminal activity). Brenner indicates that these states generally consider "simple hacking a misdemeanor and aggravated hacking a felony" (p. 84). However some states use a single statute for both activities, while others, such as Hawaii, use up to five different classifications.

So there are a variety of means by which hackers can be punished. While imprisonment is one of the most commonly cited punishments, fines can also be implemented. As mentioned earlier in the case of Gary McKinnon, it is also possible to be extradited, and as was seen in the case of Kevin Mitnick, the hacker's access to technology may be limited. Nevertheless, it has yet to be fully determined if any of these punishments can act as an appropriate deterrent for hackers. Young, Zhang and Prybutok (2007) surveyed hackers and other attendees at a DefCon (a large hacker convention) conference in Las Vegas. They found that even though hackers perceive that they would be subject to severe judicial punishment if apprehended (thus demonstrating the effectiveness of the US Government in communicating the seriousness of illegal hacking), they continued to engage in illegal hacking activities. However, the hackers felt that there was a low likelihood of this punishment occurring. This is of note as severity of punishment has little effect when the likelihood of punishment is low (Von Hirsch, Bottoms, Burney & Wickstrom, 1999) whereas increased likelihood of punishment has been found to work as a deterrent (Killias, Scheidegger & Nordenson, 2009*).* Young et al (2007) also found that hackers perceived high utility value from their hacking activities, perceiving the gains from hacking to outweigh the potential losses. It seems likely that until this is reversed hackers are unlikely to reduce their offending behaviours.

PREVENTION METHODS AND EFFICACY

Rennie and Shore (2007) indicate that several controls are required to combat hacking. These include the intervention of both parents and peers to teach children about the criminal nature of hacking and reduce its perceived attractiveness. Police patrols that identify the early signs of hacking behaviours in a potential offender would also be required, and supplemented with the use of formal warnings and acceptable behaviour contracts. Rennie and Shore also indicate that the availability of hacker tools needs to be curtailed, so that the script-kiddies commencing their hacking careers find it too difficult to begin, and hence are not subjected to the flow experience. Finally, this needs to be supported by increased system security that would reduce the effectiveness of the hacking scripts and tools, which would also prevent the flow experience.

Overall, in our efforts to prevent hacking behaviours, a two-pronged approach is required – those methods that focus on improving the security systems themselves (such as better encryption and firewall software) and those methods that focus on the human element in security. No amount of technological improvements in safety will solve the problem if social engineering techniques are still effective. Users need to be made aware of how to ensure that systems remain secure, and how passwords and other confidential information should be protected. Simple safeguards such as ensuring that computers are not left logged in when unattended, doors to computers which hold critical information are locked, and training is given on how to create secure passwords could reduce the opportunities available to hackers.

DIFFICULTIES IN HACKER RESEARCH

There is an inevitable difficulty in studying hackers. Obviously, it is difficult to persuade the offenders to admit to their offences, as many of them remain uncaught, and they would run considerable risks by disclosing details of their activities. It is also possible that there may be individuals on the Internet posing as hackers, and who participate in research studies in that capacity, even though they may not have completed much (or any) hacking activity. And so the researcher is caught in a vicious circle – asking for sufficient information to verify that the hacker is legitimate will most likely put the real criminals off responding to the research, for fear of legal consequences. Some authors (e.g. Mitnick & Simon, 2005) have succeeded in including detailed case studies of specific hacking attacks in their work, however this is mainly because Mitnick is a former hacker, who had previously been incarcerated for similar offences. Mitnick suggests that "… they trust me. They know I've done time myself, and they are willing to rely on my not betraying them in a way that could put them in that position." (Mitnick & Simon, 2005, p. ix). Most academic researchers do not have this card to play, and must rely on a delicate balance in their study – asking sufficient (but relatively vague) questions to determine if the respondent is legitimate, without putting off the individual from responding in the first place.

One method by which this could be overcome involves setting tests for the hacker which they must complete before they participate in the research. This may involve defacing a website which has been created by the researcher, or initiating a Denial of Service attack on that website. Yet this is far from ideal, as it places additional demands on participants who may not be willing to invest so much time in the research. Wilful damage to a website may also be a legal grey area, despite permissions given by the researcher, and therefore something which must be avoided. Finally this technique still does not verify that the respondent is indeed a hacker (they may have asked a friend to do it for them) nor does it ensure that all hackers could succeed at this task. For example, a hacker who specialises in social engineering may not be able to complete the task, but may have previously completed several successful hacks.

For the moment, it appears that hacker research is subject to similar caveats as most types of psychological research, especially those studies that involve mail, telephone or online surveys. The researcher is dependent on the participant's honesty, in the hope that if the participant derives no obvious benefit from deceit, then they are unlikely to lie.

FUTURE TRENDS AND RESEARCH

Despite the significantly higher proportion of research on hackers than most other areas of cybercrime, there are still many unanswered questions. Little research has been done on the psychological profile of hackers, and the field would benefit from more studies which examine specific psychological characteristics. This research would be of particular benefit if the studies were to employ appropriate controls, which have been rare in the studies to date. It is necessary to compare hackers to computer users who spend significant amounts of time online in order to eliminate the confounding variable of time spent with technology.

Finally, it is also likely that continuous research into the psychology and culture of hackers will be required. It does appear that there have been significant differences in these since the first hacker communities, as is evident by the changes in the hacker ethic and demographics (such as gender). It is likely that these will continue to change as technology becomes more advanced. Even setting aside the incomplete knowledge of the present, it would be useful to be able to track the changes in hacker culture and psychology over time, in the hope of being able to predict future trends more accurately.

CONCLUSION

While hackers have caught the public and academic imagination in ways that most other cybercriminals have not, it seems that there is still relatively little reliable empirical knowledge about them. What does exist is somewhat contradictory, and it is difficult to develop an overall picture of what a hacker is like. The problems inherent in studying hackers are probably partly to blame for this, along with an incomplete understanding of hacker techniques by researchers. It is also important that computer users are adequately informed of the techniques that hackers use, in order to tighten security, especially in large companies and organisations. Overall, while a considerable amount is known about the psychology of hackers, there are many gaps in the research, and much of the theory which has been put forth in the area needs to be empirically investigated before it can be considered reliable.

REFERENCES

Ainsworth, P.B. (2001). *Offender Profiling and Crime Analysis.* Cullompton, Devon: Willan Publishing.

Ajzen, I. (1985). *Action-control: from cognition to behaviour* (pp. 11–39). New York: Springer-Verlag.

Ajzen, I. (1991). The Theory of Planned Behaviour. *Organizational Behavior and Human Decision Processes, 50,* 179–211. doi:10.1016/0749-5978(91)90020-T

Alison, L. (2005). The Forensic Psychologist's Casebook: Psychological Profiling and Criminal Investigation. *Cullompton, Devon: Willan Publishing.*

BBC News Online. *(9ᵗʰ June 2009).* Hacker 'too fragile' to extradite. *Retrieved 24ᵗʰ February 2010 from* http://news.bbc.co.uk/2/hi/uk_news/8090789.stm

BBC News Online. *(28th July2009)*. Hacker's 'moral crusade' over UFO. *Retrieved24thFebruary2010 from*http://news.bbc.co.uk/go/pr/fr/-/2/hi/uk_news/8172842.stm

BBC News Online. *(31st July2009)*. Hacker loses extradition appeal. *Retrieved24thFebruary2010 from*http://news.bbc.co.uk/go/pr/fr/-/2/hi/uk_news/8177561.stm

BBC News Online. *(10thDecember2009)*. Hacker to appeal over extradition. *Retrieved24thFebruary2010 from*http://news.bbc.co.uk/2/hi/uk_news/8406643.stm

BBC News Online. *(24thFebruary2010)*. Robin Hood Hacker Exposes Bankers. *Retrieved25thFebruary2010from*http://news.bbc.co.uk/go/pr/fr/-/2/hi/technology/8533641.stm

Beveran, J. V. (2001). A Conceptual Model of Hacker Development and Motivations. *The Journal of Business*, *1*(Issue 2). Retrieved from http://www.dvara.net/HK/beveren.pdf.

Bissett, A., & Shipton, G. (1999). Some human dimensions of computer virus creation and infection. *International Journal of Human-Computer Studies*, *52*, 899–913. doi:10.1006/ijhc.1999.0361

Boyd, C. (2008). *Profile: Gary McKinnon.* On BBC News Online (30th July 2008). Retrieved 24th February 2010 from http://news.bbc.co.uk/2/hi/uk_news/7839338.stm

Brenner, S. W. (2006). Defining Cybercrime: A Review of State and Federal Law. In Clifford, R. D. (Ed.), *Cybercrime: The Investigation, Prosecution and Defense of a Computer Related Crime* (2nd ed., pp. 13–95). Durham, NC: Carolina Academic Press.

Bryant, R., & Marshall, A. (2008). Criminological and Motivational Perspectives. In *Robin Bryant & Sarah Bryant (2008). Investigating Digital Crime* (pp. 231–248). Chichester: Wiley.

Calcutt, A. (1999). *White Noise: An A-Z of the Contradictions in Cyberculture*. London: MacMillan Press Ltd.

Canter, D., & Youngs, D. (2009). *Investigative Psychology: Offender Profiling and the Analysis of Criminal Action*. Chichester: Wiley.

Chesebro, J. W., & Bonsall, D. G. (1989). *Computer-Mediated Communication: Human Relationships in a Computerised World*. Tuscaloosa, AL: The University of Alabama Press.

Chiesa, R., Ducci, S., & Ciappi, S. (2009). *Profiling Hackers: The Science of Criminal Profiling as Applied to the World of Hacking*. Boca Raton, FL: Auerbach Publications.

Computer Security Institute. *(2009)*. CSI Computer crime and security survey 2009. *Retrieved8thMarch2010from*http://gocsi.com/survey

Cushing, K. (2001, May10). Would you turn to the dark side? Computer Weekly, *p. 34*.

Donato, L. (2009). An Introduction to How Criminal Profiling Could be used as a support for computer hacking investigations. *Journal of Digital Forensic Practice*, *2*, 183–195. doi:10.1080/15567280903140946

Douglas, J. E., & Olshaker, M. (1995). *Mind hunter: Inside the FBI's elite serial crime unit.* New York: Mindhunters.

Fötinger, C. S., & Ziegler, W. (2004). *Understanding a hacker's mind – a psychological insight into the hijacking of identities*. Danube-University Krems, Austria: RSA Security.

Furnell, S. (2010). Hackers, viruses and malicious software (pp. 173 – 193). In Yvonne Jewkes and Majid Yar (2010) *Handbook of Internet Crime (eds)*. Cullompton, Devon: Willan Publishing.

Garlik (2009). UK Cybercrime Report 2009. Published September 2009. By Stefan Fafinski, *Neshan Minassian of Invenio Research*. Retrieved 8th March 2010 from http://www.garlik.com/cybercrime_report.php

Gunkel, D. J. (2005). Editorial: Introduction to hacking and hacktivism. *New Media & Society*, 7, 595–597. doi:10.1177/1461444805056007

Halsey, M., & Young, A. (2002). The Meanings of Graffiti and Municipal Administration. *Australian and New Zealand Journal of Criminology*, 35, 165–186. doi:10.1375/acri.35.2.165

Hayes, D. (1989). *Behind the Silicon Curtain: The Seductions of Work in a Lonely Era*. London: Free Association Books.

Home Office. *(2005)*. Fraud and Technology Crimes: findings from the 2002/03 British Crime Survey and 2003 Offending, Crime and Justice Survey. *(Home Office Online Report 34/05). Retrieved on 26th July 2005 from* www.homeoffice. gov.uk/rds/pdfs05/rdsolr3405.pdf

Kabay, M. E. *(1998)*. ICSA White Paper on Computer Crime Statistics. *Retrieved on 29th April 2005 from* www.icsa.net/html/library/whitepapers/ crime.pdf

Killias, M., Scheidegger, D., & Nordenson, P. (2009). Effects of Increasing the Certainty of Punishment: A Field Experiment on Public Transportation. *European Journal of Criminology*, 6, 387–400. doi:10.1177/1477370809337881

Kirwan, G. H. *(2006)*. An Identification of Demographic and Psychological Characteristics of Computer Hackers Using Triangulation. *PhD Thesis, Institute of criminology, College of business and law, School of law. University College Dublin. June 2006*

Lafrance, Y. *(2004)*. Psychology: A Previous Security Tool. *Retrieved on 29th April 2005 from* http:// cnscentre.future.co.kr/resource/security/hacking/1409.pdf

Levy, S. (1984). *Hackers: Heroes of the Computer Revolution*. London: Penguin Books.

Loper, D. K. (2000, November). *Profiling Hackers: Beyond Psychology*. Paper presented at the Annual Meeting of the American Society of Criminology, San Francisco, CA. Retrieved on 29th April 2005 from http://webpages.csus.edu/~doc/ ASC2000_ProfilingHackers.pdf

Maslow, A. H. (1970). *Motivation and Personality* (2nd ed.). New York: Harper & Row.

Meinel, C. P. (1998). How hackers break in… and how they are caught. *Scientific American*, 279, 98–105. doi:10.1038/scientificamerican1098-98

Mitnick, K. D., & Simon, W. L. (2002). *The Art of Deception: Controlling the Human Element of Security*. Indianapolis, IN: Wiley Publishing Inc.

Mitnick, K. D., & Simon, W. L. (2005). *The Art of Intrusion: The Real Stories Behind the Exploits of Hackers, Intruders and Deceivers*. Indianapolis, IN: Wiley Publishing Inc.

Mizrach, S. *(n.d.)*. Is there a Hacker Ethic for 90s Hackers? *Retrieved on 16th June 2010 from* http:// www.fiu.edu/~mizrachs/hackethic.html

Murphy, C. (2004, June). Inside the Mind of the Hacker. *Accountancy Ireland*, 36, 12.

Platt, C. (1994, November Issue 2.11). Hackers: Threat or Menace? *Wired*, 82-8. Retrieved from http://www.wired.com/wired/archive/2.11/hack. cong.html

Rantala, R. R. (for the US Dept of Justice, Bureau of Justice Statistics; 2008). *Cybercrime against Businesses, 2005*. Published Sept 2008; NCJ 221943. Retrieved 8th March 2010 from http://bjs. ojp.usdoj.gov/content/pub/pdf/cb05.pdf

Rennie, L., & Shore, M. (2007). An Advanced model of hacking. *Security Journal*, 20, 236–251. doi:10.1057/palgrave.sj.8350019

Rock, P. *(2007). Sociological Theories of Crime (pp. 3-42). In Mike Maguire, Rod Morgan and Robert Reiner's (eds)* The Oxford Handbook of Criminology (4th edition). *Oxford: Oxford University Press*.

Rogers, M. *(2000).* A New Hacker Taxonomy. University of Manitoba, [Online]. *Retrieved on-6ᵗʰMarch2010 from*http://homes.cerias.purdue.edu/~mkr/hacker.doc

Sanders-Reach,C.(2005, May16). Beware Pharming and Other New Hacker Scams. New Jersey Law Journal.

Schneier, B. (2003, November/December)... *IEEE Security and Privacy, 1,* 6.

Shernoff, D. J., Csikszentmihalyi, M., Schneider, B., & Shernoff, E. S. (2003). Student engagement in high school classrooms from the perspective of Flow Theory. *School Psychology Quarterly, 18,* 158–176. doi:10.1521/scpq.18.2.158.21860

Spinello, R. (2000). Information Integrity. In Langford, D. (Ed.), *Internet Ethics* (pp. 158–180). London: MacMillan Press.

Spitzner, L. (2003). *Honeypots: Tracking Hackers.* Boston, MA: Addison-Wesley Inc.

Sterling, B. (1992). *The Hacker Crackdown: Law and Disorder on the Electronic Frontier.* New York: Penguin.

Tavani, H. T. (2007). *Ethics and Technology: Ethical Issues in an Age of Information and Communication Technology* (2nd ed.). Hoboken, NJ: Wiley.

Taylor, P. (1999). *Hackers.* London: Routledge. doi:10.4324/9780203201503

Taylor, P. (2001). Hacktivism: in search of lost ethics? In Wall, D. S. (Ed.), *Crime and the Internet* (pp. 59–73). London: Routledge.

Taylor, P. A. (2003). Maestros or misogynists? Gender and the social construction of hacking (pp. 126-146). In Yvonne Jewkes (2003) *Dot. cons: Crime, deviance and identity on the Internet.* Cullompton, Devon (UK): Willan Publishing.

Torres, A. N., Boccaccini, M. T., & Miller, H. A. (2006). Perceptions of the validity and utility of criminal profiling among forensic psychologists and psychiatrists. *Professional Psychology, Research and Practice, 37,* 51–58. doi:10.1037/0735-7028.37.1.51

Voiskounsky, A. E., & Smyslova, O. V. (2003). Flow-based model of computer hacker's motivation. *CyberPsychology and Behaviour, 6,* 171–180. doi:10.1089/109493103321640365

Von Hirsch, A., Bottoms, A. E., Burney, E., & Wickstrom, P. O. (1999). *Criminal deterrence and sentence severity.* Oxford: Hart.

Warren, M., & Leitch, S. (2009). Hacker Taggers: A new type of hackers. *Information Systems Frontiers.* doi:.doi:10.1007/s10796-009-9203-y

Woo, H. J. *(2003). The hacker mentality: Exploring the relationship between psychological variables and hacking activities.* Dissertation Abstracts International, 64, 2A, *325.*

Woo, J. J., Kim, Y., & Dominick, J. (2004). Hackers: Militants or merry pranksters? A content analysis of defaced web pages. *Media Psychology, 6,* 63–82. doi:10.1207/s1532785xmep0601_3

Young, R., Zhang, L., & Prybutok, V. R. (2007). Hacking into the Minds of Hackers. *Information Systems Management, 24,* 281–287. doi:10.1080/10580530701585823

ADDITIONAL READING

Beveran, J. V. (2001). A Conceptual Model of Hacker Development and Motivations. *The Journal of Business, 1*(Issue 2). Retrieved from http://www.dvara.net/HK/beveren.pdf.

Chiesa, R., Ducci, S., & Ciappi, S. (2009). *Profiling Hackers: The Science of Criminal Profiling as Applied to the World of Hacking.* Boca Raton, FL: Auerbach Publications.

Donato, L. (2009). An Introduction to How Criminal Profiling Could be used as a support for computer hacking investigations. *Journal of Digital Forensic Practice*, 2, 183–195. doi:10.1080/15567280903140946

Fötinger, C. S., & Ziegler, W. (2004). *Understanding a hacker's mind – a psychological insight into the hijacking of identities*. Danube-University Krems, Austria: RSA Security.

Furnell, S. (2010). Hackers, viruses and malicious software (pp. 173 – 193). In Yvonne Jewkes and Majid Yar (2010) *Handbook of Internet Crime (eds)*. Cullompton, Devon: Willan Publishing.

Gunkel, D. J. (2005). Editorial: Introduction to hacking and hacktivism. *New Media & Society*, 7, 595–597. doi:10.1177/1461444805056007

Levy, S. (1984). *Hackers: Heroes of the Computer Revolution*. London: Penguin Books.

Loper, D. K. (2000, November). *Profiling Hackers: Beyond Psychology*. Paper presented at the Annual Meeting of the American Society of Criminology, San Francisco, CA. Retrieved on 29th April 2005 from http://webpages.csus.edu/~doc/ASC2000_ProfilingHackers.pdf

Mitnick, K. D., & Simon, W. L. (2002). *The Art of Deception: Controlling the Human Element of Security*. Indianapolis, IN: Wiley Publishing Inc.

Mitnick, K. D., & Simon, W. L. (2005). *The Art of Intrusion: The Real Stories Behind the Exploits of Hackers, Intruders and Deceivers*. Indianapolis, IN: Wiley Publishing Inc.

Mizrach, S. *(n.d.)*. Is there a Hacker Ethic for 90s Hackers? *Retrieved on16[th]June2010 from*http://www.fiu.edu/~mizrachs/hackethic.html

Murphy, C. (2004, June). Inside the Mind of the Hacker. *Accountancy Ireland*, 36, 12.

Rennie, L., & Shore, M. (2007). An Advanced model of hacking. *Security Journal*, 20, 236–251. doi:10.1057/palgrave.sj.8350019

Rogers, M. (2000). *A New Hacker Taxonomy*. University of Manitoba, [Online]. Retrieved on 6th March 2010 from http://homes.cerias.purdue.edu/~mkr/hacker.doc

Sterling, B. (1992). *The Hacker Crackdown: Law and Disorder on the Electronic Frontier*. New York: Penguin.

Taylor, P. (1999). *Hackers*. London: Routledge. doi:10.4324/9780203201503

Taylor, P. (2001). Hacktivism: in search of lost ethics? In Wall, D. S. (Ed.), *Crime and the Internet* (pp. 59–73). London: Routledge.

Taylor, P. A. (2003). Maestros or misogynists? Gender and the social construction of hacking (pp. 126-146). In Yvonne Jewkes (2003) *Dot. cons: Crime, deviance and identity on the Internet*. Cullompton, Devon (UK): Willan Publishing.

Voiskounsky, A. E., & Smyslova, O. V. (2003). Flow-based model of computer hacker's motivation. *CyberPsychology and Behaviour*, 6, 171–180. doi:10.1089/109493103321640365

Warren, M., & Leitch, S. (2009). Hacker Taggers: A new type of hackers. *Information Systems Frontiers*. doi:.doi:10.1007/s10796-009-9203-y

Woo, H. J. *(2003). The hacker mentality: Exploring the relationship between psychological variables and hacking activities*. Dissertation Abstracts International, 64, 2A, *325*.

Woo, J. J., Kim, Y., & Dominick, J. (2004). Hackers: Militants or merry pranksters? A content analysis of defaced web pages. *Media Psychology*, 6, 63–82. doi:10.1207/s1532785xmep0601_3

Young, R., Zhang, L., & Prybutok, V. R. (2007). Hacking into the Minds of Hackers. *Information Systems Management*, 24, 281–287. doi:10.1080/10580530701585823

Chapter 5
Malware:
Can Virus Writers be Psychologically Profiled?

ABSTRACT

Most computer users are likely to have some exposure to malware (malicious software), in the form of spyware, computer viruses, worms or Trojans. This chapter aims to determine if malware developers, and in particular virus writers, can be psychologically profiled. Initially, the chapter will clarify the distinctions between different types of malware, and provide a brief history of some of the most famous malware programs which have been developed. It is important to remember that malware producers and hackers are not necessarily the same individuals, although there is no doubt that at least some individuals engage in both behaviours and the terms are sometimes used interchangeably in the media. A key researcher in the psychology of virus writers, Sarah Gordon, distinguishes between hackers and virus writers "In general, hackers frown upon virus writers. After all, hacking requires system knowledge and skill and is somewhat "sexy" in today's counterculture, while virus writing is still looked down upon, mostly for its indiscriminate damage and lack of required skill" (PBS Frontline, n.d., no pagination). The psychology of hackers and the skills required to engage in hacking activities have previously been described in Chapter 4, and while there is some overlap, it is certain that there are differences between the methods, motives and skills of the two groups.

Malware is prolific, and the known prevalence rates for infection, as well as the quantity of known malware programs, will be identified. A brief overview of how malware applications are developed and distributed will be considered, especially in light of the use of social psychology in encouraging individuals to download and distribute the programs. However there is a lack of empirical psychological study relating to virus writers, and much of the literature is based on case studies and individual interviews. Nevertheless, some tentative explanations for the motives of virus writers can be put forward, and there is some limited information available regarding the psychological profile and personality characteristics of virus writers.

DOI: 10.4018/978-1-61350-350-8.ch005

In particular, similarities with the psychology of vandalism will be explored, in order to determine if similar theories might explain both phenomena. The chapter will also explore methods of reducing and preventing damage done by malware, and it will explore the psychological mechanisms that can predict if a computer user is likely to engage in safe online behaviour. Finally consideration will be given to future trends in malware development, such as the increasing threat of malware on portable devices, and suggestions for important future research in the area.

BACKGROUND

An early computer virus type program was known as 'cookie monster'. This relatively benign virus would prevent the user from using the computer by requesting a cookie. If the user typed in the word 'cookie', the message would disappear, only to reappear a while later requesting another treat. The 'cookie monster' virus was an irritation, but more modern viruses can have considerably more serious consequences.

In September 2010, the Stuxnet worm inflicted damage on computers and networks, mostly in Iran. While it was first detected in June 2010, it was in September 2010 that it was revealed that the worm had infected computers at Iran's first nuclear power station (BBC News, 2010a). The Stuxnet worm specifically targets systems used to manage utilities such as water, oil rigs and power plants. It is a highly tailored worm, and is thought to be the first worm designed to target such facilities. Instead of using the Internet to distribute itself it infects Windows via portable memory devices such as USB keys. Because of this it can target systems that are not connected to the Internet for security reasons. Once infected, the worm can reprogram the software which gives instructions to industrial machinery, such as motors and coolers, telling them to turn on or off at given signals. As this worm looks for very specific configurations, and does not actively affect the system unless it finds them, this case has obvious implications for the potential of cyberterrorism (see Chapter 11), although at the time of writing, there is insufficient evidence to determine who wrote the worm or what its intended target was (BBC News, 2010b).

However, Ralph Langner (an industrial computer expert) is quoted by BBC News (2010b) as saying that "With the forensics we now have it is evident and provable that Stuxnet is a directed sabotage attack involving heavy insider knowledge" (no pagination).

Definitions and Categories of Malware

Edgar-Nevill and Stephens (2008) define malware as "any piece of software devised with malicious intent" (p. 91). The term is taken from the phrase 'malicious software' and is used to describe any software program that spreads from one computer to another and that interferes with computer operation. Kramer and Bradfield (2010) indicate that while malware is intuitively considered to be "software that harmfully attacks other software, where to harmfully attack can be observed to mean to cause the actual behaviour to differ from the intended behaviour" (p. 105). However, Kramer and Bradfield claim that this definition is insufficient, as the intended behaviour is infrequently defined, and so a more accurate definition of malware needs to also consider the concept of "software system correctness" (p. 105), and proceed to define this in technical terms. They go on to define other related concepts including 'benware' (benign software) and 'anti-malware' ('antibodies' against malware).

Important terms relating to malware include 'payload' and 'in the wild'. 'In the wild' refers to how widespread the malware is. Malware such as viruses are not always released, and may be developed as a 'proof of concept' which remains limited to a small network of computers or devices. When a piece of malware escapes or is intentionally released so that it spreads to unsuspecting users on other systems, it is considered to be 'in the wild'. 'Payload' is what the malware will actually do – its raison d'etre, and according to Furnell (2010) it is the least predictable aspect of the program. In the 'cookie monster' example above, the payload refers to the application's demand for a 'cookie', thus preventing the user from continuing their work. The payload for the Stuxnet worm appears to be the program's ability to gain access over the industrial plant. Furnell (2010, p. 189) identifies three main categories of payload. These include 'damage and disruption' (such as corrupting or deleting files), 'stealing information' (such as using a keylogger to capture information, or copying files to the computer), and 'hijacking systems' (enabling remote control of the system, perhaps to create a botnet – a distributed network of computers controlled by an unauthorized user). It is likely that different motives underlie each of these types of payload. A piece of malware may use several types of software in order to deliver the payload, a brief description of some of these is provided below.

Types of Malware

There are many types of malware, of which the computer virus is probably the best known type. However, there are several other types of malware and payloads, including worms, Trojan horses, spyware, keyloggers, logic bombs and rootkits. In addition to these, virus hoaxes are sometimes also considered to be a type of malware, due to their ability to cause destruction through the actions of users who follow the instructions contained in the hoax. Definitions of all types of malware can vary from researcher to researcher, and so those definitions which appear to be most commonly used are described here. It is important to remember that each type of malware is not necessarily independent - Edgar-Nevill and Stephens (2008)

indicate that there can be 'blended attacks' where several types of malware are used in combination. However the differences, at least from the victim's perspective, can be minor, and Bocij (2006, p.33) indicates that for most users malware such as viruses and worms are very similar, and can have virtually the same effect on their systems.

A *virus* is a self-replicating program, similar to the viral infections that cause human illness. In the same way as biological viruses need a host, computer viruses need a file to spread from one computer to another. Many definitions of computer viruses indicate that the virus needs some form of human action to run and propagate. This human action may be as simple as opening an infected document running an infected program.

A *worm* is very similar to a virus by design and also spread from computer to computer, but unlike a virus, it does not need a file to travel in, and most definitions agree that worms have the capability to travel autonomously, without any human action required. As such worms are capable of both self-replication and self-transmission, and can send out thousands of copies of themselves. Tavani (2007) indicates that worms can spread more quickly than viruses, as they do not need a human operator. He provides the example of the 'Code Red Worm'. This worm became prevalent in 2001, using a vulnerability in the Microsoft NT 4.0 operating system. It was designed to infect systems on days 1 to 18 of a given month, and then activated its payload on the 19th day. On this day, the computer would "flood a target site with bogus data" (p. 173). It would then lie dormant until the end of the month, before starting to propagate again on the first of the next month.

Spyware is a type of malware which collects information about the computer user, forwarding it to the creator of the spyware or a third party. This can put personal and corporate data at risk by divulging passwords, bank account details, and browsing history. Furnell (2010) indicates that spyware always has the same objective – to invade privacy. This distinguishes it from other forms of malware which are less predictable in what they aim to do. Thompson (2005) indicates that as well as the privacy problems, spyware can also significantly slow down a computer, resulting in lost work hours. A specific type of spyware involves *keyloggers,* software devices, sometimes hidden in Trojan Horses, that monitor the keystrokes of the user, such as passwords, usernames, and confidential documents and correspondence, and then sends out a copy to the person who distributed the virus.

Trojan horses or *Trojans* are named after the mythological event where Greek soldiers created a giant wooden horse, which they left outside the gates of the city of Troy after a lengthy siege. The Greek army then pretended to sail away, while the Trojans brought the horse inside the city walls as a victory trophy. Unknown to them, there were thirty Greek soldiers hiding inside the horse, who crept out during the night and let the remainder of the Greek army inside the city. In malware terms, a Trojan Horse will, at first glance, appear to be some type of benign or useful software, such as a picture or useful application. But once installed, the Trojan Horse will show its true purpose, causing damage to the system, or allowing another individual to gain control of the computer. In some cases, the Trojan Horse may still appear to perform the promised useful function. This is especially the case for Trojans with spyware payloads, where the distributor of the program would prefer if the user did not discover the spyware software.

Tavani (2007) indicates that a *logic bomb* is a piece of software that checks for certain conditions in a computer system and then executes when they arise. As such, it may form part of another piece of malware which determines when the payload executes. A *rootkit* replaces the process management capabilities of a system so as to hide the type of malware which is installed. It is "used to hide the installation of any files and other system details that should not be present on a victim's computer" (Stephens, 2008, p. 127). If a rootkit is used in a malware program, and the user proceeds to check the status of their system, they will see a false projection of the true nature of their system, which may hide the malware from view.

While not necessarily including an actual software application, *virus hoaxes* can still cause problems by taking up user time and effort or by persuading users that a file on their system is a virus and must be deleted, while the file is actually important for the efficient running of the system. One of the first known hoaxes emerged in 1994, and was known as 'Good Times'. It warned of a virus with the power to erase a recipient's hard drive, and encouraged the reader to forward the warning to all their friends. The 'Good Times' virus did not actually exist, but the hoax did succeed in using up system resources, bandwidth, and user time and effort as it was widely distributed by well meaning users.

A Brief History of Malware

Bocij (2006) indicates that while computer viruses have existed for some time, with "naturally" occurring versions appearing as early as 1974 as part of programming glitches, most references to computer viruses did not appear until the early 1980s. One of the first known computer viruses to exist in the wild was known as Elk Cloner. It first appeared in 1982, targeting Apple operating systems and spreading via floppy disk. It was not destructive, but it did display a poem about itself every fiftieth time that the contents of the disk were run.

It will get on all your disks

It will infiltrate your chips

Yes its Cloner!

It will stick to you like glue

It will modify ram too

Send in the Cloner!

Another early computer virus – '©Brain' - appeared around 1985/1986 and is widely referred to as the first IBM-PC virus. This virus was designed to infect any computer running a pirated copy of software which was legitimately written and distributed by the creators of the virus. Despite these early viruses, Bocij (2006) indicates that the public first became widely aware and uneasy with viruses in the late 1980s. Tavani (2007) cites the example of a worm created by Robert Morris, a graduate student at Cornell University, in 1988. This worm significantly damaged internet activity and was important as it demonstrated that cybercrime could have a significant disruptive effect on Internet users. Morris was apprehended, and argued that he had not intended to cause the damage, but that his program "was just an experiment that got out of control" (Tavani, 2007, p. 198). Due to problems classifying the damage in the legal system, Morris was finally sentenced to probation and community service.

The payloads of some viruses indicated that the authors had an interesting sense of humour. The Cascade virus, evident in the late 1980s and early 1990s, had a payload that made text fall down the screen and land in a heap at the bottom. In 1988, the Stoned or Marijuana Virus displayed the message *"Your computer is stoned. Legalize Marijuana"* while the 1998 HPS virus was activated on Saturdays and flipped uncompressed bitmap files horizontally – effectively turning pictures into mirror images of themselves.

Other viruses and worms have been less humorous, causing large amounts of disruption and financial damage. In 1999, the Melissa virus infected thousands of computers using Microsoft Outlook, causing an estimated $80 million in damage. In the year 2000, the infamous "I Love You" virus infected millions of computers, as users were persuaded to open an infected attachment which pretended to be a love letter to the recipient. The 'Slammer' virus caused considerable damage in 2003, reputedly causing a large scale denial of service on the Internet, crashing computers at a nuclear power plant and disrupting a major bank's ATM network. Malware is not limited to desktop and laptop computers. In 2004 the Skulls Trojan horse infected Nokia cellphones with a worm which prevented users from any activities except making and receiving calls, and replaced icons on the screen with images of skulls and crossbones.

Some malware, such as 2004's 'Opener' and 2008's 'Conficker' programs allows the distributor to gain remote access to the computer. This can be used to steal confidential information, to invade privacy, and to use the computers as a remote-controlled 'botnet' (a collection of infiltrated computers) which may be used to carry out distributed denial of service attacks (see Chapter 4). Nevertheless, many malware applications, such as the recent "Here you have email" virus (2010) still rely on spreading via email, and using social engineering techniques to persuade users to click on links embedded in the email.

Bocij (2006) suggests that there have been significant changes over time relating to the phenomenon of malware. He suggests that current malware producers are now somewhat older than they were in the 1990s, with most being in their twenties rather than teenagers. He also suggests that there has been an increase in female virus writers. Bocij also proposes that there have been changes in the motives behind virus writing. While originally virus writers claimed to write because of curiosity or altruistic reasons (such as discovering system vulnerabilities), he indicates that now a higher proportion of malware producers are concerned with financial gain. These motives are considered in more detail below. Bocij also suggests that there has been a recent increase in spyware, rather than viruses, as spyware software can be used more obviously for financial gain via identity theft. This may also be reflected in increased interest in malware by organized crime gangs and terrorist groups, who see the potential of using malware to attain their goals.

Known Prevalence Rates and Costs Associated with Malware

Despite the relatively long history of malware, the problem seems to still be growing. Symantec attempts to quantify the amount of malware by examining the number of new malicious code signatures that are created to detect threats (Symantec, 2010). In 2009, Symantec created almost three million new malicious code signatures, a 71% increase over 2008 (Symantec, 2010). Of all the malicious code signatures ever created by Symantec, 51% were created just in 2009.

While Symantec is a commercial company, with an obvious interest in highlighting the dangers of malware, the increase in risk is also reflected by the Computer Security Insitute (CSI) Survey in 2009. The CSI survey indicates that 64.3% of businesses claim to have been the victim of a malware infection. This was an increase of approximately 14% on the previous year, but is still less than the 2005 figure where seventy-four percent of respondents reported being infected. When compared to other threats, such as denial of service, password sniffing or financial fraud, malware infection was found to be the most prevalent incident. McAfee and the National Cyber Security Alliance (2007) found that viruses are also a major problem for home users, with over half of surveyed homes having experienced a virus, and 44% believing that they were currently infected with spyware.

Furnell (2010) notes that while CSI surveys suggest that virus incidents are not associated with very large financial losses (with an average of just over $40,000 reported), that it is possible that a high number of low-cost incidents could be a threat to even the largest of businesses. Bocij (2006) also indicates that the cost of downtime associated with virus infection is also an issue for companies, as users are prevented from achieving their full productivity due to slow-running systems.

Methods of Malware Production and Distribution

Furnell (2010) indicates that as malware generally requires a method of distribution, those who write and release the code need to get the programs to contexts where users will find them. He indicates that this can be linked to whatever new online service is in favour with the online community. Historically, early viruses were spread via floppy disk. New viruses were relatively rare, and it could take a long time for an infection to spread if the computer was not connected to the internet and distribution by floppies was relied on. In the late 1990s transmission by disk was frequently eschewed as infection via email became the preferred method. Since then, infection methods have progressed to other popular services, such as instant messaging, peer-to-peer sharing, and social network sites (Furnell, 2010). Collins (2006) lists several methods by which computer viruses and malware can be contracted, including opening e-mail attachments, opening files, accessing webpages with malicious code, downloading software from the internet and sharing infected drives. As can be seen with Stuxnet, virus writers who are targeting offline systems are now returning to virus propagation by disk, specifically USB keys. After a virus is produced, it may remain an active threat for a long time, as the original writers or others produce new variations of the program so as to bypass the methods used by anti-virus software products (Furnell, 2010). In some cases, the malware can metamorphise into new variants on its own.

Virus writers do not need to develop the malware from scratch. There are many malware development kits that can be easily obtained (Ollmann, 2008). Yar (2006, p. 32) describes how one of these development kits was used to create the 'Anna Kournikova' worm, which appeared in 2001. The author admitted that it was his first attempt to create a virus, and it only took a minute to prepare, due to a toolkit called the

'Vbs Worm Generator', which allowed users to custom design a worm with a variety of destructive payloads. Despite the ease and speed with which a virus or a botnet can be created using a malware development kit, custom programs are sometimes preferred as they are less likely to be detected by antivirus software.

Furnell (2010) reports the importance of social engineering in infecting systems, as the propagation system may still require user input to be successful. He indicates that many viruses have been linked to notable dates, such as Christmas, Valentines Day or April Fool's day, as by doing so, virus writers and distributors feel that they have better chances of success. Rusch (2002) indicates that malware developers and distributors make use of several key social psychological principles when preparing the program so as to ensure that users are more likely to run the application or distribute the file. He indicates that people's use of heuristics to shorten decision-making time may play an important role. Because of a reliance on heuristic decision making, the more similar an application looks like a requested or useful file, the more likely a person is to open it without proper evaluation of the potential risk. Rusch also indicates that it is possible that users place too much trust in online sources and information, especially when the sender utilizes friendly language and language that suggests that the recipient knows them. He also lists other reasons why people may be more likely to accept and open a malware program, such as claims of authority in the email (perhaps suggesting the email is from a trusted source such as a well known corporation or public body or that the email has already been scanned for viruses). As such, Rusch indicates that social engineering is an important tactic in the generation and distribution of malware products, which can be an essential facet if the malware engineer is to achieve their motive.

MOTIVES OF MALWARE PRODUCERS

As with most types of crime, there is no single motive that explains all malware production and distribution. Furnell (2010) suggests that it is the payload that reflects the motivation of the malware developer. He suggests that "it used to be a question of what the malware would do *to* the user's system or data, but it has increasingly become a case of what might be done *with* it" (p. 189). Furnell indicates that this distinction is important – in the first instance the damage, however extensive, is limited to the system. Files may be deleted or corrupted, and the system may become unusable, but the damage goes no further. On the other hand, if the system is compromised and is used to achieve other goals, then the system may be hijacked, or it may be used to acquire data about the user or others. In this case, the system is less obviously infected, and may be used for other purposes, such as creating spam or being used as a 'zombie' or 'bot' in a denial of service attack. In many cases these malicious activities are carried out on the computer without the knowledge of the user. A combination of these computers is known as a 'botnet' or a 'zombie army'.

A malware developer may have financial motives, and Bocij (2006) suggests that virus writers gain financially from their work in two main ways – paid employment and extortion. In some cases, the virus writer may threaten to make confidential information (such as customer accounts) public, unless the company pays a sum of money. Bocij also suggests that virus writers may wish to gain paid employment either from anti-virus software manufacturers or from other criminals who hire them to create custom viruses. In addition to these, malware developers may profit financially by collecting information about the user, such as bank account details, usernames, passwords, or other personal information that makes them vulnerable to identity theft. This information may be used directly by the malware developer, or may be sold on to a third party.

Nevertheless, it does not seem that financial gain is the primary motive for all malware developers. Thompson (2004) indicates that while the best virus writers can spend hours working on programs, they often have little interest in spreading them into the wild. His interview with a virus writer called 'Philet0as3r' uncovered that the developer was afraid of being caught by the police, and so did not distribute the code. But Philet0as3r also stated that his ethical principles prevent him from damaging another person's computer. Thompson (2004) suggests therefore, that virus writers complete their acts for the intellectual challenge. He suggests that most virus authors are initially victimized by another virus, and as a result of this event, become curious as to how they work. Bocij (2006) agrees that some viruses are created as a test of knowledge or out of curiosity – a form of proof of concept. Thompson (2004) suggests that some virus writers indicate that they are not accountable for the actions of those who disseminate their viruses – that they have an interest in writing the programs, and that it is not their responsibility if others disseminate them. However, as many virus writers post their code to the Internet, for others to examine and copy, this seems like a shallow defense. According to Thompson, security professionals suggest that virus writers are aware that by publishing the code on the internet, it will be picked up by a 'script-kiddie' (a person who cannot write good code themselves, but who will use code created by others). Thompson indicates that the virus writer is pleased to see the virus in the wild, even though they did not release it themselves. On the other hand, he indicates that some of the virus writers he spoke to claim to send a copy of the virus they wrote to the antivirus companies before they circulate it on the internet, to ensure that it cannot be used for negative purposes. Bocij (2006) echoes this, and indicates that some virus writers see their work as a service to heighten security.

It may be that producing and distributing malware fulfills some need for attention or peer recognition that is craved by the developer. Thompson (2004) indicates that virus writers get a thrill when their work appears on an anti-virus company's website as a new 'alert'. He also indicates that peer acceptance is important, and that the virus writers he spoke to often work in groups, publish online magazines together, and email their work to their friends. Thompson tells the story of another virus writer, Vorgon, who had little social contacts, but who felt empowered by his virus creations. Bocij (2006) also indicates that peer recognition is important. He suggests that a virus writer experiences an increase in status if they create a particularly well-written or widespread program, especially if the virus becomes notorious and is discussed in the media and online.

It is possible that malware production is less about the developer, and more about the people and organizations around them, who they may want to seek vengeance against. Thompson reports that the virus writer Vorgon created a worm which targeted those companies who did not give him a job. Bocij (2006) suggests that in some cases virus writers will fight amongst themselves, or others involved in computer security. He cites the example of the female virus writer 'Gigabyte' who targeted Graham Clueley, a professional in the anti-virus industry. He tells how Gigabyte became angry about Clueley's disparaging remarks about virus writers, and about how he perpetuated the stereotype of the male virus writer. She went on to release several viruses that specifically attempted to ridicule Clueley through the form of games and quizzes that users were forced to partake in. More disturbingly, Bocij indicates that computer viruses have been used as weapons, including some which have been linked to Al Qaeda sympathizers. He describes many other viruses with political links, including the Fu Manchu/Jerusalem virus which altered documents by replacing the names of political leaders, such as Margaret Thatcher and Ronald Reagan, with expletives. Bocij also indicates that some countries may consider virus writers as heroes if they seem to be writing for patriotic reasons.

Another potential motive for virus writing may be as simple as boredom, with malware producers seeking to gain enjoyment from the activity. The virus writer 'Philet0ast3r', in his interview with Thompson (2004), describes developing a virus which installed two chatbots (artificially intelligent agents who engage in conversations) on the infected computer, making them appear in a pop-up window. The chatbots hold a nervous conversation, visible to the user, where they wonder if the computer's antivirus software will find them. This aspect of 'fun' can also be seen in some of the more humorous payloads described above. Nevertheless, it cannot be denied that many malware programs are not created simply to entertain the developer. This is evident from some of the more sinister payloads which have been observed to date, as with the Stuxnet case. It has been proposed that some types of malware development may be more appropriately compared to vandalism, and so this possibility will now be considered.

VANDALISM AND MALWARE

Bocij (2006) compares virus writing to acts of vandalism, indicating that there are some obvious comparisons. For example, those malware applications that write messages on users' screens could be seen as comparable to engaging in non-artistic types of graffiti[1]. Destructive malware, such as damaging or deleting files, could be seen as similar to intentionally scratching a car or puncturing tyres. Bocij suggests that virus writers and vandals may therefore share motives for their behaviours, and proposes that some of these include "boredom, misplaced anger, or an urge to rebel against authority" (p. 50).

Goldstein (1996) describes how the central behaviour of vandalism is aggression – intentional physical or psychological injury. Nevertheless, he indicates that despite several potential avenues for research in this area, vandalism has generally been ignored by psychological inquiry. Goldstein lists three potential theories of vandalism proposed by the literature – the 'enjoyment theory', the 'aesthetic theory' and the 'equity-control' theory.

The enjoyment theory suggests that vandalism has an intrinsic reward. The vandal gains satisfaction from the activity, which they may not be able to find through other activities such as schoolwork. A similar situation may be evident in malware developers – those who are capable of producing complex and effective code may not feel that they are being sufficiently challenged in school, and as such seek fulfillment elsewhere. In this sense, malware development may have similar etiology to other types of juvenile delinquency, a theory which is supported by the evidence that many virus writers 'age-out' of the activity as they get older (see the work by Sarah Gordon below).

The aesthetic theory suggests that vandalism is motivated by a desire to enjoy the artistic qualities of the object, such as novelty, organization and complexity. This may explain those involved in aesthetically appealing graffiti, who may be attempting to create artistic content while simultaneously leaving evidence of their presence in a given location. The malware developer may also be seeking to develop artistic content, although in their case the artistry may be expressed through a well-written piece of code. Another aspect of the aesthetic theory suggests that vandals may be motivated by a desire to take away the aesthetic qualities of a place or object, reducing it to a lesser state. Again, this may be applicable to malware developers, who wish to witness their creation reduce a previously functioning system to a worthless piece of equipment.

The final equity-control theory suggests that if a person perceives themselves to be in an inequitable situation, with little ability to modify the existing arrangements, they are more likely to engage in vandalism. The destruction or damaging of another's property appears to be a solution to resolving the inequity through quick and cheap means that are not beyond the vandal's control. This theory suggests that those who perceive themselves as having high inequity and low control are more likely to be engaged in vandalism. The equity-control model may also be an appropriate psychological explanation for malware production, as it would appear to fit well with the vengeance motive described above. There is also empirical support for this model with educated samples (see for example DeMore, Fisher & Baron, 1988, who found support for the equity-control theory in university students). However, as with the enjoyment and the aesthetic theories, there have not yet been studies examining the equity-control theory's applicability to malware development.

Given the apparent success in applying theories of vandalism to malware development, it is worthwhile considering the empirical research examining the characteristics of vandals. For example, Martin, Richardson, Bergen, Roeger and Allison (2003) studied a community sample of 2,603 adolescents and found that those who engaged in vandalism were more likely to experience a number of other problems, including family, parental, behavioural and psychological difficulties. These included increased reports of depression, anxiety, hopelessness, risk-taking behaviours and self-esteem. The adolescent vandals also had higher levels of family pathology, parental overprotection, parental criticism and drug use. It would be interesting to examine the characteristics and backgrounds of malware developers in a similar fashion in order to determine how similar malware development is to vandalism. Nevertheless, some preliminary work attempting to profile virus writers has been completed.

PROFILE AND PERSONALITY CHARACTERISTICS OF VIRUS WRITERS

As with many other areas of computer crime, there is relatively little empirical research which has been conducted by the psychologists on virus writers (Rogers, Siegfried & Tidke, 2006). However, Rogers, Siegfried and Tidke (2006) also argue that "computer crime and digital forensics is as much about the individuals involved in this deviant behaviour as it is about the technology... Therefore research focusing on people is vital if we have any real hope of coming to grips with the phenomena of computer crime" (p. S119).

Of what psychological research has been done, Sarah Gordon's is probably the most influential, although it is now somewhat dated. Gordon (1993) initially wrote a piece attempting to describe the mind of a male virus writer called 'Dark Avenger'. In this paper Gordon indicates that privately, virus writers display frustration, anger and general dissatisfaction, but also some evidence of conscience, and indicates that during an interview with Dark Avenger, he demonstrated sorrow for his actions. Dark Avenger described his reasons for writing viruses, which mostly related to curiosity and interest in the concept of virus distribution. Unfortunately, this paper does not allow for inferences to be drawn regarding other virus writers as it is in most part simply a transcription of an interview between Gordon and the virus writer.

In her other early work (Gordon, 1994), she presented four case studies of virus writers, using data she had gathered using mixed methods research. She indicates that it is important that the heterogeneity of virus writers be considered, that virus writers vary with regard to circumstances, skills, personality and ambition. In this regard, Gordon (1994) identified four main types of virus writer – a young adolescent, a college student, a professional and a mature, reformed ex-virus writer. She particularly focused on moral development, and examined the virus writers in light of Kohlberg's (1969) moral development theory. Kohlberg's theory suggests that there are six stages of moral development through which children and adults can progress during their lives. Progressing through the levels depends on the extent to which moral standards are internalized and self-accepted moral principles are developed. It is interesting to note that it is possible to reach the highest levels of Kohlberg's stages and still be engaged in criminal activity, depending on how the individual rationalizes their actions. However, it is generally accepted that criminals normally remain limited to the early stages of the model. Gordon (1994) identifies adolescent virus writers as being ethically normal and of average or above average intelligence. These virus writers showed respect for their parents, and understood right from wrong, but typically did not accept responsibility for the effects of their viruses. The college student virus writers also appeared to be ethically normal, and again were not concerned about the results of their actions. The adult virus writers were the smallest group, and appeared to be below the level of ethical maturity normal for their age. The ex virus writers were ethically normal, and indicated that they had ceased their virus writing because of lack of time or boredom with the activity. They generally seemed to be socially well adjusted and undecided about the ethical acceptability of virus writing. Gordon described four case studies, including one example of each group and she concludes that the four individuals are different in personal characteristics, with each being at an appropriate stage of development for their age, excepting the adult virus writer's lower moral development stage. The small sample involved in this early research allows few conclusions to be made, but it did illustrate that not all virus writers are the same, and that there is variation in age, income, education, location and social interaction, amongst other characteristics.

Gordon continued her research in a second paper relating to the heterogeneity and characteristics of virus writers (1996). Again she emphasizes that all virus writers are not the same, and indicates that it is impossible to draw conclusions about the psychology of virus writers as if they were a homogenous group. In this study, she follows up on three of the cases described in the earlier (1994) paper. She found that the adult virus writer continued to distribute viruses, and that the adolescent had moved on from just virus writing to also becoming involved in virus distribution. However the college student had stopped writing viruses and had become a professional. These findings supported Gordon's theory that virus writers 'age-out', becoming more likely to give up virus writing as they become older. This is similar to much research relating to criminology in general, with most individuals who are involved in crime as children and young adults being unlikely to become lifetime persistent offenders (see for example Farrington, 1990). With this in mind, it may be useful to consider the characteristics of persistent, life-long offenders in other types of crime in order to determine which virus writers may desist from a life-long career, and which ones will continue to develop malware. Howitt (2009, pp. 88-89) lists some of these characteristics, including family traits, educational abilities and scores on antisocial personality tests. It would be interesting to apply these to youth-limited and life-course persistent virus writers too.

Gordon (1996) cites the interesting case of the student who had given up virus writing. She indicates that he previously had said that he wrote viruses primarily for his own personal learning, and that while it was wrong, it was alright if it was not harmful. The student had subsequently been confronted by a user who had been victimized by one of his viruses. This initiated a change in his perspective so that he then publicly stated that virus writing was wrong for both himself and other people, regardless of intent, and that he would no longer write viruses. While this is still just one case study, it is of interest to note the change in perspective of the virus writer when forced to consider the consequences of his actions. It suggests that if virus writers were more aware of the consequences, then perhaps fewer would continue with the behavior. Gordon (1996) also suggests that as virus writers become older, peer pressure becomes less important, and morality develops, until they retire from virus writing. As such, she indicates that for most virus writers, as for most juvenile offenders, the antisocial activity eventually ends on its own. Unfortunately, as new generations discover viruses, younger individuals start to replace those who have aged out. On approaching the 'next generation' of virus writers, Gordon found that while they initially appeared to be more aggressive and technologically advanced than earlier virus writers, they were generally similar in skill level to their predecessors. However, there were exceptions, which she classified as the 'New Age Virus Writers', who were older, generally employed, and more private. Gordon suggests that as these virus writers are already older, they are less likely to 'age-out'. Nonetheless, again Gordon's work is mostly based on a small number of participants, and it is difficult to assess whether these findings can be generalized to a wider sample of virus writers.

In 2000, Gordon considered the impact of high profile legal intervention, such as arrests and visits by law enforcement personnel, on the virus writing communities. She suggests that for the adults who continue to write viruses, it is not the law that is important, but the individual's perception of likelihood of prosecution. Gordon concludes that laws have some limited effect for some individuals, but that laws that are considered to infringe an individual's freedom of speech (or freedom to write viruses) could result in a backlash in the United States. She therefore suggests that any aggressive legislation relating to virus writing would be unlikely to have any positive impact on reducing the problem.

While Gordon's research is interesting, there has been relatively little large-scale evaluation of the psychological profile of computer virus writers. In addition, most of her work relating to the psychology of virus writers is now quite dated. Other authors, such as Bocij (2006), have reviewed some of the early literature relating to virus writer characteristics and indicate that the traditional stereotype of the socially inept teenager who writes viruses as a form of revenge against society may have some truth behind it. Yet a satisfactory, recent empirical study of malware developer psychology remains elusive.

The most relevant study of recent years was completed by Rogers, Siegfried and Tidke (2006) who investigated self-reported criminal behaviour, including virus-writing and virus-use, amongst students. They found that 88% of their sample of seventy-seven students were classified as computer criminals, and that introversion was a significant predictor of engaging in computer criminal behaviour. Other personality characteristics, such as internal moral choice, social moral choice, hedonistic moral choice, conscientiousness, neuroticism, openness to experience and agreeableness were not found to be predictors of cybercriminal behaviour. Unfortunately Rogers, Siegfried and Tidke's (2006) study does not differentiate between different types of computer criminal – as well as being involved in computer viruses, the students were classified as computer criminals if they guessed passwords, used another person's password without permission, looked at or changed other people's files without permission, obtained another person's credit card information without permission or used a device to obtain free telephone calls. Therefore, it is difficult to be certain that introversion is directly linked to virus-writing or virus-use, as the other types of computer criminal may have skewed the results. Rogers, Siegfried and Tidke (2006) do not report what percentage of the group were involved in virus writing or virus use. They also indicate that these findings were in contrast to an earlier study completed by Rogers, Smoak and Liu (2006), which found that there were differences between self-reported computer criminals and non-criminals on moral choice and exploitive/manipulative behaviours. Rogers, Siegfried and Tidke (2006) indicate that the differences in moral reasoning findings between the two studies may relate to methodological factors in the construction of the instrument, rather than a true difference in scores. On the other hand, Rogers, Siegfried and Tidke (2006) do not suggest a reason for the difference in exploitive/manipulative behaviours between the two studies, except for differences in the academic disciplines of the students studied in each. Rogers, Siegfried and Tidke (2006) also indicate that it is premature to consider all computer criminals to hold these characteristics, based on single studies with relatively small numbers of participants.

Overall, the empirical psychological research relating to the characteristics of virus writers is remarkably limited, especially given the comparatively massive library of work which has been done examining the psychology of computer hackers. Nevertheless, there has been some research which has examined how psychology can influence a user's intention to engage in safe online behavior, which will now be examined.

HOW CAN DAMAGE DUE TO MALWARE BE PREVENTED?

Tavani (2007) states that "the effects of malware can range from minor annoyances with individual computer systems, to preventing an entire organization from operating, to shutting down computer networks, to disrupting major segments of the internet" (p. 174). With this in mind, it is important that infection by malware programs be prevented whenever possible. At the time of writing, Scott Charney of Microsoft is proposing that computers that are infected with malware should be prevented from accessing the internet, in order to avoid the spread of infection and the use of botnets (BBC News, 2010c). There are however many problems with such severe measures, and

it is likely that the current position will continue, where "Software companies are in a constant arms race… to fix vulnerabilities before they are exploited" (Brown, Edwards and Marsden, 2009, p. 673). The most common preventative measure taken against malware is anti-virus software, which should be used in conjunction with firewall software for intrusions. Most anti-virus software can not only detect viruses, but can also delete them. In some cases they can also repair damaged files, and remove infected sectors of disk drives.

Furnell (2010) indicates that as anti-malware software has developed, malware has had to do the same, so as to ensure that it has the opportunity to release its payload. He indicates that a key method of doing this is for the malware to avoid detection if possible. Furnell describes how some malware also actively defends itself against anti-malware software, including blocking access to the antivirus vendor's website so as to prevent security updates and changing system configurations so that the antivirus does not run automatically on start up.

As malware becomes more advanced, the human element in security becomes more important. According to Huang, Rau and Salvendy (2010), "no matter how well designed, security methods rely on individuals to implement and use them" (p. 221). From this perspective, psychology has some insights into the behaviour and attitudes of potential victims. For example, Lee, Larose and Rifon (2008) indicate that individual Internet users play important roles in preventing the distribution of malware. If they open email attachments or download infected software, Lee et al claim that it puts them and others at risk. Lee et al (2008) emphasise the importance of people's cognitive appraisal of threats in generating a motivation to protect themselves, and they apply this to anti-malware. They use the example of Protection Motivation Theory, devised by Rogers (1975, 1983), which proposes that there are six main components that influence the intention to protect the self from a threat. These include the perceived severity of the threatened event, the perceived probability of the threat, the perceived response efficacy of preventative measures, the perceived self-efficacy in using preventative measures, potential rewards and potential costs. When applied to malware, these can be considered as follows. Perceived severity of the threatened event relates to the individual's beliefs regarding the payload and damage the malware can do to the system. The perceived probability of the threat relates to the person's belief that they are likely to be victimized. The perceived response efficacy of preventative measures relates to the person's belief that anti-malware software will be effective (for example, perhaps they feel that most malware are zero-day exploits, and therefore anti-malware will be ineffective). The perceived self-efficacy in using preventative measures relates to the individual's beliefs regarding their ability to keep the anti-malware up to date, or their ability to avoid dangerous software. The potential rewards refers to the person's expectations of maintaining a malware-free system, and the potential costs relates to the sacrifices the person may have to make, such as the financial cost of the antivirus software or the slower system they may have to tolerate.

Consistent with this theory, Lee et al (2008) found that a number of variables predicted intention to adopt virus protection behaviour in a sample of college students. These variables included perceived self-efficacy in using virus protection measures, perceived response efficacy of virus protective measures, positive outcome expectations of virus protection measures, prior virus infection experiences and perceived vulnerability to virus threats. However, conversely they found no significant relation between perceived severity of virus attacks and negative outcome expectancies on intention to adopt protective measures. They conclude that in order to increase security, it is important to both increase individuals' awareness of the likelihood of virus attacks and also conduct interventions to increase self-efficacy and response efficacy beliefs. Lee et al (2008) believe that this

might be accomplished through Bandura's (1997) three basic approaches to increasing self-efficacy. These are verbal persuasion (perhaps implemented via traditional information campaigns, which might be targeted at high-risk users), anxiety reduction strategies (that might indicate that the user will have peace of mind if they follow the advice, similar to advertising strategies used by insurance companies, or by reducing any stresses involved in taking the action, such as simple instructions for downloading anti-virus software) and progressive mastery (building self-efficacy through completing successively difficult tasks, so helping users to learn step-by-step how to protect their systems themselves, instead of relying on others to do this for them). However, Lee et al do admit that their findings are limited due to a small sample of convenience.

Several other studies have examined the variables that predict users' intentions to engage in safer online behavior. Huang, Rau and Salvendy (2010) found that six factors characterized people's perceptions of threats to information security. These factors were knowledge, impact, severity, controllability, awareness and possibility, and bear strong similarity to the variables identified by Lee et al (2008). Huang et al (2010) also found that the user's computer experience had a significant effect on perception of information security, with experienced users having more knowledge about threats. Experienced computer users also felt that it would be easier to reduce the effects of the threats.

In the same vein, Ng, Kankanhalli and Xu (2009) used the Health Belief Model to study users' computer security behavior. The Health Belief Model was developed by Rosenstock (1966) and is used in psychology to predict both health behaviors and responses to treatment in ill patients. It proposes that behavior results from a set of core beliefs, including susceptibility to illness, severity of illness, the costs and benefits involved in carrying out the behavior, and cues to action (such as the perception of symptoms). In later forms of the model, other core beliefs, such as health motivation and perceived control, have been added. With relation to computer security behavior, Ng et al (2009) found that perceived susceptibility, perceived benefits and self-efficacy explain email related security behavior. However, the Health Belief Model has several criticisms, which may also apply to computer security behavior. These include that it focuses a great deal on conscious processing of information – it is possible that computer users do not consider online security in such detail.

Ng and Rahim (2005) used the Theory of Planned Behavior to investigate user's intention to practice home computer security. The Theory of Planned Behavior suggests that the stronger a person's intention to behave in a particular way, the more likely they are to actually do so (Ajzen, 1998; 1991). Ng and Rahim tested to see if home computer users intended to regularly update their anti-virus software, as well as backing up critical data and using a personal firewall. They found that attitude and subjective norm were associated with intentions. Other important factors found to influence home users were perceived usefulness, family and peer influence, mass-media influence and self-efficacy.

These factors are not just useful for predicting the security intentions of personal computer users. Similar studies have been completed with business executives. For example, Lee and Larsen (2009) found that the intention of the executives of small and medium sized businesses to adopt anti-malware software was predicted by their appraisal of the level and type of threat involved, as well as their appraisal of how well they would cope with an infection. Lee and Larson also noted that there was considerable variance between the executive's intent to adopt and whether or not they actually adopted the software, with this variance being caused by social influence from key stakeholders and variables specific to the situation, such as budget and support matters. Similar variables affect intentions of security professionals. Lee and Larson (2009) also found

that the intent to adopt anti-malware software by information security experts and information technology intensive industries was primarily affected by threat appraisal and social influence, as well as vendor support. In contrast, intent to adopt by non-information security experts and non-information technology intensive industries was more influenced by coping appraisal and budget issues.

Despite the regularity with which threat appraisal determines intent to engage in online security behaviors, there is evidence to indicate that we are probably not capable of accurately judging threat appraisal. Campbell, Greenauer, Macaluso and End (2007) found that students believed that positive internet events were more likely to happen to them and negative internet events were less likely to happen to them compared to the average student. Interestingly, heavy internet users were more optimistic than light users were, despite increased time spent online.

Lee et al (2008) propose several measures which may both improve online security and increase users' intention to take preventative measures to protect their systems. These measures include appropriate standardization of anti-virus software applications, such as a requirement to include anti-virus software with all new personal computers and the use of filtering technology on all email applications. Lee et al (2008) also suggest other methods of improving security, including guidelines for public notification, and a legal requirement for website proprietors to reveal the risk of virus infection from downloading files from their website. Lee et al (2008) also suggest that automated warnings each time a user tries to open an attachment or download a file could be beneficial, especially if they were coupled with an automated check of the recency of the current version of the user's anti-virus software. These warnings may be particularly useful with the increased popularity of smartphones.

FUTURE TRENDS AND RESEARCH

To date, there have been relatively few malware programmes which threaten smartphones, but some examples do exist. Some malware has been discovered which infects 'jailbroken' iPhones (iPhones where the operating system has been unlocked allowing users to install applications on the device which have not been approved by Apple). One example of this malware is the 'ikee' worm, which replaces the wallpaper on the phone with a photograph of 1980s pop star Rick Astley, supplemented with the message "ikee is never going to give you up". Apart from this action, and continuing to spread, the worm does not seem to do any other damage. In this way it is similar to some of the earliest malware for computers, where malware developers seemed to be more focused on the enjoyment and challenge of writing new code than using the malware for more sinister purposes. It has yet to be seen whether or not malware developers will take a greater interest in smartphones, which now have processing capacity far in excess of the computers targeted by early viruses.

From a psychological perspective, the lack of research into the personality and profile of malware developers is disheartening. It is unclear why most of the research so far has focused on hackers, with very little attention given to virus writers. Most large scale studies in this area have focused their efforts on understanding why users engage in security measures, probably because it is considerably easier to access populations of general computer users than it is to access virus writers. The possibility of overlap between vandalism and malware development is an area which requires further investigation, especially from a psychological perspective, as it may provide some key insights into the motives and traits of both groups.

CONCLUSION

Despite the lengthy history of malware development, psychology has so far played a very minor role in furthering our understanding of the phenomenon. This is unfortunate, as the little research that has been done does appear to be quite promising in explaining the psychology of malware developers. While Sarah Gordon seems to be correct in her statement that virus writers are not a homogenous group, the same could be said for most types of criminals, including serial killers and sexual predators, where psychological profiling has been of assistance. The potential similarities with vandals are also of interest, and may provide a useful starting place for large scale studies. Apart from the studies examining computer users' intentions to engage in safer online behaviour, there has been little psychological evaluation of the victims of malware, and their perceptions of the crime and criminal, which may be of interest. Similarly, methodological studies examining the effectiveness of various educational strategies that attempt to increase user awareness of the risks and preventative measures are required, so that governments and corporations can more successfully persuade users to protect their systems adequately, thus protecting both themselves, and others, by reducing the numbers of botnets. Despite the lack of large scale studies to date, it is evident that psychology has a lot to offer to the greater understanding of malware and its developers.

REFERENCES

Ajzen, I. (1988). *Attitudes, Personality and Behaviour*. Milton Keynes, UK: Open University Press.

Ajzen, I. (1991). The Theory of Planned Behaviour. *Organizational Behavior and Human Decision Processes, 50*, 179–211. doi:10.1016/0749-5978(91)90020-T

Bandura, A. (1997). *Self-Efficacy: The exercise of control*. New York: WH Freeman and Company.

BBC News (2010a, September 24). *Stuxnet worm hits Iran nuclear plant staff computers*. Retrieved from http://www.bbc.co.uk/news/world-middle-east-11414483

BBC News (2010b, September 23). *Stuxnet worm 'targeted high-value Iranian assets*. Retrieved from http://www.bbc.co.uk/news/technology-11388018

BBC News (2010c, October 6). *Sick PCs should be banned from the net says Microsoft*. Retrieved from http://www.bbc.co.uk/news/technology-11483008

Bocij, P. (2006). *The Dark Side of the Internet: Protecting yourself and your family from online criminals*. Westport, CT: Praeger Publishers.

Brown, I., Edwards, L., & Marsden, C. (2009). Information Security and Cybercrime. In Edwards, L., & Waelde, C. (Eds.), *Law and the Internet* (pp. 671–692). Portland, OR: Hart Publishing.

Campbell, J., Greenauer, N., Macaluso, K., & End, C. (2007). Unrealistic optimism in internet events. *Computers in Human Behavior, 23*, 1273–1284.. doi:10.1016/j.chb.2004.12.005

Collins, J. M. (2006). *Investigating Identity Theft: A Guide for Businesses, Law Enforcement, and Victims*. Hoboken, NJ: John Wiley & Sons.

Computer Security Institute (CSI). (December, 2009). *14th Annual CSI Computer Crime and Security Survey, Executive Summary*. Retrieved 7th October 2010 from http://pathmaker.biz/whitepapers /CSISurvey2009.pdf

DeMore, S. W., Fisher, J. D., & Baron, R. M. (1988). The equity-control model as a predictor of vandalism among college students. *Journal of Applied Social Psychology, 18*, 80–91. doi:10.1111/j.1559-1816.1988.tb00007.x

Edgar-Nevill, D., & Stephens, P. (2008). Countering Cybercrime. In Bryant, R. (Ed.), *Investigating Digital Crime* (pp. 79–96). Chichester, England: Wiley.

Farrington, D. P. (1990). Age, period, cohort and offending. In Gottfredson, D. M., & Clarke, R. V. (Eds.), *Policy and Theory in Criminal Justice: Contributions in Honour of Leslie T. Wilkins* (pp. 51–75). Aldershot: Avebury.

Frontline, P. B. S. (nd). *Studying the psychology of virus writers and hackers: an interview with researcher Sarah Gordon*. Retrieved 26th September 2010 from http://www.pbs.org/wgbh/pages/frontline/ shows/hackers/whoare/psycho.html

Furnell, S. (2010). Hackers, viruses and malicious software. In Jewkes, Y., & Yar, M. (Eds.), *Handbook of Internet Crime* (pp. 173–193). Cullompton, England: Willan.

Goldstein, A. P. (1996). *The Psychology of Vandalism*. New York: Plenham Press.

Gordon, S. (1993). Inside the Mind of the Dark Avenger. *Virus News International, January 1993*. Abridged version retrieved on 7th October 2010 from http://www.research.ibm.com/antivirus/SciPapers/Gordon/Avenger.html

Gordon, S. (1994). *The Generic Virus Writer. Presented at the 4th International Virus Bulletin Conference*. Jersey. 8-9th September. Retrieved on 7th October 2010 from http://vx.netlux.org/lib/asg03.html

Gordon, S. (1996). The generic virus writer II. In *Proceedings of the 6th International Virus Bulletin Conference*, Brighton, UK, 19th-20th September. Retrieved on 7th October 2010 from http://vx.netlux.org/lib/static/vdat/epgenvr2.htm

Gordon, S. (2000). Virus writers: The End of the Innocence? In *Proceedings of the 10th International Virus Bulletin Conference.* Orlando, FL, 28-29th September. Retrieved on 7th October 2010 from http://www.research.ibm.com/antivirus/SciPapers/VB2000SG.htm

Howitt, D. (1999). *Introduction to Forensic & Criminal Psychology* (3rd ed.). Harlow, England: Pearson Education Ltd.

Huang, D., Rau, P. P., & Salvendy, G. (2010). Perception of information security. *Behaviour & Information Technology, 29,* 221–232. doi:10.1080/01449290701679361

Kohlberg, L. (1969). State and sequence: the cognitive-developmental approach to socialization. In Goslin, D. A. (Ed.), *Handbook of Socialization Theory and Research.* Chicago: Rand McNally.

Kramer, S., & Bradfield, J. C. (2010). A general definition of malware. *Journal in Computer Virology, 6,* 105–114. doi:10.1007/s11416-009-0137-1

Lee, D., Larose, R., & Rifon, N. (2008). Keeping our network safe: a model of online protection behaviour. *Behaviour & Information Technology, 27,* 445–454. doi:10.1080/01449290600879344

Lee, Y., & Larson, K. R. (2009). Threat or coping appraisal: determinants of SMB executives' decision to adopt anti-malware software. *European Journal of Information Systems, 18,* 177–187. doi:10.1057/ejis.2009.11

Martin, G., Richardson, A., Bergen, H., Roeger, L., & Allison, S. (2003). Family and Individual characteristics of a community sample of adolescents who graffiti. Presented at the *Graffiti and Disorder Conference,* Brisbane, Australia. 18-19 August. Retrieved 8th October 2010 from http://www.nograffiti.com/martinstudy.pdf

McAfee-NCSA. (2007). *McAfee-NCSA Online Safety Study – Newsworthy Analysis,* October 2007. http://download.mcafee.com/products/ manuals/en-us/McAfeeNCSA_Analysis09-25-07.pdf

Ng, B. Y., Kankanhalli, A., & Xu, Y. C. (2009). Studying users' computer security behaviour: A health belief perspective. *Decision Support Systems, 46,* 815–825. doi:10.1016/j.dss.2008.11.010

Ng, B. Y., & Rahim, M. A. (2005). *A Socio-Behavioral Study of Home Computer Users' Intention to Practice Security.* The Ninth Pacific Asia Conference on Information Systems, 7 - 10 July, Bangkok, Thailand.

Ollmann, G. (2008). The evolution of commercial malware development kits and colour-by-numbers custom malware. *Computer Fraud & Security, 9,* 4–7. doi:10.1016/S1361-3723(08)70135-0

Rogers, M. K., Siegfried, K., & Tidke, K. (2006). Self-reported computer criminal behaviour: A psychological analysis. *Digital Investigation, 3S,* S116–S120. doi:10.1016/j.diin.2006.06.002

Rogers, M. K., Smoak, N., & Liu, J. (2006). Self-reported criminal computer behaviour: a big-5, moral choice and manipulative exploitive behaviour analysis. *Deviant Behavior, 27,* 1–24. doi:10.1080/01639620600605333

Rogers, R. W. (1975). A protection motivation theory of fear appeals and attitude change. *The Journal of Psychology, 91,* 93–114. doi:10.1080/00223980.1975.9915803

Rogers, R. W. (1983). Cognitive and physiological processes in fear appeals and attitude change: a revised theory of protection motivation. In Cacioppo, J., & Petty, R. (Eds.), *Social Psychophysiology* (pp. 153–176). New York: Guildford Press.

Rosenstock, I. M. (1966). Why people use health services. *The Milbank Memorial Fund Quarterly, 44,* 94–124. doi:10.2307/3348967

Rusch, J. J. (2002, June 21). *The social psychology of computer viruses and worms.* Paper presented at INET 2002, Crystal City, Virginia. Retrieved 8th October 2010 from http://m4dch4t.effraie.org/vxdevl/papers/ avers/g10-c.pdf

Stephens, P. (2008). IPR and Technological Protection Measures. In Bryant, R. (Ed.), *Investigating Digital Crime* (pp. 121–131). Chichester, England: Wiley.

Symantec (2010, April). *Symantec Global Internet Security Threat Report (Volume XV)*. Retrieved 7th October 2010 from http://eval.symantec.com/mktginfo/enterprise/white_papers/b-whitepaper_internet_security _threat_report_xv_04-2010.en-us.pdf

Tavani, H. T. (2007). *Ethics and Technology: Ethical Issues in an Age of Information and Communication Technology* (2nd ed.). Hoboken, NJ: John Wiley & Sons.

Thompson, C. (2004, February 8). The Virus Underground. *The New York Times Magazine, pp 30-33, 72, 79-81.*

Thompson, R. (2005). Why spyware poses multiple threats to society. *Communications of the ACM, 48,* 41–43. doi:10.1145/1076211.1076237

Yar, M. (2006). *Cybercrime and Society*. London: Sage.

ADDITIONAL READING

Campbell, J., Greenauer, N., Macaluso, K., & End, C. (2007). Unrealistic optimism in internet events. *Computers in Human Behavior, 23,* 1273–1284.. doi:10.1016/j.chb.2004.12.005

Edgar-Nevill, D., & Stephens, P. (2008). Countering Cybercrime. In Bryant, R. (Ed.), *Investigating Digital Crime* (pp. 79–96). Chichester, England: Wiley.

Furnell, S. (2010). Hackers, viruses and malicious software. In Jewkes, Y., & Yar, M. (Eds.), *Handbook of Internet Crime* (pp. 173–193). Cullompton, England: Willan.

Gordon, S. (1993). Inside the Mind of the Dark Avenger. *Virus News International, January 1993.* Abridged version retrieved on 7th October 2010 from http://www.research.ibm.com/antivirus/SciPapers/Gordon/Avenger.html

Gordon, S. (1994). *The Generic Virus Writer.* Presented at the 4th International Virus Bulletin Conference, Jersey. 8-9th September. Retrieved on 7th October 2010 from http://vx.netlux.org/lib/asg03.html

Gordon, S. (1996). The generic virus writer II. In *Proceedings of the 6th International Virus Bulletin Conference*, Brighton, UK, 19th-20th September. Retrieved on 7th October 2010 from http://vx.netlux.org/lib/static/vdat/ epgenvr2.htm

Gordon, S. (2000). Virus writers: The End of the Innocence? In *Proceedings of the 10th International Virus Bulletin Conference.* Orlando, FL, 28-29th September. Retrieved on 7th October 2010 from http://www.research.ibm.com/antivirus/SciPapers/VB2000SG.htm

Huang, D., Rau, P. P., & Salvendy, G. (2010). Perception of information security. *Behaviour & Information Technology, 29,* 221–232. doi:10.1080/01449290701679361

Kramer, S., & Bradfield, J. C. (2010). A general definition of malware. *Journal in Computer Virology, 6,* 105–114. doi:10.1007/s11416-009-0137-1

Ng, B. Y., Kankanhalli, A., & Xu, Y. C. (2009). Studying users' computer security behaviour: A health belief perspective. *Decision Support Systems, 46,* 815–825. doi:10.1016/j.dss.2008.11.010

Ng, B. Y., & Rahim, M. A. (2005). *A Socio-Behavioral Study of Home Computer Users' Intention to Practice Security.* The Ninth Pacific Asia Conference on Information Systems, 7 - 10 July, Bangkok, Thailand.

Rogers, M. K., Siegfried, K., & Tidke, K. (2006). Self-reported computer criminal behaviour: A psychological analysis. *Digital Investigation*, *3S*, S116–S120. doi:10.1016/j.diin.2006.06.002

Rogers, M. K., Smoak, N., & Liu, J. (2006). Self-reported criminal computer behaviour: a big-5, moral choice and manipulative exploitive behaviour analysis. *Deviant Behavior*, *27*, 1–24. doi:10.1080/01639620600605333

Rusch, J. J. (2002, June 21). *The social psychology of computer viruses and worms*. Paper presented at INET 2002, Crystal City, Virginia. Retrieved 8th October 2010 from http://m4dch4t.effraie.org/vxdevl/papers /avers/g10-c.pdf

ENDNOTE

[1] It should be noted that there are many graffiti artists who make public spaces more aesthetically pleasing through their work, and these are not included in this comparison with malware developers. Graffiti can be considered by many as true artistic works, and some graffiti artists have become famous due to their creations. The comparison of graffiti with malware production described in this chapter relates only to destructive graffiti, which defaces property and detracts from the aesthetic appeal of its surroundings.

Section 3
Online Variations of Offline Crimes

Chapter 6

Identity Theft and Online Fraud:
What Makes Us Vulnerable to Scam Artists Online?

ABSTRACT

Probably the type of online crime with which most people have direct experience involves attempts at identity theft and fraud. Most individuals have received an email involving an attempt to get them to part with their money. This chapter aims to describe some of the common types of identity theft and fraud which can occur online, as well as attempting to determine what makes us vulnerable to such attacks. To do this, the chapter will examine some aspects of human decision making, as well as identifying the social engineering tactics used by prospective fraudsters. The chapter will describe the known prevalence rates and costs of online identity theft and fraud, and will compare these types of offences to offline fraud schemes. The methods of attack will be described, including phishing, keyloggers, social engineering, advance fee frauds, and other techniques. An attempt will be made to determine what the psychology of the identity thief and fraudster is, based on comparisons to similar offline offenders. In addition to this, the effects on the victim will be considered, including the phenomenon of victim blaming, where others place partial blame on the victim for the criminal event. Possible methods of preventing identity theft and online fraud will be considered, along with potential future trends and research.

BACKGROUND

Sarah regularly uses her credit card online. When purchasing clothes from an online shop, she became distracted, and she failed to notice that the site was not secure. Her credit card details were stolen, and the thief has used her credit card to make payments of over $2,000. Sarah was not aware of her victimization until her credit card was refused after a meal at a restaurant.

DOI: 10.4018/978-1-61350-350-8.ch006

James uses profiles on several social networking websites to stay in touch with friends. The profiles include many personal details about him, including his date of birth, hometown and contact details. On applying for a loan, he discovered that he had a bad credit rating, although he has always paid his credit card, mortgage and bills on time. He runs a credit check, and discovers that a motor loan has been taken out in his name, although he never applied for it. No repayments have been made on the loan. He eventually realizes that he has been the victim of identity theft, and that the offender used the personal information available on his social networking profile along with other online information about him to apply for the loan.

Definitions and Key Terms

The above scenarios describe how easily individuals can become victims of identity theft. There are other examples of identity theft. In some cases these can be relatively harmless, where an individual leaves their social networking profiles unprotected and a friend or relation has used the opportunity to post embarrassing comments on their profile. This 'impersonation' of the other is not normally performed with criminal intent, but rather is an attempt to play a prank on a friend or family member. That said, there have been cases where celebrities have been impersonated in online social networking websites, with the impostor sometimes portraying them in a negative light. In other identity theft cases individuals might use weak passwords for online activities, which are easy to guess with only limited knowledge of the person (such as their address or date of birth).

Smith (2010) describes identity theft as "one of the most pressing financial crime problems that has faced developed societies in recent years" (p. 273). He indicates that while it is not a new criminal activity, it is facilitated by information technology, which makes it easier to access personal information and to fabricate important identity documents. Several definitions of identity theft have been proposed. For example, McQuade (2006) defines identity theft as "acquiring and then unlawfully using personal and financial account information to acquire goods and services in someone else's name" (p. 69).

Marshall and Stephens (2008) suggest that in order to understand the concept of identity theft, the term 'identity' needs to be sufficiently defined. They suggest that identity, from the point of view of the individual, is "an awareness of one's own existence in the world" (p. 180), which is comprised of a variety of factors including membership of a family, a circle of friends, career, physical traits, behaviour and preferences. However they suggest that from the perspective of another, a person's identity is somewhat simpler, where only recognition of the individual is required in order to confirm identity. Marshall and Stephens relate how this recognition becomes less reliable if the person has never been encountered before. If this happens online, they indicate that it is necessary for the person to present some kind of 'trusted token' to either validate their identity or confirm that they have the authorization to complete the action they are attempting. This may involve a password or special documentation, which lets the system know that it is alright for the person to proceed. As such, Marshall and Stephens argue that identity theft should really be considered 'authority fraud'.

Finch (2003) distinguishes between individual identity (the person's sense of self), social identity (the external view of the person) and legal identity (a set of characteristics that are unique to the individual and provides a way in which people can be differentiated from each other). Finch (2003) indicates that neither individual nor social identity can be stolen, but that legal identity can. She indicates that the birth certificate is the foundation of legal identity, and that whenever legal and individual identity conflict, legal identity prevails. An example of this involves a nickname – it may be part of the person's social and individual identity, but it is not permissible for legal documentation. Legal identity can be verified through production of specific documents or the possession of certain knowledge, and identity theft "involves the misuse of information that is specific to an individual in order to convince others that the imposter is the individual, effectively passing oneself off as someone else" (pp. 89-90).

Finch (2003) indicates that identity theft may be short or long-term. She cites an example of a case where a man had assumed the identity of his deceased flatmate for fifteen years. In other cases, the identity theft may last for only a few minutes, as stolen credit card information is used to make a purchase. Finch therefore suggests that there should be a twofold categorization of identity theft – 'total identity theft' where there is a permanent adoption of the victim's details, and 'partial identity theft' where the use of the person's details is temporary (p. 90) – which Finch indicates appears to be the most prevalent use of identity theft.

Known Prevalence Rates

As with many other types of online crime, it is impossible to know the true extent of the problem. It is certain that online fraud and identity theft have reached a level of prevalence where books have been developed for both personal and corporate users advising them on how to improve their security in this regard (see for example Lininger & Vines, 2005; Collins, 2006). Nevertheless, it is likely that many individuals and organizations are victimized or targeted but that these events are never reflected in estimates of the extent of the activity. Smith (2010) indicates that it is very difficult to determine the true extent of the problem of identity theft for several reasons. These include the lack of clarity regarding the definition of the concepts involved and fear by victims of reporting the offence as criminals may implicate them in the criminal event (this may be especially true for victims of advance fee fraud scams – see below). Victims may also be afraid of secondary victimization (Smith, 2010, p. 287), where they feel that they may be blamed by others for activities which could be seen as having enabled their victimization. This is also a topic which will be considered in more depth later in the chapter. Levi (2001) indicates that other reasons why threat levels may be inaccurate include that victims may not be asked about their victimization, or are unaware of their victimization. Yar (2006) also indicates that there is a lack of systematic information about the amount of Internet fraud. He suggests that victims may not report the crime due to the loss of relatively small amounts of money. Yar also suggests that the victim may be embarrassed that they were deceived, or they may not know who to report it to. They might also feel that it is unlikely that they will get their money back, so there is little point in going to the trouble of reporting it. It is also probable that many potential victims would not report the event if they received an email suspected to be fraudulent, but they were not deceived into losing any money.

Despite these difficulties in calculating the true levels and costs of identity theft and fraud, there are some estimates available from a number of sources. The UK National Fraud Authority (NFA) reported that in the year prior to October 2010, stolen identities had affected 1.8 million people, with the fraudsters gaining GBP £1.9 billion in that time (BBC News, 2010). Smith (2010), based on a review of several studies regarding the extent of identity theft, estimates that losses for major countries are in excess of GBP£1 billion annually per country, although it should be noted that much of this identity theft occurs offline. Jewkes (2010) cites a 2007 US Federal Trade Commission report that indicated that over a twelve month period, 8.3 million Americans had been victims of identity theft. She also cites a report by the credit-checking agency Experion, covering the same time period that reported a growth of 69% in identity theft in the United Kingdom.

A specific strategy used by identity thieves and online fraudsters involves 'phishing' (a description of which is provided below). The Anti-Phishing Working Group (APWG) is the global association which attempts to eliminate fraud and identity theft resulting from phishing and related incidents. Their 'Phishing Activity Trends Report' for the first quarter of 2010 indicates that unique phishing reports reached a record high of over forty thousand reports in August 2009. They indicated that by quarter end, almost thirty thousand unique phishing websites were detected, with almost three hundred brands being hijacked by phishing campaigns (Anti-Phishing Working Group, 2010).

Despite the inability to accurately assess the extent of identity theft and fraud online, the studies above clearly indicate that it is a severe problem. However, these are not new offences, and offline versions of these crimes have existed for many years.

Similar Offline Offences

There have been a wide variety of fraudulent schemes utilised by confidence artists.

In these cases, the potential victim is often referred to as a 'mark'. Historically, some travelling salesmen sold assorted potions which claimed to have medicinal properties, capable of curing all manner of illnesses and inflictions. Sometimes these salesmen had accomplices who they would plant in the audience. The accomplice would claim to have been healed of a specific ailment by the potion, thus encouraging the marks to invest in the medicine. Similar 'pharma-fraud' exists online today, and is discussed below.

Bocij (2006) describes 'Ponzi' schemes, named after Charles Ponzi (1882-1949). Ponzi offered an investment scheme where he promised a specific return that was very tempting for investors. However, the promised return was usually very ambitious and unobtainable, and money obtained from newer investors was used to repay dividends and capital to the early investors. This scheme was unsustainable, as eventually Ponzi ran out of investors. Other types of fraud include pyramid schemes, where each individual in the scheme is required to invest a given amount of money, as well as recruiting new investors to the scheme. Each new investor is promised a return from those lower in the pyramid than themselves – specifically the individuals that they recruit, and those that their recruits later draw into the scheme. Similarly to Ponzi schemes, pyramid schemes are also unsustainable due to the large numbers of new investors required to pay the earlier investors. Pyramids rapidly reach a point where more investors are required than there are individuals on the planet (if each individual is required to recruit just two others, this point is reached before thirty-five tiers of the pyramid are complete). Of course, pyramid schemes always collapse long before this point, and often the only individuals who profit from the scheme are those at the very highest levels.

There are other types of fraudulent schemes which prey on some of the poorest members of society. An example of this involves employment fraud. In these cases, an individual may be tempted by an advertisement which promises income for working at home. The type of work involved may vary – it may be production of specific goods such as clothes, or it may involve office work, such as stuffing envelopes for mass mailing. On applying for the work, the individual is told that they need to make an initial investment to cover materials for the products, the list of addresses for the mass-mailing, and/or administrative costs. The individual is then provided with the materials required to start work, but they are unlikely to see any return. The office work roles sometimes require the individual to attempt to recruit others into the same scheme, for which the individual may receive a small sum of money for each new applicant recruited, but rarely so much that their initial investment is returned. The production work schemes generally involve the purchase of a significant quantity of materials, and the individual is required to prepare a sample of the finished product for inspection. Almost invariably the sample is considered to be of inadequate quality, and the individual is left with a large quantity of useless materials which they have paid for, with no means of selling their work.

Many of these types of fraud schemes are still in existence today. For example, Bernard Madoff was found guilty of a Ponzi type scheme in 2008, resulting in a loss of billions of dollars for his investors. However, there are a variety of other techniques used by online fraudsters and identity thieves.

METHODS OF ATTACK FOR ONLINE SCHEMES

Jaishkankar (2008) indicates that identity-related cybercrime is perpetrated more easily than offline identity-related crime. It also has a larger impact than offline crime, due to the speed at which it can occur, its international nature, and its association with other criminal activities such as terrorism (Jaishkankar, 2008). Different strategies for online identity theft and fraud utilise different underlying mechanisms. For example, some strategies involve the offender searching for useful information about the mark online, perhaps through social networking or dating websites. Similarly, such information could be gathered using technical tools, such as keyloggers, or by searching through the person's garbage for confidential information. However, many other strategies involve social engineering mechanisms, which Marshall and Stephens (2008) describe as "encompassing a number of related ideas, all emphasizing the importance of the human element in the transfer of trusted token from one person to another, particularly in relation to identity theft and fraud" (p. 184). Several of these different strategies will be described below, along with an overview of the possible reasons why individuals may fall for online scams.

Social Networking and Dating Websites

Many social networking profiles include significant quantities of personal information useful to a potential identity thief. These can include present place of employment, previous educational institutions, date of birth, names of close contacts, and so on. These could be used in conjunction with some of the social engineering techniques described in Chapter 4 to obtain confidential information about the mark which could then be used to access email or bank accounts.

Similarly, potential offenders can create profiles on dating websites to gain information about suitable victims, tailoring their characteristics to suit the specific mark (Finch, 2007). The offender may engage in communication with the mark in order to obtain more information as required. This information can then be supplemented with details obtained from other sources to build a sufficient body of knowledge to engage in fraud or identity theft.

Keyloggers and Help Desk Attacks

Keyloggers are devices, either hardware or software, that monitor the keystrokes of the user. These keystrokes can include passwords, usernames, and confidential documents and correspondence. Other personal data might also be logged. For example, many online websites use security questions to allow individuals to retrieve lost passwords. These security questions are often similar to the security questions used by financial institutions to verify identity (such as a mother's maiden name). The log of these keystrokes is sent to the potential fraudster, who can then utilize the information for identity theft or other fraudulent reasons. Keyloggers are often distributed using malware (see Chapter 5), although hardware keyloggers can also be used and connected to a specifically targeted computer terminal.

Marshall and Stephens (2008) describe related, but less technological techniques - help desk attacks. These types of attack have two main forms. Either the offender might call a help desk, asking for information which might be used in identity theft attacks, or they might eavesdrop on exchanges between an individual and a true helpdesk official, such as in a bank, later using the information for the identity theft. A third possibility involves the identity thief masquerading as the helpdesk official, directly calling the mark and getting them to confirm or provide sensitive information.

Dumpster Diving

'Dumpster diving' refers to a potential identity thief searching in the garbage bins of a company or individual for useful items. These may include scraps of paper with user names and passwords, old computer hard drives which may still have sensitive information on them, or even confidential files that may have been discarded without being properly shredded. Wall (2007) refers to this as *trashing* and indicates that it is a difficult, lengthy and local activity, with low yield. Nevertheless, it is a popular method for targeted attacks.

Pharming

The term 'pharming' has various meanings, but for the purposes of this chapter it refers to redirecting a web browser to a fake website. To do this, software on the user's computer can intercept any web addresses entered by the user, redirecting the browser away from the desired location and to the fake website which has been generated by the offender. It is also possible to alter the information at a Domain Name Server (or DNS) – redirecting websites from the central location and so eliminating the need for widespread distribution of malware. This strategy is sometimes known as *DNS cache poisoning*. Pharming frequently targets banks, especially larger banks, as this increases the chance that an individual will go to the website and use internet banking. Often the user is unaware that the redirection has taken place, and will continue with their online activities as normal. The fake website can have various levels of sophistication. Sometimes the website appears to be fully functional, other websites may have many broken links with only a minimum number of functioning pages. In general, the webpages requiring the user's login information appear to be functional, so the user unintentionally provides the identity thief with their username and password. After the login screen the fake website often displays an error message, telling the user that the website is currently unavailable and that they should try to login later.

Phishing

Phishing uses emails directed at the user to obtain critical information such as passwords and other information. In this case, the identity thief sends out large numbers of emails claiming to be from an organization that would have legitimate reasons to access the individual's information, such as a bank or the revenue services. These phishing emails may also be accompanied by the logos of the companies, and email addresses are often created that are similar to those used by the company or agency.

There are several main tactics that might be used in phishing. The first is to engage fear in the potential victim. This might be done by suggesting that their account information has already been compromised. The email gives reasons as to why the user needs to click on a link in the email urgently, such as for a system update. The link on the email may appear to direct the user to a legitimate website, but in fact it is linked to a bogus website, set up by the identity thief, in order to access the information. One common phishing scam targets users of an online auction site, using text similar to the following:

Dear Sir

We recently have determined that different computers have logged onto your account, and multiple password failures were present before the logons. We strongly advise that you change your password.

If this is not completed by March 8, we will be forced to suspend your account indefinitely, as it may have been used for fraudulent purposes. Thank you for your cooperation.

Click here to change your password

We apologize for any inconvenience

Thank you for using our service.

Of course, such an email is unlikely to create fear in a mark who does not have an account with the online auction company. However phishing emails are often prepared so as to appear to be from large companies or organizations, thus increasing the probability that the recipient will feel that the warning is legitimate. Nevertheless, businesses are not the only fronts used by identity thieves in these circumstances. The United States Revenue service has also been impersonated in attempts to gain personal information. In this case, the fraudsters generate fear in users by suggesting that they owe taxes to the system. Such a sample phishing email is included below.

From: *Internal Revenue Service [mailto:no-reply@irs.gov]*

Subject: *Notice of Underreported Income*

Tax Type: INCOME TAX

Issue: Unreported/Underreported Income (Fraud Application)

Please review your tax statement on Internal Revenue Service (IRS) website by clicking here

Internal Revenue Service

In addition to phishing emails designed to elicit fear in as many individuals as possible, such as those described above, other phishing techniques are aimed at very specific victims. Spear-phishing is a type of phishing attack which is targeted at a specific individual or organisation. Fraudsters might spend a great deal of time learning the names of important individuals at that organisation, as well as learning the protocols for certain procedures and gathering email addresses for individuals with certain responsibilities in the organisation. They then use this information to send targeted emails to those individuals, specifically tailored to obtain the desired response.

Whatever the type of phishing attack, there are some shared characteristics. Yar (2006) suggests that phishing scams rely on our willingness to trust others. He indicates that if others look and behave according to how we would expect them to, given their self-description, then we tend to accept them to be who they say they are. As such, the more professional the email and website appears to be, perhaps including the use of logos and brand names, the more likely they are to deceive the recipient.

Internet Auction Fraud

Yar (2006) states that most reported Internet fraud relates to events which occur on online auction sites (p. 81). This may include fencing stolen goods, non-delivery of items, product inauthenticity or misrepresentation and shill bidding (placing of fake bets to increase the auction price). Nonetheless, online auction sites are becoming more aware of these problems, and customer satisfaction ratings can help to reduce these problems. Despite this, Yar indicates that this system is not fool proof, and that sellers can leave false positive feedback for themselves by having multiple accounts.

Nigerian Scams and Advance Fee Fraud

Instead of using the fear tactics outlined above, other fraud-related emails sometimes attempt to deceive the mark by using promises of financial gain. This type of attack relies on 'advance fee fraud' – where the mark is persuaded to supply a sum of money upfront, on the promise that a larger sum of money will be returned to them later. It is sometimes known as the Nigerian scam fraud, as many examples of this involve the potential fraudsters and identity thieves masquerading as wealthy Nigerian individuals. It is also known as the 419 scheme, after the anti-fraud section of the criminal code in Nigeria. However, it is not uncommon for variations of the scheme to profess to be from other countries. Below is an example of a recent email of this type received by one of the authors.

Subject: *reply me urgently*

Dearest,

Please, I do not have former relationship with you but because of my present predicament I want to confide my life to you, I know I am taking risk but it is my best option at present please, accept me.

I want you to help me to transfer my inheritance for investment purpose in your country. Please, I am anticipating your urgent reply

Thanks

In some cases, the mark is not asked to provide money, but is required to provide bank account details with personal identification numbers (PINs). The identity thief then removes the cash from the account, having sufficient information to impersonate the account owner. One variant on this scheme involves an email which suggests that the mark could claim a large inheritance from a recently deceased individual who shares the same last name. In another, the sender of the email pretends to be an individual who requires a foreign bank account to transfer money out of a country, and promises to share his windfall with the mark if the mark provides his bank details to be used for this purpose. Edelson (2003) describes several of the common themes used during advance fee frauds. These include a banker trying to close the account of a dead customer, using the mark as the next of kin. Another theme involves the fraudster pretending to be the relative of a military or political individual who has died, with the fraudster indicating that they are trying to claim the inheritance.

While these scams sound obvious, some very educated people have fallen for them. Zuckoff (2006) cites the example of a Massachusetts psychotherapist who received such an email. When the psychotherapist responded to the email indicating that he would help, the sender engaged in prolonged correspondence, taking care to tailor his responses to reinforce the psychotherapist's beliefs regarding why he had been chosen to receive the offer. The psychotherapist became suspicious when the swindler sent him a check which turned out to be an altered duplicate of a legitimate payment. Despite his reservations, the psychotherapist eventually transferred large amounts of his cash, as well as some of the cash belonging to one of his patients, to help the swindler transfer the money. When checks did arrive from the scammers, they were fraudulent, and by the time that the psychotherapist decided to exit the scheme, he had been apprehended by the US authorities on charges of bank fraud, money laundering and possession of counterfeit checks. He was eventually sentenced to two years in prison, plus restitution of nearly six hundred thousand dollars, as well as being personally at a loss of approximately eighty thousand dollars due to the transfers made to the scammers and related charges. The psychotherapist was lucky, as he had not followed the scammer's instructions to travel to South Africa. Zuckoff indicates that some of those who have traveled to Nigeria at the invitation of scammers have been kidnapped or murdered.

Other Online Fraud

Not all such scams involve the transfer of funds from foreign bank accounts. Similar scams can involve fake charity and disaster relief frauds or fake lotteries where the recipient is told that they have won a significant prize. In other schemes, the prize may in fact be real, and the 'winner' is told that they have won an item from a list of expensive sounding prizes. One of the prizes is actually of low value (say for example a small-value gift voucher, or a worthless 'golden' bracelet). The 'winner' is told that in order to receive their prize, they must pay a processing charge, which comes to significantly more than the value of the 'prize' they eventually receive. Another internet fraud scheme - 'pharma-fraud', involves the advertisement of medicines online in a similar fashion to the early medicinal fraud schemes. In many cases the individual who pays for such medicines receives a worthless placebo, or an unregulated substance which may be harmful. One final example of internet fraud schemes involves a type of internet dating fraud where the mark, who has normally identified themselves as interested in starting a romantic relationship through online profiles, is approached by a potential bride who is resident in a foreign country. The mark is persuaded to send his potential bride money so that she can travel to visit and marry the victim. In many cases neither the money, nor the potential bride, are ever seen again.

Human Susceptibility to Online Fraud and Identity Theft Techniques

While many of these scams sound very obvious, and it is tempting to think of any victim of fraud or identity theft as being quite naïve, there are a number of psychological explanations for why humans are susceptible to such attacks. There is a considerable body of research examining human decision making, some of which is useful in helping to understand why individuals might decide to go along with a suggested course of behaviour, despite the potential for harm.

Firstly, the fake websites used by fraudsters can be very persuasive. Dhamija, Tygar and Hearst (2006) showed twenty websites to participants. Thirteen of the websites were fabricated, and ninety percent of the participants were deceived by those websites considered to be good quality. Almost one in four participants relied only on the website content to establish its authenticity, without looking at the website address or security indicators to validate its author. This finding has a base in the psychology of human decision mak-

ing. Payne (1980) examined how the salience (or attention-attracting properties) of a cue (a specific element in a person's perceptual field) can affect how well it will be attended to and weighted when making a decision. A salient piece of information, such as a large logo, or a personalised message, can therefore help to persuade a user that the email is legitimate. As an example of this, Griffin and Tversky (1992) found that evaluators, forming impressions of an applicant on the basis of letters of recommendation, tended to give more weight to the tone or enthusiasm of the letter (a salient feature) than to the credibility or reliability of the evidence. Returning to identity theft and fraud, this finding may suggest that users will pay more attention to the content of the fraudulent email than to establishing its true source.

The projected authority of the offender is also important. Marshall and Stephens (2008) indicate how the easiest way to steal a billiards table from a bar involves arriving in a lorry and wearing a high visibility jacket. If the thief acts confidently enough, staff are less likely to challenge the behavior, and may allow the table to be taken away. In a way, the person's clothes and props are sufficient to create a belief in the potential victim that they are legitimate. A similar situation seems to occur online – if the person seems legitimate enough, acts in a confident enough manner and presents their email or website appropriately, people often believe that this is sufficient to prove their identity. Tversky and Kahneman (1974) discuss the representativeness heuristic, where individuals are assumed to draw conclusions by evaluating the extent to which the evidence provided corresponds with the information that they have about that situation which is stored in long-term memory. As such, if the person views a fraudulent email and finds that it includes the logo for their bank, appears to be official in nature, and refers to them by name, this may be quite representative of their personal construct of what a letter from their bank looks like. As such, they might be more likely to interpret the email as coming from their bank, and hence follow the instructions in it.

Marshall and Stephens (2008) go on to describe how the criminal often poses as an authority figure, where there is often a suggestion of potential threat involved if the authority figure is unhappy with the interchange because of a lack of helpfulness on the part of the mark. Frequently, the emails indicate that it is important that the recipient respond quickly in order to access a specific fund, or to prevent them from losing money or privileges. Svenson and Maule (1993) found that such time pressure is another key influence on human decision making.

With regard to advance fee frauds, Holt and Graves (2007) completed a qualitative analysis of over four hundred fraudulent email messages, and found that multiple writing techniques were used to encourage responses. As well as the types of scenarios listed by Edelson, they also identified fraudulent emails that claimed that the recipient was the winner of a lottery, as well as emails from people claiming to have a terminal illness who wanted to transfer their money to the recipient for donation to charity. Holt and Graves noted several techniques that were used by scammers. These included the use of critical and serious tone in the subject line (such as 'Urgent Attention' or 'Payment Agent Needed'). Others included cordial greetings (such as 'Hello Friend') which may make the recipient feel emotionally linked to the sender. Holt and Graves indicated that seventy-five percent of messages gave no indication of how the sender chose the recipient, though a small number of messages indicated that they had found the recipient through an online search for 'reliable and honest' people. Most messages requested confidentiality and a rapid response, with half of the emails requesting personal information, sometimes bank account details. However, some messages simply sought an indication of whether or not the recipient would help them. This may be an attempt to get a 'foot in the door', hoping that once the individual has committed themselves to helping the scammer, then they will be more likely

to follow this with further information and action later. Nhan, Kinkade and Burns (2009) examined similar suspect unsolicited emails and found that "relationship-building social engineering methods" (p. 452) were preferred to direct requests for sensitive information. They found that scammers rarely requested bank account or social security numbers in initial emails, with only 3.2% and 2.5% of emails requesting each respectively. They also discovered that the scammers tended to pose as financial institutions and reputable companies. Holt and Graves indicate that some emails also use links to news stories in order to help to support their claims, while others use religious language, presumably in the hope of evoking an emotional or spiritual response. They also found that spelling, typographical and grammatical errors were very common (present in over eighty percent of emails), and indicate that these errors may actually be included on purpose, in order to reinforce the belief that the sender is a foreigner.

Finally, it is also possible that once we reach the conclusion that an email is genuine, it is more difficult to change our minds. Einhorn and Hogarth (1978) describe the confirmation bias, a tendency for people to seek information and cues that confirm their tentatively held hypothesis or belief, and not seek those that support an opposite conclusion. Due to this bias, ambiguous cues will be interpreted in a manner that supports the favoured belief. This puts users at risk of only attending to the information that confirms that the sender of the email is who they claim to be, and ignoring other information (such as unusual email addresses) which is in opposition to their conclusion. To worsen this, Bremmer, Koehler, Liberman and Tversky (1996) noted that people in general are overconfident in their state of knowledge or beliefs, becoming unlikely to seek additional information (which may refute the hypothesis) even when it is appropriate to do so. As such, victims of identity theft may not liaise with their bank to see if the email was legitimate before clicking on the link provided.

PROFILE AND PERSONALITY CHARACTERISTICS OF OFFENDERS

Despite the obvious financial motives for these offences, it is too simple to say that these crimes are committed simply for financial reasons. Many other individuals with similar levels of intelligence have the same ability to fool others to such an extent that they can be taken advantage of, but do not. What are the differences between these individuals, and those who go on to commit the crime? It is possible that some of the literature relating to the offline fraudsters and white-collar criminals might be of use.

Duffield and Grabosky (2001) state that just a combination of greed and dishonesty is too simple an explanation to explain fraudsters – they argue that many people are "aggressively acquisitive but generally law abiding" (p. 2), and that there are also dishonest people who do not commit fraud. They suggest that no psychological characteristics had been identified at that time which were both valid and reliable indicators of a potential fraudster. Duffield and Grabosky suggest that common elements that explain fraud include financial strain (perhaps feeling a pressure to have similar earnings as peers, or to support expenses such as compulsive gambling), and ego or power aspects (where the fraudster feels delight from manipulating their victim). Duffield and Grabosky also highlight the technique of neutralization, where individuals rationalize their criminal activities by "nullifying internal moral objections" (p. 3). They explain that the offender might justify their actions by suggesting that the victim can afford to be defrauded, especially if the victim is a large and impersonal organization. In other cases the offender may justify their criminality by suggesting that the victim deserves to be targeted, or that everyone engages in fraudulent behavior of some kind. Nelken (2007) indicates that some motives such as greed and power have been ascribed to white-collar criminals. He argues that most individuals who have opportunity do not engage in white collar crime due to their investment in relationships and society which they do not want to risk, suggesting that many potential offenders do consider such activities at some time, but decide against it in order to maintain their social status.

Blickle, Schlegel, Fassbender and Klein (2006) examined white-collar criminals and found that this type of criminality is predicted by several demographic and psychological characteristics, including being male, having low behavioral self-control, high levels of hedonism, high levels of narcissism and high levels of conscientiousness. However Blickle et al specifically examined high-level white collar crime in business, and it is unknown whether these characteristics are also evident in other types of fraudsters. It is also possible that some research relating to fraudulent claims of social welfare benefits may be applicable here. Hessing, Elffers, Robben and Webley (1993) found that while there was no difference between financial strain and social norms between an honest and fraudulent group of unemployment benefit claimants, other characteristics did vary. Those in the fraudulent group were less well educated, were more alienated, more inclined to take risks, had more opportunities, and more positive attitudes towards a variety of kinds of fraud.

EFFECTS ON VICTIMS

In addition to the psychology of offenders, an insight into the experiences of victims can also be important in understanding identity theft and online fraud. These types of offences can have both financial and psychological effects on the victims, both of which will be considered here.

Financial Effects on Victims

For many individuals, the financial effects of identity theft are relatively short lived. In many cases the bank or credit organization will cover the losses involved, although this is not always so, and it is usually not the case for fraud. In one Canadian study, Winterdyk and Thompson (2008) found that 46% of non-students and 52% of students reported that it cost them nothing to restore their identity. Thirty percent of non-students and twenty-six percent of students spent up to three hundred Canadian dollars to repair the damage, while the experience cost a small minority of individuals over eight hundred Canadian dollars.

Some of the financial effects of identity theft involve short-term credit rating problems, or lack of access to credit cards and bank accounts until the issue is resolved. There can be some confusion and inconvenience for the victim before their financial situation returns to normal. The Federal Trade Commission (2006) indicated that 31% of identity theft victims required over forty hours to rectify their credit issues. Almost half (48%) faced harassment by creditors, one in four had loan applications rejected, and twelve percent faced criminal investigations.

Winterdyk and Thompson (2008) found that students are slightly more at risk, but are better informed than adult non-students about identity theft. They noted that 23% of non-students and 44% of students noticed their victimization within days, with 35% of student victims realizing their victimization within minutes or hours of the incident, compared to only 15% of non-students. Approximately 62% of non-student victims and 22% of student victims only realized their victimization after several weeks or months had passed. Nearly 70% of non-students and 78% of students estimated it took between a few hours and a few days to resolve the issue. However almost 23% of non-students and 17% of students indicated it took weeks or months to solve the issue, with some respondents indicating that it took over a year to sort out their finances.

Psychological Effects on Victims

While for some it may only take time and finances to resolve identity theft victimisation, for others, there may also be psychological effects. Ess (2009) considers the impact on the victim of identity theft. He suggests that it is more harmful to us personally than theft of other property, indicating that property can generally be replaced, but that it is not possible to "buy a replacement identity" (p. 58). He argues that it is a harm against the person, not just their property. Carey (2009) indicates that victims of phishing scams may develop symptoms similar to post-traumatic stress disorder (PTSD), with symptoms such as embarrassment and depression being noted. Sharp, Shreve-Neiger, Fremouw, Kane and Hutton (2004) completed an exploratory study of the impact of identity theft on victims by examining thirty-seven victims using focus groups and questionnaires. Sharp et al found that the majority of participants experienced increased maladaptive psychological and somatic symptoms, particularly those with unresolved cases.

Victims of online fraud and identity theft may also experience secondary victimization, where the victim's family, friends and even the authorities may place some blame on the victim for the experience. Mendelsohn (1956) suggested that there is a spectrum of shared responsibility between the victim and the offender. This spectrum ranges from the completely innocent victim, who could have done nothing to prevent the crime (for example, if they are a passenger on a plane which is hijacked by terrorists) to the victim who is actually an offender (for example, a person who pretends to have been the victim of a burglary in order to commit insurance fraud). Between these extremes lie victim facilitation and victim precipitation. In victim facilitation, the victim may have carried out an act (or failed to take certain precautions), which enabled the offender to commit the crime. This may include failing to fit a suitable house alarm, or leaving the keys to their car in the ignition. In the case of victim precipitation, the victim may have played a more active part in their victimisation – for example they may have insulted the offender who went on to physically attack them.

While the concept of shared responsibility is obviously quite controversial, particularly when used in the defence cases of suspected sex offenders and rapists, there has been considerable support for the phenomenon (see for example Amir, 1971; Klinger, 2001; Grubb & Harrower, 2008).

Kirwan (2009) examined the concept of victim blaming and shared responsibility in identity theft. She attempted to determine if facilitation of an online crime by the victim affects victim blaming behaviours in mock jurors. She presented four scenarios of identity theft to 128 participants using an online survey. Almost half of the participants had been the victim of cybercrime. For each scenario, the participants were asked to indicate if they would award damages to the victim or not, and in the four scenarios potentially confounding variables such as age, gender, and financial losses were kept constant. Three scenarios were included in which the victim could be considered to have facilitated the crime in some way. These included scenarios involving online shopping and auction fraud, along with a scenario describing the distribution of personal information using a social networking site which is outlined below for illustrative purposes:

"A woman puts up some personal information about herself on a social networking site. Later, she discovers that the information that she put up has been used by an identity thief to steal $4,000 from her. She has brought the social networking site to court, in an attempt to sue them for damages. She says that the social networking site should have warned her before allowing her to put up such personal information. The social networking site is counter-arguing that it is up to the user to be careful of the information they make available."

In addition to these three 'high facilitation' scenarios, a fourth scenario was included where the victim had taken all reasonable precautions, and could therefore be considered to have low victim facilitation. This scenario involved an online shopping incident, outlined below:

"A woman uses her credit card online regularly. One of the online shops that she has bought from has recently been hacked into, and her credit card details were among those stolen, even though the site indicated that the transaction was secure at the time. The thief has used her credit card to steal $4,000 from her. The woman has brought the online shop to court, in an attempt to sue them for damages. She says that the online shop is at fault because they inadequately protected her details. The online shop is counter-arguing that they have stated in their terms and conditions that all information is supplied at the user's own risk."

As hypothesised, in all the scenarios except for the low victim facilitation scenario, the majority of respondents chose not to award damages to the victim. This indicates that victim blaming does occur in identity theft cases, with individuals more likely to withhold financial compensation from victims who are seen to have facilitated the crime. Interestingly, previous victimisation of cybercrime did not have a significant relationship with likelihood to award damages to the hypothetical victims, and those who had experienced victimisation were just as likely to withhold compensation as those who had not.

SOLUTIONS: PREVENTION METHODS AND EFFICACY

Despite the damage which can be caused by online fraud and identity theft, there are a number of specific solutions which can be suggested. For example, Marshall and Stephens (2008) indicate that some methods to reduce the likelihood of identity theft include more rigorous measures for applications for certain documents, such as passports. Currently it is quite easy to order important documentation, such as birth certificates online, using only limited knowledge of the potential victim. This initial piece of identification can then be used in conjunction with other pieces of information to obtain further important documents or to open bank accounts. Similarly, the advent of online banking and online shopping has made the work of the identity thief easier. It is now possible to apply for bank loans online, without ever visiting a branch in person. In addition, fraudulent use of credit cards has been made easier as individuals can shop online without being asked for identification. If the credit card has been cancelled, identity thieves are less likely to call attention to themselves during a failed online purchase, rather than if a purchase at a shop counter is refused.

Marshall and Stephens (2008) also indicate that it is important to raise public awareness regarding the problem. This does not just apply to protecting the details of their financial accounts, but also other items of information that may help an identity thief. Finch (2003) states that "many Internet users are cautious about the safety of Internet transactions that require them to provide their debit or credit card details but there appears to be an almost reckless disregard for basic security precautions in relation to publication of any other personal information on the Internet" (p. 94). Vast quantities of information are available about many people online through a variety of sources, including staff profiles on employer's websites, personal profiles on social networking websites, telephone directories, registers of electors, business listings, and so on. If a person is using an unsecured wireless network, other confidential information can be collected by simply being within range of the network with the appropriate technology. A potential identity thief can even check the credit rating of a potential victim online in order to determine if it is worthwhile attempting to get credit in their name. It is likely that one of the key preventative measures which can be taken by individuals involves ensuring that they carefully control what information about them is publicly available, or available with little effort.

Users should also be informed about the importance of appropriate security measures for online accounts. Tam, Glassman and Vandenwauver (2009) found that while computer users know what makes a good and bad password, they engage in bad password-management behaviors because they do not see any immediate negative consequences to themselves and because of the 'convenience-security tradeoff'. They found that users were willing to share their passwords with trusted others (such as family, friends and co-workers), even taping their passwords next to the computer. Tam et al found that users want easy to remember passwords, only choosing stronger passwords and sacrificing convenience for accounts where there is an immediate negative consequence to the individual if they are compromised (such as online banking, rather than email accounts). It seems that users are less concerned about the large quantities of personal information that may be made available to an identity thief should their email account be hacked. Tam et al also found that users were more worried about personal information being exposed to friends and family than they were about fraud and identity theft. They found that users were not concerned about their behavior if they felt that the immediate and negative consequences only affected others. This provides interesting insights into potential public information strategies, and Tam et al suggest that in order to ensure better password management, users need to feel a personal loss if their account is compromised. It is therefore preferable that future information strategies focus on highlighting to users the personal losses involved in identity theft cases in order to improve personal security measures.

Wang, Yuan and Archer (2006) describe a complex contextual framework for combating identity theft. Their framework involves interactions between the identity owner, the identity issuer (such as a government), identity checkers (such as the retailer) and identity protectors (such as law enforcement and government officials).

Wang et al argue that their framework can be used to help people to understand the nature of risks and vulnerabilities, to identify the role of stakeholders, to analyse the relationships between these stakeholders, to develop systematic and effective security strategies, and to evaluate the effectiveness of identity theft solutions. They suggest several key mechanisms for prevention. These include education and guidance that inform users on how to check if they have been the victim of identity theft, and what to do if they are victimized. These educational materials may take the form of government materials, pamphlets and websites. Another prevention mechanism involves companies educating their customers about the risk (such as a bank indicating on their online banking system that they will never email users asking for personal details). Wang et al suggest that it would also be useful to have early identity theft detection measures, as earlier detection reduces potential losses. This could be promoted by encouraging individuals to regularly check their online banking records, rather than waiting for bank statements. Stiffer penalties could also be implemented for convicted identity thieves, and better background checks could be carried out on individuals in companies and organizations who would legitimately handle personal information. Finally Wang et al suggest that newer technologies, such as biometrics and smart cards, could also be useful prevention methods, and this possibility is considered in more depth below.

FUTURE TRENDS AND RESEARCH

Biometrics are identity measures based on the physical characteristics of the person. These may include technologies which many people are familiar with, such as fingerprints and DNA matching, but also less familiar technologies such as retinal scanning. Finch (2003) indicates that these measures are useful in preventing identity theft as they are not as easily replicated as currently popular methods of identity checking, specifically the use of usernames, passwords, and identification numbers. Finch (2003) indicates that these current methods, including documentation and pieces of information that are supposedly only known to the user, are unreliable, and are open to theft. It is significantly more difficult to fabricate biometric evidence such as fingerprints.

While this sounds expensive to implement, the use of biometrics in home computing has been available for some time, with fingerprint scanners integrated in some laptop computers for security purposes. Fingerprint scanners which can be attached to most computers via standard USB connectors can be bought for less than $100. It would seem reasonable that important financial transactions such as online shopping and online banking may one day soon require both passwords and fingerprint scans to be processed. Fingerprint recognition is not the only biometric possibility, and Smith (2007) outlines many more. These include hand geometry, DNA matching, facial thermography, blood pulse measurement and nailbed identification as well as facial, iris, signature, voice, keystroke pattern, retina, vein, ear shape, gait, odour and skin pattern recognition. Of these, voice and signature recognition are probably the biometric identification methods which could be relatively easily implemented as technologies for checking these are relatively cheap and prevalent.

Despite the advantages of biometric identification methods, Smith (2007) emphasizes the need for proper enrollment systems in their use. This is important as identity theft issues can arise when a specific imprint is being registered to an individual. For example, it may be possible to fraudulently assign an incorrect fingerprint to a specific identity. Smith lists several other problems with biometrics, including questions such as efficiency of the system, invasion of privacy, user acceptance, cost and problems regarding where the information regarding the identity is kept (for example, would the information be kept on a personal identity card, or on a central database).

In addition to examining the potential procedures for implementing biometric identifiers, as well as their impact on users, other avenues for future research include more detailed examinations of the psychology of both offenders and victims. While it is likely that the decision making strategies described within cognitive psychology probably apply to the decisions which users make when considering responding to a fraudulent email, these have yet to be empirically tested. Similarly further support is required for the limited research to date on blame ascribed to victims of online fraud and identity theft, as well as more thorough insights into their psychological experiences. Finally the characteristics of perpetrators of identity theft and online fraud need to be psychologically examined, although this is admittedly the area of research which will probably be the most difficult to implement due to the evasive nature of these individuals.

CONCLUSION

Despite the prevalence of identity theft attempts and fraudulent emails, little empirical research has been conducted to date in this area. Nevertheless, psychology can provide some very important insights into the behaviour of both offenders and victims, due to research into the nature of decision making, persuasive techniques and victimisation. The key issue for psychologists and online security professionals now is to test the applicability of these insights to ensure that they hold true for these crimes. It would also be of interest to determine what psychologically differentiates those who do become the victim of online fraud from those who received the same invitation but did not respond, and so were not victimised. Identity theft and online fraud is an expensive issue for modern society, as even though financial institutions sometimes accept the costs of their customers' identity theft, these costs are eventually passed on to the consumer through interest rates and insurance premiums. A deeper psychological understanding of the offenders and victims of these offences could therefore save many millions of dollars, as well as encouraging potential users who are currently fearful of being victimised to have richer online experiences.

REFERENCES

Amir, M. (1971). *Patterns of Forcible Rape*. Chicago, IL: University of Chicago Press.

Anti-Phishing Working Group. (APWG, 2010, September 23). *Phishing Activity Trends Report, 1ˢᵗ Quarter, 2010*. Retrieved 11ᵗʰ October 2010 from http://www.antiphishing.org/reports/apwg_report_Q1_2010.pdf

BBC News (2010, October 18). *Identity fraud now costs £1.9 bn, says fraud authority.* Retrieved 21 October 2010 from http://www.bbc.co.uk/news/business-11553199

Blickle, G., Schlegel, A., Fassbender, P., & Klein, U. (2006). Some personality correlates of business white-collar crime. *Applied Psychology: An International Review, 55,* 220–233. doi:10.1111/j.1464-0597.2006.00226.x

Bocij, P. (2006). *The Dark Side of the Internet: Protecting yourself and your family from online criminals*. Westport, CT: Praeger Publishers.

Bremmer, L. A., Koehler, D. J., Liberman, V., & Tversky, A. (1996). Overconfidence in probability and frequency judgements: A critical examination. *Organizational Behavior and Human Decision Processes, 65,* 212–219. doi:10.1006/obhd.1996.0021

Carey, L. (2009, July 29). Can PTSD affect victims of identity theft: Psychologists say yes. *Associated Content*. Retrieved on 21 October 2010 from http://www.associatedcontent.com/article/ 2002924/can_ptsd_affect_victims_of_identity.html

Collins, J. M. (2006). *Investigating Identity Theft: A Guide for Businesses, Law Enforcement, and Victims*. Hoboken, NJ: John Wiley & Sons.

Dhamija, R., Tygar, J. D., & Hearst, M. (2006). Why Phishing Works. [Montreal: CHI.]. *CHI, 2006*(April), 22–27.

Duffield, G. & Grabosky, P. (2001, March). The Psychology of Fraud. *Australian Institute of Criminology: Trends & Issues in crime and criminal justice, No. 199*.

Edelson, E. (2003). The 419 scam: Information warfare on the spam front and a proposal for local filtering. *Computers & Security, 22*, 392–401. doi:10.1016/S0167-4048(03)00505-4

Einhorn, H. J., & Hogarth, R. M. (1978). Confidence in judgement: Persistence of the illusion of validity. *Psychological Review, 85*, 395–416. doi:10.1037/0033-295X.85.5.395

Ess, C. (2009). *Digital Media Ethics*. Cambridge, England: Polity Press.

Federal Trade Commission. (2006). *Identity theft survey report*. Retrieved 21 October 2010 from http://www.ftc.gov/os/2007/11/ SynovateFinalReportIDTheft2006.pdf.

Finch, E. (2003). What a tangled web we weave: identity theft and the internet. In Jewkes, Y. (Ed.), *Dot.cons: Crime, deviance and identity on the internet* (pp. 86–104). Cullompton, England: Willan Publishing.

Finch, E. (2007). The problem of stolen identity and the Internet. In Jewkes, Y. (Ed.), *Crime Online* (pp. 29–43). Cullompton, England: Willan Publishing.

Griffin, D., & Tversky, A. (1992). The weighting of evidence and the determinants of confidence. *Cognitive Psychology, 24*, 411–435. doi:10.1016/0010-0285(92)90013-R

Grubb, A., & Harrower, J. (2008). Attribution of blame in cases of rape: An analysis of participant gender, type of rape and perceived similarity to the victim. *Aggression and Violent Behavior, 13*, 396–405. doi:10.1016/j.avb.2008.06.006

Hessing, D. J., Elffers, H., Robben, H. S. J., & Webley, P. (1993). Needy or Greedy? The social psychology of individuals who fraudulently claim unemployment benefits. *Journal of Applied Social Psychology, 23*, 226–243. doi:10.1111/j.1559-1816.1993.tb01084.x

Holt, T. J., & Graves, D. C. (2007). A Qualitative analysis of advance fee fraud e-mail schemes. *International Journal of Cyber Criminology, 1 (1)*. Retrieved 21 October 2010 from http://www. cybercrimejournal.com/ thomas&danielleijcc.htm

Jaishkankar, K. (2008). Identity related crime in cyberspace: Examining phishing and its impact. *International Journal of Cyber Criminology, 2*, 10–15.

Jewkes, Y. (2010). Public policing and Internet crime. In Jewkes & M. Yar (eds.) *Handbook of Internet Crime* (pp. 525-545). Cullompton, England: Willan Publishing.

Kirwan, G.H. (2009). *Victim facilitation and blaming in cybercrime cases*. Proceedings of Cyberspace 2009. Brno, Czech Republic. November 20-21.

Klinger, D. A. (2001). Suicidal intent in victim-precipitated homicide: Insights from the study of "suicide-by-cop." *Homicide Studies, 5*(3), 206–226. doi:10.1177/1088767901005003002

Levi, M. (2001). "Between the risk and the reality falls the shadow": Evidence and urban legends in computer fraud (with apologies to T.S. Eliot). In Wall, D. (Ed.), *Crime and the Internet* (pp. 44–58). London, New York: Routledge.

Lininger, R., & Vines, R. D. (2005). *Phishing: Cutting the Identity Theft Line*. Indianapolis, IN: Wiley Publishing Inc.

Marshall, A., & Stephens, P. (2008). Identity and Identity Theft. In Bryant, R. (Ed.), *Investigating Digital Crime* (pp. 179–193). Chichester, England: John Wiley & Sons.

McQuade, S. C. III. (2006). *Understanding and Managing Cybercrime*. Boston, MA: Pearson Allyn and Bacon.

Mendelsohn, B. (1956). A New Branch of Bio-Psychological Science: La Victimology. *Revue Internationale de Criminologie et de Police Technique, 10*, 782–789.

Nayar, P. K. (2010). *An Introduction to New Media and Cybercultures*. Chichester, England: Wiley Blackwell.

Nelken, D. (2007). White-collar and corporate crime. In Maguire, M., Morgan, R., & Reiner, R. (Eds.), *The Oxford Handbook of Criminology* (4th ed., pp. 733–770). Oxford: Oxford University Press.

Nhan, J., Kinkade, P., & Burns, R. (2009). Finding a pot of gold at the end of an internet rainbow: Further examination of fraudulent email solicitation. *International Journal of Cyber Criminology, 3*, 452–475.

Payne, J. W. (1980). Information processing theory: Some concepts and methods applied to decision research. In Wallsten, T. S. (Ed.), *Cognitive processes in choice and decision behaviour*. Hillsdale, NJ: Erlbaum.

Sharp, T., Shreve-Neiger, A., Fremouw, W., Kane, J., & Hutton, S. (2004). Exploring the psychological and somatic impact of identity theft. *Journal of Forensic Sciences, 49*, 131–136.

Smith, R. G. (2007). Biometric solutions to identity-related cybercrime. In Jewkes, Y. (Ed.), *Crime Online* (pp. 44–59). Cullompton, England: Willan Publishing.

Smith, R. G. (2010). Identity theft and fraud. In Jewkes, Y., & Yar, M. (Eds.), *Handbook of Internet Crime* (pp. 173–301). Cullompton, England: Willan Publishing.

Svenson, S., & Maule, A. (1993). *Time pressure and stress in human judgement and decision making*. New York: Plenum.

Tam, L., Glassman, M., & Vandenwauver, M. (2009). The psychology of password management: a tradeoff between security and convenience. *Behaviour & Information Technology, 29*, 233–244.. doi:10.1080/01449290903121386

Tversky, A., & Kahneman, D. (1974). Judgement under uncertainty: Heuristics and biases. *Science, 211*, 453–458. doi:10.1126/science.7455683

Wall, D. S. (2007). *Cybercrime: The Transformation of Crime in the Information Age*. Cambridge, England: Polity Press.

Wang, W., Yuan, Y., & Archer, N. (2006). A contextual framework for combating identity theft. *IEEE Security & Privacy, 4*, 30–38. doi:10.1109/MSP.2006.31

Winterdyk, J., & Thompson, N. (2008). Student and non-student perceptions and awareness of identity theft. *Canadian Journal of Criminology and Criminal Justice, 50*, 153–186. doi:10.3138/cjccj.50.2.153

Yar, M. (2006). *Cybercrime and Society*. London: Sage.

Zuckoff, M. (2006). The Perfect Mark: How a Massachusetts psychotherapist fell for a Nigerian e-mail scam. *The New Yorker, May 15,* pp. 36-42.

ADDITIONAL READING

Blickle, G., Schlegel, A., Fassbender, P., & Klein, U. (2006). Some personality correlates of business white-collar crime. *Applied Psychology: An International Review, 55*, 220–233. doi:10.1111/j.1464-0597.2006.00226.x

Bocij, P. (2006). *The Dark Side of the Internet: Protecting yourself and your family from online criminals*. Westport, CT: Praeger Publishers.

Carey, L. (2009, July 29). Can PTSD affect victims of identity theft: Psychologists say yes. *Associated Content*. Retrieved on 21 October 2010 from http://www.associatedcontent.com/article/ 2002924/can_ptsd_affect_victims_of_identity.html

Collins, J. M. (2006). *Investigating Identity Theft: A Guide for Businesses, Law Enforcement, and Victims*. Hoboken, NJ: John Wiley & Sons.

Dhamija, R., Tygar, J. D., & Hearst, M. (2006). Why Phishing Works. [Montreal: CHI.]. *CHI, 2006*(April), 22–27.

Duffield, G. & Grabosky, P. (2001, March). The Psychology of Fraud. *Australian Institute of Criminology: Trends & Issues in crime and criminal justice, No. 199*.

Edelson, E. (2003). The 419 scam: Information warfare on the spam front and a proposal for local filtering. *Computers & Security, 22*, 392–401. doi:10.1016/S0167-4048(03)00505-4

Finch, E. (2003). What a tangled web we weave: identity theft and the internet. In Jewkes, Y. (Ed.), *Dot.cons: Crime, deviance and identity on the internet* (pp. 86–104). Cullompton, England: Willan Publishing.

Finch, E. (2007). The problem of stolen identity and the Internet. In Jewkes, Y. (Ed.), *Crime Online* (pp. 29–43). Cullompton, England: Willan Publishing.

Holt, T. J., & Graves, D. C. (2007). A Qualitative analysis of advance fee fraud e-mail schemes. *International Journal of Cyber Criminology, 1 (1)*. Retrieved 21 October 2010 from http://www.cybercrimejournal.com/ thomas&danielleijcc.htm

Jaishkankar, K. (2008). Identity related crime in cyberspace: Examining phishing and its impact. *International Journal of Cyber Criminology, 2*, 10–15.

Marshall, A., & Stephens, P. (2008). Identity and Identity Theft. In Bryant, R. (Ed.), *Investigating Digital Crime* (pp. 179–193). Chichester, England: John Wiley & Sons.

Nhan, J., Kinkade, P., & Burns, R. (2009). Finding a pot of gold at the end of an internet rainbow: Further examination of fraudulent email solicitation. *International Journal of Cyber Criminology, 3*, 452–475.

Sharp, T., Shreve-Neiger, A., Fremouw, W., Kane, J., & Hutton, S. (2004). Exploring the psychological and somatic impact of identity theft. *Journal of Forensic Sciences, 49*, 131–136.

Smith, R. G. (2010). Identity theft and fraud. In Jewkes, Y., & Yar, M. (Eds.), *Handbook of Internet Crime* (pp. 173–301). Cullompton, England: Willan Publishing.

Winterdyk, J., & Thompson, N. (2008). Student and non-student perceptions and awareness of identity theft. *Canadian Journal of Criminology and Criminal Justice, 50*, 153–186. doi:10.3138/cjccj.50.2.153

Chapter 7
Internet Child Pornography:
A Stepping Stone to Contact Offences?

ABSTRACT

Internet child pornography is a topic which is eliciting greater attention from society and the media, as parents and caregivers become more aware of the risks to their children and law enforcement agencies become more aware of the techniques and strategies used by offenders. Sheldon and Howitt (2007) indicate that at least in terms of convictions, internet child pornography is the major activity that constitutes Internet related sex crimes. However, the distribution of child pornography in itself is not a new offence, but rather one which has been facilitated by the introduction of new technologies such as digital photography and the internet. Before the popularity of the internet, public concern and academic interest in child pornography was quite low as it was considered to be a small and specialist issue. However, the proliferation of images of child sexual abuse online has altered public opinion considerably. This chapter considers how online distribution of child pornography is different to offline distribution. It also considers the psychology of the online child pornography offender and considers the difference between these individuals and contact offenders, attempting to determine if online offenders later progress to offend offline as well. The chapter will then examine what psychological effects child pornography can have on the victims involved, and finally examines the rehabilitation techniques that have been used on these offenders.

BACKGROUND

Sophie is a 38 year old survivor of child sexual abuse. She was abused by her uncle, and has undergone many years of therapy to help her to emotionally overcome the traumas she endured. Only recently has she begun to fully enjoy her life. She has a successful career as a lawyer and a loving husband, and she is expecting her second child.

However, she has now learned that her uncle took photographs of her abuse, and has been posting the images to file-sharing websites. Although the photographs are almost thirty years old, Sophie is afraid that she is still recognizable in the images. She has no idea how many people have downloaded or seen the images. Every time a passerby makes eye contact with her in the street, she wonders if the person has recognized her from the images. Her confidence in the courtroom has been shattered, as she wonders if her opponent or the jury

DOI: 10.4018/978-1-61350-350-8.ch007

have seen the pictures. During her last case, she found herself preoccupied with these fears, and she had a panic attack in the middle of her opening statement. She stopped going to work and refuses to even go out to buy groceries anymore. She has been diagnosed with agoraphobia.

Jack is a happy and healthy six year old boy. Occasionally he visits Graham, his next door neighbour, and helps him with the gardening. Recently Graham has started touching Jack, and Jack is unsure about if this is okay or not. Graham assures him that it's fine, and perfectly normal. Graham turns on his computer and shows Jack pictures of other little boys who are also being touched. The other little boys seem to be enjoying it, and there are lots of pictures. Jack thinks that perhaps it is normal, even though he's still a little unsure.

While the two accounts above are fictional, they represent the thousands of children who are affected by child pornography online. One example of a real life case involves Ian Green, a 45 year old unemployed convicted sex offender from West Sussex. In August 2010, Green admitted to making, possessing and distributing child pornography. He used eleven difference accounts on the social networking site Facebook to distribute both still images and videos. Green created private groups on Facebook, and only allowed others to join when they had verified their trustworthiness, normally by uploading images of child pornography themselves (BBC News, 2010).

It is difficult to establish one commonly accepted definition of child pornography. The acceptability of images that depict minors in nude or sexually explicit scenes has varied throughout history and across cultures, with some of the most famous examples being depictions of Shakespeare's *Romeo and Juliet*, in which Juliet is just thirteen years old. Tate (1990) indicates that sexualised images of children were being traded and collected soon after cameras became more widely available in the early nineteenth century, although the early images were generally

of poor quality and difficult to obtain (Wortley & Smallbone, 2006). As technology has developed, the quality of the images and the ease of access have improved dramatically.

While most individuals intuitively feel that child pornography is easily identifiable, there are several classification systems available, some of which would include images that are present in most family photo albums. This has resulted in making child pornography difficult to define in a legal sense. Wortley and Smallbone (2006) outline the history of child pornography laws in the United States of America, indicating that the first federal law regarding the issue was passed in 1978, with the first laws regarding computers and child pornography being passed ten years later, with the laws being progressively tightened since then. In brief, the content of the images does not have to involve obscene behaviour, but may include suggestive explicit content of any person under the age of eighteen. It is not only an offence to produce or trade the image, but also simply to possess it, and the image only needs to have been accessed, not saved to the offender's own computer. Definitions in academic literature are also quite diverse (Endrass et al, 2009), and confusion is added by phenomena such as 'barely-legal pornography' (where the individuals in the image are close to the age of consent, often just eighteen years old), and ageplay, where an adult may pretend to be a child, often wearing a costume. In other cases, the image may be of an adult, but the person's head has been replaced with a child's, or virtual child characters (actually controlled by adults) may be used to create pornographic images (as was the case in the 'Wonderland' area of Second Life as reported by Sky News in October 2007).

Before the popularity of the Internet, child pornography was more limited – images tended to be manufactured and traded locally, and distributers needed a considerable amount of equipment to develop and copy the images (Wortley & Smallbone, 2006). With the advent of digital cameras and webcams, images and videos can now be made more cheaply, in higher quality, and with less equipment. They are also easier to distribute. Early child pornography rings online favoured Usenet groups, but more recently, primary forms of distribution include social networking sites and file-sharing or 'peer-to-peer' websites. However, older forms of distribution such as e-mail and traditional websites still appear to be used by some.

The Internet allows for wider distribution of the images with global rather than local distribution. Cooper, Delmonico and Berg (2000) indicate that the 'Triple A Engine' of the internet (Accessibility, Affordability and Anonymity) greatly facilitate the distribution and consumption of child pornography. Gathering a collection of child pornography images is now easier and cheaper than before, and the offender has the added protection of perceived anonymity (Quayle, Vaughan & Taylor, 2006), as they do not need to contact a dealer in person and the individual can search for and collect images at home. Nevertheless, as police forces use newer technologies and have advanced powers to determine the geographical location of the IP address used by the offender, the anonymity provided by the internet is considerably reduced.

Prevalence of Child Pornography Online

It is very difficult to quantify the amount of child pornography online at any one time (Taylor & Quayle, 2003; Calder, 2004). There are several reasons for this. Firstly, child pornography distributors use a wide variety of distribution methods, including e-mail, websites, discussion groups, bulletin boards and peer-to-peer networks, and there can be considerable overlap between the content on these. Secondly, each of these sources can be quite transient, with distribution techniques constantly being added and removed in order to avoid being uncovered by authorities. For example, a distributor may set up a website with child pornography content which will be accessible for only a few hours or days. The website

may then be advertised using a less public technique, such as a discussion group, before being removed. The website will also likely be given a title and description that make it unlikely to be uncovered using simple search techniques. Finally, academic research which attempts to quantify the amount of child pornography is relatively rare, as some countries do not give legal protection to researchers attempting to study this area. As downloading and making child pornography can, in some jurisdictions, be considered equivalent in law, this can make researching this area quite perilous. When coupled with the potential trauma a researcher may experience when working with such upsetting images, most researchers choose to study a different topic.

Despite these issues, there have been several studies which have attempted to quantify the extent of internet child pornography. Early research by Mehta (2001) examined 9,800 images from 32 sexually oriented Usenet groups. Twenty percent of these images involved children or adolescents, although 5.1% of the images were of nude children who were not engaged in sexual activity. However, this research was completed in 1995 and 1996, and as such probably only reflects the early adopters of the internet for this purpose.

The most highly prized images on child pornography distribution rings are those of new children, and Taylor, Quayle and Holland (2001) found that each month, approximately two new children appeared on newsgroups, with over one thousand illegal photographs per week being posted. Renold et al (2003) found that over a six week period in 2002, child pornography images of twenty new children were posted, with a total of over 140,000 child images posted. Taylor and Quayle (2003) also noticed an increase in homemade production. It is unclear how many child abuse victims appear in child pornography. Cawson et al (2000) found that less than one percent of adults said that they had pornographic videos or photographs taken of them as children. Scott (2001) found that of a sample of thirty-six self-defined survivors of sexual abuse, only thirteen had been used in the development of pornographic content.

Research by Ropelato (2006) suggests that the child pornography industry is worth approximately $3 billion annually, and it should be remembered that many offenders involved in child pornography distribution may be solely motivated by financial gain. Ropelato also suggested that at the time, there were approximately 100,000 websites offering illegal child pornography. In October 2007, Interpol stated that the Child Abuse Image Database contained more than 512,000 images (Interpol, 2007 as cited by Elliott et al, 2009).

Siegfried, Lovely and Rogers (2008) completed an online survey regarding internet child pornography use, and found that 15.9% of the males and 5.5% of the females who responded to the survey had used child pornography. However, it should be remembered that this was a self-selecting sample, and it may not be an accurate reflection of the overall distribution of child pornography users online. Also, it is unclear as to exactly how the survey was distributed – while Siegfried et al indicate that they advertised the survey on chat rooms, bulletin boards and discussion forums, they do not indicate how they chose which of the countless examples of each of these that exist online to recruit from. Siegfried et al (2008) do admit that there may be individual differences between those who completed the survey and those who only completed part, or those who chose not to answer the survey at all. They are also aware that there may be volunteer bias, and that the information provided is not verifiable. With all this in mind, Siegfried et al's (2008) study is still a useful starting point in attempting to determine how many internet child pornography users there are.

Steel (2009) attempted to quantify the distribution and nature of child pornography on peer-to-peer networks by analyzing queries and query hits. The study found that while the most prevalent query was child pornography related, only 1% of all queries were related to the subject. Similarly while the top two most prevalent filenames returned as query hits were child pornography related, only 1.45% of all query hits were related to child pornography. This finding is consistent with a previous, smaller study by Hughes et al (2008).

Ratings of Material

As with adult pornography, there is considerable variation in the type of child pornography material available. The COPINE (Combating Paedophile Information Networks in Europe) project completed by University College Cork developed a database of child pornography and used it to develop a system by which the content could be rated. The material used was taken from sixty newsgroups, with images which could be defined as old (more than fifteen years since produced), recent (ten to fifteen years since produced) and new, which had been produced in the past ten years (Taylor, Quayle & Holland, 2001).

The COPINE project described ten levels of content (Taylor, Holland & Quayle, 2001). The first few levels would not normally lead to prosecution, and it is unlikely that pictures at levels 4 and 5 would be illegal (Jones, 2003)

- Level 1 is labelled 'Indicative'. These images are non-sexualised pictures, such as bathing costumes, and may be collected from commonly available sources such as clothing catalogues.
- Level 2 is labelled 'Nudist'. These images may be of naked or semi-naked children, but taken at legitimate nudist settings. For example, photographs of babies or children during bath time would often fall under Level 2.
- Level 3 is termed 'Erotica'. These are photos taken of naked or semi-clothed children which are taken surreptitiously.
- Level 4 is termed 'Posing', where the naked or semi-clothed children are deliberately posed, but not in sexualised postures.

- At Level 5, 'Erotic Posing' the child appears in a provocative or sexualised posture, in varying degrees of nakedness.
- Level 6, 'Explicit erotic posing', involves images that emphasise the child's genital areas
- In images at Level 7, 'Explicit sexual activity', there is sexual activity involving children (such as touching, masturbation or oral sex), but adults are not seen in the image
- Level 8 is labelled 'Assault', and involves a record of the child being assaulted by an adult using their fingers
- At Level 9, 'Gross assault', images may include penetrative sex, masturbation or oral sex with an adult.
- Finally, at Level 10, 'Sadistic/bestiality', the child is subjected to pain or there is sexual activity with an animal.

The COPINE scale remains one of the most exhaustive and detailed taxonomies of child pornographic content available, and has been adapted by other bodies, such as the United Kingdom's Sentencing Advisory Panel, who utilise the 'SAP Scale'. SAP uses a five point scale, with the following levels:

- *Level 1 - Images depicting erotic posing with no sexual activity*
- *Level 2 - Non-penetrative sexual activity between children, or solo masturbation by a child*
- *Level 3 - Non-penetrative sexual activity between adults and children*
- *Level 4 - Penetrative sexual activity involving a child or children, or both children and adults*
- *Level 5 - Sadism or penetration of, or by, an animal*

(Sentencing Guidelines Council, 2007, p. 109):

The panel also specifies that "Pseudo-photographs should generally be treated as less serious than real images. However, they can be just as serious as photographs of a real child, for example where the imagery is particularly grotesque and beyond the scope of normal photography." (Sentencing Guidelines Council, 2007, p. 109). As such, the guidelines also take into account the digitally produced or enhanced images which modern technology is capable of, and consider that these images can have other negative consequences, such as use in grooming of children for sexual behaviour, or the contentious issue of whether or not the use of child pornography is linked to child sexual assault.

BACKGROUND AND PSYCHOLOGY OF CHILD PORNOGRAPHY OFFENDERS

When considering the psychology of child pornography offenders, several issues are of concern. Primarily, these relate to being able to profile a collector or distributor of child pornography. In addition, a key argument in the literature also relates to whether those who use online pornography but have no history of contact offences are qualitatively different to those that have. Researchers have raised the question as to if these are two separate types of offenders, thus requiring different treatments and interventions, and posing related but largely separate risks to society, or if the use of child pornography might be a stepping stone for those who may later become contact offenders. Also of interest to psychologists are the cognitive distortions that these offenders use to justify their actions and behaviours.

Cognitive Distortions

Taylor and Quayle (2003) indicate that child pornography may be justified by the user through various distortions in thinking processes. Cognitive distortions in forensic contexts are "offence-supportive attitudes, cognitive processing during an offence sequence, as well as post-hoc neutralisations or excuses for offending" (Maruna & Mann, 2006, p. 155). Effectively they are the excuses and rationale that the offender provides themselves (and sometimes others) with, which justify the offending behaviour to themselves. It should be remembered that cognitive distortions are not always rational, and while the offender may feel that they are reasonable reasons for committing a crime, many others will find them unacceptable. While cognitive distortions are frequently associated with sexual offenders (see for example Ward & Casey, 2010; Marziano, Ward, Beech & Pattison, 2006; Thakker, Ward & Navathe, 2007) they can also be evident in other offenders, and even non-offending populations (see for example Sears & Kraus, 2009).

Howitt and Sheldon (2007) indicate that these types of cognitive distortions are held by a considerable number of both internet and contact offenders. A common cognitive distortion of child pornography users is the belief that the child is enjoying the experience, or that it is a natural behaviour for the child to engage in. Many child pornography images and videos are created to give the impression that the child enjoys the encounter, in order to encourage the sexual fantasy of the user. Thus the user may hold the cognitive distortion that the child is a willing participant, or that the child is being taught about their sexuality in an appropriate way. Other users may feel that as the image or video of the child already exists, and therefore the action has already been completed, that they are not harming the child or society by viewing and engaging with pornography. The offender may think that as long as they do not carry out the abuse themselves, or pay for the pornography, then they are not doing any real harm. Of course, there are several arguments against these distortions.

Taylor and Quayle (2003) describe how the demand created by users of child pornography fuels the market for new images and video, and hence leads to the victimisation of new children. They also describe how the trauma for the victim does not end following the production of the pornography, but is maintained for as long as the record exists. If the pornography is distributed online, it is also harder to destroy all the copies of the production, and the victim is unlikely to ever feel that they have eradicated all the evidence.

Quayle and Taylor (2002) indicate that it is possible that those who regularly view child pornography online may be fuelling a need to sexually abuse other children. It is possible that they become accustomed to the material, and begin to perceive it as a 'normal' behaviour, thus feeling justified in engaging in the behaviour themselves. However, other researchers such as Howitt and Cumberbatch (1990) and Seto et al (2001) argue that there is no evidence for this. The differences and link between contact and non-contact offenders will be returned to later in this chapter.

Finally, Burgess and Hartman (1987) describe how child pornography can be used to groom children into sexual abuse by densensitising them. As the child is exposed to numerous images of many children being abused, and apparently enjoying it, they may become easier targets of abuse themselves.

Thus while users of child pornography online may attempt to justify their behaviour through a variety of excuses, it is clear that there is a vicious circle of victimisation related to this offence, which may extend far beyond the original abuse victim. With this in mind, it is useful to consider the background and psychological profile of internet child pornography users and distributors.

Background and Online Behaviour of Offenders

While many individuals may feel that they would probably realize if they knew a person who views online child pornography, realistically there is no easy way to recognize such an offender (Wortley

& Smallbone, 2006). In fact, it is possible that having such a preconceived notion of what an internet child sex offender is like may be distracting for the police officers involved (Simon, 2000). However, despite this, there are some recurring findings regarding the characteristics of internet child pornography users.

Users of internet child pornography are predominately male (Frei, Erenay, Dittmann & Graf, 2005; Seto & Eke, 2005; Webb, Craissati & Keen, 2007) to the extent that some researchers have suggested that female child pornography consumers do not exist (Quayle, Erooga, Wright, Taylor & Harbinson, 2006). Conversely, as outlined earlier, Siegfried, Lovely and Rogers (2008) found that one in three of the internet child pornography users who responded to their online survey were female. Wortley and Smallbone (2006) note that offenders are more likely to be white, male and between the ages of 26 and 40. Siegfried, Lovely and Rogers (2008) found that 80% of child pornography users were 35 years of age or younger, with 63.3% being single, never married. They may also experience some symptoms of internet dependence (Blundell et al, 2002; Schneider, 2000).

The internet child pornography users are generally well educated. Riegel (2004) found that 77% of alleged child pornography consumers had graduated from college. Wolak, Finkelhor and Mitchell (2005) found that 38% of convicted child pornography consumers had completed high school. Burke, Sowerbutts, Blundell and Sherry (2002), Frei, Erenay, Dittman and Graf (2005) and O'Brien and Webster (2007) also generally found child pornography users to be in employment and/or highly educated. Siegfried, Lovely and Rogers (2008) found that 82.1% of the child pornography users who responded to their online survey had completed some level of college. Calder (2004) notes that judges, teachers, academics, dentists, rock stars, police officers and soldiers are among those who have been arrested for online child pornography crimes.

With regard to preferred content, Steel (2009) found that the median age searched for on peer-to-peer networks was thirteen years old. Most queries were gender neutral, but of those that did specify a gender-related term, the majority (79%) were female oriented. Most searches were for movies (at 99%), but still images were more prevalent in availability. Quayle and Taylor (2002) indicate that users of child pornography are very specific in the type of images they seek, with their preferences typically corresponding to preexisting sexual fantasies. Thus a child pornography consumer may only be interested in images of children of a particular gender and age, with certain eye, skin and hair colour, engaging in specific behaviours.

Krone (2004) suggests a typology of nine categories of offending in internet child pornography, depending on factors such as their interaction with other offenders, their involvement in the creation and distribution of the material and their expertise in avoiding detection. The categories include:

- Browsers, who save images of child pornography they happen across online but do not interact with other offenders
- Trawlers, who actively seek out images, and may engage in some networking with other offenders
- Secure collectors, who engage in high levels of security behaviours and are often members of secure child pornography rings. Their collecting can reach obsession level.
- Non-secure collectors, who use non-secure sources and open content. They engage in high levels of networking, but do not employ security strategies.
- Physical abusers, who sexually abuse children and who may record these abuses for personal use, but also seek other child pornography online
- Producers, who create child pornography for the purpose of disseminating it to others, rather than for personal use.

- Distributers, who are involved in disseminating abuse images – sometimes just for financial reasons.
- Private fantasisers, who create digital images using electronic means, such as morphing photographs, for personal use.
- Groomers, who send child pornography to other children online in order to try to initiate a sexual relationship with them.

These categories are not mutually exclusive, and an offender in one category (such as non-secure collectors) may also be classifiable in another category (such as groomers). While it is estimated that between one-fifth and one-third of users of child pornography before the internet were also involved in child sex offending (Dobson, 2003; Wellard, 2001), it is now much easier for individuals to seek out these stimuli. As such it is possible that the advent of the Internet may encourage more casual users of child pornography (Wortley & Smallbone, 2006), who may not be involved in contact offending. Krone's taxonomy, while useful for classification purposes, does not inform us greatly about the psychology behind each type of offender, or the potential evolution of an offender from one typology to another. Nonetheless, Krone's taxonomy does aid in distinguishing between internet only offenders and contact offenders, which provides a useful starting point for considering the personality differences between these two types of offender.

Personality of Internet Child Pornography Offenders

Until relatively recently, there had been little empirical work done examining the psychology of internet child pornography offenders. However, literature did exist relating to the personality of consumers of pornography offline (see Fisher & Barak, 2001) which is of use for comparative purposes. More recently, there have been a number of studies which have attempted to determine the psychometric traits of internet child pornography offenders, in comparison to both contact offenders and non-offenders. Quayle and Taylor (2002) completed one of the first studies in this area, and interviewed thirteen men convicted of downloading child pornography about the photographs they accessed. They found that the Internet plays an important role for users in increasing sexual arousal to child pornography, while also distancing the respondent from personal agency and facilitating the objectification of children.

Siegfried, Lovely and Rogers (2008) compared those who used internet child pornography with those who did not on a number of personality measures. The internet child pornography users demonstrated higher exploitive-manipulative amoral dishonesty (EMAD) traits than non-offenders. They also displayed lower scores on internal moral choice than non-offenders. This result suggests that they do not have the same personal, moral compass that non-users do when determining right from wrong, despite being aware of society's laws or regulations regarding the same issue. As such, while they might recognize the use of child pornography as illegal and unacceptable socially, they may not believe it is immoral for them personally. However, other psychological factors, including moral choice hedonistic values, moral choice social values, extraversion, neuroticism, openness to experience, agreeableness, and conscientiousness, were not found to be significantly related to child pornography use. Unfortunately, it is uncertain how reliable these results are due to the relatively small number of child pornography users in the sample (thirty) and the fact that respondents self-selected to complete an online survey.

With regard to the Ward and Siegert (2002) pathways model of paedophilic behaviour (see Chapter 8), Middleton, Elliott, Mandeville-Norden and Beech (2006) attempted to assign internet offenders to one of the four pathways. They found that most of the offenders were assigned to either the intimacy deficits or emotional dysregulation pathways, but that about 40% of the sample showed deficits indicative of more than one pathway, and so could not be clearly assigned to any one of the pathways. Those in the emotional dysregulation pathway were more likely to use child pornography as a mood altering strategy when in a negative mood. While the study has been criticized for not including a social desirability measure, and for the questionable lack of evidence found for deviant arousal or cognitive distortions (Elliott et al, 2009), the finding is supported by Quayle, Vaughan and Taylor (2006) who also indicate that "for some offenders, but not all, accessing images on the Internet may function as a way of avoiding or dealing with difficult emotional states" (p. 10).

Webb, Craissati and Keen (2007) compared ninety internet sex offenders with 120 contact child sex offenders. They found that both types of offenders had experienced childhood difficulties, although the contact offenders were more likely to have experienced physical child abuse. The internet offenders were predominately white, compared to more mixed ethnicity of contact offenders, and the internet offenders were significantly younger than the contact offenders. While Webb et al (2007) found no major differences between the groups in personality or mental health functioning, more internet offenders had contact with mental health services, and they had fewer live-in relationships than contact offenders. Both groups demonstrated relatively high levels of self-reported pathology, and forty percent reported having a personality disorder, specifically schizoid, avoidant and dependent behaviours. The internet offenders had fewer previous sexual convictions, and they were significantly less likely to reoffend over eighteen months than contact offenders.

Laulik, Allam and Sheridan (2007) compared internet sex offenders to the normal population and found that they differed with regard to warmth, dominance and depression on the Personality Assessment Inventory (PAI), with internet offenders possibly experiencing deficits in interpersonal functioning and affective difficulties. They also found significant correlations between the PAI scales assessing schizophrenia, borderline features, depression and warmth and the hours per week spent accessing child pornography. These findings lend further support to the previous findings that internet sex offenders appear to have specific psychological difficulties, and may help in the design of appropriate treatment measures.

Reijnen, Bulten and Nijman (2009) carried out a study of twenty-two internet child pornography offenders, examining their backgrounds, characteristics and profiles on the Minnesota Multiphasic Personality Inventory (MMPI), a commonly used psychometric scale of a wide variety of psychological traits. The child pornography users were compared to a control sample of 112 offenders of other crimes. When compared to other sexual offenders, the child pornography users were younger, more likely to be single, and in most cases lived alone with no children. Reijnen et al do note that these variables are associated with each other – younger men are less likely to be married with children than older ones. Interestingly Reijnen found no specific differences between the child pornography offenders and other offenders on the MMPI.

Elliott, Beech, Mandeville-Norden and Hayes (2009) compared large samples of internet (N = 505) and contact (526) sex offenders on a variety of psychological traits. While contact offenders had more cognitive distortions and victim empathy distortions, the internet offenders identified more with fictional characters and had increased scores on scales of fantasy and underassertiveness. The contact offenders also showed increased scores on locus of control, perspective taking, overassertiveness, empathic concern and cognitive impulsivity. This research adds further support to the evidence that internet and contact sex offenders are qualitatively different personality types.

Bates and Metcalf (2007) compared internet and contact sex offenders, and also found that the internet offenders scored higher rates of underassertiveness (but that this was not statistically significant) and lower scores on locus of control. The internet offenders also had higher rates of socially desirable responding, and lower scores on sexualized attitudes towards children, emotional congruence with children and empathy distortions with regard to victims of child abuse. With regard to cognitive differences, both Burke, Sowerbutts, Blundell and Sherry (2002) and O'Brien and Webster (2007) found higher scores of intelligence in internet child pornography offenders compared to contact offenders.

Several studies have investigated the use of child pornography by contact offenders. Kingston, Fedoroff, Firestone, Curry and Bradford (2008) found that the use of illegal pornography was a risk factor for contact offending. However, Howitt (1995) disagreed, and concluded that an association between contact offences and use of child pornography could not be established, as the contact offenders he examined reported that they not only used child pornography but also cognitively manipulated legal adult pornography. Neither Kingston et al's (2008) study, nor Howitt's (1995) study allows a causal inference to be made, as both studies only examined contact offenders, rather than a general sample of child pornography users. As such, the studies do not allow us to predict that all child pornography users will go on to become contact offenders. There are also conflicting findings. Smallbone and Wortley (2000) found that only about ten percent of those convicted of sexually abusing children also use and collect child pornography.

Riegel (2004) attempted to determine if paedophiles felt that child pornography increased their desire for contact offences with children. The majority of the respondents to their online study, who self-identified as 'Boy-Attracted Paedosexual Males', indicated that the material 'rarely' or 'never' increased that desire. However, this study may be critically flawed in that the study asked participants to self-report, and there may be a strong element of altering responses due to social desirability. Seto, Cantor, and Blanchard (2006) discovered that use of child pornography

is a better diagnostic indicator of sexual attraction to children than actual contact offending is. The majority of the child pornography consumers they studied, whether or not they had previous convictions for contact offences, showed greater sexual arousal to child pornography than did a group of contact offenders. Buschman (2007) interviewed a clinical sample of child pornography users, most of whom admitted to being sexually aroused by children.

Other studies, such as Frei, Erenay, Dittmann and Graf (2005) found that none of their sample of child pornography consumers had a criminal record, and that the use of child pornography greatly exceeds the prevalence of child sexual abuse. While this of course does not account for any offences they may have committed but had not been arrested and convicted of, nor the possibility that the offenders may have gone on to commit contact offences in the future, it does lend some evidence to the possibility that not all users of child pornography are engaged in contact offending. However, conflicting findings are reported by Bourke and Hernandez (2009) who compared child pornography offenders with and without contact sex offence convictions. They found that the internet child pornography consumers were significantly more likely than not to have sexually abused a child. However, the internet child pornography users in Bourke and Hernandez's sample had self-selected to engage in a treatment programme, and it is possible that this is indicative of a different type of offender than those who would not engage in contact offences.

Endrass et al (2009) therefore indicate that the best research design in order to determine if child pornography use can predict future contact offending requires a longitudinal study of a sample of users of child pornography. Seto and Eke (2005) completed such a study, and found that less than one in four of their sample of convicted child pornography consumers had been convicted of a contact offence. Seto and Eke (2005) also found that recidivism rates were low at a 30 month follow up.

To conclude, the literature and research in this area is quite conflicting, but overall there does not seem to be definitive evidence of a causal link between consumption of child pornography and the committing of contact offences. Nevertheless, as has already been noted, the victim of child pornography may still be further victimized due to the continued presence of the material online, and the psychological effects of this victimization will now be considered.

PSYCHOLOGY OF VICTIMS

Lanning (2001) emphasizes that even though a child pornography consumer may never become a contact offender, they still "play a role in the sexual exploitation of children" (p. 86). The user may be willing to pay considerable amounts of money for a suitable image, and in some cases users may request a specific type of image or video, which will later be produced for them. Even if they are not fuelling the industry financially, the user may be contributing to the survival of the online society through other means, such as encouraging other users' beliefs that the behaviour is acceptable, or by forwarding images from their collection for free. But the psychological effect on each of the children portrayed in the images should not be underestimated. This section will not consider the psychological effects of the actual sexual abuse itself, but rather will consider the effects of the continued existence and distribution of the material on the victim of abuse.

In many cases the producer of the child pornography is a trusted adult, such as the father. The fact that the child is rarely abducted (Wortley & Smallbone, 2006; Taylor & Quayle, 2003) would support this. Most children portrayed in child pornography productions have not been physically forced to participate (Lanning & Burgess, 1989), but they can still experience severe physical, psychological and social effects (Klain, Davies & Hicks, 2001). The victim's initial psychological

distress can last for many years (Silbert, 1989), due in part to the fact that the production of the pornography results in a permanent record of the abuse (Calcetas-Santos, 2001). Frequently a child will not disclose their abuse, because of fear of the abuser's reaction, and/or shame regarding their part in the incident (Silbert, 1989), to the extent that most children involved are identified through investigation rather than disclosure (Taylor & Quayle, 2003).

Taylor and Quayle (2003) also emphasise the ongoing nature of the abuse created by the existence of the pornography, and indicate that the abuse will continue for as long as the pornographic material exists. As the internet allows multiple copies of the material to be produced quickly and cheaply, and the material can easily be distributed to any networked computer worldwide, it becomes difficult or impossible for the victim to know for sure if all evidence of the abuse has been removed. As such, it is not surprising that these victims encounter symptoms in addition to those experienced by survivors of child sexual abuse that have not been used for pornographic production. Silbert (1989) noted that victims' initial feelings of shame and anxiety intensified as time passed, sometimes being replaced with feelings of deep despair, worthlessness and hopelessness. Silbert also noted that their victimization left them with difficulties in forming normal sexual relationships as adults, as well as a distorted model of sexuality.

Overall, there appears to have been little research completed in response to Taylor and Quayle's (2003) conclusion that there is a dearth of empirical knowledge available regarding the long-term consequences for victims of internet child pornography. There is, however, some anecdotal evidence of these effects. O'Donnell and Milner (2007, p. 71) quote 'Sandra':

"When I was four years old until I was fifteen I was taken to people's houses as a child prostitute. Pictures were also taken of me... After it was over and I would go home I was always worried and

scared where those pictures would wind up, and who would see me. I still have those same concerns at age thirty. Those pictures could be anywhere."

Taylor and Quayle (2003) indicate that "Victim issues need to be at the very top of the agenda in both investigations and social welfare or probation interventions" (p. 210). However, to date, there appears to be relatively little focus on the victims of internet child pornography, with greater emphasis being placed on discovering methods to identify offenders and gather appropriate forensic evidence.

PUNISHMENT AND REHABILITATION OF OFFENDERS

A major role for forensic psychologists involves the development and provision of rehabilitation programmes for many types of offenders, including sex offenders. In this regard, a key question relating to child pornography use is if such a treatment programme is required, and if so, how could it be designed. Endrass et al (2009) examined the recidivism rates for Internet child pornography users, and found that at a six year follow up, only three percent of the sample had recidivated with a violent and/or sex offence, although a slightly larger group of nearly four percent had recidivated with a non-contact sex offence. Less than one percent had recidivated with a contact sex offence. As such, Endrass et al (2009) conclude that it is unlikely that internet child sex offenders would re-offend. This would indicate that the development and implementation of a treatment programme for internet child pornography users may not be the most suitable use of available funds.

Public perception of the severity of the offence can have a significant impact on how the offender is treated. Lam, Mitchell and Seto (2010) investigated how university students perceived the offence and possession of child pornography.

They found that the possession offence was rated as more severe depending on the child's age, with younger victims being seen as more serious offences. While the age and gender of the offender did not impact perceptions of risk severity, male offenders were considered to be at higher risk of recidivism. As has been previously stated, many jurisdictions do not distinguish between the manufacture or distribution of child pornography, and the possession of it. As a result of this, there have been cases of extremely lengthy sentences being handed out for relatively minor offences. For example, in Arizona, there is a mandatory minimum sentence of ten years for sexual exploitation of a minor. As a result of this, one Arizona man who was found in possession of twenty child pornography images received a two hundred year sentence. While taking into account the ongoing effects on victims outlined above, it is still questionable as to whether or not such a lengthy sentence is an appropriate use of expensive and limited prison resources, given the relatively low recidivism rates noted.

Similarly, there seems to be high levels of public support for sex offender treatment (Mears et al, 2008). However, to date the assessment and treatment programmes used for internet child sex offenders tend to be adapted from generic sex offender programmes (Middleton, 2004). This is based on the assumption that the internet offenders have similar traits and risk factors to other sex offenders, specifically interpersonal functioning, deviant sexual arousal, general self-regulation problems, and offense-supportive cognitions (Beech, 1998; Beech & Ward, 2004; Hanson & Harris, 2000; Thornton, 2002). Given the differences already noted between internet and contact sex offenders, it is possible that this may not be the most appropriate treatment approach. However, there has been relatively little research completed evaluating the treatment programmes for Internet child pornography users (Middleton, 2004) although Middleton (2009) suggests that despite the absence of "reliable offence-specific research, practitioners" (p. 212) a reliance on literature and findings relating to contact child sex offenders is a valid approach. Middleton (2009) suggests that there is enough overlap of predisposing factors in contact and internet offenders to suggest that, for at least the time being, similar assessment tools can be used for both groups.

Middleton (2008) describes the development of the Internet Sex Offender Treatment Programme (i-SOTP), which aims to prevent further viewing behaviour and escalation to contact offending. It includes steps to:

- *Increase motivation, decrease denial and identify and reduce discrepancy between perceived pro-social values and behaviour (addressing distorted attitudes)*
- *Challenge offence-supportive attitudes and behaviours (addressing distorted attitudes)*
- *Build an empathic response to identifying that children depicted in the indecent images are real victims of child abuse (addressing distorted attitudes and socio-affective functioning).*
- *Reduce use of sex as a strategy for coping and emotional avoidance, replacing it with effective problem-solving strategies (addressing socio-affective functioning and self-management).*
- *Develop adequate relationship, intimacy and coping skills; improve self-esteem and internal locus of control (social adequacy factors and self-management).*
- *Develop realistic relapse-prevention strategies and new pro-social lifestyle goals (addressing self-management and socio-affective functioning).* (Middleton, 2008, p 57-58)

The i-SOTP is run individually in ninety minute sessions. Between twenty and thirty sessions are required. A variation of the programme to be run in groups was also developed. In late 2006 the i-SOTP was given accreditation for use in the community by the National Probation Service of England and Wales. Middleton, Mandeville-Norden and Hayes (2009) report on the effectiveness of the programme on a sample of 264 convicted offenders, indicating that the programme improved socio-affective functioning and decreased pro-offending attitudes. While this indicates good support for the programme, it is yet to be seen how effective it is in reducing recidivism rates.

Overall, while there have been some recent advances in the rehabilitation of internet child pornography users, it is difficult as yet to determine their effectiveness in reducing recidivism, and without a complete understanding of the psychology of the offenders involved, it is uncertain that the interventions are targeting the appropriate behaviours.

FUTURE TRENDS AND RESEARCH

While internet child pornography is one of the online offences which has generated the most research from psychologists to date, it is evident that there is still a vast quantity of knowledge missing from the literature. It is clear that the problem of child pornography online will not be solved soon, as the producers and distributors find new methods of circulating the material as new online technologies develop – they have already moved from Usenet groups to websites to file-sharing networks and it is likely that they will evolve and change with future developments too. One of the key difficulties for police forces involves determining new methods of intercepting disseminations as quickly as possible after they are devised.

From a psychological perspective, the conflicting findings regarding the influence of pornography viewing on contact offences is worrying. There have been few longitudinal studies examining the process, and most studies to date rely heavily on self-reporting of offending from participants. Greater understanding is required of the psychological profiles of the two groups, and in particular attention should be placed on those who engage in either viewing or contact offences, but not both, in order to understand the key differences and similarities between the groups. With this knowledge, more precise assessment and intervention techniques can be developed, with greater confidence of their effectiveness. In addition to this, follow-up research on the effectiveness of the i-SOTP, along with an assessment of recidivism rates, is required. It would be useful to know if this programme demonstrates more effectiveness than standard sex offender treatment programmes that have been modified for use with internet offenders.

Finally, the dearth of academic research investigating the effects of victimisation is disappointing, especially as the rights of the victim have been identified as so crucial by key researchers such as Taylor and Quayle (2003). While completing research in this area would not be a simple task to undertake, it would inform therapeutic processes for these individuals. In particular, attention should be focused on the additional trauma that child pornography victims experience in relation to those who are abused without a record being made. It would also be helpful if it could be predicted what characteristics would put a child at increased risk of this victimisation, so that additional efforts could be made to protect these individuals. Researchers and policy makers should also consider if it is appropriate and helpful to inform children that child pornography exists as part of stay-safe programmes in order to prevent child predators from using the images during the grooming process. However, if implemented, this would need to be done extremely carefully and sensitively.

CONCLUSION

While internet child pornography is a major concern for much of society, much of the psychological research to date has been inconclusive or contradictory. While this is understandable given the difficulty of studying the topic and the evolution of the offenders involved, it is important that more stringent research designs are developed, particularly in relation to comparing contact and internet-only offenders. To date, the evidence linking these two types of offenders is insufficient to allow a concrete conclusion to be drawn, and it cannot be said with certainty if viewers of child pornography online are truly at higher risk of going on to sexually abuse children offline. If this research was completed, it would then better equip psychologists to effectively treat and assess child sex offenders. On the other hand, the question of the impact of online child pornography on the victim also requires urgent attention, so that appropriate help can be provided to these individuals. Despite the relatively high quantity of psychological publications relating to internet child pornography, there is still a great deal of work to be done if we are to claim that we completely understand the phenomenon.

REFERENCES

Bates, A., & Metcalf, C. (2007). A psychometric comparison of internet and non-internet sex offenders from a community treatment sample. *Journal of Sexual Aggression*, *13*, 11–20. doi:10.1080/13552600701365654

BBC News (2010, August 26). *Facebook child abuse images ringleader jailed*. Retrieved from http://www.bbc.co.uk/news/uk-england-11101149

Beech, A. R. (1998). A psychometric typology of child abusers. *International Journal of Therapy and Comparative Criminology*, *42*, 319–339. doi:10.1177/0306624X9804200405

Beech, A. R., & Ward, T. (2004). The integration of etiology and risk in sex offenders: A theoretical model. *Aggression and Violent Behavior*, *10*, 31–63. doi:10.1016/j.avb.2003.08.002

Blundell, B., Sherry, M., Burke, A., & Sowerbutts, S. (2002). Child Pornography and the Internet: Accessibility and Policing. *Australian Police Journal*, *56*(1), 59–65.

Bourke, M. L., & Hernandez, A. E. (2009). The 'Butner Study' Redux: A report of the incidence of hands-on child victimization by child pornography offenders. *Journal of Family Violence*, *24*, 183–191. doi:10.1007/s10896-008-9219-y

Burgess, A. W., & Hartman, C. (1987). Child abuse aspects of child pornography. *Psychiatric Annals*, 248–253.

Burke, A., Sowerbutts, S., Blundell, B., & Sherry, M. (2002). Child Pornography and the Internet: Policing and Treatment Issues. *Psychiatry, Psychology and Law*, *9*, 79–84. doi:10.1375/pplt.2002.9.1.79

Buschman, J. (2007). *The position of child pornography in sex offending: First Dutch polygraph findings.* Poster presented at the 26th Annual Conference of the Association for the Treatment of Sexual Abusers, San Diego, CA.

Calcetas-Santos, O. (2001). Child pornography on the internet. In Arnaldo, C. A. (Ed.), *Child abuse on the internet* (pp. 57–60). Paris: UNESCO.

Calder, M. (2004). *Child Sexual Abuse and the Internet: Tackling the New Frontier. Lyme Regis.* United Kingdom: Russell House Publishing.

Cawson, P., Wattam, C., Brooker, S., & Kelly, G. (2000). *Child Maltreatment in the UK: A Study of the Prevalence of Child Abuse and Neglect.* London: NSPCC.

Cooper, A., Delmonico, D.L. & Burg, R. (2000). Cybersex users, abusers, and compulsives: New findings and implications. *Cybersex: The dark side of the force A special issue of the Journal of Sexual Addiction & Compulsivity, 7,* 5-27.

Dobson, A. (2003). Caught in the Net. *Care and Health*, Feb. 13 pp. 6–9.

Elliott, I. A., Beech, A. R., Mandeville-Norden, R., & Hayes, E. (2009). Psychological profiles of internet sexual offenders: Comparisons with contact sexual offenders. *Sexual Abuse, 21,* 76–92. doi:10.1177/1079063208326929

Endrass, J., Urbaniok, F., Hammermeister, L. C., Benz, C., Elbert, T., Laubacher, A., & Rossegger, A. (2009). The consumption of Internet child pornography and violent and sex offending. *BMC Psychiatry*, *9*, 43..doi:10.1186/1471-244X-9-43

Fisher, W., & Barak, A. (2001). Internet pornography: A social psychological perspective on internet sexuality. *Journal of Sex Research*, *38*(4), 312–323. doi:10.1080/00224490109552102

Frei, A., Erenay, N., Dittmann, V., & Graf, M. (2005). Paedophilia on the internet – a study of 33 convicted offenders in the Canton of Lucerne. *Swiss Medical Weekly, 135,* 488–494.

Greenhouse, L. (2007, February 27). Justices decline case on 200-year sentence for man who possessed child pornography. *The New York Times,* p. A13.

Hanson, R. K., & Harris, A. J. R. (2000). Where should we intervene? Dynamic predictors of sexual offense recidivism. *Criminal Justice and Behavior, 27,* 6–35. doi:10.1177/0093854800027001002

Howitt, D. (1995). Pornography and the paedophile: Is it criminogenic? *The British Journal of Medical Psychology*, *68*, 15–27. doi:10.1111/j.2044-8341.1995.tb01810.x

Howitt, D., & Cumberbatch, G. (1990). *Pornography: Impacts and Influences. A Review of Available Research Evidence on the Effects of Pornography.* London: Home Office Research and Planning Unit.

Howitt, D., & Sheldon, K. (2007). The role of cognitive distortions in paedophilic offending: Internet and contact offenders compared. *Psychology, Crime & Law*, *13*, 469–486. doi:10.1080/10683160601060564

Hughes, D., Rayson, P., Walkerdine, J., Lee, K., Greenwood, P., Rashid, A., et al. (2008). *Supporting law enforcement in digital communities through natural language analysis.* In Proceedings of IWCF'08 Washington, DC, USA, August, 2008

Jones, T. (2003). Child abuse or computer crime? The proactive approach. In MacVean, A., & Spindler, P. (Eds.), *Policing paedophiles on the Internet. John Grieve Centre for policing and Community Safety.* Bristol: The New Police Bookshop.

Kingston, D. A., Fedoroff, P., Firestone, P., Curry, S., & Bradford, J. M. (2008). Pornography use and sexual aggression: the impact of frequency and type of pornography use on recidivism among sexual offenders. *Aggressive Behavior, 34,* 341–351. doi:10.1002/ab.20250

Klain, E., Davies, H., & Hicks, M. (2001). *Child Pornography: The Criminal-Justice-System Response.* Washington, D.C.: National Center for Missing & Exploited Children. www.missingkids.com/en_US/publications/NC81.pdf.

Krone, T. (2004). *A Typology of Online Child Pornography Offending.* Trends & Issues in Crime and Criminal Justice, No. 279. Canberra: Australian Institute of Criminology. www.aic.gov.au/publications/tandi2/tandi279.pdf.

Lam, A., Mitchell, J., & Seto, M. C. (2010). Lay Perceptions of Child Pornography Offenders. *Canadian Journal of Criminology and Criminal Justice, 52,* 173–201. doi:10.3138/cjccj.52.2.173

Lanning, K. (2001). *Child Molesters: A Behavioral Analysis* (4th ed.), Washington, DC: National Center for Missing and Exploited Children. Retrieved June 23, 2010 from http://www.ncmec.org/en_US/publications/ NC70.pdf

Lanning, K., & Burgess, A. (1989). Child Pornography and Sex Rings. In Zillmann, D., & Bryant, J. (Eds.), *Pornography: Research Advances & Policy Considerations.* Hillsdale, New Jersey: Lawrence Erlbaum.

Laulik, S., Allam, J., & Sheridan, L. (2007). An investigation into maladaptive personality functioning in Internet sex offenders. *Psychology, Crime & Law, 13,* 523–535. doi:10.1080/10683160701340577

Maruna, S., & Mann, R. E. (2006). A fundamental attribution error? Rethinking cognitive distortions. *Legal and Criminological Psychology, 11,* 155–177..doi:10.1348/135532506X114608

Marziano, V., Ward, T., Beech, A. R., & Pattison, P. (2006). Identification of five fundamental implicit theories underlying cognitive distortions in child abusers: A preliminary study. *Psychology, Crime & Law, 12,* 97–105.. doi:10.1080/10683160500056887

Mears, D. P., Mancini, C., Gertz, M., & Bratton, J. (2008). Sex Crimes, Children and Pornography: Public Views and Public Policy. *Crime and Delinquency, 54,* 532–559. doi:10.1177/0011128707308160

Mehta, M. D. (2001). Pornography in Usenet: a study of 9,800 randomly selected images. *Cyberpsychology & Behavior, 4,* 695–703. doi:10.1089/109493101753376641

Middleton, D. (2004). Current treatment approaches. In Calder, M. (Ed.), *Child sexual abuse and the Internet: Tackling the new frontier* (pp. 99–112). Lyme Regis, UK: Russell House Publishing.

Middleton, D. (2008). From Research to practice: The development of the internet sex offender treatment programme (i-SOTP). *Irish Probation Journal, 5,* 49–64.

Middleton, D. (2009). Internet Sex Offenders. In Beech, A. R., Craig, L., & Browne, K. D. (Eds.), *Assessment and treatment of sex offenders: A handbook* (pp. 199–215). Chichester: Wiley.

Middleton, D., Elliott, I. A., Mandeville-Norden, R., & Beech, A. R. (2006). An investigation into the application of the Ward and Siegert pathways model of child sexual abuse with Internet offenders. *Psychology, Crime & Law, 12,* 589–603. doi:10.1080/10683160600558352

Middleton, D., Mandeville-Norden, R., & Hayes, E. (2009). Does treatment work with internet sex offenders? Emerging findings from the internet sex offender treatment programme (i-SOTP). *Journal of Sexual Aggression, 15,* 5–19. doi:10.1080/13552600802673444

O'Brien, M. D., & Webster, S. D. (2007). The construction and preliminary validation of the Internet Behaviours and Attitudes Questionnaire (IBAQ). *Sexual Abuse, 19,* 237–256. doi:10.1177/107906320701900305

O'Donnell, I. & Milner, C. (2007). *Child Pornography: Crime, Computers and Society.* Cullompton, Devon: Willan Publishing.

Quayle, E., Erooga, M., Wright, L., Taylor, M., & Harbinson, D. (2006). Abuse Images and the Internet. In *Only Pictures? Therapeutic work with Internet sex offenders.* Edited by: Quayle E, Erooga M, Wright L, Taylor M, Harbinson D. Lyme Regis: Russell House Publishing Ltd; 2006:1-11.

Quayle, E., & Taylor, M. (2001). Child Seduction and Self-Representation on the Internet. *Cyberpsychology & Behavior, 4*(5), 597–608. doi:10.1089/109493101753235197

Quayle, E., & Taylor, M. (2002). Child pornography and the Internet: perpetuating a cycle of abuse. *Deviant Behaviour: An Interdisciplinary Journal, 23,* 365–395.

Quayle, E., Vaughan, M., & Taylor, M. (2006). Sex offenders, internet child abuse images and emotional avoidance: The importance of values. *Aggression and Violent Behavior, 11,* 1–11. doi:10.1016/j.avb.2005.02.005

Reijnen, L., Bulten, E., & Nijman, H. (2009). Demographic and Personality Characteristics of Internet Child Pornography Downloaders in Comparison to Other offenders. *Journal of Child Sexual Abuse, 18,* 611–622. doi:10.1080/10538710903317232

Renold, E., Creighton, S. J., Atkinson, C., & Carr, J. (2003). *Images of Abuse: A Review of the Evidence on Child Pornography.* London: The National Society for the Prevention of Cruelty to Children.

Riegel, D. L. (2004). Effects on boy-attracted pedosexual males of viewing boy erotica. *Archives of Sexual Behavior, 33,* 321–323. doi:10.1023/B:ASEB.0000029071.89455.53

Ropelato, J. (2006). *Internet Pornography Statistics.* Retrieved June 23, 2010, from Internet Filter Review Web Site: http://internet-filter-review.toptenreviews.com/internet-pornography-statistics.html

Schneider, J. P. (2000). Effects of Cybersex Addiction on the Family: Results of a Survey. In Cooper, A. (Ed.), *Cybersex: The Dark Side of the Force.* New York: Brunner/Mazel.

Scott, S. (2001). *The Politics and Experience of Ritual Abuse. Beyond Disbelief.* Buckingham: Open University Press.

Sears, S., & Kraus, S. (2009). I think therefore I am: cognitive distortions and coping style as mediators for the effects of mindfulness meditation on anxiety, positive and negative affect, and hope. *Journal of Clinical Psychology, 65,* 561–573.. doi:10.1002/jclp.20543

Sentencing Guidelines Council. (2007). *Sexual Offences Act 2003: Definitive Guideline.* April 2007. Retrieved 5th July 2010 from http://www.sentencing-guidelines.gov.uk/ docs/0000_SexualOffencesAct1.pdf

Seto, M., Maric, A., & Barbaree, H. (2001). The role of pornography in the etiology of sexual aggression. *Aggression and Violent Behavior, 6*, 35–53. doi:10.1016/S1359-1789(99)00007-5

Seto, M. C., Cantor, J. M., & Blanchard, R. (2006). Child pornography offenses are a valid diagnostic indicator of pedophilia. *Journal of Abnormal Psychology, 115*, 610–615. doi:10.1037/0021-843X.115.3.610

Seto, M. C., & Eke, A. W. (2005). The criminal histories and later offending of child pornography offenders. *Sexual Abuse, 17*, 201–210. doi:10.1177/107906320501700209

Sheldon, K., & Howitt, D. (2007). *Sex Offenders and the Internet*. Chichester: Wiley.

Siegfried, K. C., Lovely, R. W., & Rogers, M. K. (2008). Self-Reported Online Child Pornography Behaviour: A Psychological Analysis. *International Journal of Cyber Criminology, 2*, 286–297.

Silbert, M. (1989). The Effects on Juveniles of Being Used for Pornography and Prostitution. In Zillmann, D., & Bryant, J. (Eds.), *Pornography: Research Advances & Policy Considerations*. Hillsdale, New Jersey: Lawrence Erlbaum.

Simon, L. (2000). An Examination of the Assumptions of Specialization, Mental Disorder, and Dangerousness in Sex Offenders. *Behavioral Sciences & the Law, 18*, 275–308. doi:10.1002/1099-0798(200003/06)18:2/3<275::AID-BSL393>3.0.CO;2-G

Sky News. (October 31, 2007). *Paedophiles target Virtual World*. Retrieved 6th July 2010 from http://news.sky.com/skynews/Home/Sky-News-Archive/Article/20080641290719

Smallbone, S., & Wortley, R. (2000). *Child Sexual Abuse in Queensland: Offender Characteristics and Modus Operandi*. Brisbane: Queensland Crime Commission.

Steel, C. M. S. (2009). Child pornography in peer-to-peer networks. *Child Abuse & Neglect, 33*, 560–568. doi:10.1016/j.chiabu.2008.12.011

Tate, T. (1990). *Child Pornography: An Investigation*. London: Methuen.

Taylor, M., Holland, G., & Quayle, E. (2001). Typology of paedophile picture collections. *The Police Journal, 74*, 97–107.

Taylor, M., & Quayle, E. (2003). *Child Pornography: An Internet Crime*. Hove: Brunner-Routledge.

Taylor, M., Quayle, E., & Holland, G. (2001). Child pornography, the Internet and offending, ISUMA. *The Canadian Journal of Policy Research, 2*, 94–100.

Thakker, J., Ward, T., & Navathe, S. (2007). The Cognitive Distortions and Implicit Theories of Child Sexual Abusers. In Gannon, T. A., Ward, T., Beech, A. R., & Fisher, D. (Eds.), *Aggressive Offenders' Cognition: Theory, Research and Practice* (pp. 11–29). Chichester, West Sussex: John Wiley & Sons Ltd. doi:10.1002/9780470746295.ch1

Thornton, D. (2002). Constructing and testing a framework for dynamic risk assessment. *Sexual Abuse, 14*, 139–154. doi:10.1177/107906320201400205

Ward, T., & Casey, A. (2009). Extending the mind into the world: A new theory of cognitive distortions in sex offenders. *Aggression and Violent Behavior, 15*, 49–58. doi:10.1016/j.avb.2009.08.002

Ward, T., & Siegert, R. J. (2002). Toward a comprehensive theory of child sexual abuse: A theory knitting perspective. *Psychology, Crime & Law, 8*, 319–351. doi:10.1080/10683160208401823

Webb, L., Craissati, J., & Keen, S. (2007). Characteristics of Internet Child Pornography Offenders: A Comparison with Child Molesters. *Sexual Abuse, 19*, 449–465.

Wellard, S.S. (2001). Cause and Effect. *Community Care,* March 15–21, pp. 26–27.

Wolak, J., Finkelhor, D., & Mitchell, K. J. (2005). *Child-Pornography Possessors Arrested in Internet-Related Crimes: Findings From the National Juvenile Online Victimization Study.* Alexandria: National Center for Missing & Exploited Children.

Wortley, R., & Smallbone, S. (2006). *Child pornography on the internet.* Retrieved June 23 2010, from http://www.cops.usdoj.gov/files/ric/Publications/e04062000.pdf

ADDITIONAL READING

Bates, A., & Metcalf, C. (2007). A psychometric comparison of internet and non-internet sex offenders from a community treatment sample. *Journal of Sexual Aggression, 13,* 11–20. doi:10.1080/13552600701365654

Blundell, B., Sherry, M., Burke, A., & Sowerbutts, S. (2002). Child Pornography and the Internet: Accessibility and Policing. *Australian Police Journal, 56*(1), 59–65.

Bourke, M. L., & Hernandez, A. E. (2009). The 'Butner Study' Redux: A report of the incidence of hands-on child victimization by child pornography offenders. *Journal of Family Violence, 24,* 183–191. doi:10.1007/s10896-008-9219-y

Burke, A., Sowerbutts, S., Blundell, B., & Sherry, M. (2002). Child Pornography and the Internet: Policing and Treatment Issues. *Psychiatry, Psychology and Law, 9,* 79–84. doi:10.1375/pplt.2002.9.1.79

Elliott, I. A., Beech, A. R., Mandeville-Norden, R., & Hayes, E. (2009). Psychological profiles of internet sexual offenders: Comparisons with contact sexual offenders. *Sexual Abuse, 21,* 76–92. doi:10.1177/1079063208326929

Frei, A., Erenay, N., Dittmann, V., & Graf, M. (2005). Paedophilia on the internet – a study of 33 convicted offenders in the Canton of Lucerne. *Swiss Medical Weekly, 135,* 488–494.

Howitt, D., & Sheldon, K. (2007). The role of cognitive distortions in paedophilic offending: Internet and contact offenders compared. *Psychology, Crime & Law, 13,* 469–486. doi:10.1080/10683160601060564

Krone, T. (2004). *A Typology of Online Child Pornography Offending.* Trends & Issues in Crime and Criminal Justice, No. 279. Canberra: Australian Institute of Criminology. www.aic.gov.au/publications/tandi2/tandi279.pdf.

Mehta, M. D. (2001). Pornography in Usenet: a study of 9,800 randomly selected images. *Cyberpsychology & Behavior, 4,* 695–703. doi:10.1089/109493101753376641

Middleton, D. (2008). From Research to practice: The development of the internet sex offender treatment programme (i-SOTP). *Irish Probation Journal, 5,* 49–64.

Middleton, D., Elliott, I. A., Mandeville-Norden, R., & Beech, A. R. (2006). An investigation into the application of the Ward and Siegert pathways model of child sexual abuse with Internet offenders. *Psychology, Crime & Law, 12,* 589–603. doi:10.1080/10683160600558352

Middleton, D., Mandeville-Norden, R., & Hayes, E. (2009). Does treatment work with internet sex offenders? Emerging findings from the internet sex offender treatment programme (i-SOTP). *Journal of Sexual Aggression, 15,* 5–19. doi:10.1080/13552600802673444

O'Donnell, I. & Milner, C. (2007). *Child Pornography: Crime, Computers and Society.* Cullompton, Devon: Willan Publishing.

Quayle, E., Erooga, M., Wright, L., Taylor, M., & Harbinson, D. (2006). Abuse Images and the Internet. In Quayle E, Erooga M, Wright L, Taylor M, Harbinson D. Lyme Regis(eds).*Only Pictures? Therapeutic work with Internet sex offenders.* Russell House Publishing Ltd; 2006:1-11.

Quayle, E., Vaughan, M., & Taylor, M. (2006). Sex offenders, internet child abuse images and emotional avoidance: The importance of values. *Aggression and Violent Behavior, 11,* 1–11. doi:10.1016/j.avb.2005.02.005

Reijnen, L., Bulten, E., & Nijman, H. (2009). Demographic and Personality Characteristics of Internet Child Pornography Downloaders in Comparison to Other offenders. *Journal of Child Sexual Abuse, 18,* 611–622. doi:10.1080/10538710903317232

Sheldon, K., & Howitt, D. (2007). *Sex Offenders and the Internet.* Chichester: Wiley.

Siegfried, K. C., Lovely, R. W., & Rogers, M. K. (2008). Self-Reported Online Child Pornography Behaviour: A Psychological Analysis. *International Journal of Cyber Criminology, 2,* 286–297.

Steel, C. M. S. (2009). Child pornography in peer-to-peer networks. *Child Abuse & Neglect, 33,* 560–568. doi:10.1016/j.chiabu.2008.12.011

Taylor, M., & Quayle, E. (2003). *Child Pornography: An Internet Crime.* Hove: Brunner-Routledge.

Webb, L., Craissati, J., & Keen, S. (2007). Characteristics of Internet Child Pornography Offenders: A Comparison with Child Molesters. *Sexual Abuse, 19,* 449–465.

Chapter 8
Online Child Predators:
Does Internet Society Make Predation Easy?

ABSTRACT

There has been significant media interest in the possible dangers of child predation on the internet, but it is not necessarily a new type of offence (Wolak, Finkelhor, Mitchell & Ybarra, 2008). Indeed, in many cases it seems to bear more resemblance to statutory rape than paedophilia. Nevertheless, the Internet does seem to provide an easier route for child predators to encounter and engage with children and teenagers, and the question as to if it enables child predators in their acts should be considered. This chapter will attempt to address this question. Initially paedophilia will be defined, and problems with its diagnosis will be considered. An attempt will be made to quantify the problem of online child predation, and the techniques used by online child predators will be described. The psychology of child predators will be considered, including an overview of some of the main theories of paedophilic behaviour. The psychology of victims will also be considered, with an overview of the risk factors of online predation, along with the psychological effects on victims. Potential solutions will then be reviewed, including re-habilitation efforts and prevention methods. Finally, future trends in online predation will be considered.

BACKGROUND

Sophie is fifteen years old, and has recently started using social networking websites. She received a friend request from Jim, a boy who she does not know. His profile says that he is sixteen years old,

and lives in the next town. Jim is actually a twenty-seven year old man from a different country. Sophie notices that he is listed as a friend of some of her schoolmates, so she accepts his friend request as she does not want to seem rude. Jim starts to send her private messages, and as he looks quite cute in his profile, Sophie feels flattered. The messages

DOI: 10.4018/978-1-61350-350-8.ch008

start to turn sexual in nature, and Jim asks her to send him photographs of her in her underwear. Sophie has never had a boyfriend, and she is not sure what to do, but Jim persuades her that it is normal to swap sexy photos. She takes the photo and sends it to him, and he replies that she is very beautiful, but that it would be even better if she was naked. After a little more persuasion she sends him a photo of herself completely naked. Over time his demands become more and more difficult for Sophie to accept. Eventually Jim asks her to use a webcam, saying that he wants to watch her carry out sexual acts on herself in real time. Sophie feels very uncomfortable at this request and refuses. Jim starts to get very angry, he calls her a tease, and says that if she does not comply to his requests, he will put her naked photo on his profile so that all of her friends will see it. She consults her friends for advice about Jim, and then realises that they do not know him either – they accepted his friend request without knowing who he was. Although she is very embarrassed, Sophie tells her parents the whole story. Her parents then report the issue to the police.

George is a twenty-two year old man with paedophilic tendencies. He spends a lot of time on the internet searching for suitable teenage girls to approach. He finds a profile of Judy on a social networking website. Judy is fourteen years old and lives locally. She seems a little shy, and does not have many friends on the website. George makes contact with her, and he does not hide the fact that he is much older than her. Soon they are in contact several times a day, and as the relationship progresses, George starts to discuss various sexual activities and fantasies with her. She seems receptive to his ideas, so George eventually feels confident enough to suggest meeting up in real life. Judy agrees, and they set a date for the next day at her house, as she says her parents will be out at work. She tells him to bring the sex toys that he has mentioned in his messages. When George arrives at the house, he is arrested. Judy was actually a thirty-four year old undercover

police officer. The sex toys that he brought with him were used as evidence that he intended to engage in sexual activity with an underage girl.

The scenarios mentioned above are both entirely fictional, but are based on mostly typical events that can occur during online child predatory events. As will be outlined later in the chapter, most victims are adolescents rather than younger children, and most are female. Many involve discussion of sexual activities in advance of physical meetings, and a gradual 'grooming' of the youth to prepare them for a sexual encounter. The reporting of the events to the police in the first scenario is unusual however, as it is likely that most cases of online child predation never come to the attention of the authorities. The terms used to describe the events and individuals involved in these attacks are sometimes confusing, however, and so it is important that these are appropriately defined.

Definitions of Paedophilia

While the media image of paedophilia frequently involves violent, predatory and sensational crimes (Brown, 2005), in practice few sexual offences against children involve severe brutality, sexual mutilation or significant physical injury (West, 1996). The definition of a paedophile is quite specific in the Diagnostic and Statistical Manual (Fourth edition, text revised – DSM-IV-TR) of the American Psychiatric Association (2000). The DSM-IV-TR indicates that in order to receive a clinical diagnosis of paedophilia, the individual must have experienced intense and recurrent sexually arousing fantasies over a minimum of six months, or urges or behaviours that involve sexual activities with a prepubescent child or children. In addition to this, the individual will experience significant distress, or impairment in social, occupational or other functioning, due to the presence of these fantasies, urges or behaviours. Finally, the individual must be at least sixteen years of age, and at least five years older than their victims.

There are obvious problems with such a narrow definition of paedophilia. Marshall (1997) indicates that, at most, only 25-40% of child sex offenders exhibit the fantasies, urges or behaviours at the frequency and intensity outlined in the DSM. Even among those that do, in many cases paedophiles do not experience the disruption or distress outlined in the DSM, and many maintain otherwise normal lives and relationships. The DSM-IV-TR does allow for this however, as societal judgements of impairment may be substituted for the person's own judgement of impairment (Blanchard, 2009). In addition, the DSM does not mention significant cognitive and psychological factors such as the cognitive distortions that are prevalent in paedophiles (see discussion on this below), or the difficulties in self-regulation that are experienced by child sex offenders.

The publication of the fifth edition of the DSM (due in 2013) offers the possibility of revising this definition of paedophilia. Blanchard (2009) indicates that such a revision is necessary, outlining a large number of changes that should be made including a revision of the requirements regarding duration of symptoms, clearer definitions of terms (such as 'intense' and 'recurrent', and the inclusion of those individuals who are attracted to pubescent children who have not reached sexual maturity. These 'hebephiles' (as coined by Glueck in 1955) specific erotic age preference was verified by Blanchard et al (2008), and it seems negligent that they are not fully considered under the current version of the DSM.

Yar (2006) indicates that online child sex abuse can be of two main forms. Firstly, some forms of abuse remain 'virtual' and are "restricted to communicative abuses committed via the Internet" (p. 131). In this case the youth and the offender may communicate at length online, often in chatrooms or via instant messenger, discussing sexual activities, while the communicants engage in masturbatory behaviour. It may also involve the use of webcams or the swapping of images with sexual content. The first scenario above describes

such abuse. Under some jurisdictions, including the United Kingdom, inciting a child to engage in such behaviour can be illegal (as outlined by Yar, 2006, p. 132), so even if the predator and the child never actually meet, they may still be indicted for child sex abuse. The second form involves using the online communications as a preparation for later physical contact, and is termed 'grooming'. In this case, the offender may solicit a variety of different actions from the youth, including those outlined above, but also a request to meet at an offline location. For the purpose of this chapter, the terms 'predator' and 'solicitor' will be used to describe these offenders, rather than the term 'paedophile', which may not be accurate in all cases. The term 'aggressive solicitations' will be used to describe occasions where the predator requests to meet the victim offline.

Known Prevalence Rates

It is extremely difficult to estimate how many paedophiles there are, as it is expected that many have managed to persuade their victims not to report their experiences through a variety of methods. In addition to this, it is possible that there are some individuals who have a specific sexual interest in children, but who have never acted on it (Blanchard, 2009).

The Child Exploitation and Online Protection (CEOP) centre in the UK indicate that in 2009-2010 alone they protected 278 children from sexual abuse and arrested 417 suspected child sexual offenders, as a result of intelligence reports from CEOP and the deployment of CEOP resources. This resulted in a total of 624 children protected and 1,131 arrests since 2006 (Child Exploitation and Online Protection, 2010). Sheldon and Howitt (2007) indicate that in 2004 there were 3,400 paedophiles in UK prisons.

In the US, the National Centre for Missing and Exploited Children (2007) estimated that there were approximately 603,000 registered sex offenders in the US at that time. Over 56,000 cases of child sexual abuses were reported and substantiated in 2007 (US Department of Health and Human Services, 2007), although Finkelhor (2009) indicates that only about 30% of cases are reported to authorities. Similarly, Finkelhor and Lewis (1988) found through a telephone survey that ten percent of males admitted being sexually abused as a child, which would further support the suggestion that a relatively small number of child sexual abuse cases are reported.

Wolak, Finkelhor and Mitchell (2009) indicate that arrests for online child exploitation crimes increased almost threefold between the years 2000 and 2006 (from 2,577 to 7,010), although this included figures for child pornography possession and distribution. Over three thousand of the cases involved the use of undercover investigators posing as minors, while just over six hundred involved online predation. Wolak, Finkelhor and Mitchell (2006) indicate that approximately one in seven young internet users receive unwanted sexual solicitations. However only one in twenty-five received *aggressive* solicitations, where the solicitor attempted to make offline contact with the youth. Similarly, four percent of all youth users said online solicitors asked them for nude or sexually explicit photographs. Interestingly, fourteen percent of the unwanted solicitations originated from offline friends and acquaintances. They also found that only five percent of solicitations were reported. Nevertheless, it should not be interpreted that the internet has led to an increase in child sex abuse. Wolak, Finkelhor, Mitchell and Ybarra (2008) indicate that increases in online sex offending may be balanced by decreases in offline victimisations, as overall the number of sex abuse cases substantiated by child protective agencies between 1990 and 2005 fell by over fifty percent.

Bryce (2010) concludes that the "prevalence of online sexual exploitation is relatively small given the wider context of sexual offending against young people in society" (p. 322). Nevertheless, Bryce also concurs that it is likely that official records of online child predation prevalence do not reflect the full extent of the problem due to the difficulties in reporting and recognition of such offences.

THE GROOMING PROCESS ONLINE

The process by which internet child sex predators approach children is a gradual one, during which the predator 'grooms' the child into agreeing to meet. Edgar-Nevill (2008) indicates that there are a number of steps involved in the grooming procedure. Initially, the predator requires access to children or adolescents. Before the internet, this would require the predator to physically stalk their victim, or to know them through legitimate reasons (such as youth work or family). However, as the internet has become more popular, predators have a wide variety of methods by which to access their victims, including e-mail, forums, chatrooms, blogs, instant messaging, and social networking websites. From these, the predator then selects a victim with which they can initiate contact. During this contact, the predator may pretend to be a teenager, often one or two years older than the intended victim. However, while it is possible that the internet child sex predator will engage in deception, pretending to be younger than they actually are, Wolak, Finkelhor and Mitchell (2004) found that only five percent of offenders pretended to be teens, and that the stereotype of the offender who uses trickery and violence is largely inaccurate.

Edgar-Nevill (2008) suggests that while the grooming may start in a relatively public online space, such as the victim's profile, the predator will often try to move the communications to a more private space as quickly as possible. Communications become more frequent and personal, and the predator begins to build a profile of the victim. At this stage, the predator tries to use the conversation to develop the victim's empathy and trust. Using publicly available information, they may gather information about the victim which they can use in conversations, increasing the likelihood that the victim will disclose more sensitive information. The victim may begin to enjoy the interactions and attention, and at this stage the predator might ask the victim to take some specific action such as appearing on a webcam, talking on the phone, or meeting in person.

Dombrowski, LeMasney, Ahia, and Dickson (2004) echo some aspects of Edgar-Nevill's description of the grooming process, again indicating that initial contact would be prosocial in nature, where the perpetrator gains the youth's affection and trust (pp. 66-67). Dombrowski et al indicate that most children and adolescents find this attention appealing. The predation escalates with the exchange of gifts or pictures, and if the victim seems to be receptive, the grooming escalates and the predator may start overt communication about sexuality. Dombrowski et al suggest that the predator may provide the victim with pornographic material to desensitize the youth to sexual content. Again, if the victim is accepting of this, the predator may try to establish a meeting, where again a gradual process of increasingly sexual behaviours may occur. The predator may then use a variety of techniques in order to ensure the victim does not discuss the sexual activity, including psychological manipulation or physical threats.

O'Connell (2003) outlines another similar series of steps used during the grooming process. Again the predator initially identifies their victim, and then the offender initiates a conversation or relationship through computer mediated communication. These early stages of the relationship can be quite similar to the development of other, benign online friendships. But during this stage the offender might indicate that they are interested in developing the relationship, hinting at romance, exchanging images or future meetings. At this stage, O'Connell (2003) indicates that the offender assesses the risks involved in pursuing the relationship further, and may ask the victim about the security measures their family uses in order to prevent sexual predators. The offender

then develops the trust of the victim, and makes changes to the relationship so that it becomes more sexually explicit. They may try to persuade the victim to use a webcam, or send the victim sexually explicit material. If necessary, offenders may become threatening or harassing to persuade the victim to comply with the requests. If the offender becomes sexually gratified without actually meeting the victim, they may choose to end the relationship then, leaving the victim feeling hurt and humiliated by their deception (O'Connell, 2003). But the relationship may proceed to contact sexual relations.

Technologies Used by Predators

Predators use a variety of techniques to communicate with and identify potential victims. Three quarters of men who perpetrated or attempted to perpetrate contact sex offences against minors using the Internet monitored chat room dialogue while one half reviewed the online profiles of the children and teenagers to identify victims (Malesky, 2007).

Mitchell, Finkelhor, Jones and Wolak (2010) found that social networking sites (SNSs) can be used by online predators to communicate with and initiate sexual relationships with a potential victim. They found that in 2006, an estimated 2,322 arrests for internet sex crimes against minors involved the use of social networking sites. The SNS can also be used to find out information about the victim, to disseminate photographs, and to communicate with the victim's friends. Nevertheless, Mitchell, Wolak and Finkelhor (2008) found that while bloggers posted more personal information online, they were at no increased risk for sexual solicitation as long as they did not interact with people they met online and did not know in person. This was in contrast to increased media reports indicating that there might be a link.

In addition, Wolak, Finkelhor & Mitchell (2006) indicated that 37% of incidents happened while youths were in chatrooms, while 40% began with instant messages. They also describe cases of interactions in online gaming and online dating websites. Overall, it seems that predators are willing to use a wide variety of online technologies in order to contact youths.

Comparison to Offline Techniques Used by Offenders

Online grooming techniques appear to be different to those of offline offenders, primarily because there appears to be a major difference in the likelihood of the victim knowing the offender beforehand. Offline, victims frequently know or trust the perpetrators (Elliott, Browne & Kilcoyne, 1995), and warnings of 'stranger-danger' may misrepresent the reality of the offence (Brown, 2005). For offline offences, children are in most danger in private locations (Elliott et al, 1995), such as their home. However, online predators are normally people that the victim met online, and did not know in person. Wolak, Mitchell and Finkelhor (2006) indicate that victims only knew their predators in fourteen percent of cases.

Nevertheless, in some ways, the online and offline offences are quite similar. In most cases, violence is not used in order to gain access to the child. Also in both cases, children are frequently made to feel special and deserving of attention by the offender, characteristics the offender then exploits to gain sexual access. Wolak, Mitchell and Finkelhor (2006) found that almost one-third of online solicitations involved attempted offline contact with the minor involved, with most of these asking to meet the youth in person, sometimes buying travel tickets for the youth to enable the meeting. Interestingly, twelve percent of solicitation incidents involved money or gifts for the minor, which indicates some overlap of grooming behaviour online and offline. Wolak, Mitchell and Finkelhor (2006) also indicate that solicitors asked youths for photographs of themselves in over half of the solicitation incidents they studied, and twenty-seven percent of cases

involved requests for sexual photographs of the minor. In some cases, solicitors also sent sexual photographs of themselves to the youth.

Wolak, Finkelhor, Mitchell and Ybarra (2008) indicate that rather than resembling offline paedophilic encounters, online predations more often resemble a model of statutory rape. They suggest that offenders are generally honest about their sexual interests in the encounter, with sex often being discussed online in advance of any meeting. Wolak, Finkelhor, Mitchell and Ybarra (2008) suggest that most victims who meet their online predator go to the meetings expecting to engage in sexual activity, and that any deception by the predator usually involves the predator promising love and romance, when their intentions are primarily sexual.

Wolak, Finkelhor, Mitchell and Ybarra (2008) question whether the internet makes youths more accessible to child molesters, and deduce that this is likely as it creates more opportunities for predators to be alone with victims and it allows offenders to find victims more easily. The rapid and private communications possible through the Internet can also aid the predator, along with a potentially higher tendency among adolescents to talk about more personal matters with strangers online rather than face to face. Wolak, Finkelhor, Mitchell and Ybarra suggest that this may lead to faster development of feelings of intimacy between the predator and the victim, and so sensitive topics such as sex may be brought up much sooner than would occur if communication only occurred offline. However Wolak, Finkelhor, Mitchell and Ybarra do indicate that there is a lack of empirical evidence to support these theories.

PSYCHOLOGY OF OFFENDERS

While considerable research has been done on the psychology of paedophiles, Howitt (2009) indicates that there does not seem to be any specific personality characteristics that are associated with paedophilia. Sheldon and Howitt (2007) indicate that in many cases paedophiles seem to be aware from an early age that they are sexually oriented towards children, and so it would seem important to search for precursors to paedophilia at this time. They indicate that various psychological disciplines explain the development of paedophilia in diverse ways, including disruptions to psychosexual development, developmental events related to deviant sexual interests, childhood masturbation and insecure attachment styles. Sheldon and Howitt conclude that in general, Internet and mixed sex offenders report similar early childhood experiences, particularly of "parental non-supervision, violence, and institutional care" (p. 137).

Groth and Birnbaum (1978) indicate that there are two main types of paedophiles, depending on the usual sexual orientation of the offender. Repressed offenders have a usual sexual orientation to adults, but some variable causes them to regress to sexual involvement with children. This may be stress or life pressures. Repressed offenders are more likely to be in a long term relationship with an adult, and may even be married. They are most likely to offend against children they are related to. In contrast, fixated offenders rarely marry, and they are primarily sexually oriented towards children from adolescence. Fixated offenders are more likely to victimize strangers or acquaintances. In efforts to better understand the phenomenon, various theories of paedophilia have been proposed.

Theories of Paedophilia

Several researchers have attempted to explain why some individuals show paedophilic tendencies. These include Finkelhor's (1984, 1986) 'Four Preconditions Model of Paedophilia', Hall and Hirschman's (1991) 'Quadripartite Model', and Ward and Siegert's (2002) 'Pathways Model'. The relative merits of each of these models are considered below.

Finkelhor's Four Preconditions Model

Finkelhor (1984, 1986) suggested the 'Four Preconditions Model of Paedophilia'. This model assumes that there are multiple determinants of child sex offending, with four preconditions that need to be present for a sex offence to occur. It is the foundation for many cognitive-behavioural therapies for paedophilia. Initially, the offender has to have the motivation to commit the crime. They may believe that alternative sources of sexual gratification will not satisfy them, or are unavailable, and as such the child is the only source of sexual gratification. Finkelhor suggests that the offender then has to overcome internal inhibitors. He indicates that, as with the rest of society, paedophiles are socialised to inhibit sexual approaches to young people, but that this must be overcome for the abuse to occur. The paedophile has a number of alternatives available to them to accomplish this. They may partake of drugs or alcohol to reduce their inhibitions, or they may attempt to justify their actions through a variety of excuses (see the section on cognitive distortions below).

Having overcome their internal inhibitors, the paedophile must then overcome external inhibitors. This means that the offender must create a situation where there is the potential for abuse. However, children tend to be well protected in society – very young children are normally protected by parents or caregivers for the majority of the time, so if the offender's preference is for a very young child they may need to target family members. As the child becomes older, there are fewer external inhibitors, as the child becomes more independent and more likely to be interacting with people outside of their immediate family. Eventually the child is likely to develop an online presence, which allows offenders to contact them easily without drawing attention from caregivers. Finally, the paedophile must overcome the victim's resistance through the grooming process. Offline, this may involve using treats or gifts as bribes.

This can then be followed by gradually introducing sexual activities, perhaps through the introduction of the victim to child pornography materials.

While Finkelhor's model is of use in understanding the process of offending, it fails to explain the behaviour itself (Ward, Polaschek & Beech, 2006), and is lacking in substantial empirical evidence to support it (Howitt, 2006).

Hall and Hirschman's (1991) Quadripartite Model

Hall and Hirschman's (1991) Quadripartite Model also identifies four factors in offending behaviour, and attempts to determine the difficulties that may cause the offending behaviour. Different offenders can have different dominant factors, and the treatment approach will vary according to which factor is dominant (Ward, 2001). These factors include affective dyscontrol – an inability to identify and manage emotions. This may mean that the individual who is feeling lonely, and whose loneliness is decreased by the presence of a younger companion, may confuse this with a sexual attraction. A second difficulty may include personality problems, such as attachment difficulties, which could be rooted in early childhood experiences with parents or other adults. A third factor is physiological sexual arousal, which has been noted in many studies of child sexual offenders.

The final factor in offending behaviour is the presence of cognitive distortions. Cognitive distortions are justifications that people make in order to excuse their actions or behaviours. In the case of child sex offenders, the cognitive distortions are used by the offender to argue for the acceptability or their actions, both to themselves and others. The presence of cognitive distortions suggests that the paedophile has normal sexual scripts (personal narratives that dictate how sexual relationships should develop, and the types of sexual behaviour that are acceptable), but that they also have pro-criminal attitudes and beliefs. They may have a

sense of superiority, and feel that the laws and social norms regarding children and sex should not apply to them. Ward and Siegert (2002) list some cognitive distortions that may be held by child sex offenders. These include a belief that the offender is entitled to sex with an individual who they are physically attracted to, whether or not that person is a child. They may indicate that they have no control over their behaviour and that they are ruled by their sexual urges, or that sex with adults can be dangerous but that children are not a threat. Some of the more common cognitive distortions involve the belief that the child enjoys sex, is mature enough to consent to sexual acts, or that the child is not harmed by the encounter. Some may even justify the act by suggesting that the sexual encounter is beneficial to the child, and helps to educate them about sexuality. Others justify the child sexual abuse by indicating that the current Western age of consent is a recent, culturally defined phenomenon. There are many examples of historical and literary cases where sexual activity with minors was considered the norm. In addition to this, some modern cultures maintain much lower ages of consent than Westernised countries. Some child predators with cognitive distortions use this evidence as justification for their activities in modern, Western civilisation.

Ward and Siegert's (2002) 'Pathways Model'

Cognitive distortions are also an element in Ward and Siegert's (2002) 'Pathways Model'. Ward and Siegert critiqued previous models of sexually offensive behaviour, including those proposed by Finkelhor, Hall and Hirschman, and a model by Marshall and Barbaree (1990). Ward and Siegert developed their model by integrating the best elements of each of the previous models. Their model suggests that there are four different potential pathways to becoming a paedophile, and hence four different types of offender. The use of cognitive distortions is one of these pathways.

A final, fifth pathway may involve dysfunctions across multiple areas. Ward and Siegert argue that vulnerability to committing a sexual offence derives from a combination of developmental experiences and environmental factors.

An alternative to the cognitive distortions pathway involves the presence of deviant sexual scripts. Through socialization, humans develop sexual scripts but the production of these depends a great deal on developmental experiences. Those individuals who have been sexually abused or prematurely sexualized are at highest risk of possessing deviant sexual scripts, potentially missing those scripts that stigmatise sexual relationships with minors. Potential paedophiles in this pathway have distorted sexual scripts and dysfunctional relationship schema – they may find it difficult to differentiate between sex and intimacy. This can result in unsatisfying relationships that are transient, and the offender may seek sex with children after they've been rejected by an adult.

A third pathway involves intimacy deficits. This type of offender has normal sexual scripts, but experiences deficits in intimacy and social skills. The main cause for development of paedophilic tendencies is insecure attachment styles, and as such the offender experiences difficulties in forming adult relationships. They may experience low self-efficacy, critical self-evaluation and personal dissatisfaction. The resulting loneliness and social isolation may result in the individual becoming particularly vulnerable to offending.

The fourth pathway involves dysfunctional emotional regulation. While this is characterized by normal sexual scripts, the potential offenders in this pathway may experience two kinds of emotional dysfunction. Firstly, these individuals may express anger through abuse of children as a method of punishing partners. Alternatively, the person may use sex to calm their mood. Cortoni and Marshall (2001) suggest that it is possible that engaging in compulsive masturbation during adolescence to improve self-esteem and mood may create an early link between sex and emo-tional wellbeing, and this may be a factor in the development of paedophilic tendencies.

The fifth and final pathway, involving multiple dysfunctions, may involve dysfunctions in some or all of the previous four pathways. These individuals are likely to have a history of sexual abuse or activity from a young age, and their preferred sexual partners will be children. Hence they are likely to be described as 'pure paedophiles'. As with Hall and Hirschman's model, treatment approaches based on Ward and Siegert's model are dependent on the pathway involved. If the offender has multiple dysfunctions, it should be identified if there is a dominant dysfunction, which would need the most attention during the therapeutic process.

Consideration of the Ward and Siegert model in relation to internet child sex offences has been carried out by Middleton, Elliott, Mandeville-Norden and Beech (2006), but only in relation to possession of child pornography (see Chapter 7 for a discussion of this). However, Bryce (2010) indicates that while a similar pattern of pathways for Internet related contact offending may be found, there are no published studies to date regarding this. Bryce (2010) also suggests that it is possible that some internet related contact offenders may not be classifiable to the identified pathways, and so further research is required for this group in order to better understand them in terms of risk, assessment and treatment approaches.

Demographic and Psychometric Traits of Offenders

Wolak, Finkelhor and Mitchell (2006) indicate that online predators are mostly male. However, the stereotype of the older male predator seems to be false, as they found that over forty percent of solicitations came from those under eighteen. A further thirty percent were aged between eighteen and twenty-five. However it should be remembered that most of the victims involved (eighty-five percent) were not certain of the solicitor's age.

Wolak, Finkelhor, Mitchell and Ybarra (2008) indicate that online child molesters are generally not paedophiles (due to an apparent preference for adolescents rather than prepubescent children). This seems to be mainly due to the fact that younger children are not as accessible online, and are more likely to be supervised during their online activities. Nevertheless, it is possible that paedophiles may use the Internet to contact parents or other adult offenders, or they may use it to collect child pornography (see Chapter 7 for an overview of this phenomenon). As such, it appears that online child predators more closely fit the definition of hebephilia rather than paedophilia. Hines and Finkelhor (2007) indicate that adult men who pursue adolescent girls in offline environments are more likely to have less education, feelings of inadequacy, a criminal history, and arrested psychosocial development, although it is possible that there may be a difference between online and offline hebephiles. Motives for adults who pursue sex with adolescents can vary. Lanning (2001) suggests that they include impulse, anger, curiosity, or desire for power, while Nuñez (2003) suggests that it may be a wish to relive adolescent experiences or to seek admiration from victims.

Wolak, Finkelhor, Mitchell and Ybarra (2008) also indicate that online predators tend not to be violent or sadistic, with most online predators being patient enough to develop the relationships with their victims. Wolak, Finkelhor, Mitchell and Ybarra (2008) also indicate that abductions are rare, and most victims meet their solicitor of their own accord. However, a minority of cases do involve violence or abduction, but these cases are rare. Wolak, Finkelhor, Mitchell and Ybarra suggest that online child molesters are not generally impulsive, aggressive or violent, although they fear that this pattern may change as Internet access becomes more widespread.

PSYCHOLOGY OF VICTIMS

Offline, there are a variety of characteristics of youths who are more vulnerable to sexual predators. These include physically attractive youths with low self-esteem (Elliott, Browne & Kilcoyne, 1995); youths from dysfunctional families (Kenny & McEachern, 2000) and youths from impoverished backgrounds (Kenny & McEacher, 2000; Derezotes & Snowden, 1990). Wolak, Finkelhor & Mitchell (2006) found that seventy percent of youths who experienced online solicitations were girls. Of the boys who were targeted, virtually all the offenders were male (Wolak, Finkelhor & Mitchell, 2004). Wolak et al's studies seem to indicate that most male victims were either gay or were questioning their sexual orientations. Wolak et al (2006) suggest that these youths may be more willing to search for sexual information online and may be more likely to seek advice or sexual partners in online environments where there is less concern about social stigma and confidentiality. This puts them at greater vulnerability for sexual solicitations.

Over eighty percent of victims in Wolak et al's (2006) study were fourteen years old or older, and the most aggressive and distressing solicitations were concentrated amongst the older minors, with less than thirty percent of each happening to under-fourteens. Wolak et al (2006) indicate that this may be because younger children are more likely to be supervised when online, and they may spend less time online than teenagers. It seems likely that those youths who are most curious about romance and sexuality were manipulated into meetings for sexual purposes (Wolak, Finkelhor & Mitchell, 2004) and as this interest tends to develop in teenage years, this may be another reason why younger children were less likely to be targeted.

Mitchell, Finkelhor and Wolak (2007) indicate that youths who send personal details to strangers, or who talk to strangers online about sex, are more likely to receive aggressive sexual solicitations. Also at higher risk were those youths who visited chatrooms. In addition, youths who had histories of abuse (either physical or sexual), or who had other offline problems, such as rule-breaking behaviour, depression or social interaction problems were at higher risk (Wolak, Finkelhor, Mitchell and Ybarra, 2008).

Wolak, Finkelhor, Mitchell and Ybarra (2008) indicate that posting personal information online alone does not appear to be particularly risky. They indicate that posting such information online is prevalent, in their 2005 study more than half of youths aged between ten and seventeen had posted personal information, and it would be expected that the prevalence of social networking sites since then will have increased this statistic. Wolak, Finkelhor, Mitchell and Ybarra indicate that it is difficult to make predictions about relatively rare activities (such as online predation) based on behaviours engaged in by large proportions of the population (such as posting personal information). They determine that it is interactive behaviours, such as communicating with strangers about sex, that demonstrate greater risk of victimisation.

Wolak, Finkelhor, Mitchell and Ybarra (2008) do indicate that it may be a combination of different activities that put youths at higher risk of victimisation. These activities included interacting online with unknown people, friending unknown people on social networking sites, seeking pornography online and being rude or nasty online. The more activities that youths engaged in, the higher the probability that they would be sexually solicited.

Psychological Effects on Victims

While there are no universal post-abuse symptoms, Dombrowski (2003) indicates that sexual abuse can adversely impact many areas of a child's life, including cognitive, physical, academic and psychological development. Dombrowski, Le-Masney, Ahia and Dickson (2004) describe how negative effects can continue much later into life, sometimes evolving into depression, substance abuse, suicidal ideation, and other psychological and personal difficulties.

Wolak, Finkelhor & Mitchell (2006) found that most youths dealt relatively well with online solicitations. Most (66%) removed themselves from the situation, often by leaving the website or the computer or blocking the predator. Others (16%) confronted the solicitor, warned them, or told them to stop. A further 11% ignored them. Only 5% of incidents were reported to authorities or law enforcement, 12% were handled by parents, and 2% by teachers or other school personnel. In 56% of cases, the youth did not tell anyone.

In most cases (66%) youths said that they were not particularly upset or frightened by the event. Just over a quarter said it left them feeling very or extremely upset, with one in five feeling very or extremely afraid. These figures increase for aggressive incidents, where attempts are made to meet the victim offline. In these cases just over a third left the youth feeling very or extremely upset, and 28% left youth feeling very or extremely afraid. Some youths showed symptoms of stress, some stayed away from the internet (or a particular website or application within it), were unable to stop thinking about it, felt irritable or jumpy, and/or lost interest in things. Some youths were also extremely embarrassed by the incidents.

Bryce (2010) lists several negative outcomes associated with sexual abuse, including "delinquency, depression, substance abuse, guilt, post-traumatic stress disorder" (p. 335), as well as psychiatric disorders in later life, but also indicates that less is known about the consequences for victims of online sexual abuse. Bryce suggests that the impact may be similar, but that the involvement of technology may intensify the victimisation and its potential outcomes.

SOLUTIONS

Having considered the procedures involved in online child grooming, and the effects of victimization, it is heartening to know that there are a number of potential solutions to the problems involved. Some are reactive, involving rehabilitation and assessment of offenders or support for the victim and their families, but some are preventative in nature.

Rehabilitation of Offenders

There are a wide variety of treatment programmes available for child sex offenders. Schmucker and Lösel (2008) conducted an international meta-analysis of studies of many of the potential treatments that are available for sex offenders. They found that overall, the majority of studies in this field confirm that there is a positive effect to offenders undergoing treatment, with a 37 percent difference between treatment and control groups recidivism levels. Schmucker and Lösel found that the strongest effects were for surgical castration, but that these studies had confounding variables. Other treatment approaches such as medications controlling hormones, and cognitive-behavioural approaches also had a positive effect, but that non-behavioural treatments did not show significant results.

Much therapy for sex offenders is based on cognitive-behavioural therapies and relapse prevention. Some of these programmes target the cognitive distortions outlined above, others treat problems such as using sex to regulate emotions, while others target social skills deficits that may prevent offenders from developing satisfying sexual relationships with peers (Yates, 2005). Wolak, Finkelhor, Mitchell and Ybarra (2008) indicate that most of these approaches are also likely to be applicable to online offenders, and that it is possible that online predators already have higher social functioning which may make therapy more successful than similar techniques

with offline offenders. Wolak, Finkelhor, Mitchell and Ybarra (2008) emphasise that it is important to recognize the diversity of online child predators, and that assessments should allow specialized treatment and social control options to be developed that correspond to the needs and problems of the specific offenders.

Risk of Recidivism

When attempting to determine if an offender has been rehabilitated, recidivism is predicted based on the outcomes of previous cases, a process known as 'actuarial' prediction (Hall, 1996). Here, an analysis is made of previous offenders about whom recidivism rates are already known, and the characteristics of the current offender are compared to the information known about these previous offenders. It can then be estimated as to whether the current offender is likely to reoffend or not (Bickley & Beech, 2001). When attempting to estimate probability of recidivism, two main types of variables are considered – static and dynamic risk factors. Static risk factors are most commonly used, and do not vary over a lengthy period of time (Bonta, 1996). These include variables such as a tendency to choose victims who are males or strangers. It will also include the number of previous offences, and the age of first offence. Hanson and Bussiere (1998) indicate that these static risk factors are the best predictor of long-term recidivism.

However, the use of static risk factors as the sole predictor would suggest that an offender cannot be rehabilitated and will always be a danger to society. This is not always the case, and so risk assessment also considers dynamic risk factors. These are characteristics that can change over time (Bonta, 1996), and may result in a change in recidivism risk. Within dynamic risk factors there is a further subdivision into stable and acute dynamic risk factors. Stable dynamic risk factors are expected to remain unchanged for long periods of time, and are those often targeted by interventions (Hanson & Harris, 2000). They include the presence of factors such as cognitive distortions and deviant sexual scripts, which are difficult but not impossible to amend. Acute dynamic risk factors change rapidly over very short periods of time. These can include access to victims, drug or alcohol levels, and presence of stress. These acute dynamic risk factors are harder to assess and difficult to control for, but they could be useful in determining if the treatment approaches used to address stable dynamic risk factors have been successful. There have been few studies to date determining what the most accurate risk factors for online predator recidivism are, and this is an area that would benefit from further research, as it would allow more effective rehabilitation programmes to be developed.

Support for Victims and Families

Wolak, Finkelhor, Mitchell and Ybarra (2008) indicate that there is little information available about treatment strategies for victims of statutory rape or internet-initiated sex crimes. This is in part due to the likelihood that these youths do not experience the events as traumatic, and so standard treatment models for sexual abuse may not be applicable. In fact, the victim may feel that they are being victimized by parents or authorities, rather than the predator, to whom they may feel love and allegiance. Wolak, Finkelhor and Mitchell (2004) indicate that most victims meet and have sex with the perpetrator on more than one occasion, and that half of the victims were described as being in love with or feeling very close to the offender.

Wolak, Finkelhor, Mitchell and Ybarra (2008) indicate that there is a need for assessment protocols for these victims, as well as strategies for building alliances with the victims. They indicate that it may be hardest to communicate with younger adolescents, who may not be aware of the risks that were involved in the situation. They also propose that the most suitable approach may

mimic those used with drug addicts and victims of domestic violence, who may not commence the treatment with a desire to change. Wolak, Finkelhor, Mitchell and Ybarra also suggest that some family interventions may be useful, particularly those that focus on parent-child relationships, supervision, and family conflict.

Prevention Methods and Efficacy

Wolak, Finkelhor, Mitchell and Ybarra (2008) indicate that much media coverage of internet dangers emphasise young children as the victims, or demonstrate violence, deception and abduction. However, as these researchers have demonstrated, this is a false portrayal of the risks involved, and so these descriptions should be avoided. Wolak, Finkelhor, Mitchell and Ybarra also suggest that prevention efforts and strategies should be targeted at adolescents rather than parents, as even though parents may be a more receptive audience for the message, it is not guaranteed that the adolescents will respond to parents' interventions. Wolak, Finkelhor and Mitchell (2006) suggest that most parents and guardians (almost ninety percent) had talked to their children about various aspects of online safety but that fewer youths (closer to half) had acknowledged hearing these messages. This may indicate that the parents responded in what they believed to be a socially desirable way (indicating that they had warned their children about these behaviours) or it may mean that the adolescents did not pay sufficient attention to their parents' warnings. Wolak, Finkelhor, Mitchell and Ybarra (2008) also emphasise the importance of good sex education for adolescents, and especially education about the wrongfulness of the seduction techniques that may be used by predators both online and offline, as well as focusing the prevention strategies on the interactive aspects of internet use, rather than on posting of personal information. The behaviours outlined above that put youths most at risk of victimization should be specifically targeted.

Dombrowski, LeMasney, Ahia and Dickson (2004) suggest that both technological and psychoeducational methods can be used to protect minors from online child predation, but that technological methods alone are insufficient due to the fact that they can be circumvented by predators. Technological interventions include monitoring browser history, using privacy filtration and application tracking and usage. However it is possible that older youths, in particular adolescents, may uncover methods of overcoming these methods, particularly as they have access to the Internet in a wider variety of ways including computers at schools or friends houses, and the increasing popularity of smartphones. Particular issues of ethics and trust also surround the high level of supervision that caregivers may need to employ using these means. Dombrowki et al (2004) therefore suggest that psychoeducational methods should also be employed, including discussing internet dangers with youths, establishing caregiver-child contracts of internet use, and placing the computer in public locations.

Bryce (2008) found that educational messages are successful in raising awareness amongst youths of the dangers of communicating with strangers online, but later concludes (Bryce, 2010) that a significant number of young people still engage in risky online behaviours, despite awareness of these risks. Bryce (2010) suggests that educational strategies need to place more emphasis on the potential negative consequences of these behaviours. While there has been recent controversy regarding the presence or absence of 'panic buttons' on some social networking sites, Mitchell, Finkelhor, Jones and Wolak (2010) suggest that prevention methods should be targeted at specific youth behaviours, rather than the online locations that youths frequent. If the youths are educated as to safe and unsafe behaviours, then they can use this knowledge in all aspects of online behaviour, rather than being limited to those online locations that provide safety functions.

Policing Investigations

Mitchell, Wolak and Finkelhor (2005) investigated whether police impersonation of juveniles online is an effective method of apprehending online predators. They found that these proactive investigations lead to a quarter of all arrests for internet sex crimes against minors, and that prosecution of these cases led to high rates of guilty pleas and low rates of dropped cases.

These proactive investigations can take a number of formats – the investigator may impersonate the youth themselves, as in the case described earlier in this chapter, or they may pose as mothers of children who "are seeking men to "teach" their children about sex" (p. 242). In other cases, the police may take over a real juvenile's online identity when they discover that they have been solicited.

These techniques require the police officers to undergo considerable training, and need to be completed very carefully, adhering to explicit guidelines. However, Mitchell et al question whether these offenders are really those who would be otherwise targeting real juveniles. They cite Delmonico, Griffin and Moriarity (2001) who suggest that a disproportionate number of perpetrators apprehended due to proactive investigations were part of a *discovery group* that had no previous history of problematic sexual behaviour. However, Mitchell, Wolak and Finkelhor (2005) found that thirteen percent of the offenders arrested in undercover operations had molested a minor, and that over forty percent of them possessed child pornography. Nevertheless, they also found that these offenders tended to be older than offenders of juvenile victims, and more likely to be employed full time and on a high income. Despite these caveats, as these offenders went to meetings where they expected to meet minors for sexual activity, this indicates that they are indeed a risk to youths.

FUTURE TRENDS AND RESEARCH

Livingstone (2009) argues that "online risks do not merit a moral panic, and nor do they warrant seriously restricting children's internet use, especially as this would deny them many benefits" (p. 178). Her point is well made – it is important that accurate risk assessments be made of the likelihood of online predation, and it is also important that any security measures put in place to counteract risks do not result in unnecessary restrictions on the child's internet access. To do so does not ensure the child's safety, but rather makes it more likely that the child will not be able to deal with such an encounter effectively if they are unfortunate enough to experience it.

Wolak, Finkelhor, Mitchell and Ybarra (2008) indicate that there is a dearth of research in this field, and suggest four key directions in which research should be taken in order to base policy and practice. Firstly, they suggest that the nature of online sexual behaviour by youths needs to be monitored, particularly in light of the rapidly changing uses of technologies such as cellphones. Secondly, studies should be made of internet sex-offenders, in order to determine if there are new groups of offenders online and to determine the pathways to offending behaviour allowed by the Internet. Thirdly, research should be carried out in order to better understand characteristics, prior experiences and attitudes of victims and potential victims. Finally, Wolak, Finkelhor, Mitchell and Ybarra suggest that evaluations should be made of policy in this area, and particularly with regard to the efficacy and implementation of prevention messages and strategies.

Our use of the internet has changed a great deal since the advent of networked home computers, and online predators have taken advantage of this. With the advent of greater interactivity online, and the growing numbers of youths who have access to personal devices capable of accessing the internet, it becomes more difficult to monitor their online behaviour to ensure their safety. As more mobile devices include cameras to allow videocalls, such as the iPhone 4, it may lead to increased pressure on young people to engage in sexual acts dictated by online predators within their own homes.

On a more positive note, it seems that in most cases victims are not adversely affected by many solicitations, with most indicating that they did not feel upset by the event. The influence of social networking websites on victimisation rates currently seems unclear, and this would benefit from further research. Specifically, it would be of great interest to determine how adolescents choose whether or not to allow a stranger onto a friend list, and if they have removed a person from the friend list due to unsolicited sexual messages.

It is possible that in the future, more unsolicited sexual messages will be received by youths from people that they already know in real life. The messages received may be from a person who is known both by the youth and by their circle of friends, and while the predator may be someone closer in age to the youth, the recipient may find it more difficult to escape from interacting with them.

CONCLUSION

It is clear from the research to date in this field that, while it may be easier for predators to identify and communicate with youths using the Internet, there is a significant difference between the truth of online predation and the public perception of the risk. Those youths who are most at risk are teenage girls who are sexually curious to the extent that they will communicate with strangers about sexual matters online. While this is a worrying phenomenon, it is clear that much could be done to prevent youths from engaging in such risky behaviours, through a combination of adequate sex education and guidance in online safety measures. Perhaps the most difficult aspect of this will be persuading the youths of the dangers that these behaviours involve, as well as informing them that in most cases, the interest of the child predator is limited to sexual activity, rather than the love and romance that they may promise.

Information regarding differences between online child predators and offline offenders is limited, perhaps mostly due to the limited research on hebephilia to date. Amendments to the Diagnostic and Statistical Manual may help to encourage further research in this area, which may in turn allow for clearer distinctions between online and offline offences. This would allow for the development of more appropriate treatment and assessment protocols, along with more structured approaches for working with victims who may not see their predator as an offender. It is likely that, at the very least, amendments to the theories of paedophilia will need to be developed in order to more accurately reflect these offenders.

Finally, it is somewhat heartening to learn from the literature that violence and abduction is rare in these cases, but the willingness of youths to voluntarily meet for sex with adults who they have met online is disturbing. It is clear that society needs to reconsider the safety messages given to youth in light of the development of online technology.

REFERENCES

American Psychiatric Association. (2000). *Diagnostic and Statistical Manual of Mental Disorders (Fourth Edition, Text Revision)*. Washington, DC: American Psychiatric Association.

Bickley, J. A., & Beech, A. R. (2001). Classifying child abusers: its relevance to theory and clinical practice. *International Journal of Offender Therapy and Comparative Criminology, 45*, 51–69. doi:10.1177/0306624X01451004

Blanchard, R. (2009). The DSM Diagnostic Criteria for Pedophilia. *Archives of Sexual Behavior, 39*, 304–316. doi:10.1007/s10508-009-9536-0

Blanchard, R., Lykins, A. D., Wherrett, D., Kuban, M. E., Cantor, J. M., & Black, T. (2008). Pedophilia, Hebephilia, and the DSM-V. *Archives of Sexual Behavior, 38*, 335–350. doi:10.1007/s10508-008-9399-9

Bonta, J. (1996). Risk-needs assessment and treatment. In Harland, A. T. (Ed.), *Choosing correctional options that work* (pp. 18–32). Thousand Oaks: Sage.

Brown, S. (2005). *Treating sex offenders: An introduction to sex offender treatment programmes*. Oregon: Willan.

Bryce, J. (2008). *Bridging the Digital Divide: Executive Summary*. London: Orange and the Cyberspace Research Unit.

Bryce, J. (2010). Online sexual exploitation of children and young people. In Y. Jewkes and M. Yar (eds.) *Handbook of Internet Crime* (320-342). Cullompton, England: Willan Publishing

Child Exploitation and Online Protection (CEOP) Centre. (2010). Annual Review 2009-2010. Retrieved from http://www.ceop.police.uk/Documents/ CEOP_AnnualReview_09-10.pdf

Cortoni, F., & Marshall, W. L. (2001). Sex as a coping strategy and its relationship to juvenile sexual history and intimacy in Sexual Offenders. *Sexual Abuse, 13*, 27–43. doi:10.1177/107906320101300104

Derezotes, D., & Snowden, L. (1990). Cultural factors in the intervention of child maltreatment. *Child and Adolescent Social Work, 7*, 161–175. doi:10.1007/BF00757652

Dombrowski, S. C. (2003). Mandated reporting for mental health professionals: An overview. *Directions in Rehabilitation Counselling, 14*, 71–80.

Dombrowski, S. C., LeMasney, J. W., Ahia, C. E., & Dickson, S. A. (2004). Protecting children from online sexual predators: Technological, Psychoeducational and Legal Considerations. *Professional Psychology, Research and Practice, 35*, 65–73. doi:10.1037/0735-7028.35.1.65

Edgar-Nevill, D. (2008). Internet Grooming and Paedophile Crimes. In Bryant, R. (Ed.), *Investigating Digital Crime* (pp. 195–209). Chichester: Wiley.

Elliott, M., Browne, K., & Kilcoyne, J. (1995). Child sexual abuse prevention: What offenders tell us. *Child Abuse & Neglect, 19*, 579–594. doi:10.1016/0145-2134(95)00017-3

Finkelhor, D. (1984). *Child Sexual Abuse. New Theory and Research*. New York: Free Press.

Finkelhor, D. (1986). *A Source Book on Child Sexual Abuse*. London: Sage.

Finkelhor, D. (2009). The Prevention of Childhood Sexual Abuse. *The Future of Children, 19*, 169–194. doi:10.1353/foc.0.0035

Finkelhor, D., & Lewis, I. A. (1988). An epidemiologic approach to the study of child molesters. In Quinsey, R. A., & Quinsey, V. L. (Eds.), *Human Sexual Aggression; Current Perspectives. Annals of the New York Academy of Sciences*. New York: Plenum.

Glueck, B. C. Jr. (1955). *Final report: Research project for the study and treatment of persons convicted of crimes involving sexual aberrations, June 1952 to June 1955*. New York: New York State Department of Mental Hygiene.

Groth, A. N., & Birnbaum, H. J. (1978). Adult sexual orientation and attraction to underage persons. *Archives of Sexual Behavior, 7*, 175–181. doi:10.1007/BF01542377

Hall, G. C. (1996). *Theory-Based Assessment, Treatment and Prevention of Sexual Aggression*. Oxford: Oxford University Press.

Hall, G. C., & Hirschman, R. (1991). Towards a theory of sexual aggression: a quadripartite model. *Journal of Consulting and Clinical Psychology, 59*, 662–669. doi:10.1037/0022-006X.59.5.662

Hanson, R. K., & Bussiere, M. T. (1998). Predicting relapse: a meta-analysis of sexual offender recidivism studies. *Journal of Consulting and Clinical Psychology, 66*, 348–362. doi:10.1037/0022-006X.66.2.348

Hanson, R. K., & Harris, A. J. R. (2000). Where should we intervene? Dynamic predictors of sexual offence recidivism. *Criminal Justice and Behavior, 27*, 6–35. doi:10.1177/0093854800027001002

Hines, D., & Finkelhor, D. (2007). Statutory sex crime relationships between juveniles and adults: A review of social scientific research. *Aggression and Violent Behavior, 12*, 300–314. doi:10.1016/j.avb.2006.10.001

Howitt, D. (2006). Paedophilia prevention and the Law. In Moss, K., & Stephens, M. (Eds.), *Crime Reduction and the Law. Abington*. Routledge.

Howitt, D. (2009). *Introduction to Forensic & Criminal Psychology* (3rd ed.). Harlow, England: Pearson Education.

Kenny, M. C., & McEachern, A. G. (2000). Racial, ethnic and cultural factors of childhood sexual abuse: A selected review of the literature. *Clinical Psychology Review, 20*, 905–922. doi:10.1016/S0272-7358(99)00022-7

Lanning, K. V. (2001). Child molesters and cyber paedophiles: A behavioural perspective. In Hazelwood, R., & Burgess, A. W. (Eds.), *Practical aspects of rape investigation: A multidisciplinary approach* (3rd ed., pp. 199–220). Boca Raton, FL: CRC Press. doi:10.1201/9781420042375.ch11

Livingstone. S. (2009). *Children and the Internet: Great Expectations, Challenging Realities*. Cambridge, England: Polity.

Malesky, L. A. Jr. (2007). Predatory Online Behaviour: modus operandi of convicted sex offenders in identifying potential victims and contacting minors over the internet. *Journal of Child Sexual Abuse, 16,* 23–32. doi:10.1300/J070v16n02_02

Marshall, W. L. (1997). Pedophilia: Psychopathology and theory. In Laws, D. R., & O'Donohue, W. (Eds.), *Sexual deviance: Theory, assessment, and treatment* (pp. 152–174). New York: Guilford Press.

Marshall, W. L., & Barbaree, H. E. (1990). An integrated theory of the etiology of sexual offending. In Marshall, W. L., Laws, D. R., & Barbaree, H. E. (Eds.), *Handbook of Sexual Assault: Issues, Theories and Treatment of the Offender* (pp. 257–275). London: Plenum Press.

Middleton, D., Elliott, I. A., Mandeville-Norden, R., & Beech, A. R. (2006). An investigation into the applicability of the Ward and Siegert Pathways Model of child sexual abuse with Internet offenders. *Psychology, Crime & Law, 12,* 589–603. doi:10.1080/10683160600558352

Mitchell, K. J., Finkelhor, D., Jones, L. M., & Wolak, J. (2010). Use of Social Networking Sites in Online Sex Crimes Against Minors: An Examination of National Incidence and Means of Utilization. *The Journal of Adolescent Health.* doi:10.1016/j.jadohealth.2010.01.007

Mitchell, K. J., Finkelhor, D., & Wolak, J. (2007). Youth internet users at risk for the most serious online sexual solicitations. *American Journal of Preventive Medicine, 32,* 532–537. doi:10.1016/j.amepre.2007.02.001

Mitchell, K. J., Wolak, J., & Finkelhor, D. (2005). Police posing as juveniles online to catch sex offenders: Is it working? *Sexual Abuse, 17,* 241–267. doi:10.1177/107906320501700302

Mitchell, K. J., Wolak, J., & Finkelhor, D. (2008). Are blogs putting youth at risk for online sexual solicitation or harassment? *Child Abuse & Neglect, 32,* 277–294. doi:10.1016/j.chiabu.2007.04.015

National Centre for Missing and Exploited Children. (2007, February 28). *Press Release: National Centre for Missing and Exploited Children Creates New Unit to help find 100,000 missing sex offenders and calls for states to do their part.* Retrieved from http://www.missingkids.com/ missingkids/ servlet/NewsEventServlet?LanguageCountry =en_US&PageId=3081

Nuñez, J. (2003). Outpatient treatment of the sexually compulsive ephebophile. *Sexual Addiction & Compulsivity, 10,* 23–51. doi:10.1080/10720160309047

O'Connell, R. (2003). *A Typology of Child Cyberexploitation and Online Grooming Practices. Lancashire: Cyberspace Research Unit.* University of Central Lancashire.

Schmucker, M., & Lösel, F. (2008). Does sexual offender treatment work? A systematic review of outcome evaluations. *Psicothema, 20,* 10–19.

Sheldon, K., & Howitt, D. (2007). *Sex Offenders and the Internet.* Chichester, England: Wiley.

U.S. Department of Health and Human Services. (2007). *Child Maltreatment. Administration for Children and Families.* Retrieved from http://www.acf.hhs.gov/programs/cb/pubs/cm07/cm07.pdf

Ward, T. (2001). Hall and Hirschman's quadripartite model of child sexual abuse: a critique. *Psychology, Crime & Law, 7,* 363–374.

Ward, T., Polaschek, D., & Beech, A. R. (2006). *Theories of Sexual Offending.* Chichester, England: Wiley.

Ward, T., & Siegert, R. (2002). Toward a comprehensive theory of child sexual abuse: a theory of knitting perspective. *Psychology, Crime & Law, 8,* 319–351. doi:10.1080/10683160208401823

West, D. (1996) Sexual Molesters. In: N.Walker *Dangerous People,* London: Blackstone Press.

Wolak, J., Finkelhor, D., & Mitchell, K. (2004). Internet-initiated sex crimes against minors: Implications for prevention based on findings from a national study. *Journal of Adolescent Health, 35,* 424.e11–424.e20.

Wolak, J., Finkelhor, D., & Mitchell, K. (2008). Is talking online to unknown people always risky? Distinguishing online interaction styles in a national sample of youth internet users. *Cyberpsychology & Behavior, 11,* 340–343. doi:10.1089/cpb.2007.0044

Wolak, J., Finkelhor, D., & Mitchell, K. (2009). Law Enforcement Responses to Online Child Sexual Exploitation Crimes: The *National Juvenile Online Victimization Study,* 2000 & 2006. Retrieved from http://www.unh.edu/ccrc/pdf/LE_Bulletin_final_Dec_09.pdf

Wolak, J., Finkelhor, D., Mitchell, K., & Ybarra, M. (2008). Online "Predators" and Their Victims: Myths, Realities, and Implications for Prevention and Treatment. *The American Psychologist, 63,* 111–128. doi:10.1037/0003-066X.63.2.111

Wolak, J., Mitchell, K., & Finkelhor, D. (2006). Online victimization of youth: Five years later. *National Center for Missing & Exploited Children Bulletin - #07-06-025.* Alexandria, VA. Retrieved from http://www.unh.edu/ccrc/pdf/CV138.pdf

Yar, M. (2006). *Cybercrime and Society.* London: Sage Publications Ltd.

Yates, H. (2005). *A review of evidence-based practice in the assessment and treatment of sex offenders: Pennsylvania Department of Corrections: Office of Planning.* Research, Statistics and Grants.

ADDITIONAL READING

Bickley, J. A., & Beech, A. R. (2001). Classifying child abusers: its relevance to theory and clinical practice. *International Journal of Offender Therapy and Comparative Criminology, 45,* 51–69. doi:10.1177/0306624X01451004

Blanchard, R. (2009). The DSM Diagnostic Criteria for Pedophilia. *Archives of Sexual Behavior, 39,* 304–316.doi:10.1007/s10508-009-9536-0

Blanchard, R., Lykins, A. D., Wherrett, D., Kuban, M. E., Cantor, J. M., & Black, T. (2008). Pedophilia, Hebephilia, and the DSM-V. *Archives of Sexual Behavior, 38,* 335–350.doi:10.1007/s10508-008-9399-9

Bryce, J. (2010). Online sexual exploitation of children and young people. In Y. Jewkes & M. Yar (eds.) *Handbook of Internet Crime* (320-342). Cullompton, England: Willan Publishing

Child Exploitation and Online Protection (CEOP) Centre. (2010). *Annual Review 2009-2010.* Retrieved from http://www.ceop.police.uk/Documents/ CEOP_AnnualReview_09-10.pdf

Dombrowski, S. C., LeMasney, J. W., Ahia, C. E., & Dickson, S. A. (2004). Protecting children from online sexual predators: Technological, Psychoeducational and Legal Considerations. *Professional Psychology, Research and Practice, 35,* 65–73. doi:10.1037/0735-7028.35.1.65

Edgar-Nevill, D. (2008). Internet Grooming and Paedophile Crimes. In Bryant, R. (Ed.), *Investigating Digital Crime* (pp. 195–209). Chichester, UK: Wiley.

Finkelhor, D. (1984). *Child Sexual Abuse. New Theory and Research.* New York: Free Press.

Hall, G. C., & Hirschman, R. (1991). Towards a theory of sexual aggression: a quadripartite model. *Journal of Consulting and Clinical Psychology, 59,* 662–669. doi:10.1037/0022-006X.59.5.662

Lanning, K. V. (2001). Child molesters and cyber paedophiles: A behavioural perspective. In Hazelwood, R., & Burgess, A. W. (Eds.), *Practical aspects of rape investigation: A multidisciplinary approach* (3rd ed., pp. 199–220). Boca Raton, FL: CRC Press. doi:10.1201/9781420042375.ch11

Livingstone. S. (2009). *Children and the Internet: Great Expectations, Challenging Realities.* Cambridge, England: Polity.

Malesky, L. A. Jr. (2007). Predatory Online Behaviour: modus operandi of convicted sex offenders in identifying potential victims and contacting minors over the internet. *Journal of Child Sexual Abuse, 16*, 23–32. doi:10.1300/J070v16n02_02

Middleton, D., Elliott, I. A., Mandeville-Norden, R., & Beech, A. R. (2006). An investigation into the applicability of the Ward and Siegert Pathways Model of child sexual abuse with Internet offenders. *Psychology, Crime & Law, 12*, 589–603. doi:10.1080/10683160600558352

Mitchell, K. J., Finkelhor, D., Jones, L. M., & Wolak, J. (2010). Use of Social Networking Sites in Online Sex Crimes Against Minors: An Examination of National Incidence and Means of Utilization. *The Journal of Adolescent Health.* doi:10.1016/j.jadohealth.2010.01.007

Mitchell, K. J., Finkelhor, D., & Wolak, J. (2007). Youth internet users at risk for the most serious online sexual solicitations. *American Journal of Preventive Medicine, 32*, 532–537. doi:10.1016/j.amepre.2007.02.001

Mitchell, K. J., Wolak, J., & Finkelhor, D. (2005). Police posing as juveniles online to catch sex offenders: Is it working? *Sexual Abuse, 17*, 241–267. doi:10.1177/107906320501700302

Mitchell, K. J., Wolak, J., & Finkelhor, D. (2008). Are blogs putting youth at risk for online sexual solicitation or harassment? *Child Abuse & Neglect, 32*, 277–294. doi:10.1016/j.chiabu.2007.04.015

O'Connell, R. (2003). *A Typology of Child Cyberexploitation and Online Grooming Practices. Lancashire: Cyberspace Research Unit.* University of Central Lancashire.

Sheldon, K., & Howitt, D. (2007). *Sex Offenders and the Internet.* Chichester, England: Wiley.

Ward, T. (2001). Hall and Hirschman's quadripartite model of child sexual abuse: a critique. *Psychology, Crime & Law, 7*, 363–374.

Ward, T., & Siegert, R. (2002). Toward a comprehensive theory of child sexual abuse: a theory of knitting perspective. *Psychology, Crime & Law, 8*, 319–351. doi:10.1080/10683160208401823

Wolak, J., Finkelhor, D., & Mitchell, K. (2004). Internet-initiated sex crimes against minors: Implications for prevention based on findings from a national study. *Journal of Adolescent Health, 35*, 424.e11–424.e20.

Wolak, J., Finkelhor, D., & Mitchell, K. (2008). Is talking online to unknown people always risky? Distinguishing online interaction styles in a national sample of youth internet users. *Cyberpsychology & Behavior, 11*, 340–343. doi:10.1089/cpb.2007.0044

Wolak, J., Finkelhor, D., Mitchell, K., & Ybarra, M. (2008). Online "Predators" and Their Victims: Myths, Realities, and Implications for Prevention and Treatment. *The American Psychologist, 63*, 111–128. doi:10.1037/0003-066X.63.2.111

Chapter 9
Cyberbullying and Cyberstalking:
Are They as Serious as Their Offline Counterparts?

ABSTRACT

This chapter considers two of the most personal forms of online attack – cyberbullying and cyberstalking. While not always technically criminal events, in some jurisdictions cyberbullying acts are offences, especially when they include direct threats or physical assault. Indeed Jewkes (2010) indicates that cyberbullying occupies "a grey area between social harms and illegal acts, depending on their severity and the legal jurisdiction in which they take place" (p. 526). Cyberstalking may also be included in the stalking laws of many jurisdictions. This chapter aims to determine if cyberbullying and cyberstalking are as severe as their offline counterparts, particularly from a psychological perspective. Case studies of both cyberbullying and cyberstalking are provided, along with definitions of both activities. Known prevalence rates of the phenomena are provided, although as with most types of criminal events, the true prevalence rates of these activities is unknown. Descriptions are provided of some of the techniques used during cyberbullying and cyberstalking attacks, and differences between online and traditional stalking and bullying are considered. The demographic and psychological traits of cyberstalkers and cyberbullies are described, along with the traits of their victims, and the psychological effects of victimisation. Possible solutions for these problems are considered, including both preventative measures and suitable responses. Finally, potential future trends in the area are considered, including the possible use of online gaming and social networking sites for harassment, as well as the underexamined phenomenon of workplace cyberbullying.

DOI: 10.4018/978-1-61350-350-8.ch009

BACKGROUND

Rebecca is a fifteen year old girl who has repeatedly been the victim of cyberbullying. She regularly has to remove derogatory comments from other people which are posted on her social networking profiles. She also gets many text messages from phone numbers that she does not recognise, most of which are insulting and some of which contain threats of physical abuse. Recently she was sent a picture message where an image of her head had been placed onto someone else's naked body. When Rebecca went to school the next day, she discovered that the picture message had been circulated around all her classmates. She feels humiliated and upset, even though she knows that the photograph has been faked. Rebecca received more humiliating text messages throughout the day, and they did not stop when she returned home. Late that night her cell phone rang, but the caller remained silent when she answered. This happened eight more times until she gave up and turned off her phone. While she is very upset, Rebecca does not want to tell her parents about the bullying as she fears that they will take away her cell phone.

Stacy is a thirty year old woman who has recently broken up with her ex-boyfriend due to his abusive tendencies. Since the break-up, her ex-boyfriend has sent her at least ten emails every day, asking her to reconsider and to take him back. While she initially answered these emails, indicating that she was not willing to give the relationship another try, she quickly realised that this only encouraged his behaviours. He has cyberstalked her in other ways, including posting replies to every social networking post she writes, and initiating instant messaging conversations whenever she is online. He has also started to stalk her offline as well, using information about her whereabouts derived from her online activity. In the past few weeks his online communications have started to become more hostile, as he realised that Stacy was starting a new relationship. He began to send derogatory emails to Stacy, suggesting that she is sexually promiscuous and threatening to physically harm both her and her new boyfriend.

Definitions and Key Terms

The above case studies indicate how harmful and distressing cyberbullying and cyberstalking can be. Nevertheless, there has been little consensus as to suitable definitions for these two phenomena, nor are reliable estimates available of the prevalence of these activities.

Several definitions of cyberbullying have been proposed by academics and practitioners working in the field. Hinduja and Patchin (2009) define cyberbullying as "willful and repeated harm inflicted through the use of computers, cell phones, and other electronic devices" (p. 5). Belsey (n.d.) suggests that "Cyberbullying involves the use of information and communication technologies to support deliberate, repeated, and hostile behaviour by an individual or group, that is intended to harm others" (p 3). Willard (2007, p. 1) defines cyberbullying as "sending or posting harmful material or engaging in other forms of social aggression using the Internet or other digital technologies" while Shariff and Gouin (2005) indicate that cyberbullying "consists of covert, psychological bullying, conveyed through the electronic mediums" (p. 3). Bhat (2008) cites Hazler's (1996) description of bullying. This indicates that an action is bullying when the victim is being harmed by the physical, verbal or socio/emotional actions of the bully. Secondly, there is a power imbalance between the victim and the bully and thirdly that the actions are repeated over time. Bhat (2008) indicates that cyberbullying "involves the use of ICT to intimidate, harass, victimise or bully an individual or a group of individuals" (p 54). This may involve the use of the Internet, mobile phones, or other ICT devices.

A similar concept is cyberstalking. Stalking can also be seen as a repeated engagement in threatening or harassing behaviours (Ashcroft,

2001). While Huss (2009) indicates that people tend to associate stalking with celebrities, this type of stalking tends to be quite rare, and most stalkers do not target celebrities. Ashcroft describes offline stalking behaviours (including following the victim, appearing at their home or workplace, vandalism of the person's property, or leaving written messages or objects in places that the victim will find them) and indicates that the Internet provides an additional mechanism for stalkers to both identify potential victims, and to target them. Ashcroft (2001) defines cyberstalking as "the use of the Internet, e-mail and other electronic communication devices to stalk another person" (p. 1). Mishra and Mishra (2008) define cyberstalking as "when a person is followed and pursued online. Their privacy is invaded, their every move watched. It is a form of harassment and can disrupt the life of the victim and leave them feeling very afraid" (p. 216). Other definitions of cyberstalking include "the persistent and targeted harassment of an individual via electronic communication such as email" (Yar, 2006, p. 122) and "the use of information and communications technology (ICT) in order to harass one or more victims" (Bocij, 2006, p. 160). Bocij (2006) indicates that cyberstalking has only gained widespread public attention since the late 1990s. He indicates that harassment refers to any act that causes distress for the victim, and that intent to cause this distress is not required. As such, it should be noted that the stalker may not intend to cause any upset to their victim, but this does not necessarily detract from the offence.

Known Prevalence Rates

As with many types of criminal activity and online phenomena, it is difficult to determine exactly how much cyberbullying and cyberstalking exists. This problem is exacerabated by a lack of awareness of some victims that what they are experiencing is a criminal event, a potential sense of shame or embarassment because of their victimisation,

a fear of the repercussions of reporting such events, or even a lack of awareness that they are being victimised (for example, if an individual's actions are being tracked by a cyberstalker, but the victim is unaware of this). Nevertheless, there have been several attempts to estimate the extent of these problems.

Prevalence of Cyberbullying

Smith, Mahdavi, Carvalho and Tippett (2006) found that 22% of British participants had been cyberbullied, with 6.6% having been cyberbullied frequently. They found that most cyberbullying comes from a small number of students, normally in the same year group, and while most incidences last only about a week, some last much longer, particularly phone call bullying. United Press International (2008) indicated that more than 40% of teens in the USA had been victimized by cyberbullying, but that only one in ten tell their parents about it. Kowalski and Limber (2007) found that eleven percent of 6th to 8th grade students had experienced cyberbullying at least once in the past couple of months. Seven percent were bully/victims and four percent were bullies only. The Pew Internet and American Life Project (Lenhart, 2007) found that 32% of teenagers say that they have experienced online harassment of some kind, including actions such as receiving threatening messages or having an embarassing picture posted.

Li (2007) found that almost 54% of students were victims of traditional bullying, and that over a quarter of them had been cyber-bullied. Almost one third had bullied others traditionally, and almost fifteen percent had cyber-bullied. Most did not report the incidents to adults. Microsoft (2009) discovered that almost a third of European teenagers had been the victim of online bullying, with over half (53%) feeling that it is easier to bully due to the Internet. Hinduja and Patchin (2010b) found that about twenty percent of 11-18 year old students surveyed in 2010 indicated that they had been a victim of cyberbullying in their lifetime. A similar number admitted to cyberbullying others over their lifetime. Approximately ten percent indicated that they were both cyberbullies and cybervictims. Dehue, Bolman and Völlink (2008) found that sixteen percent of children had engaged in bullying using either the Internet or text messages. About 23% had been victims of cyberbullying.

There are, however, some problems with the consistent use of definitions of cyberbullying when attempting to estimate prevalence levels. For example, Wolak, Mitchell and Finkelhor (2007) surveyed 1500 Internet users aged between ten and seventeen years, and found that nine percent had experienced online harassment over the previous year. Of these, 43% were by known peers, with 57% by online acquaintances. Wolak et al (2007) indicate that most of the incidents could not be classified as bullying as they lacked aggression, repetition or an imbalance of power. They suggest that because of this, a more appropriate term is "online harassment" (p. S51), and that it should not be considered to be bullying unless it is related to offline contacts or offline bullying.

It should also be remembered that cyberbullying, like traditional bullying, is not restricted to children. Privitera and Campbell (2009) found that 34% of their participants in the workplace were bullied face to face, with 10.7% experiencing cyberbullying (all those cyberbullied were also bullied face to face). However, despite the considerable number of research studies examining the phenomenon of cyberbullying amongst children and adolescents, there appears to be very little research to date examining workplace cyberbullying.

Prevalence of Cyberstalking

Fewer studies have attempted to determine the prevalence of cyberstalking than have examined the prevalence of cyberbullying. Yar (2006) indicates that it is difficult to determine the amount of cyberstalking as there is little large-scale systematic research in the area, and what research there is often involves varying definitions of cyberstalking.

However, there has been some limited work done in this area. For example, Spitzberg and Hoobler (2002) found that almost one third of university students reported some form of computer-based unwanted pursuit, most of which was relatively harmless but harassing. Working to Halt Online Abuse (WHOA, 2010a), a volunteer organisation that aims to help victims of online abuse, indicate that they receive approximately 50-75 online harassment or cyberstalking cases per week. Yet it is expected that these estimates are conservative for a number of reasons.

Ashcroft (2001) suggests that many cyberstalking victims do not report the behaviour for one of two reasons – either they feel that the behaviour has not reached the extent of a criminal event, or they feel that law enforcement agencies may not take them seriously enough. On the other hand, Joseph (2003) suggests that it is difficult to determine how much cyberstalking exists as some victims may not consider it to be dangerous, or they may be unaware that they are being stalked. Irrespective of the reasons, it is highly likely that a significant number of cyberstalking cases are not captured in any academic or official estimates.

METHODS OF CYBERBULLYING AND CYBERSTALKING

The increasing number of online applications and behaviors facilitates the activities of cyberbullies and cyberstalkers. Social networking websites, online communication mechanisms, cell phones and video-sharing websites are all widely used by these types of offenders in the course of their activities.

Methods of Cyberbullying

Cyberbullying acts can be perpetrated over many aspects of online communication. Internet technologies, such as websites, blogs, email, instant messaging and chat rooms have all been used by cyberbullies. The recent popularity of social networking sites (SNS) has also facilitated the activities of cyberbullies. As well as creating personal profiles, SNS can be used by bullies to post photos of their victim, share videos, share files, write blogs, enable discussion groups to converse about the victim, as well as messaging the victim either synchronously (through instant messaging), or asynchronously (through e-mail type messages). In addition to the Internet, cyberbullies can also take advantage of cell phone technology, bullying their victims through the use of text and picture messages, as well as leaving voicemails or directly calling the victim. The cameras inbuilt in many modern cell phones also permit users to take pictures or videos of the victim, with or without the victim's knowledge, which can later be distributed to a wider audience. Bhat (2008) suggests that many forms of digital communication can be used as bullying tools. These include "email, instant messaging, social network sites, chat rooms, web sites, blogs, and text messages, pictures, or video clips via mobile phones" (p. 54).

There is some disagreement among researchers as to what the most common technologies used by cyberbullies are. Smith et al (2006) found that the most common forms of cyberbullying were phone calls, text messages and emails; with chat room bullying being the least common. Conversely, Kowalski and Limber (2007) report that the most common methods for cyberbullying involved instant messaging, chatrooms and emails. On the other hand, the Pew Internet and American Life Project (Lenhart, 2007) found that the most common form of cyberbullying involved making private information public, with 15% of teenagers reporting that it had happened to them. Dehue,

Bolman and Völlink (2008) found that the most commonly used harassments were name-calling and gossiping.

Bhat (2008) indicates that bullying actions can include the spreading of rumors, ridiculing, social exclusion, telling secrets and gathering support for physical attacks. It may also include the dissemination of embarrassing information about the individual or their loved ones, photographs and video clips taken with or without the victim's consent, or excluding a person from a list of friends and contacts, a form of social exclusion. Hinduja and Patchin (2009) also describe a number of techniques used by cyberbullies. These include sending harassing communications (such as emails or instant messaging), posting slanderous or insulting messages to public online spaces, such as bulletin boards or social networking websites, or the development of specific websites to disseminate negative content. In addition to these, the cyberbully may send text messages to the victim's cellphone. Hinduja and Patchin (2009) also describe how cyberbullies can use voting or rating websites where visitors judge aspects of a person's physical attractiveness as part of the bullying strategies. A public judgment that the victim is 'not attractive' may add to the victim's emotional reaction. Hinduja and Patchin (2009) also list other methods by which cyberbullying may occur, including blogs, virtual worlds and online gaming.

A specific example of cyberbullying described by Hinduja and Patchin (2009) and Jewkes (2010) involves 'happy-slapping', where an incident of a person being physically bullied is recorded and uploaded to a website or otherwise distributed. Jewkes (2010) also describes 'sexual bullying', and cites an example where in 2007 a 16 year old boy was accused of sexually assaulting a 14 year old girl, while another boy was charged for filming the attack and distributing the images on his cellphone. Jewkes (2010) also describes 'sexting', "where an individual sends nude or suggestive photos of themselves over their mobile phone" (p. 531). She cites the example of an 18 year old girl who committed suicide in 2008 after nude images that she had sent to her boyfriend ended up in circulation, initially in her high school in Cincinnati, but later over a much further distance. A related type of bullying is described by Hinduja and Patchin (2009), who indicate that photos of victims may be modified so that they are "placed in a compromising or embarrassing context or scene" (p. 35). This image can then be distributed widely.

Wolak, Mitchell and Finkelhor (2007) found that over half of those engaged in online peer harassment sent or posted messages in public online spaces, such as gossip and rumors. They found that harassment by known peers tended to involve multiple harassers, and generally were more likely to require the involvement of an adult, such as a parent or a teacher, to resolve the issue. Hinduja and Patchin (2009) indicate that in some cases personal communications, meant only for the recipient, are later forwarded by the recipient to a large number of people and confidentiality is broken. This may be a particularly painful form of cyberbullying as it is initiated by someone the victim previously trusted.

A final form of cyberbullying is described by Hinduja and Patchin (2009), who suggest that in some cases a victim may be impersonated online – perhaps if their bully knows their username and password. The bully can then make it appear that messages originate from the victim, and the recipients of the messages may not know that the impersonation has occurred. This may extend to changing the victim's password after the impersonation, so that the victim has less opportunity to limit the damage caused by deleting the content. Overall, a wide array of bullying techniques are available to the cyberbully, and these techniques can be completed using a variety of online tools and technologies. Similarly, cyberstalkers utilize numerous tools and techniques to achieve their goals.

Methods of Cyberstalking

Bocij (2006) indicates that cyberstalking can include identity theft, distribution of offensive online messages, and damage to files or equipment. He lists a number of possible cyberstalking behaviors, including physical assault, although he indicates that this is rare. Other behaviors noted by Bocij include making threats, false accusations made about the victim, the sending of abusive messages, gathering information about the victim, impersonating the victim, encouraging other people to harass the victim, ordering goods or services for the victim (in some case causing embarrassment, by sending potentially humiliating products to the victim's workplace), and attempting to meet the victim.

McQuade (2006) indicates that cyberstalkers may "psychologically terrorize [victims] by leaving surveillance photographs, symbolic objects, or other items in conspicuous locations where they will be found by victims" (p. 96). This indicates the potential for overlap between the online and offline varieties of stalking – the cyberstalker may use the Internet to determine where the target will be at a given time, and then physically be there or place objects there to be found. Mishra and Mishra (2008) indicate that cyberstalking can be direct or indirect. Direct forms involve directly contacting the victim (such as through cell phones, e-mail, and so on). Indirect cyber stalking involves using the internet to display messages more publicly, such as via webpages or on bulletin boards. Philips and Morrissey (2004) examine the cyberpredators of adults, particularly in relation to sexual harassment. They indicate that such online harassment can include obscene emails and the posting of false personal advertisements suggesting the victim is available for sex, and can lead to actual sexual violence and death. Philips and Morrissey (2004) suggest that stalkers may even use keyloggers (for a description of keyloggers, see Chapter 5) to control and examine their victim. They admit that cyberstalking is not always sexual in nature, and that while it seems that women are the majority of victims, men have also been targeted. In addition, Wykes suggests that cyberstalking may involve "electronic sabotage" (p. 137) by sending vast quantities of spam or computer viruses. She also indicates that cyberstalkers may impersonate their victims, hijacking their email accounts.

Working to Halt Online Abuse (WHOA, 2010b) found that for most people harassment began by email (34%), although harassment starting via instant messaging was also high (13%), and Facebook and Myspace accounted for 5.5% of initial harassment each. In 66% of cases the cyberstalking escalated, mostly by email, but also including phone calls, text messages, websites and social networking services, and in over sixteen percent of cases there were threats of offline or physical violence. In over seventy percent of cases the victim reported the harassment, normally to the police or their Internet Service Provider (ISP). However, WHOA do recognise that their sample is incomplete, and while they invite all victims who contact them to complete their online questionnaire, many do not.

In some cases cyberstalking is linked to an offline abusive partner, who Finn and Atkinson (2009) indicate may "monitor email through a keystroke-logging device or spyware program, assume a victim's identity online or send their picture to socialization sites so that she/he will be harassed by email or telephone responses". In addition to this, the victim may be stalked by monitoring their online history, tracking their car, checking their cell phone logs or placing a hidden camera in their home. Finn and Atkinson (2009) carried out and evaluated a training system to increase awareness of technology safety issues for domestic violence victims and survivors. They carried out a survey with the trainees, and found that satisfaction levels were high, and that they found the training useful. However they found that of those who completed the training system, one in four had experienced someone checking their browser history to find out what they had visited.

Almost the same amount (23.6%) had received repeated emails from someone that threatened, insulted or harassed them. Eighteen percent of women had someone monitor their emails, with other forms of privacy invasion (such as impersonation) also occurring.

While there is some overlap between online and offline harassment types, some characteristics of the Internet seem to augment the activities of cyberbullies and cyberstalkers. These will be explored in the following section.

Comparison to Offline Bullying and Stalking Techniques and Activities

Cyberbullying

There are several key differences between traditional bullying and cyberbullying, although it is noted that often the same bullies and victims are involved in each type. For example, Raskauskas and Stoltz (2007) found that students' roles in traditional bullying were similar to cyberbullying – being a victim online was related to being a victim in school, and traditional victims were not necessarily found to be cyberbullies.

One key difference between traditional bullying and cyberbullying relates to gender. For example, Kowalski and Limber (2007) found that traditionally, boys are more likely to be the bully, but online, girls are more likely to engage in bullying behaviours. A second difference relates to the anonymity provided by the Internet (as noted by Kowalski & Limber, 2007; Li, 2007), which can make it easier to engage in cyberbullying, and also makes the activity harder to prevent and investigate. Shariff (2005) also describes how the bully has the option of remaining anonymous online, and as such many victims may not know the identity of their bully or bullies, which may be even more traumatising for the victim. Hinduja and Patchin (2009) also indicate that the anonymity and pseudonymity provided by the Internet can enable cyberbullies. They suggest that this may release the individual from traditional constraints of conscience, morality and ethics. Hinduja and Patchin (2009) indicate that cyberbullies "do not have to deal with the immediate emotional, psychological or physical effects of face-to-face bullying on their victim" (p. 22). The cyberbully does not receive response clues as to the inappropriateness of their actions. Bhat (2008) also suggests that the cyberbully may not realize the ramifications of their actions. What they may see as a relatively harmless prank may have a severe impact on their victim, but the lack of visibility of the effects of their actions may not prevent the bully from repeating the behavior. Kowalski and Limber (2007) also describe how the bully may not realize how much of an effect their comments have had as they cannot see the victim's emotional reactions.

Willard (2007) indicates that disinhibition relates to how people on the Internet are more willing to say or do things that they would not in the real world. She explains that this is a neutral aspect of online behavior, leading to either positive or negative results (p. 78). She describes how online, people can perceive themselves to be anonymous (even though they may not necessarily be as anonymous as they feel they are). She suggests that this perceived invisibility leads people to believe that they will not be punished for their actions, and so she suggests that strategies that threaten legal action in cyberspace are unlikely to succeed. Willard indicates that disinhibition may distance people from the realization of the harm that they have caused due to the lack of tangible feedback normally achieved through face-to-face interactions. This may also lead people to feel that they have not really harmed the other. Twyman, Saylor, Taylor and Comeaux (2009) found that almost two thirds of cyberbully/victims were also traditional bully/victims. However, they also found that some of the online bullies were not traditional bullies, which they attributed to online disinhibition.

A third characteristic of online bullying relates to the size of the potential audience. This is much larger online than offline (Kowalksi & Limber, 2007). Shariff (2005) indicates that the online nature of the victimisation allows for the potential that the victimisation may be witnessed by others. For example, this may occur if the bully posts a derogatory message on the victim's profile on a social networking site – although the victim may be able to remove the message, they will be aware that others may have seen it before they removed it. The Pew Internet and American Life Project (Lenhart, 2007) suggested that cyberbullying was popular because it was easy to replicate and transmit the content.

This point is elaboarated by Hinduja and Patchin (2009), who indicate that the viral nature of cyberbullying differentiates it from traditional bullying. The hurtful information or files can be distributed to a much larger number of people in a much shorter period of time using the internet than traditional bullying allows. Hinduja and Patchin (2009) indicate that this relates to the concept of repetition and repeat victimization in bullying, as even though there may only be one image or remark involved, it is repeated many times, and exposed to a much wider number of people, who may then go on to join in the harassment.

Finally, Hinduja and Patchin (2009) indicate that cyberbullying is different to offline bullying as there are a greater number of methods for bullies to contact targets. Bullying is no longer confined to school settings, but the target can be bullied in their own bedroom. As many individuals now keep cell phones turned on permanently, there is a constant link between the bully and the target if the bully knows the cellphone number. In addition, with the growing number of smartphones currently available, which allow access to social networking websites and other online applications, the cell phone allows the bully to reach the target at any time, using a variety of both public and private avenues.

Cyberstalking

Similar to the literature on cyberbullying, much of the research on cyberstalking has identified the anonymous nature of the activity. Ashcroft (2001) indicates that the anonymity provided by the Internet "allows the perpetrator to exercise power and control over the victim by threatening the victim directly or posting messages that lead third parties to engage in harassment and threatening behavior toward the victim" (p. vii).

Philips and Morrissey (2004) suggest that most cyberstalking incidents occur between strangers, with the stalker not deliberately targeting any individual. They suggest that the stalker will claim that they did not mean any harm if they are caught, and they indicate how the anonymity provided by the Internet protects the identity of the stalker. Wykes (2007) indicates that the Internet provides greater potential for stranger stalking due to the large quantity of personal data available there. She also indicates that cyberstalking is more likely to be carried out anonymously and from a distance, and that it may involve abusive or threatening communication. Philips and Morrissey (2004) suggest that while cyberstalking incidents may occur over much larger distances than offline stalking, they should still be considered dangerous, as it may progress to real-life stalking.

Finally, Finn and Banach (2000) suggest that on the Internet, there is a sense of 'electronic propinquity', where "people feel in proximity to each other online despite the physical distance" (p. 248). Finn and Banach also suggest that potential cyberstalkers may misinterpret the meaning of messages that they receive, developing idealized perceptions of the individual. They also feel that other factors, such as anonymity and disinhibition, may be related to cyberstalking behaviors. The following section considers the psychology of both the perpetrators and the victims of cyberbullying and cyberstalking.

PSYCHOLOGY OF CYBERBULLYING AND CYBERSTALKING

Psychological Traits of Cyberbullies

There has been considerable research into the psychology of cyberbullies, examining personality traits, cognitive abilities and motives. Bhat (2008) reviews the literature relating to the psychological traits of bullying, and identifies several important characteristics. These include that bullies tend to be more impulsive, acting without fully considering the consequences. They may react more quickly to anger than others do, perceive hostility in the actions of others, hold rigid beliefs and use aggressive actions to protect their image. They may also have little empathy for others. Bhat (2008) indicates that this impulsivity may be especially important for cyberbullies (as opposed to traditional bullies), as the internet permits actions to be taken quickly in retaliation to any real or imaginary offending action. Patchin and Hinduja (2010) found that strain is an important indicator of cyberbullying, with those who experience strain being more likely to engage in both traditional and nontraditional types of bullying.

Strom and Strom (2005) indicate that the motive behind cyberbullying is to threaten, humiliate or harm the victim, as well as creating fear and helplessness in them. Bhat (2008) suggests that the cyberbully's aim is the same as the offline bully – "to embarrass, threaten, shame, hurt, or exclude the victim" (p. 58). Hinduja and Patchin (2009) indicates that cyberbullies "seek implicit or explicit plesure or profit through the mistreatment of another individual" (p. 17). Pew Internet & American Life Project (Lenhart, 2007) indicate that intolerance may be a cause of online bullying, such as targeted attacks on minority groups such as homosexual individuals.

With regard to demographic characteristics, Hinduja and Patchin (2008) found that gender and race were not significantly related to involvement in cyberbullying or being victimised online.

Conversely, Li (2007) found that over half of cyberbullies were males, but that females prefer to use the electronic communication medium to bully others.

Ybarra and Mitchell (2004) claim that males and females are equally involved in cyberharassing others, and that those who are victims of bullies offline are significantly more likely to bully others online.

Hinduja and Patchin (2008) found the computer proficiency and the amount of time that the adolescent spent online had a positive correlation with both cyberbullying victimization and cyberbullying offending. Offline problems also associated with cyberbullying included school problems, traditional bullying, being assaultive, and substance abuse. Twyman, Saylor, Taylor and Comeaux (2009) also found that those engaged in cyberbullying or who were cyberbullying victims were more likely to spend more time on the Internet, instant messaging, social networking, or e-mailing.

Psychological Traits of Cyberstalkers

There is limited empirical evidence regarding the psychological traits of cyberstalkers, although some of the research regarding traditional stalkers may be of use. For example, Joseph (2003) suggests that cyberstalkers are, like traditional stalkers, "motivated by a desire to exert control over their victims and engage in similar types of behaviour to accomplish this end" (p. 106). She indicates that as with offline stalking, the victim and stalker are often acquainted or have had a previous relationship, and the majority of cyberstalkers are men, with the majority of victims being women. Similarly, Yar (2006) cites the statistics of The New York Police Department's Computer Investigation and Technology Unit (CITU), who found that offender characteristics in cyberharassment cases showed similarities and differences from traditional stalkers. About 80%

of cyberstalkers were male (similar to offline), but females made up 52% of victims, much less than the estimated 75-80% of offline victims. Slightly different findings are reported by Working to Halt Online Abuse (WHOA, 2010b), who report that in one in five cases, the gender of the harasser was unknown, but in 45% of cases it was male, and in 35% of cases it was female. In 61% of cases the victim had a prior relationship with the harasser. Over forty percent of these cases involved an ex partner; with 22% being online acquaintances and fourteen percent being family members.

However, there may be differences between the two types of stalking. Yar (2006) suggests that cyberstalking is more likely than traditional stalking "to remain mediated and at a distance" (p. 129), and so the predator and victim are less likely to meet. However, this does not eliminate the potential for psychological harm to be done to the victim, and in some cases cyberstalkers do physically track down their victim, sometimes with violent consequences.

Ashcroft (2001) suggests that many stalkers, online or offline "are motivated by a desire to exert control over their victims" (p. 2). While Ashcroft indicates that most evidence is anecdotal in nature, he indicates that the majority of cyberstalkers are men, with the majority of victims being women, although this is not always the case. He indicates that in many cases the cyberstalker had a prior relationship with the victim, and that the cyberstalking commenced when the victim tried to break up with the stalker. Nevertheless, Ashcroft indicates that it is also possible for individuals to be cyberstalked by strangers. Ashcroft goes on to list some similarities and differences between offline and online stalking. The similarities include that in both instances, most cases involve those who were formerly in an intimate relationship, although stalking by strangers can also occur in both cases. Similarly, most victims are women and most stalkers are men in both cases, and in both cases stalkers tend to be motivated by a desire to control their victim. Differences between online and offline stalking include the distances involved – cyberstalking may involve individuals who live much further apart. Online stalking may also involve the cyberstalker getting other individuals to harass and threaten their target. This might be done by the stalker leaving controversial messages on bulletin boards, pretending to be the target, and thus encouraging readers of the messages to send malicious messages to the victim. Ashcroft (2001) suggests that people who otherwise would not engage in stalking behavior may be more likely to do so due to the anonymous, impersonal and non-confrontational aspects of online communication.

Some typologies have been suggested of offline stalkers, which may be relevant to cyberstalkers. Bocij (2006) cites research by Zona, Sharma and Lane (1993) who propose a typology of stalkers, involving *erotomanics, love obsessionals* and *simple obsessionals.* Erotomanics tend to feel that they are loved by the person that they stalk, despite a lack of previous relationship. These are usually females, with a focus on celebrities. Love obsessionals also frequently believe that their victims love them, but not always, and their delusions derive from psychotic illness. These individuals also usually focus on celebrities, but tend to be male. Simple obsessionals are characterized by a previous relationship with the victim, although it may be a professional or personal relationship rather than an intimate one. Simple obsessionals are equally likely to be male or female. Meloy (2000) claims that most stalkers are 'simple obsessional', with about a quarter being 'love obsessional' and a small minority being 'erotomanic'.

Bocij (2006) also cites a classification system of stalkers by Mullen, Pathé, Purcell and Stuart (1999) which differentiates between five types of stalker. These include *rejected stalkers* (who pursue a former intimate partner, and are motivated by reconciliation or revenge), *intimacy seekers* (who believe that a romantic relationship is destined to happen), *incompetent stalkers* (who are not in love with the victim but are trying to establish

contact with them), *resentful stalkers* (who are seeking revenge and wish to scare the victim) and *predatory stalkers* (probably the most dangerous type, who use stalking as a method of preparing to sexually assault the victim).

A further typology is proposed by Mishra and Mishra (2008), this time specifically for cyberstalkers. They suggest that there are three types of cyberstalker – the 'common obsessional cyberstalker' (who previously had a relationship with the victim, and who refuses to let go of the relationship); the 'delusional cyber stalker' (who may be suffering from a mental illness that leads them to the false belief that they have a romantic relationship with the victim, even though they have not met – these stalkers are more likely to choose celebrities or those in the helping professions such as teachers or doctors); and finally the 'vengeful stalker' (who is angry at their victim due to some minor indiscretion).

Douglas and Dutton (2001) indicate that stalkers have extreme emotional dysregulation, being more likely to experience substance abuse and depression. They also tend to be more angry and jealous, and are likely to have had poor emotional attachment to their parents. It is also possible that the disinhibition phenomenon outlined in relation to cyberbullying above also relates to cyberstalking, with Meloy (1998) suggesting that cyberstalkers may become disinhibited due to the lack of social constraints online, so that they are more comfortable expressing their emotions and desires directly to the victim. In addition to this, the lack of physicality involved online may mean that fantasy becomes more important for the stalker, and may fuel their behavior.

Psychological Traits of Cyberbullying Victims

There has been some information relating to profiles of cyberbullying victims. Li (2007) found that almost sixty percent of cybervictims were females. Similarly, the Pew Internet and American

Life Project (Lenhart, 2007) indicated that girls were more likely to be targets of cyberbullying with 38% of online girls being bullied, as opposed to 26% of online boys. Older girls in particular were found to be most at risk. Other research by Smith et al (2006) found no significant differences in age, but they found that girls were significantly more likely to be cyberbullied, especially by text messages and phone calls. With regard to reporting the victimization, Li (2006) reports that female cyberbully victims are more likely to inform adults than males are. Kowalski and Limber (2007) found that 15% of girls and 11% of boys had been cyber victimized whereas, 3.6% of girls and 4.1% of boys were bully/victims and 9.5% of girls and 6.8% of boys had cyberbullied someone else. So overall girls were more involved in cyberbullying, as a victim or a bully (with only 71.8% not involved) than boys (with 78% not involved).

Kowalski and Limber (2007) indicate that almost half of cyberbullying victims did not know who their bully was, and as such, the anonymity perceived by cyberbullies seems to be quite real. This has further repercussions for the victims of cyberbullies, as they may become distrustful of many of their friends because they do not know who they are being victimized by. Finally, the Pew Internet and American Life Project (Lenhart, 2007) found that teenagers who share their thoughts and identities online are more likely to be targets of cyberbullying. Those who used social networking sites and those who used the Internet daily were more likely to say that they had been cyberbullied. This is an aspect of online life that is under the control of the potential victim, and provides a possible mechanism of preventing cyberbullying.

Psychological Traits of Cyberstalking Victims

As with cyberbullying, there is a strong relationship between gender and victimization in cyberstalking cases. Working to Halt Online Abuse (WHOA, 2010b) report that in 2009, their sample

of cyberstalking victims were mostly female (78%) and Caucasian (69.5%). Most were single (43%), with 27% married and over eleven percent divorced. Bocij (2006) found that females made up the majority of cyberstalking victims, and most were over the age of thirty. He found that over three-quarters of his sample of cyberstalking victims were married or cohabiting with a partner. Over forty percent did not know the identity of their harasser. Conversely, Alexy, Burgess, Baker and Smoyak (2005) found that male students were statistically more likely than female students to have been cyberstalked. Also, for those individuals who were cyberstalked, the stalking perpetrator was most likely to be a former intimate partner.

As with cyberbullying victims, there is one known characteristic of cyberstalking victims which can be directly targeted in intervention strategies. Finn and Banach (2000) suggest that those who seek help and advice online may be at higher risk of cyberstalking, due in part to the higher amount of personal information revealed. As some people provide large quantities of personal information online in order to seek more accurate advice from others, this also enables cyberstalkers to identify them more easily, and possibly to determine their physical location. This tendency to provide large quantities of personal information online is another aspect of the online disinhibition effect described above, and while it can in some cases be useful (such as by allowing the person to gain useful advice), in other cases it can be detrimental to the victim by enabling cyberstalkers.

Psychological Effects on Cyberbullying Victims

While there is a shortage of empirical work examining the psychosocial impact on cyberbullying victims (Bhat, 2008, p. 55), some research has been completed in this area. Patchin and Hinduja (2006) indicate that the effects of cyberbullying on victims can be psychological, emotional and/

or social in nature, and may last for years. Specifically Burgess-Proctor, Patchin and Hinduja (2009) describe how victimization of cyberbullying may undermine the victim's ability to explore the more positive aspects of online life. Beran and Li (2005) found that cyber harassment (which they use interchangeably with the term cyberbullying) victims in their sample reported feeling angry, hurt, anxious, sad, or fearful. They found that 21% of their students had been harassed several times, with three percent admitting to engaging in harassment. They also found that the majority of students who were victims of cyberharassment were also victimized at school. They found that the severity of the incidents ranged from annoying, to the occurrence of death threats. They indicate that some of their victims of cyber-harassment's emotional reactions may have impaired their ability to fulfill their academic potential.

Conversely, Wolak, Mitchell and Finkelhor (2007) found that once-off online harassment of teenagers, whether by known or unknown harassers, was not distressing for targets. The circumstances under which it was found to be distressing involved cases where repetition was involved (where there were a series of incidents), or if the harasser was over the age of eighteen (possibly suggesting a power imbalance). Youths were also distressed if harassers asked for pictures.

Consequences of cyberbullying can be quite severe. Ybarra (2004) reported a relationship between internet harassment and depressive symptoms. Hinduja and Patchin (2010a) found that youths who experienced cyberbullying, either as an offender or as a victim, had more suicidal thoughts and were more likely to attempt suicide than those who had not. These feelings are compounded by the fact that "victims of cyber bullying do not feel that they have any safe haven or sanctuary" (Bhat, 2008, p. 55). No longer is home a safe place from bullies – the omnipresence of mobiles phones and Internet access means that the victim is rarely out of reach of the cyberbully.

Finally, it is possible that different forms of cyberbullying have varying effects on the victim. Smith et al (2006) found that their participants perceived picture/video clip and phone call bullying to have more impact on the victim than traditional forms of bullying, with website and text message bullying seen as similar in impact to traditional bullying, and chatroom, IM and email bullying were perceived as having less of an impact than traditional forms of bullying.

Psychological Effects on Cyberstalking Victims

Yar (2006) indicates that victims of traditional stalking may experience fear, anxiety, lost time from work and making adjustments to their normal lives (such as increased home security or changing telephone numbers). It is possible that similar responses are seen in victims of cyberstalking. For example, Philips and Morrissey (2004) suggest that victim reactions to cyberstalking can vary from annoyance to distress, with the potential that the person may eventually begin to fear for their lives. Conversely, other research, such as Sheridan and Grant (2007) found that there were no significant differences in psychological and medical effects of cyberstalking on the victim.

The consequences for victims of cyberstalking can be quite complex. Philips and Morrissey (2004) suggest that the victim may feel that they are in some way responsible for what happened to them and they indicate that reactions can range from irritation to trauma. This suggests that there is some evidence that cyberstalking victims self-blame for their victimization, adding a feeling of guilt to their other reactions. This may be compounded by the actions of the cyberstalker. For example, Alexy, Burgess, Baker and Smoyak (2005) found that cyberstalking was more likely to include threats of suicide by the stalker. The victim may feel compelled to respond to the stalker's advances in order to prevent the stalker from taking their own life, so feeling even more trapped in their situation. Nevertheless, there are some possible solutions and preventative measures that can be employed to help victims of both cyberbullying and cyberstalking.

SOLUTIONS

Potential solutions to the problems of cyberbullying and cyberstalking have taken two main approaches. Firstly, efforts are made to prevent such events from occurring in the first place, and most of these preventative measures have specifically targeted cyberbullying. Secondly, suggestions have been made for dealing with incidents of cyberbullying and cyberstalking. In some cases these responses are formal in nature, involving interventions by schools or police, while in other cases informal measures can be taken by the victim themselves.

Preventative Measures

One of the primary methods of preventing cyberbullying involves monitoring children's use of the Internet, and educating children about the phenomenon and the harm it can do. Kowalski and Limber (2007) describe how it is important that parents proactively discuss cyberbullying with their children. They indicate that adolescents are reluctant to report cases that do not involve death threats, as they are afraid that their parents will restrict their time on the internet. So Kowalski and Limber (2007) suggest that it is important that parents set up appropriate guidelines for their children's use of technologies. Similarly, Microsoft (2009) suggest that some of the best ways to deal with cyberbullying involve putting internet enabled devices in central locations in the home, discussing children's online activities with them, discuss cyberbullying with older children who are more likely to use the Internet outside of the home environment, and ensuring that children feel comfortable reporting bullying to the parent. Bhat

(2008) also suggests that parents should monitor their children's use of information technologies, and should encourage open discussions with the children about cyberbullying. Hinduja and Patchin (2010b) also indicate that parents need to inform their children about what is and is not appropriate behavior online, and that the child should be monitored online. Internet use and cell phone use contracts may be employed so that children are clear about the appropriateness of different online activities.

Hinduja and Patchin (2009) discuss that part of the cyberbullying problem is the lack of supervision involved – for many online communications there is no monitoring of content to see if it is offensive. This problem is exasperated by the fact that teenagers have increased unsupervised access to the Internet, either through computers in their bedrooms or through cell phones. Willard (2007) suggests that younger children's online activities should be limited to *safe* places that are deemed to be appropriate by an adult. She then indicates that teenagers should be taught to recognize that others online are real people, who will experience emotional reactions to the bullying. Conversely, some research (such as Mesch, 2009) found that the location of the computer does not affect the risk of being a cyberbullying victim. Similarly, restrictive parental mediations, where the parents try to block access to certain online content or to record online activities did not have a significant effect on victimization. However, by setting rules on which websites adolescents were allowed to visit, their risk of victimization was reduced.

Some researchers suggest that schools, as well as parents, need to play a role in preventing cyberbullying. Bhat (2008) suggests several strategies that could be undertaken by school personnel to combat cyberbullying. Bhat indicates that as the cyberbullying has an impact on what happens in school, even if it does not happen on school grounds, it is important that schools deal with the problem. Bhat suggests that school counselors should offer training to parents and students about cybersafety and cyberbullying. In addition to this, efforts to develop character traits such as empathy, and teaching social skills should be continued. Similarly, Hinduja and Patchin (2010b) indicate that schools should be sure that students are informed about acceptable use, and that signs should be used in computer labs to ensure that students are reminded of these. In addition, harassment and bullying policies in schools should be reviewed to ensure that they cover cyberbullying, with appropriate penalties set and adhered to, up to and including expulsion if necessary.

Finally, Brown, Jackson and Cassidy (2006) suggest that students should have a say in the development of policies in the area, to ensure that the policies are more consensual than imposed, and that the policies need to be evaluated to determine if they are achieving their goals.

Responses to Cyberbullying Attacks

Despite the best efforts of parents and schools, it seems unlikely that the problem of cyberbullying will be completely eradicated. As such, it is important that the most efficient methods of dealing with such problems are identified and implemented as soon as possible after an incident of cyberbullying occurs. This can be difficult to achieve, as it is estimated that only about a third of cyberbullying victims had told anybody about their victimization (Smith et al, 2006). This is compounded by the low rate of bystander intervention. Li (2007) reports that many adolescent bystanders of cyberbullying do not report the incident to adults, possibly because they feel that adults would not help.

Even if the cyberbullying is reported, it is not always clear what the best approach to deal with it is. Microsoft (2009) suggest that parents carefully consider the right strategy to take if their child is the victim of bullying, and that parents clearly indicate the consequences that will occur if their child engages in cyberbullying. United Press

International (2008) indicate that some methods of preventing cyberbullying include blocking communication with cyberbullies, reporting cyberbullying to adults, and refusing to pass along cyber-bullying messages. Dehue, Bolman and Völlink (2008) indicate that cybervictims tend to respond to cyberbullying by ignoring it (or at least pretending to), or by bullying the bully.

Hinduja and Patchin (2010b) propose that parents need to be supportive of children who are cyberbullied. They indicate that it may be appropriate to discuss the matter with teachers, school administrators, the Internet Service Provider, and the parents of the bully. If physical threats are involved, the police should also be informed. Hinduja and Patchin (2010b) indicate that if a parent discovers that their child is a cyberbully, they should teach the child about the harm caused by the behavior, and appropriate consequences should be applied. Tracking or filtering software may be employed, if required, or the child's technology access should be withdrawn for a set time.

Responses to Cyberstalking Attacks

Similar to cyberbullying incidents, in many cases cyberstalking incidents are not formally reported. Philips and Morrissey (2004) suggest that investigations of cyberpredation and cyberstalking are made more difficult as the victim is often hesitant to report their experiences, possibly due to shame, a lack of awareness of who can help, or a lack of awareness of the fact that the incident is criminal in nature. When cyberstalking does occur, a number of responses are both appropriate and suitable, depending on the circumstances.

Philips and Morrissey (2004) suggest that if harassment does happen, the victim should take some actions to reduce the extent of the incident. These include avoiding retaliation, so that the harasser is not rewarded with a response. Incidents should be reported to the administrator of the website or service it happens on. If necessary, communications from the offender should be saved so that they can be used as evidence to be passed on to the police. Joseph (2003) suggests that there are several things a cyberstalking victim can do to protect themselves. These include being careful of including personal information in public profiles, being cautious about meeting people that they met online in real life, logging off if a situation becomes hostile, reporting incidences to the police, and deleting emails from certain addresses if they have inappropriate content. While Joseph also suggests that emails from harassers should be blocked, there are problems with doing this. For example, Ashcroft (2001) indicates that it may not be appropriate for victims of cyberstalking to block emails and communications from the stalker, as they may be unaware of threats that are sent, until such a time that the stalker attempts to carry out the threat.

Official bodies also need to take appropriate action when cyberstalking cases come to their attention. Ashcroft (2001) suggests that law enforcement officers need more training in dealing with cyberstalking cases, and that they need to become more sensitive to the impact of cyberstalking on victims. He also indicates that Internet Service Providers (ISPs) need to provide suitable support for victims. He suggests that the educational materials available for parents to help protect children online may be useful for victims of cyberstalking too, as they often discuss measures such as limiting personal information online.

Of course, the cyberstalker themselves should not be forgotten when various responses are considered. Sheridan and Davies (2004) indicate that different stalkers respond in different ways to attempted interventions. They suggest that while some stalkers will respond to counseling, others will "view police interference as a challenge to overcome whilst still maintaining control of the victim" (p. 206). As such, even though the law seldom differentiates between different types of stalkers, interventions should bear in mind the typology of the stalker in order to reduce reoffending.

FUTURE TRENDS AND RESEARCH

As the Internet becomes a more common daily activity for larger numbers of people, it is possible that we will see increased frequencies of cyberbullying and cyberstalking. In particular, the growing popularity of Social Networking Sites may facilitate cyberstalking incidents due to the large amount of personal information which is made available on the profiles of potential victims, including date of birth, hometown, and attendance at upcoming events. Bocij (2006) suggests that online gaming may also be an increasing area for cyber harassment, suggesting that members of an online group in the game may repeatedly attack the victim's avatar, or may refuse to interact with the player in the game. The victim may also be insulted or threatened in the game.

There is a need for increased research into the effectiveness of cyberbullying and cyberstalking interventions and preventative measures. While most of the measures suggested so far seem to be intuitively correct, not all research to date has supported this, and more thorough, larger-scale research needs to be completed. Specifically, research into preventative measures for cyberstalking is notably scarce, and this is possibly an area which requires urgent attention.

Finally, there is limited information to date on workplace cyberbullying. Society has become more aware that bullying is not limited to children and adolescents, but that it can extend to adults as well, particularly where there is an imbalance of power. Research is required to examine the extent to which cyberbullying occurs in workplace settings, the forms that it takes, and the reactions of victims to such events. While it is important that research focuses on protecting the most vulnerable in society, including children, it must also be remembered that other individuals can experience similar victimization.

CONCLUSION

Bullying and stalking have been serious problems in offline settings for many years, and modern technologies such as the Internet and cell phones have provided perpetrators with new tools and techniques for engaging in such behaviors. It is also possible that these new technologies also encourage individuals to bully or stalk where they would not have contemplated such behaviors without the anonymity that these new media provide. While there are now several high-profile research studies relating to cyberbullying, the empirical work on cyberstalking is still limited, and there is a specific need for more research on the effects that such incidents have on victims, as well as the effectiveness of interventions and preventative measures. It would seem that for at least some victims, the effects of such attacks are as severe as similar offline victimization, due to modern society's tendency to be (almost) always online, in one form or another. Because of this, there is limited respite from the stalker and bully, and this may have a more severe impact on the victim than if the activity was more intermittent. In addition to this, as the evidence to date seems to suggest that many of those who are cyberbullied also experience traditional forms of bullying, it is difficult to determine which type of bullying actually has the most severe effect on the victim. As such, it is difficult to conclude with certainty which types of activity have the most severe impact, and instead it is probably of more benefit to focus attention on determining the most effective methods of reducing both traditional and cyber-forms of both stalking and bullying.

REFERENCES

Alexy, E. M., Burgess, A. W., Baker, T., & Smoyak, S. A. (2005). Perceptions of Cyberstalking Among College Students. *Brief Treatment and Crisis Intervention, 5*, 279–289. doi:10.1093/brief-treatment/mhi020

Ashcroft, J. (2001, May). *Stalking and Domestic Violence: Report to Congress.* Retrieved November 4, 2010 from http://www.ncjrs.gov/pdffiles1/ojp/186157.pdf

Belsey, B. (n.d.). *Cyber bullying: An emerging threat to the 'always on' generation.* Retrieved November 3, 2010 from http://www.cyberbullying.ca/pdf/ Cyberbullying_Article_by_Bill_Belsey.pdf

Beran, T., & Li, Q. (2005). Cyber-Harassment: A study of a new method for an old behaviour. *Journal of Educational Computing Research, 32*, 265–277. doi:10.2190/8YQM-B04H-PG4D-BLLH

Bhat, C. S. (2008). Cyber Bullying: Overview and Strategies for School Counsellors, Guidance Officers, and All School Personnel. *Australian Journal of Guidance & Counselling, 18*(1), 53–66. doi:10.1375/ajgc.18.1.53

Bocij, P. (2006). *The dark side of the Internet: Protecting yourself and your family from online criminals.* Westport, CT: Praeger Publishers.

Brown, K., Jackson, M., & Cassidy, W. (2006). Cyber-bullying: Developing policy to direct responses that are equitable and effective in addressing this special form of bullying. *Canadian Journal of Educational Administration and Policy, 57.* Retrieved November 6, 2010 from http://www.umanitoba.ca/publications/ cjeap/articles/brown_jackson_cassidy.html

Burgess-Proctor, A., Patchin, J. W., & Hinduja, S. (2009). Cyberbullying and online harassment: Reconceptualizing the victimization of adolescent girls. In Garcia, V., & Clifford, J. (Eds.), *Female Crime Victims: Reality Reconsidered* (pp. 162–176). Upper Saddle River, NJ: Prentice Hall.

Dehue, F., Bolman, C., & Völlink, T. (2008). Cyberbullying: Youngers' Experiences and Parental Perception. *Cyberpsychology & Behavior, 11*, 217–223. doi:10.1089/cpb.2007.0008

Douglas, K. S., & Dutton, D. G. (2001). Assessing the link between stalking and domestic violence. *Aggression and Violent Behavior, 6*, 519–546. doi:10.1016/S1359-1789(00)00018-5

Finn, J., & Atkinson, T. (2009). Promoting the safe and strategic use of technology for victims of intimate partner violence: Evaluation of the Technology Safety Project. *Journal of Family Violence, 24*, 53–59. doi:10.1007/s10896-008-9207-2

Finn, J., & Banach, M. (2000). Victimisation online: The down side of seeking human services for women on the Internet. *Cyberpsychology & Behavior, 3*, 243–254. doi:10.1089/109493100316102

Hazler, R. J. (1996). *Breaking the cycle of violence: Interventions for bullying and victimization.* Bristol, PA: Accelerated Development.

Hinduja, S., & Patchin, J. (2010b). Cyberbullying *fact sheet: Identification, Prevention, and Response.* Cyberbullying Research Center. Retrieved November 6, 2010, from http://www.cyberbullying.us/Cyberbullying_Identification_Prevention_Response_Fact_Sheet.pdf

Hinduja, S., & Patchin, J. W. (2008). Cyberbullying: An exploratory analysis of factors related to offending and victimisation. *Deviant Behavior, 29*, 129–156. doi:10.1080/01639620701457816

Hinduja, S., & Patchin, J. W. (2009). *Bullying Beyond the Schoolyard: Preventing and Responding to Cyberbullying.* Thousand Oaks, CA: Sage Publications (Corwin Press).

Hinduja, S., & Patchin, J. W. (2010). Bullying, cyberbullying and suicide. *Archives of Suicide Research, 14*, 206–221. doi:10.1080/13811118.2010.494133

Huss, M. T. (2009). *Forensic Psychology: Research, clinical practice, and applications.* Chichester, England: Wiley-Blackwell.

Jewkes, Y. (2010). Public policing and Internet crime. In Jewkes, Y., & Yar, M. (Eds.), *Handbook of Internet Crime* (pp. 525–545). Cullompton, England: Willan Publishing.

Joseph, J. (2003). Cyberstalking: an international perspective. In Jewkes, Y. (Ed.), *Dot.cons: Crime, deviance and identity on the Internet* (pp. 105–125). Cullompton, England: Willan Publishing.

Kowalski, R. M., & Limber, S. P. (2007). Electronic Bullying Among Middle School Students. *The Journal of Adolescent Health, 41*, S22–S30. doi:10.1016/j.jadohealth.2007.08.017

Lenhart (2007). *Pew Internet and American Life Project: Cyberbullying and Online Teens.* Retrieved November 6, 2010 from http://www.pewinternet.org/~/media//Files /Reports/2007/PIP%20Cyberbullying% 20Memo.pdf.pdf

Li, Q. (2006). Cyber bullying in schools: A research of gender differences. *School Psychology International, 27*(2), 157–170. doi:10.1177/0143034306064547

Li, Q. (2007). New bottle but old wine: A research of cyberbullying in schools. *Computers in Human Behavior, 23*, 1777–1791. doi:10.1016/j.chb.2005.10.005

McQuade, S. C. (2006). *Understanding and Managing Cybercrime.* Boston, MA: Allyn & Bacon.

Meloy, J. R. (1998). The psychology of stalking. In Meloy, J. R. (Ed.), *The psychology of stalking: Clinical and Forensic Perspectives* (pp. 1–23). London: Academic Press.

Meloy, J. R. (2000). Stalking (obsessional following). In Meloy, J. R. (Ed.), *Violence, risk and threat assessment* (pp. 167–191). San Diego, CA: Specialised Training Services.

Mesch, G. S. (2009). Parental mediation, online activities and cyberbullying. *Cyberpsychology & Behavior, 12*, 387–393. doi:10.1089/cpb.2009.0068

Microsoft. (2009, February 10). *29% of European teenagers are victims of online bullying.* Retrieved November 6, 2010 from http://www.microsoft.com/emea/presscentre /pressreleases/OnlinebullyingPR_100209.mspx

Mishra, A., & Mishra, D. (2008). Cyber Stalking: A challenge for web security. In Janczewski, L. J., & Colarik, A. M. (Eds.), *Cyber Warfare and Cyber Terrorism* (pp. 216–225). Hershey, PA: Information Science Reference.

Patchin, J. W., & Hinduja, S. (2006). Bullies move beyond the schoolyard: A preliminary look at cyberbullying. *Youth Violence and Juvenile Justice, 4*, 148–169. doi:10.1177/1541204006286288

Patchin, J. W., & Hinduja, S. (2010). Traditional and nontraditional bullying among youth: A test of general strain theory. [published online ahead of print]. *Youth & Society*, (May): 7. doi:. doi:10.1177/0044118X10366951

Philips, F., & Morrissey, G. (2004). Cyberstalking and Cyberpredators: A threat to safe sexuality on the Internet. *Convergence, 10*, 66–79.

Privitera, C., & Campbell, M. A. (2009). Cyberbullying: The new face of workplace bullying? *Cyberpsychology & Behavior, 12*, 395–400. doi:10.1089/cpb.2009.0025

Raskauskas, J., & Stoltz, A. D. (2007). Involvement in traditional and electronic bullying among adolescents. *Developmental Psychology, 43*, 564–575. doi:10.1037/0012-1649.43.3.564

Shariff, S. (2005). Cyber-dilemmas in the new millennium: School obligations to provide student safety in a virtual school environment. *McGill Journal of Education, 40*(3).

Shariff, S., & Gouin, R. (2005). *Cyber-Dilemmas: Gendered Hierarchies, Free Expression and Cyber-Safety In Schools.* Paper presented at the Oxford Internet Institute (OII), Oxford University Conference on September 8, 2005. Retrieved November 4 2010 from http://www.oii.ox.ac.uk/microsites/ cybersafety/extensions/pdfs/papers/shaheen_shariff.pdf

Sheridan, L., & Davies, G. (2004). Stalking. In Adler, J. R. (Ed.), *Forensic Psychology: Concepts, debates and practice* (pp. 197–215). Cullompton, England: Willan Publishing.

Sheridan, L. P., & Grant, T. (2007). Is cyberstalking different? *Psychology, Crime & Law, 13*, 627–640. doi:10.1080/10683160701340528

Smith, P., Mahdavi, J., Carvalho, M., & Tippet, N. (2006, July). *An investigation into cyberbullying, its forms, awareness and impact, and the relationship between age and gender in cyberbullying.* Retrieved November 4 2010 from http://www.plymouthcurriculum.swgfl.org.uk /resources/ict/cyberbullying/Cyberbullying.pdf

Spitzberg, B., & Hoobler, G. (2002). Cyberstalking and the technologies of interpersonal terrorism. *New Media & Society, 4*, 71–92. doi:10.1177/14614440222226271

Strom, P. S., & Strom, R. D. (2005). When teens turn cyberbullies. *Education Digest, 71*, 35–41.

Twyman, K., Saylor, C., Taylor, L. A., & Comeaux, C. (2009). Comparing children and adolescents engaged in cyberbullying to matched peers. *Cyberpsychology & Behavior, 12,* 1–5.

United Press International. (2008, April 9). *Survey: Cyber-bullying affects US teens.* Retrieved November 3, 2010 from http://www.upi.com/NewsTrack/Health/2008/04/09/survey_cyberbullying_affects_us_teens/3823/

Willard, N. E. (2007). *Cyberbullying and Cyberthreats: Responding to the challenge of online social aggression, threats, and distress.* Research Press.

Wolak, J., Mitchell, K. J., & Finkelhor, D. (2007). Does online harassment constitute bullying? An exploration of online harassment by known peers and online-only contacts. *The Journal of Adolescent Health, 41,* S51–S58. doi:10.1016/j.jadohealth.2007.08.019

Working to Halt Online Abuse. (WHOA, 2010a). *Online Harassment/Cyberstalking Statistics.* Retrieved November 5, 2010 from http://www.haltabuse.org/resources/stats /index.shtml

Working to Halt Online Abuse. (WHOA, 2010b). *2009Cyberstalking Statistics.* Retrieved November 5, 2010 from http://www.haltabuse.org/resources/stats /2009Statistics.pdf

Wykes, M. (2007). Constructing crime: stalking, celebrity, 'cyber' and media. In Jewkes, Y. (Ed.), *Crime Online* (pp. 128–143). Cullompton, England: Willan Publishing.

Yar, M. (2006). *Cybercrime and Society.* London: Sage Publications Ltd.

Ybarra, M. L. (2004). Linkages between depressive symptomatology and internet harassment among young regular internet users. *Cyberpsychology & Behavior, 7,* 247–257. doi:10.1089/109493104323024500

Ybarra, M. L., & Mitchell, K. J. (2004). Online aggressor/targets, aggressors, and targets: A comparison of associated youth characteristics. *Journal of Child Psychology and Psychiatry, and Allied Disciplines, 45*(7), 1308–1316. doi:10.1111/j.1469-7610.2004.00328.x

ADDITIONAL READING

Alexy, E. M., Burgess, A. W., Baker, T., & Smoyak, S. A. (2005). Perceptions of Cyberstalking Among College Students. *Brief Treatment and Crisis Intervention, 5,* 279–289. doi:10.1093/brief-treatment/mhi020

Beran, T., & Li, Q. (2005). Cyber-Harassment: A study of a new method for an old behaviour. *Journal of Educational Computing Research, 32,* 265–277. doi:10.2190/8YQM-B04H-PG4D-BLLH

Bhat, C. S. (2008). Cyber Bullying: Overview and Strategies for School Counsellors, Guidance Officers, and All School Personnel. *Australian Journal of Guidance & Counselling, 18*(1), 53–66. doi:10.1375/ajgc.18.1.53

Burgess-Proctor, A., Patchin, J. W., & Hinduja, S. (2009). Cyberbullying and online harassment: Reconceptualizing the victimization of adolescent girls. In Garcia, V., & Clifford, J. (Eds.), *Female Crime Victims: Reality Reconsidered* (pp. 162–176). Upper Saddle River, NJ: Prentice Hall.

Dehue, F., Bolman, C., & Völlink, T. (2008). Cyberbullying: Youngers' Experiences and Parental Perception. *Cyberpsychology & Behavior, 11,* 217–223. doi:10.1089/cpb.2007.0008

Finn, J., & Atkinson, T. (2009). Promoting the safe and strategic use of technology for victims of intimate partner violence: Evaluation of the Technology Safety Project. *Journal of Family Violence, 24,* 53–59. doi:10.1007/s10896-008-9207-2

Hinduja, S., & Patchin, J. W. (2008). Cyberbullying: An exploratory analysis of factors related to offending and victimisation. *Deviant Behavior*, *29*, 129–156. doi:10.1080/01639620701457816

Hinduja, S., & Patchin, J. W. (2009). Bullying Beyond the Schoolyard: Preventing and Responding to Cyberbullying. Thousand Oaks, CA: Sage Publications (Corwin Press).

Hinduja, S., & Patchin, J. W. (2010). Bullying, cyberbullying and suicide. *Archives of Suicide Research*, *14*, 206–221. doi:10.1080/13811118.2010.494133

Joseph, J. (2003). Cyberstalking: an international perspective. In Jewkes, Y. (Ed.), *Dot.cons: Crime, deviance and identity on the Internet* (pp. 105–125). Cullompton, England: Willan Publishing.

Kowalski, R. M., & Limber, S. P. (2007). Electronic Bullying Among Middle School Students. *The Journal of Adolescent Health*, *41*, S22–S30. doi:10.1016/j.jadohealth.2007.08.017

Lenhart (2007). Pew Internet and American Life Project: Cyberbullying and Online Teens. Retrieved November 6, 2010 from http://www.pewinternet.org/~/media//Files /Reports/2007/PIP%20Cyberbullying% 20Memo.pdf.pdf

Li, Q. (2007). New bottle but old wine: A research of cyberbullying in schools. *Computers in Human Behavior*, *23*, 1777–1791. doi:10.1016/j.chb.2005.10.005

Mishra, A., & Mishra, D. (2008). Cyber Stalking: A challenge for web security. In Janczewski, L. J., & Colarik, A. M. (Eds.), *Cyber Warfare and Cyber Terrorism* (pp. 216–225). Hershey, PA: Information Science Reference.

Patchin, J. W., & Hinduja, S. (2006). Bullies move beyond the schoolyard: A preliminary look at cyberbullying. *Youth Violence and Juvenile Justice*, *4*, 148–169. doi:10.1177/1541204006286288

Patchin, J. W., & Hinduja, S. (2010). Traditional and nontraditional bullying among youth: A test of general strain theory. [published online ahead of print]. *Youth & Society*, (May): 7. doi:. doi:10.1177/0044118X10366951

Philips, F., & Morrissey, G. (2004). Cyberstalking and Cyberpredators: A threat to safe sexuality on the Internet. *Convergence*, *10*, 66–79.

Privitera, C., & Campbell, M. A. (2009). Cyberbullying: The new face of workplace bullying? *Cyberpsychology & Behavior*, *12*, 395–400. doi:10.1089/cpb.2009.0025

Sheridan, L. P., & Grant, T. (2007). Is cyberstalking different? *Psychology, Crime & Law*, *13*, 627–640. doi:10.1080/10683160701340528

Spitzberg, B., & Hoobler, G. (2002). Cyberstalking and the technologies of interpersonal terrorism. *New Media & Society*, *4*, 71–92. doi:10.1177/14614440222226271

Wolak, J., Mitchell, K. J., & Finkelhor, D. (2007). Does online harassment constitute bullying? An exploration of online harassment by known peers and online-only contacts. *The Journal of Adolescent Health*, *41*, S51–S58. doi:10.1016/j.jadohealth.2007.08.019

Wykes, M. (2007). Constructing crime: stalking, celebrity, 'cyber' and media. In Jewkes, Y. (Ed.), *Crime Online* (pp. 128–143). Cullompton, England: Willan Publishing.

Chapter 10
Music, Video and Software Piracy:
Do Offenders See Them as Criminal Activities?

ABSTRACT

Of all the types of cybercrime considered in this book, piracy, illegal file sharing and/or other types of copyright infringement are probably the offences that members of the general public are most likely to have committed. Yar (2007) indicates that piracy activity seems to be very widespread, including individuals from various social classes, although there seems to be a disproportionate number of young people engaging in the activity. This chapter aims to determine if those involved in piracy and online copyright infringement activities see themselves as criminals. It also aims to examine how such offenders justify their actions and how they can be dissuaded from such acts. Definitions of key terms in the area will be presented, along with some examples of real events relating to illegal file sharing. A description of some of the methods used during illegal file sharing and piracy will be provided, along with a historical view of how copyright infringement has developed over time. The known current prevalence rates and costs of offending will be considered, along with arguments presented from industry and academia regarding the effects of file sharing on legitimate sales. Similarly, the problem of trying to estimate the true cost of piracy and illegal file sharing will be highlighted. The psychology of offenders will be considered, and in particular, the phenomenon of the lack of insight of offenders into their own criminality will be investigated. In particular, the roles of self-control, social learning and justifications in illegal file sharing will be analysed. Some potential solutions for these crimes will be considered, including the determination of appropriate punishments and the development of suitable educational campaigns. Finally, potential future trends and research will be described.

DOI: 10.4018/978-1-61350-350-8.ch010

BACKGROUND

There have been several high profile cases of online file sharing websites in recent years.

Yar (2007) describes the case of a file-sharing service called Napster. When using this service, individuals registered online and downloaded the Napster software, which would then scan the user's computer for any digital music files (such as MP3 files). The software then sent a list of the music files on the computer to the Napster server. If another user then searched for a specific song, Napster would inspect its members' computers for copies of it, while also checking which of these computers were currently online. Napster then allowed the searcher to ask the file owner for permission to download a copy of the file for themselves. Eventually approximately seventy million individuals were using the system. In late 1999 the US recording industry took Napster to court, suggesting that the file sharing website had facilitated illegal downloading of copyrighted material. Napster eventually paid $36 million to the recording industry (Yar, 2007, p. 98).

Jewkes (2010) describes the case of 'The Pirate Bay' (p. 534). This Sweden-based website allowed people to post music, films and software, and directed users to media files available elsewhere on the Internet. 'The Pirate Bay' did not store the content or index itself, and so circumvented anti-piracy laws. Nevertheless, in 2009, the four owners of 'The Pirate Bay' were found guilty of breaking copyright law, were fined and were sentenced to a year in prison each.

In October 2010, a New York district court issued an injunction which forced 'LimeWire', a large file-sharing website, to disable some of its functions, including searching, downloading, uploading and file-trading (BBC News, 2010a).

Definitions and Key Terms

There are a large number of terms which are used in conjunction with the illegal distribution of copyrighted material. Bryant (2008) distinguishes between 'illegal filesharing' and 'commercial music piracy'. The former involves the transmission of files, while the latter involves the use of physical materials such as CDs and DVDs. However, many researchers use the term 'piracy' to refer to illegal filesharing as well. For example, Hill (2007) defines digital piracy as "the purchase of counterfeit products at a discount to the price of the copyrighted product, and illegal file sharing of copyright material over peer-to-peer computer networks" (p. 9).

Yar (2006) indicates that it has proven to be difficult to settle upon a precise and agreed definition of 'piracy', but that legal and economic uses of the term are based in Intellectual Property (IP) law and protection (p. 65). Stephens (2008) describes Intellectual Property Rights (IPR) as "encompassing the privileges accorded to the creators and owners of creative work (intellectual property, or IP) including inventions, designs, software, music, films, and written works" (p. 121). Stephens indicates that copyright does not require a registration process, and in most cases the copyrighted work can only be reproduced and used with the copyright holder's permission. If it is otherwise used, the holder has a legal right to stop the copyright breach and to seek compensation.

There are complications in defining the legality of copyright infringement. Stephens (2008) indicates that some consumers argue for 'fair use' of the content, suggesting that they should be entitled to make copies of the content for personal use. For example, a person may buy a music CD. They may then wish to make a copy of the CD to leave in their car. They may also want to copy the CD to mp3 format so that they can listen to it on their digital media player, but they may later buy an alternative portable music player that does not read mp3 files, and so they need to copy it to a different format. They may decide that they would like to use one of the tracks as their personal ringtone on their cellphone, which may require them to change the format of the file again, hence creating another version. It is possible that the consumer may have to purchase several copies of the song in order to achieve these goals legally.

Methods of Offenders

Illegal copying of music, video and software files is not a new phenomenon. Jewkes and Yar (2010) describe how Charles Dickens was possibly the first known case of 'Net piracy' when his works were transmitted to the United States by telegraph for reprinting without seeking his permission or paying him royalties (p. 3). It is somewhat ironic that most of Dickens' works are now legally available as free downloads for electronic readers (eReaders), as the copyright on his works has now lapsed. However, illegal copying of material has taken many forms over the past few decades.

While the digitalization of information allows it to be copied much more easily than previously (Bryant, 2008), illegal copying of music, software and video has existed for some time. In the 1980s, dual deck tape recorders allowed users to copy both music cassettes and the then popular software cassettes. Bryant (2008) cites how the British Phonographic Industry (BPI) launched a campaign in the early 1980s saying that 'Home Taping is Killing Music'. Similarly, dual deck video recorders were also made available, or two single video recorders could be connected in such a way that copying of tapes was possible. However, this form of copying had problems. As Bryant (2008) indicates, serial copying of video tape results in a significant deterioration of quality, so that by the third or fourth generation (that is, a copy of a copy of a copy) the tape was practi-

cally unwatchable. There was a similar reduction in quality for audio cassettes. Conversely, digital files do not deteriorate with copying, and so are open to much wider distribution than earlier forms of piracy. Digital files can also be copied much faster than analogue copies of music.

Later, CD copying became more prevalent, with Bryant indicating that most of the time, the distribution of copies was limited to creating 'back-ups', or circulating to friends and family for the most part. However, more numerous pirated CDs started to appear in the late 1980s (Bryant, 2008, p. 22). Video piracy using disks followed later, although it was hampered by the low memory of recordable DVDs, compared to the high quantity of information on commercial DVDs, coupled with copy protection software.

With regard to software piracy, Stephens (2008) describes how early versions of software were included in their entirety in disk format, which could be easily copied. More recently, systems were introduced which required additional information to install the software, normally a product key (a list of numbers and letters), which would be provided in the packaging or via communication with the company. In some early cases the same key could activate multiple versions of the software, and so the key was simply copied along with the software. In some cases, the product key could only be used once, especially if it was then registered with the company. However crackers (see Chapter 4) overcame this security measure by the creation of 'keygens' (key generators). As the software products generally used mathematical algorithms to recognise true product keys, a keygen software program could be used to 'generate' new keys which would be unique, but accepted by the software. Other software cracks created files which tricked the software into thinking that a trial version of the software had been properly activated, so that the limited time access (or any other limitations on the trial version) would be removed.

Using the Internet in Copyright Infringement

The advent of widespread Internet use has also changed the ways in which copyright infringement occurs. Yar (2007) indicates that one of the differences between online and offline offences involves the widespread distribution available online. Previously, copies could normally only be obtained from family, friends, acquaintances and illegal markets. The Internet greatly expanded the potential pool of resources, which is the basis for illegal file-sharing networks. Bryant (2008) indicates that much piracy occurs through peer-to-peer networks, but that initially file-sharing occurred on Usenet groups.

Yar (2006) indicates that the Internet offers several advantages over offline piracy. These include: reducing the costs in copying the content onto physical media, such as disks; that it is much faster to distribute soft copies; that unlimited copies can be made from a single copy hosted on the web (individual copies do not need to be made for each user); that it circumvents the risks involved in the distribution of hard media (such as confiscation and border controls), reduces the risks of detection as the distributor has more anonymity; and the point of distribution can be located in a country with little enforcement of copyright laws, while distributing to the rest of the world.

According to Bryant (2008) internet piracy became possible for several reasons, including increased speed of the internet and a reduction in file size using compression techniques and the stripping out of extras from commercial DVDs. Music files can be converted and compressed into MP3 or other format files, and movies and television programmes can be recorded, and again compressed into MP4 or similar format files. The ability to upload whole films and television series to the Internet with relatively small file sizes proved tempting for some of those engaged in copyright infringement. New release (and sometimes pre-release) films can frequently be found on the Internet. At the time of writing, the release date for the seventh movie in the Harry Potter series is still some weeks away, but several websites offer illegal copies for downloading. Similarly, it is common for new episodes of popular television series to be available online within minutes of the episode premiering.

One outcome of this is that there is a shorter gap between release dates of films and television programmes in the country of origin and release dates in other countries. For example, while previously it may take weeks or months for television programmes to appear on European channels after their release in the USA, some television channels now boast that they show the content 'days' or 'hours' after the first airing in the US. This is in the hope that viewers will not download the programme from a website, and will instead wait for the higher quality television airing. A brief examination of file-sharing websites illustrates the vast quantity of audio, video and software files that are illegally available online, but it is difficult to quantify the extent of the problem.

Known Prevalence Rates

Much of the publicly available information regarding the extent of online copyright infringement has been supplied by organizations created to protect the copyright holders. Bryant (2008) cites the British Phonographic Industry (BPI) who estimated in 2007 that illegal peer-to-peer filesharing had lost British music sales approximately GBP£1.1 billion in the previous three years. The International Federation of Phonographic Industries (IFPI, 2010) reported that global industry revenues were down approximately 30% between 2004 and 2009. The British Recorded Music Industry (nd) estimates that 95% of all music files exchanged online are unlicensed.

Yar (2006) cites the International Intellectual Property Alliance (IIPA, 2005), who claimed that the piracy of US copyrighted content costs $20-$22 billion in losses to the copyright holders. The

Motion Picture Association of America (MPAA, 2006) indicates that their movie studios lost $6.1 billion to piracy in 2005. They estimate that $2.3 billion of that loss was due to internet piracy. Meanwhile, the British Software Alliance (BSA, 2007) indicates that 35% of software in the world is pirated, with regions such as Central/Eastern Europe and Latin America having the highest rates (68% and 65% respectively) and North America having the lowest rate (22%). The BSA estimates that total losses due to software piracy at over $47 billion in 2007.

Despite these figures, it is still extremely difficult to accurately estimate the true cost of piracy (Wall, 2007), and Bryant (2008) indicates that "industry-based organizations may have a particular interest in emphasizing the seriousness of the problem" (p. 23). Yar (2006) describes several reasons why it is difficult to estimate the true quantity of piracy and infringements. These include that estimates of overall piracy levels are "often extrapolated from detection and conviction rates" (p. 72), and so the levels detected depend on the level of policing activity, either by law enforcement agencies or other bodies, such as those listed above. As such, increased levels may simply reflect increased policing efficiency and activity, rather than an actual increase in offending behavior. As is demonstrated above, many attempts to quantify the scale of the problem include the attempt to determine the financial losses due to piracy. Yar (2006) suggests that this is often based on the 'legitimate product price', presuming that each illegal copy replaces the purchase of a legitimate sale (such as one DVD, cinema ticket, CD, copy of the software, etc). Certainly it could be argued that many of the files that are downloaded may not directly replace sales of the file – some individuals may download the file as it is available for low cost or even free, but would not pay the full price for it.

Peitz and Waelbroeck (2006) suggest that the negative effect of illegal music downloading may in fact be overcompensated by 'sampling'

– as consumers are better able to match product characteristics and their own tastes, they may be willing to pay more. Peitz and Waelbroeck found that this occurs under different types of music taste and product diversity. Wall and Yar (2010) indicate that the threat of copyright infringement is not just in lost income, but also what is termed the "dilution" of its value (p. 260). This refers to a reduction of the value of the property because of its unrestricted use, and it forms part of the argument in justification of legal sanctions against illegal distributors. Nevertheless, Yar (2006) describes how at least some recording artists can profit more from illegal downloading, as it may encourage more individuals to attend concerts, where musical artists make most of their income, rather than via sales. In some cases, musicians have embraced the possibility of making names for themselves by distributing their work freely online.

Although some record companies and artists indicate that illegal distribution of music is denying the authors their dues, and may cause the end of popular music, this is contested (Wall & Yar, 2010). Wall and Yar cite a report by the Australian Institute of Criminology which suggests the music industry cannot explain how they reach the figures cited for losses. Wall and Yar also indicate that evidence suggests that illegal music downloading may actually help to promote music culture and expand the market, particularly in relation to sales of older works. Wall and Yar also indicate that it is possible that CD sales have actually risen, or at least remained constant, and that the introduction of authorized content download sites has demonstrated to be very successful.

There is some empirical evidence for this. For example, LaRose and Kim (2007) found that downloading intentions had no impact on CD purchases or subscription to online pay music services. Zentner (2004) found that those who regularly download music online are more likely to buy music. However, for users of peer-to-peer systems, piracy reduced the probability of buying music by 35%, so Zentner estimates that online music piracy may explain drops in music sales of between 7.8% and 14.5%. Conversely, other researchers (Oberholzer-Gee & Strumpf, 2007) found that downloads have a negligible effect on sales, although this study has been the subject of criticism, and most studies in the field seem to find some negative relationship between illegal file sharing and legitimate sales (Liebowitz, 2006).

PSYCHOLOGICAL INSIGHTS INTO OFFENDERS

Research provides several insights into the psychology of illegal file-sharers and copyright infringers. Firstly, it has suggested motives for involvement in such activities, as well as some insights into the demographic characteristics of such individuals. Secondly it can provide information regarding psychological characteristics of offenders, such as self-control and social learning. Finally, it provides insight into the justifications (or *neutralizations*) that illegal file-sharers provide to explain their actions.

Demographic Characteristics and Motives

Piquero (2005) summarizes several causes of intellectual property theft. She reviewed the literature relating to demographic characteristics of those involved in intellectual property violations and indicates that while some studies found that males were more likely to engage in such actions, other studies found no gender difference. Similarly, she found that older college students were more likely to engage in piracy than younger college students, but that overall, younger individuals are more likely to engage in such behaviors than older individuals.

Cronan, Foltz and Jones (2006) indicate that many students admit to illegally installing software, and used a survey to examine the demographic characteristics of students who engage in piracy and computer misuse. They found that over one third admitted to committing some form of software misuse or piracy (defined in this case as destroying or copying software, using copied software, or distributing copied software without permission). They found that students who are more familiar with computers and students in computer-related majors reported committing more misuse, with students in higher years of courses being more likely to engage in software misuse. Cronan et al (2006) also found that university computer usage policies were ineffective at preventing misuse, as many students had not read the policy, and those who had committed even more misuses than those who did not read the policies.

With regard to motive, while there have been proposed links between counterfeiting, piracy and terrorist groups, with the indication that such activities fund terrorist acts (Yar, 2007, p. 102), it is unclear to what extent this is the case with online copyright infringements. It is also unclear what proportion of such offenders have links with terrorist organizations. Nevertheless, several public information campaigns have highlighted this link, hoping to prevent users from engaging in these behaviors by associating copyright infringement with a significantly more serious offence. However, it is likely that a significant proportion of those involved in illegal file-sharing do not have terrorist links.

Bryant (2008) suggests that the most likely motive for illegally downloading music involves not just the fact that it is free, but also that it is immediately available (pp. 2-4). At the time of some of the first illegal file sharing websites there were few online sources where legitimate digital copies of songs could be accessed. Since then, several major legitimate online retailers, such as iTunes and Amazon, provide legal immediate access to such resources. However as music piracy still exists, availability cannot be considered to be the only cause, and other motives, most likely cost, must be at play.

Bryce and Rutter (2005) indicate that many Internet users view such behaviors as morally acceptable and useful for saving money on media use. They found that downloading of music files was more common than buying counterfeit CDs, with 27% of people downloading music tracks and 18% downloading entire albums in the previous year. They found that access to credit cards was seen as a barrier to young consumers preventing them from legally downloading services, and the only significant risks they noted were viruses and files that did not work properly. The most frequently cited motivations for downloading music in Bryce and Rutter's (2005) study involved the range of choice, convenience, cost and getting access to tracks not otherwise available in the country. Another motivation involved listening to albums before anyone else, as soon as possible. Being able to access content was seen as more important than being assured of the quality of the content. The most cited reasons for not copying music CDs involved preference for the legitimate version and fear of poor product quality. Other reasons cited include the lack of guarantee and potential links with organized crime.

Hsu and Shiue (2008) analyzed how much consumers were willing to pay for non-pirated versions of software in Taiwan, finding that the average price consumers were willing to pay was much lower than the suggested retail price for the software involved. They found that social norms had a strong impact on willingness-to-pay, but that the prosecution risk did not significantly increase the price that consumers were willing to pay (conversely, Liao, Lin & Liu, 2009, found that perceived prosecution risk did have an impact on intention to use pirated software). In the Hsu and Shiue study, those who were willing to pay less for the software were more likely to use pirated software. Those who were willing to pay more cited reasons such as technical support, customer service and source reliability, and Hsu and Shiue suggest that these should be used in marketing strategies.

Hinduja (2008) explored the link between deindividuation and software piracy. Deindividuation suggests that if people have a reduced sense of self, such as by using pseudonyms online, they feel less responsible for their actions, and it may be possible that those who use more pseudonyms online may be more likely to engage in illegal file sharing. However, Hinduja (2008) found no link between those who prefer anonymity and pseudonymity online and likelihood to engage in software piracy.

Finally, Becker and Clement (2006) indicate that while there are obvious motives for downloading files on peer-to-peer networks, it is not as easy to explain why people provide files, as it is not always necessary in order to complete downloads. They found that reciprocity is one of the main reasons why individuals offer files, but that many individuals do not contribute files. They found that there is a significant group of individuals that are motivated to share, even though there may be legal implications. It therefore seems that there is a strong social aspect to illegal file sharing, which is now examined alongside self-control theory.

Self-Control and Social Learning Theory

Higgins, Fell and Wilson (2006) developed a three factor model, suggesting that low self-control along with social learning theory contribute to the likelihood of engaging in digital piracy. Higgins et al (2006) indicate that individuals need to learn the behaviors involved from others. Self-control theory was linked to criminal behavior by Gottfredson and Hirschi (1990), suggesting that low self-control is a fairly stable characteristic through life, and is a result of poor or ineffective parenting. Higgins et al (2006) state that individuals with low self-control are impulsive, risk-taking, insensitive, nonverbal and do not consider the long-term repercussions of their actions. Because of their nature, these individuals may be attracted to criminal acts. Higgins et al (2006) also link social learning theory to this type of offender. Social learning theory is a complex theory, suggesting that people associate differentially with offending peers. The individual is exposed to deviant models, eventually initiating or increasing the individual's own involvement in crime. It is this social learning theory link that suggests both how individuals learn these behaviors, and also why they may not consider piracy as being morally wrong.

Morris and Higgins (2010) found that social learning theory may apply to digital piracy in a study of university students. D'Astous, Colbert and Montpetit (2005) found that intention to swap music online depended on the person's attitude towards music piracy, their perception that important others wanted the piracy to be committed, and the person's belief that they could do so, factors which may be linked to social learning theory. Similarly, Malin and Fowers (2009) also examined Gottfredson and Hirschi's theories in relation to piracy, specifically music and movie piracy in adolescents. They found that attitudes towards internet piracy were related to low self-control and affiliation with deviant peers.

Further evidence for this theory is provided by LaRose, Lai, Lange, Love and Wu (2005), who found that downloading behavior was linked to deficient self-regulation. It was reduced by dissatisfaction with poor quality downloads and fear of punishment, although LaRose et al (2005) note that regular downloaders were unlikely to stop. Nevertheless, Higgins (2007) found that while low self-control is a predictor of criminal behavior, motivation is also important, and so it is probably a combination of low self-control, social learning and motivation which lead an individual to engage in illegal file-sharing. In addition to this, many of those who commit such crimes often subsequently justify their actions.

Neutralizations and Ethical Positions

'Neutralization' is a similar phenomenon to the cognitive distortions described in Chapter 7. Sykes and Matza (1957) describe their theory on neutralization techniques, describing techniques that offenders use to counter guilty feelings associated with offending. Sykes and Matza define five techniques of neutralization, although alternative techniques have been proposed by other researchers since. The original neutralizations proposed by Sykes and Matza included: *denial of responsibility* (where offenders refused to accept responsibility for their actions, perhaps suggesting that they were forced into the action because of matters beyond their control); *denial of injury* (suggesting that the victim was not injured, or that the victim could afford the financial loss); *denial of victim* (where the victim was considered deserving of punishment); *condemnation of the condemners* (a suggestion that those who were victimized are hypocrites) and *appeal to higher loyalties* (a suggestion that their behavior was warranted because their immediate social group needed it to be carried out).

Moore and McMullan (2009) examined neutralization techniques in students using qualitative interviews, and found that multiple neutralizations were used by a relatively small number of participants. Moore and McMullan (2009) found that all their participants showed support for some neutralization technique to defend file sharing, most commonly the "denial of victim" and "denial of injury" neutralizations, along with a neutralization proposed by Coleman (1994), that "everyone else is doing it". Moore and McMullan (2009) explain these findings by suggesting that file sharers may not realize the harm they are doing to the musician because of the anonymity of the internet – they rarely see the victim except in glamorized media portrayals. Moore and McMullan also suggest that file sharers hold the belief that the activity ultimately benefits the musician as it introduces them to new consumers.

Ingram and Hinduja (2008) studied a sample of undergraduates and found that "denial of responsibility, denial of injury, denial of victim, and appeal to higher loyalties" predicted piracy participation (p. 334). They suggest that university settings might allow for a climate to develop where students put higher values on group rather than legal norms, and do not appropriately consider the potential harms of music piracy. Similarly Morris and Higgins (2009) found support for both neutralization theory and social learning theory in explaining music, software and movie downloading. However, not all studies have found a strong connection and Hinduja (2007) found that neutralization was only weakly related to experience with online software piracy.

The use of neutralization techniques in copyright infringement offenders may be indicative of an underlying lack of ethical standards in this regard. Yar (2010) describes several studies that found high levels of illegal downloading of content from the Internet, with users often seeing the behavior as acceptable. Piquero (2005) suggests that the early research in this area found that people do not perceive piracy to be an ethical problem. She suggests that engaging in piracy could be considered an unethical decision, but that people are unable or unwilling to recognize the moral issue. Similarly, Gopal, Sanders, Bhattacharjee, Agrawal and Wagner (2004) found that ethical predispositions indirectly affect digital piracy and Yar (2007) indicates that those who steal intellectual property online, such as through the downloading of copyrighted music on peer-to-peer programs would not attempt to conceal that they have done so and would otherwise feel that they are law-abiding citizens.

Stephens (2008) suggests that many consumers are either unaware or unconcerned about the illegality of copying and distributing copyrighted material. Bryce and Rutter (2005) found that consumers were aware that sharing of unauthorized copies of music files was illegal, yet downloading and owning counterfeit CDs was considered

widespread and normal, with ripped tracks and albums downloaded from the internet being seen as less 'wrong' than the buying of counterfeit CDs. They felt that downloading was less ethically dubious because of the lack of profits generated, and so downloading was considered unrelated to the claimed links between copyright infringement and organized crime. Over half of the respondents were aware of recent announcements regarding potential prosecution of downloaders, with 75% feeling that a threat of prosecution would prevent some people from illegally downloading.

Bryce and Rutter (2005) also studied consumer attitudes to downloading illegal computer games. Fifteen percent had illegally downloaded computer games in the previous year, with ten percent regularly downloading games. Again, downloading was perceived to be less ethically dubious due to the lack of profits, and downloading for personal use was viewed as more acceptable than reselling, although consumers did acknowledge that downloading games result in lost sales for the gaming companies. Many respondents had 'chipped' consoles, allowing them to play pirated games. Conversely, Bhal and Leekha (2008), when carrying out semi-structured interviews with 38 software professionals in India, found that many considered software piracy to be unethical. However they did find that for those who considered the activity not to be unethical, respondents mostly used neutralization techniques. Those who did consider it to be unethical used principled or normative logics. The study completed by Bhal and Leekha suggests that it may be possible to change the ethical position of those who engage in copyright infringement, and some of the potential methods for doing this are outlined below.

POTENTIAL SOLUTIONS

Two of the most commonly used methods to attempt to tackle the problem of illegal file sharing involve the use of information strategies to inform the public about the impact and illegality of copyright infringement and the threat and implementation of punishment in order to attempt to deter potential offenders from committing the crime. However, there are a number of other potential methods which may help to reduce the problem.

Deterrence

Piquero (2005) describes deterrence theory in relation to intellectual property crime. This theory suggests that potential criminals will not engage in criminal activity because of the penalties that they associate with it. These penalties may be certain and/or severe in nature, and relate to both specific and general deterrence. Specific deterrence is the suggestion that if an individual is punished severely enough after offending, then they are unlikely to commit further offences. General deterrence suggests that if the potential offender sees another person being severely punished for their acts, then they are less likely to commit the same acts as they do not want to be punished.

An example of general deterrence occurs when cases of individuals who have faced severe punishments for illegal file sharing are publicized. McQuade (2006) suggests that when some individuals are subjected to severe penalties, such as significant fines and long jail terms, it will deter other people from committing these crimes as well (p. 144-145). There are several examples of such severe penalties being imposed. For example, in 2007, the Recording Industry Association of America (RIAA) took legal action against Jammie Thomas-Rasset, accusing her of pirating almost 2,000 music files, but seeking damage for only 24 of them (BBC News, 2010b). She was initially found guilty, and fined $200,000, but following a re-trial in 2009 the fine was increased to $1.92 million, as US law permits recording companies to request damages of $30,000 per song, which can be increased to $150,000 per song by a jury if they believe the piracy to be wilful (BBC News, 2010b). The fine was later reduced to $54,000.

A problem with such attempts at general deterrence is that many offenders may feel that they will not be prosecuted themselves, as to prosecute all illegal file-sharers would place too extensive a burden on the legal system due to the prevalence of the criminal activity. McQuade (2006) indicates that some individuals, specifically college students, feel that they are unlikely to be prosecuted for illegally downloading a relatively small number of songs, especially as there are others out there who have downloaded many more, or who have engaged in uploading activities. McQuade agrees that generally there are insufficient resources to investigate all those who engage in illegal file sharing, and so often the investigations are restricted to the worst offenders. As such, general deterrence attempts seem unlikely to work, and prevention measures may be better focused on specific deterrence measures.

At the time of writing, some jurisdictions are attempting to penalize all those involved in illegal file-sharing activities. In some cases this involves attempts to cut off offenders' internet service, generally following the issuing of warning letters. There are attempts to introduce this policy in a number of countries, including France, Ireland and the United Kingdom (BBC News, 2010c), although it has met with considerable reluctance from some Internet Service Providers (BBC News, 2010c; 2010d). Other interventions include private agreements between Internet Service Providers (ISPs) and copyright holders where the ISP agrees to write to illegal file-sharers asking them to either pay a fine or to go to court (BBC News, 2010c).

While the specific deterrence measures outlined above may seem on the surface to be easier and more practical to implement, there are difficulties associated with this approach. Among these are attempting to enforce the punishment when an internet service is shared amongst several people. There may also be difficulties in implementation if it is shown that the computer involved had been hacked, or any other circumstance where it cannot be proven that the ISP bill payer is actually the guilty party.

Related to deterrence is learning theory, which Piquero (2005) applied to intellectual property crime. Learning theory suggests that we will continue to engage in activities that are rewarded, and we will avoid behaviors that are punished. For copyright infringement, the rewards involve the vast collection of music, software and video that we can accumulate for little or no expenditure. The potential punishments relate to the consequences if we are apprehended, as described above. For as long as the punishments seem to be unlikely or minor, while the rewards remain attractive, it is likely that offending will continue, particularly if it remains easy to commit the offence.

Piquero (2005) differentiates between preventative controls (that make criminal activities harder or less rewarding) and deterrent controls (that attempt to dissuade users from attempting to commit the act, such as the prosecutions and penalties outlined above). Examples of preventative controls include CDs that will not work in computers (Jewkes, 2010) and the encryption of digital media (Higgins, 2007). Higgins (2007) suggests that due to the low levels of self-control in these types of offenders, it may be appropriate to take preventative controls, making digital piracy more difficult, which would discourage individuals with impulsive natures. While both preventative and deterrent controls have been implemented in attempting to deal with the problem of intellectual property crime, Piquero states that they have not been appropriately evaluated, and until this is done it remains uncertain which is the best approach to take when attempting to prevent future offending.

Public Information Campaigns

In addition to deterrence measures, some anti-copyright infringement measures have involved the use of public information campaigns. Wall and Yar (2010) suggest that anti-piracy education cam-

paigns have primarily focused on young people, as they seem to be more heavily involved in illegal downloading. They indicate that these campaigns include a range of materials and exercises for use in the classroom, typically focusing on children aged eight to thirteen years old. These campaigns aim to make participants feel that illegal copying is a form of theft, and is therefore similar in morality terms to stealing a physical possession. Similar short video clips are often included at the start of many DVDs to discourage illegal distribution. Effectively, these campaigns are attempting to get individuals to see infringements as illegal acts, and to make them less acceptable to others. However, Wall and Yar indicate that such strategies may not work, and that offenders may still be able to justify their actions using neutralization techniques (p.267).

D'Astous, Colbert and Montpetit (2005) found that many anti-piracy arguments, such as stressing the negative consequences for the self, the artists or stressing the unethical nature of the behavior had no significant effect on the behavioral dynamics underlying music piracy. Nevertheless, Yar (2007) suggests that the use of a suggested link between terrorism and piracy is a powerful tool in creating public perception of a serious threat posed by piracy.

Other Solutions

In addition to deterrence and public information campaigns, there have been several alternative methods proposed for dealing with the problem of copyright infringement. For example, it is possible that technological interventions may be of use. Wolfe, Higgins and Marcum (2008) suggest that fear of computer viruses may influence people's intentions to engage in digital piracy, and this may provide a method of reducing the problem. Stephens (2008) describes the use of monitoring software by some companies. In order to obtain software patches and security updates, the user is required to also use such monitoring software, which reports to the company if illegal copies of the software are in place on the computer. Stephens also indicates that some legally downloaded files may have embedded restrictions that prevent the number of copies that can be made of the file. In other cases, downloaded files may include information about the purchaser that could later be used to identify the individual who shares or sells the music illegally at a later time.

Other interventions may focus on the psychological phenomena discussed above. Based on their finding that such behaviours need to be learned from others, Higgins, Fell and Wilson (2006) suggest that university administrators should develop policies that emphasize building friendships with non-offending peers, although they acknowledge that such policies need to be carefully evaluated and implemented. Malin and Fowers (2009) suggest that it may be suitable to focus piracy prevention efforts on high school age individuals, and specifically focus on increasing self-control. Finally, Higgins, Wolfe and Marcum (2008) examined digital piracy in undergraduate students over a four week period. They found that as the study progressed, the rate of digital piracy and neutralization decreased. Higgins, Wolfe and Marcum (2008) suggest that it is possible that participants reflected on the criminality of digital piracy as the study progressed, and as the deviant behavior decreased, so did the need to neutralize the behaviors. They therefore suggest that a way to reduce piracy might be education and efforts to improve moral conscience. Overall, there are a number of avenues that may be suitable for further research.

FUTURE TRENDS AND RESEARCH

Piquero (2005) suggests that future research in this area should take three main approaches. These include the development of data collection efforts targeting information about the prevalence of the problem, testing how well the theoretical explanations (such as deterrence) explain the phenomenon, and thirdly evaluating the effects of prevention and intervention efforts. Piquero (2005) indicates that despite considerable attention from legal perspectives, there has been little social scientific or criminological research on the area, and that this needs to be addressed.

The research regarding self-control, social learning and neutralizations shows promise in building an explanation of this type of offending, but further research needs to be completed to determine in greater detail how these three factors interact. Similarly the respective benefits of general and specific deterrence methods need to be fully evaluated in order to determine their effectiveness. It would also be useful to see how effective some of the alternative solutions outlined above may be. In addition, thorough evaluations need to be completed regarding the effectiveness of public information campaigns in order to determine if they are targeting the right individuals and if the most effective message is being sent.

One of the more interesting future trends may examine print media. While it is possible to obtain full transcripts of some bestselling books online, this does not seem to be as popular as other types of copyright infringement. This may be due in part to a general reluctance for reading long documents on monitors due to the eye strain which may occur. With the increasing popularity of eReaders (devices that use displays which cause less eye strain), there may be an increased market for illegal digital copies of books. Current eReaders tend to be limited in distribution potential, although some allow copies of the publications to be held on more than one personal device registered to the user (so for example, the purchased book may be read on a mobile phone, portable tablet device and personal computer of the purchaser, as well as the eReader device). In some cases, the retailer even allows the different versions to communicate so that they synchronise to the last read page of the book or document. Nevertheless, it is currently more difficult to copy such files than it is to copy music, game and video files. It is likely that these restrictions will be overcome relatively quickly by enthusiastic and determined copyright infringers.

CONCLUSION

Music, film and software piracy is prevalent on the Internet, but the true extent of the problem is unclear. Due to the high proportion of use of illegal copies of such files among certain groups it can be difficult to determine what psychological attributes are connected with such behaviours, although there seems to be links with low self-control and social learning theory. There appears to be widespread use of neutralizations among offenders, and strategies to reduce the problem will need to focus on lessening illegal file-sharers' use of this cognitive strategy. Overall it seems that illegal file sharers are aware that their acts are illegal, but feel they can justify their actions through a variety of neutralization techniques. Some evidence to date suggests that an effective counter-measure involves challenging these neutralizations, but as yet, the effectiveness of anti-piracy campaigns is still largely untested. Rigorous evaluations need to be completed to assess the suitability of these campaigns and only when this is complete will it be possible to develop and implement the most suitable solutions for this problem.

REFERENCES

Becker, J. U., & Clement, M. (2006). Dynamics of illegal participation in peer-to-peer networks: Why do people illegally share media files? *Journal of Media Economics*, *19*, 7–32. doi:10.1207/s15327736me1901_2

Bhal, K. T., & Leekha, N. D. (2008). Exploring cognitive moral logics using grounded theory: The case of software piracy. *Journal of Business Ethics*, *81*, 635–646. doi:10.1007/s10551-007-9537-7

British Recorded Music Industry (nd). *Protecting UK music.* Retrieved October 31 2010 from http://www.bpi.co.uk/category/protecting-uk-music.aspx

British Software Alliance. (BSA, 2010). *Fifth Annual BSA and IDC Global Software Piracy Study.* Retrieved on October 31 2010 from http://portal.bsa.org/idcglobalstudy2007/ studies/2007_global_piracy_study.pdf

Bryant, R. (2008). The Challenge of Digital Crime. In Bryant, R. (Ed.), *Investigating Digital Crime* (pp. 1–26). Chichester, England: John Wiley & Sons.

Bryce, J., & Rutter, J. (2005). *Fake Nation: A study into an everyday crime. Report for the Organized Crime Task Force – Northern Ireland Office.* Retrieved 30th October 2010 from http://digiplay.info/files/FakeNation.pdf

Coleman, J. (1994). *The criminal elite: The sociology of white collar crime*. New York: St. Martin's Press.

Cronan, T. P., Foltz, C. B., & Jones, T. W. (2006, June). Piracy, Computer Crime and IS Misuse at the University. *Communications of the ACM*, *49*, 85–89. doi:10.1145/1132469.1132472

D'Astous, A., Colbert, F., & Montpetit, D. (2005). Music piracy on the web – How effective are anti-piracy arguments? Evidence from the Theory of Planned Behavior. *Journal of Consumer Policy*, *28*, 289–310. doi:10.1007/s10603-005-8489-5

Gopal, R., Sanders, G. L., Bhattacharjee, S., Agrawal, M., & Wagner, S. (2004). A behavioral model of digital music piracy. *Journal of Organizational Computing and Electronic Commerce*, *14*, 89–105. doi:10.1207/s15327744joce1402_01

Gottfredson, M. R., & Hirschi, T. (1990). *A general theory of crime*. Stanford, CA: Stanford University Press.

Higgins, G. E. (2007). Digital piracy: An examination of low self-control and motivation using short-term longitudinal data. *Cyberpsychology & Behavior, 10*, 523–529. doi:10.1089/cpb.2007.9995

Higgins, G. E., Fell, B. D., & Wilson, A. L. (2006). Digital piracy: Assessing the contributions of an integrated self-control theory and social learning theory. *Criminal Justice Studies: A Critical Journal of Crime. Law and Society, 19*, 3–22.

Higgins, G. E., Wolfe, S. E., & Marcum, C. D. (2008). Music piracy and neutralization: A preliminary trajectory analysis from short-term longitudinal data. *International Journal of Cyber Criminology, 2*, 324–336.

Hill, C. W. (2007). Digital piracy: causes consequences and strategic responses. *Asia Pacific Journal of Management, 24*, 9–25. doi:10.1007/s10490-006-9025-0

Hinduja, S. (2007). Neutralization theory and online software piracy: An empirical analysis. *Ethics and Information Technology, 9*, 187–204. doi:10.1007/s10676-007-9143-5

Hsu, J., & Shiue, C. (2008). Consumers' willingness to pay for non-pirated software. *Journal of Business Ethics, 81*, 715–732. doi:10.1007/s10551-007-9543-9

Ingram, J., & Hinduja, S. (2008). Neutralizing music piracy: an empirical examination. *Deviant Behavior, 29*, 334–366. doi:10.1080/01639620701588131

International Federation of Phonographic Industries. (IFPI, 2010). *IFPI Digital Music Report: Music how, when, where you want it*. Retrieved October 31 2010 from http://www.ifpi.org/content/library /DMR2010.pdf

Jewkes, Y. (2010). Public policing and Internet crime. In Jewkes, Y., & Yar, M. (Eds.), *Handbook of Internet Crime* (pp. 525–545). Cullompton, England: Willan Publishing.

Jewkes, Y., & Yar, M. (2010). Introduction: the Internet, cybercrime and the challenges of the twenty-first century. In Jewkes, Y., & Yar, M. (Eds.), *Handbook of Internet Crime* (pp. 1–15). Cullompton, England: Willan Publishing.

LaRose, R., & Kim, J. (2007). Share, steal or buy? A social cognitive perspective of music downloading. *Cyberpsychology & Behavior, 10*, 267–277. doi:10.1089/cpb.2006.9959

LaRose, R., Lai, Y. J., Lange, R., Love, B., & Wu, Y. (2005). Sharing or piracy? An exploration of downloading behaviour. *Journal of Computer-Mediated Communication, 11*, 1–21. doi:10.1111/j.1083-6101.2006.tb00301.x

Liao, C., Lin, H.-N., & Liu, Y.-P. (2009). Predicting the Use of Pirated Software: A Contingency Model Integrating Perceived Risk with the Theory of Planned Behavior. *Journal of Business Ethics, 91*, 237–252. doi:10.1007/s10551-009-0081-5

Liebowitz, S. J. (2006). File Sharing: Creative destruction or just plain destruction? *The Journal of Law & Economics, 49*, 1–28. doi:10.1086/503518

Malin, J., & Fowers, B. (2009). Adolescent self-control and music and movie piracy. *Computers in Human Behavior, 25*, 718–722. doi:10.1016/j.chb.2008.12.029

McQuade, S. C. (2006). *Understanding and Managing Cybercrime*. Boston, MA: Allyn & Bacon.

Moore, R., & McMullan, E. C. (2009). Neutralizations and Rationalizations of Digital Piracy: A qualitative analysis of university students. *International Journal of Cyber Criminology, 3*, 441–451.

Morris, R., & Higgins, G. (2009). Neutralizing potential and self-reported digital piracy: A multitheoretical exploration among college undergraduates. *Criminal Justice Review, 34*, 173–195. doi:10.1177/0734016808325034

Morris, R. G., & Higgins, G. E. (2010). Criminological theory in the digital age: The case of social learning theory and digital piracy. *Journal of Criminal Justice*. Retrieved from http://dx.doi.org/10.1016/ j.jcrimjus.2010.04.016

Motion Picture Association of America. (MPAA, 2006). *Worldwide study of losses to the film industry and international economies due to piracy: Pirate profiles*. Retrieved October 31, 2010 from http://www.fact-uk.org.uk/site/media_centre/documents/2006_05_03leksumm.pdf

News, B. B. C. (2010a, October 27). *LimeWire file-sharing service shut down in US*. Retrieved October 30, 2010 from http://www.bbc.co.uk/news/technology-11635320

News, B. B. C. (2010b, January 25). *$2m file-sharing fine slashed to $54,000*. Retrieved October 30, 2010 from http://news.bbc.co.uk/2/hi/technology/ 8478305.stm

News, B. B. C. (2010c, October 12). *Irish court rules in favour of ISPs in piracy case*. Retrieved October 30, 2010 from http://www.bbc.co.uk/news/technology-11521949

News, B. B. C. (2010d, September 30). *Lawyers to continue piracy fight*. Retrieved October 30, 2010 from http://www.bbc.co.uk/news/technology-11443861

Oberholzer-Gee, F., & Strumpf, K. S. (2007). The effect of file sharing on record sales: An empirical analysis. *The Journal of Political Economy, 115*, 1–42. doi:10.1086/511995

Peitz, M., & Waelbroeck, P. (2006). Why the music industry may gain from free downloading – The role of sampling. *International Journal of Industrial Organization, 24*, 907–913. doi:10.1016/j.ijindorg.2005.10.006

Piquero, N. L. (2005). Causes and prevention of intellectual property crime. *Trends in Organised Crime, 8*, 40–61. doi:10.1007/s12117-005-1013-0

Stephens, P. (2008). IPR and Technological Protection Measures. In Bryant, R. (Ed.), *Investigating Digital Crime* (pp. 121–131). Chichester, England: John Wiley & Sons.

Sykes, G., & Matza, D. (1957). Techniques of neutralization; a theory of delinquency. *American Sociological Review, 22*, 664–670. doi:10.2307/2089195

Wall, D. S., & Yar, M. (2010). Intellectual property crime and the Internet: cyber-piracy and 'stealing' information intangibles. In Jewkes, Y., & Yar, M. (Eds.), *Handbook of Internet Crime* (pp. 255–272). Cullompton, England: Willan Publishing.

Wolfe, S. E., Higgins, G. E., & Marcum, C. D. (2008). Deterrence and Digital Piracy: A Preliminary Examination of the Role of Viruses. *Social Science Computer Review, 26*, 317–333. doi:10.1177/0894439307309465

Yar, M. (2006). *Cybercrime and Society*. London: Sage Publications Ltd.

Yar, M. (2007). Teenage kicks or virtual villainy? Internet piracy, moral entrepreneurship and the social construction of a crime problem. In Jewkes, Y. (Ed.), *Crime Online* (pp. 95–108). Cullompton, England: Willan Publishing.

Yar, M. (2010). Public perceptions and public opinion about internet crime. In Jewkes, Y., & Yar, M. (Eds.), *Handbook of Internet Crime* (pp. 104–119). Cullompton, England: Willan Publishing.

Zentner, A. (2004). *Measuring the effect of online music piracy on music sales*. Retrieved from http://economics.uchicago.edu/download/musicindustryoct12.pdf

ADDITIONAL READING

Becker, J. U., & Clement, M. (2006). Dynamics of illegal participation in peer-to-peer networks: Why do people illegally share media files? *Journal of Media Economics*, *19*, 7–32. doi:10.1207/s15327736me1901_2

Bhal, K. T., & Leekha, N. D. (2008). Exploring cognitive moral logics using grounded theory: The case of software piracy. *Journal of Business Ethics*, *81*, 635–646. doi:10.1007/s10551-007-9537-7

Bryant, R. (2008). The Challenge of Digital Crime. In Bryant, R. (Ed.), *Investigating Digital Crime* (pp. 1–26). Chichester, England: John Wiley & Sons.

Cronan, T. P., Foltz, C. B., & Jones, T. W. (2006, June). Piracy, Computer Crime and IS Misuse at the University. *Communications of the ACM*, *49*, 85–89. doi:10.1145/1132469.1132472

Gopal, R., Sanders, G. L., Bhattacharjee, S., Agrawal, M., & Wagner, S. (2004). A behavioral model of digital music piracy. *Journal of Organizational Computing and Electronic Commerce*, *14*, 89–105. doi:10.1207/s15327744joce1402_01

Higgins, G. E. (2007). Digital piracy: An examination of low self-control and motivation using short-term longitudinal data. *Cyberpsychology & Behavior*, *10*, 523–529. doi:10.1089/cpb.2007.9995

Higgins, G. E., Fell, B. D., & Wilson, A. L. (2006). Digital piracy: Assessing the contributions of an integrated self-control theory and social learning theory. *Criminal Justice Studies: A Critical Journal of Crime. Law and Society*, *19*, 3–22.

Higgins, G. E., Wolfe, S. E., & Marcum, C. D. (2008). Music piracy and neutralization: A preliminary trajectory analysis from short-term longitudinal data. *International Journal of Cyber Criminology*, *2*, 324–336.

Hinduja, S. (2007). Neutralization theory and online software piracy: An empirical analysis. *Ethics and Information Technology*, *9*, 187–204. doi:10.1007/s10676-007-9143-5

Ingram, J., & Hinduja, S. (2008). Neutralizing music piracy: an empirical examination. *Deviant Behavior*, *29*, 334–366. doi:10.1080/01639620701588131

LaRose, R., & Kim, J. (2007). Share, steal or buy? A social cognitive perspective of music downloading. *Cyberpsychology & Behavior*, *10*, 267–277. doi:10.1089/cpb.2006.9959

Malin, J., & Fowers, B. (2009). Adolescent self-control and music and movie piracy. *Computers in Human Behavior*, *25*, 718–722. doi:10.1016/j.chb.2008.12.029

Moore, R., & McMullan, E. C. (2009). Neutralizations and Rationalizations of Digital Piracy: A qualitative analysis of university students. *International Journal of Cyber Criminology*, *3*, 441–451.

Morris, R. G., & Higgins, G. E. (2010). Criminological theory in the digital age: The case of social learning theory and digital piracy. *Journal of Criminal Justice*. Retrieved from http://dx.doi.org/10.1016/j.jcrimjus.2010.04.016

Wall, D. S., & Yar, M. (2010). Intellectual property crime and the Internet: cyber-piracy and 'stealing' information intangibles. In Jewkes, Y., & Yar, M. (Eds.), *Handbook of Internet Crime* (pp. 255–272). Cullompton, England: Willan Publishing.

Yar, M. (2007). Teenage kicks or virtual villainy? Internet piracy, moral entrepreneurship and the social construction of a crime problem. In Jewkes, Y. (Ed.), *Crime Online* (pp. 95–108). Cullompton, England: Willan Publishing.

Chapter 11
Cyberterrorism:
Can Terrorist Goals be Achieved Using the Internet?

ABSTRACT

Cyberterrorism is a subject which has gained considerable interest from both researchers and media, particularly since the attacks on the United States of America on September 11th 2001. Nevertheless, there is a considerable lack of empirical research in the area, with most writings based on theoretical or anecdotal accounts, despite many calls by leaders in the field for more empirically sound methods. This is further complicated by the difficulty in even finding consensus as to what does and does not constitute cyberterrorism. This chapter aims to determine if cyberterrorism is a likely strategy to be used by terrorists, and if so, how it might be used to strike terror into the hearts of citizens. Following some illustrative scenarios of terrorist activity online, some of the conflicting definitions of the subject will be considered. The methods used by terrorists online will then be outlined, including both an examination of the possibility of using the internet for a large scale attack, and using the internet for more conventional activities such as recruitment and fundraising. The psychology of terrorism will then be examined, including investigations of the personalities and psychiatric health of terrorists, and it will be examined as to whether or not the findings relating to 'traditional' terrorists can also be applied to online terrorist activity. The potential effects of an attack on victims will also be considered. Consideration will be given as to how terrorist activity online could be prevented, while also recognising that the increasing online presence of terrorist organisations may be a double-edged sword, enabling counter-terrorism agencies to employ new strategies in their work.

DOI: 10.4018/978-1-61350-350-8.ch011

BACKGROUND

In order to illustrate the potential of the Internet for terrorist causes, two fictional scenarios are presented below.

A government has a strong online presence, maintaining official websites along with several profiles on a variety of social networking websites. One afternoon, a 'Denial of Service' attack renders their official websites useless. No legitimate user can gain access to the information or services available online, including taxation, health care appointments and corporation services. Simultaneously, unofficial access is gained to the government run social networking profiles, and status messages are posted which include insulting comments that are offensive to many members of the society, particularly those in the armed services. The government realizes that they have been the victim of an attack by a terrorist organization. While it only takes a few days to restore their online presence to its previous status, there is significant damage to the public confidence in the government. The people are worried that terrorists may have accessed their personal information, and that they are at risk of identity theft. They also have concerns that the government is unable to properly defend their online resources appropriately.

A young man is beginning to feel disillusioned. He feels that society is not treating him as well as it should, and that the regime he lives under is unfair, particularly to his ethnic group. He spends some time searching the internet, and finds the website of a terrorist organization. The website is filled with information and propaganda. There are messages from the terrorists, explaining their reasons for fighting, and the young man finds that he agrees with their position. He views pictures on the website of women and children being mistreated by the regime, and he becomes angry. He finds instructions on the website for making bombs, but is still unsure if he wants to become violent for his cause. The website includes a chat facility, within which he makes contact with members of the terrorist organization. He finds they hold the same beliefs as he does, and although he is still a little unsure, he finds their arguments very persuasive. For the first time in many years he feels that others understand his perspective. After a vetting process, he joins their organization.

In addition to these, there have been several fictional depictions of cyberterrorism in the popular media. One of the most famous of these is the 2007 film *Live Free or Die Hard* (released as *Die Hard 4.0* outside of the United States), which depicted a scenario where a terrorist organization employed computer hackers to develop code that was used to take control of various critical systems, including traffic lights and the stock market (Fottrell & Wiseman, 2007). While the above scenarios are fictional, and the world has not experienced an attack similar to that portrayed in the *Die Hard* film, terrorists are making increased use of modern technology for their causes. In September 2010 the *Stuxnet* worm (a form of malware) infiltrated some of the personal computers at Iran's first nuclear power station (BBC News, 2010a). If it ever reaches the computers designed to control the industrial machinery, such as motors and coolers, it may be able to instruct the equipment to turn on or off at given signals or equipment status settings. It is a highly tailored worm, searching for very specific configurations. While it is not yet known who the developer of the worm was, or whether their motive is cyberterrorism or something else, this case provides evidence that there is potential for cyberterrorists to cause significant harm to critical systems.

The first two scenarios, while fictional, are based on strategies that some terrorist organizations are already known to employ. For example, Denning (2001) describes an "email bombing" by the Internet Black Tigers against the Sri Lankan embassies in 1998, which flooded their system by filling staff in-boxes with spam emails that prevented them from completing their work. Similarly, Wilson (2007) indicates that an attack on the Estonian government computer systems has been labeled by some observers as a cyberterror campaign. In this attack, a series of sustained Distributed Denial of Service (DDOS) attacks were launched against the websites of government ministries and the prime minister's Reform Party. The attack resulted in the repeated shutdown of the websites for several hours at a time, blocking legitimate users.

It is also known that terrorists can use the Internet for more conventional activities, such as communication and planning. Conway (2002) reports that in the aftermath of the 11th September 2001 terrorist attacks on the United States of America, it was discovered that at least nine of the terrorists' airline tickets were booked online, that the terrorists had used the Internet to search for information about the aerial application of pesticides, and emails were used to distribute operational details of the attack. The terrorists had used both personal computers and public terminals to access the Internet. However, Wilson (2005) suggests that while many international terrorist groups do use the Internet to communicate, there is disagreement as to whether or not coordinated cyberattacks against US infrastructure could be highly damaging, or if they are really a target for furthering terrorist goals. Wilson indicates that most security experts feel that it is most likely that an attack on US computers and communications would be used to amplify the effects of a more conventional terrorist attack, using nuclear, biological or chemical means. Despite the suggestions by some that a cyberterror attack may be severe, most writers do not seem to agree. Leman-Langlois (2008) demonstrates a minority view by stating that "A 'cyber Pearl Harbour' is looming, with attackers targeting essential infrastructures in attempts to cripple economies. They will coordinate attacks on… targets selected to produce cascading failures along our highly intercon-nected infrastructures" (pp. 2-3). Nevertheless, the emergence of the Stuxnet worm, coupled with an admission in 2009 by the US government that malware had been found which could shut down the national power grid (BBC News, 2010b), may mean that experts in the field need to reappraise their position. The threat may now be more real than previously thought.

As will be discussed below, some researchers and practitioners in the field do not believe that online terrorism activities such as operational issues and planning, or even website defacements and Denial of Service attacks, should be classified as 'cyberterrorism'. For these individuals and groups, the term 'cyberterrorism' should be reserved for activities similar to those portrayed in the film plot above, which result in death or severe disruption. Denning (2001) cites hypothetical scenarios described by Collin (1997), where terrorists could cause havoc by using the Internet to increase the levels of iron in a breakfast cereal to a lethal level, or cause civilian aircraft to collide by hacking into air traffic control systems, although it is generally felt that it would either be very difficult to gain access to these systems, or that the problem would be detected before severe consequences result. Denning (2007a) indicates that likely targets for cyberterrorism include electrical power, oil, gas, water supply, telecommunications, banking, emergency services, transportation, and essential government services. Whittaker (2004, p. 123) takes a somewhat pessimistic view of what is probably the worst case scenario:

At the throw of a few switches, a saboteur, sitting in relative comfort and with highly technical equipment, can shut down power grids, unravel telephone networks, bring chaos to road and rail transport and air traffic control, and break down the operation of pharmaceutical and food processing plants. A 'logic bomb' can be timed to detonate at a certain hour and there will be irreversible damage to software. Computer viruses, if carefully ordered, will completely shut down an entire computer system. A computer can browse through databanks thought to be confidential. Surveillance systems will be entered, examined, and, if necessary, destroyed. Death and destruction can be brought into being at a distance with nobody hostile there to watch

Definitions of Cyberterrorism

It is difficult to find consensus amongst experts in the field as to what does and does not constitute cyberterrorism. It is even difficult to find consensus as to what constitutes traditional terrorism, but, for the purposes of this chapter it will refer to the use of violence or intimidation to invoke fear in a specific group in order to achieve a desired goal, which may be political, ideological or religious in nature. The objective of this chapter is not to consider terrorism in historical or general terms, although there are several key sources where the reader can find further information on these matters (see for example Sterba, 2003 or Whittaker, 2004). Here the focus will be on cyberterrorism, which Conway (2007) suggests is a term that "unites two significant modern fears: fear of technology and fear of terrorism" (p. 73).

Gordon and Ford (2003) indicate that a solid definition of cyberterrorism is elusive, and that there is a large degree of subjectivity regarding what is and is not cyberterrorism. Yet Gordon and Ford indicate that, without a good definition and understanding of cyberterrorism, a solution to it cannot be developed. Pollitt (1997, as cited by Denning, 2001) suggested that cyberterrorism "is the premeditated, politically motivated attack against information, computer systems, computer programs, and data which result in violence against non-combatant targets by subnational groups or clandestine agents" (p. 281). Wilson (2005) suggests that cyberterrorism is "the use of computers as weapons, or as targets, by politically motivated international, or sub-national groups, or clandestine agents who threaten or cause violence and fear in order to influence an audience, or cause a government to change its policies" (p. CRS-7).

Gordon and Ford (2003) describe pure cyberterrorism, where the activities are carried out primarily online, but indicate that it is also important to defend against traditional forms of terrorism in online environments, such as recruitment and organisation. Gordon and Ford (2003) suggest that pure cyberterrorism could promote the creation of new terrorist groups, given that it requires very little financing and could be quickly and easily organized. Gordon and Ford also emphasise the advantages of online anonymity for both pure and traditional cyberterrorism activities. Wykes and Harcus (2010) state, in relation to the Internet, that "It is the public space of the twenty-first century. Its global reach, chaotic structure, ease of access, anonymity and our increasing dependence on it for the information, education, entertainment and communication it offers makes it appear to be both a perfect tool for terrorists and site of terror activity, worldwide" (p. 216).

Denning (2007b, p. 71) defines cyberterrorism as

The convergence of terrorism and cyberspace… unlawful attacks and threats of attack against computers, networks and the information stored therein when done to intimidate or coerce a government or its people in furtherance of political or social objectives. Further, to qualify as cyberterrorism, an attack should result in violence against persons or property, or at least cause enough harm to generate fear. Attacks that lead to death or bodily injury, explosions, plane crashes, water contamination, or severe economic loss would be examples. Serious attacks against critical infrastructures could be acts of cyberterrorism, depending on their impact. Attacks that disrupt nonessential services or that are mainly a costly nuisance would not

Denning (2001) also suggests that "politically motivated attacks that cause serious harm, such as severe economic hardship or sustained loss of power or water, might also be characterised as cyberterrorism" (p. 281). Similarly, other researchers, such as Nelson, Choi, Iacobucci, Mitchell and Gagnon (1999) suggest that activities that harness the Internet to complete terrorist missions, by means of organization, communication etc, should not be included in the category of cyberterrorism. Nelson et al indicate that these activities should be classified as either 'cyberterror support' (the unlawful use of information systems by terrorists which is not intended, by itself, to have a coercive effect on a target audience) or 'terrorist use of the internet', which does not qualify as cyberterrorism according to Nelson et al (1999). .

Conway (2007) furthers this argument, suggesting a four tiered system to classify cyberactivism and cyberattacks. At one end of this system is 'Use' – using the internet to express ideas, which many internet users engage in legally. Hackers or hacktivists may engage in the next level 'Misuse', where the internet is used to disrupt websites or infrastructure, perhaps through Denial of Service attacks. 'Offensive Use' involves using the Internet to cause damage or to steal, which Conway (2007) suggests is completed by crackers. Finally, 'Cyberterrorism' refers to the use of the Internet to carry out an attack which would result in violence or severe economic damage, and would be carried out by terrorists.

And so there is some disagreement amongst authors as to what does and does not constitute cyberterrorism. Due to this disagreement, and for the purposes of clarity within this chapter, the term 'cyberterrorism' will be used in line with the definition by Denning (2007b) above. The more inclusive term of "terrorist activity online" will be used to describe cyberterrorim, as well as attacks such as website defacements and Denial of Service attacks, and will also include routine activities such as fundraising, organization and recruitment.

Methods Used by Cyberterrorists

Terrorists use the Internet just like everybody else, - Richard Clarke (2004, as cited by Conway, 2006).

Although not generally recognized as cyberterrorism, the terrorist use of the Internet for purposes such as propaganda and recruitment appear to be the main focus of current online terrorist activity. Wilson (2007) declared that "It is clear that terrorist groups are using computers and the Internet to further goals associated with spreading terrorism" (p. CRS-2). He indicates that terrorist organizations are using websites for recruitment, fundraising and training. Maghaireh (2008) indicates that some websites propagating Islamic rhetoric and ideology have online schools teaching hacking techniques.

Denning (2010) claims that "despite the ordinariness of much of this use, the very practice of terrorism – the ways in which terrorists disseminate documents and propaganda, recruit and train new members, and inflict harm on their victims – is being fundamentally transformed and expanded because of the Net" (p. 194). Conway (2006) indicates that there are five main ways in which terrorists use the internet – information provision, financing, networking, recruitment and information gathering. Other researchers have suggested a broader usage of the internet, including Weimann (2004) who suggests eight different ways, including psychological warfare, publicity and propaganda, planning and co-ordination, and mobilization, as well as those outlined by Conway (2006). The various forms of terrorist activity online will now be considered.

Cyberterror Attacks

Denning (2010) uses the term 'cyber-attacks' to refer to the 'pure' terrorism of Gordon and Ford (2003). She indicates that despite allowances within official definitions of cyberterrorism for attacks such as Denials of Service to be included, that government officials and academics "have been reluctant to label any cyber-attack that has occurred so far as an act of cyber-terrorism" (p. 198). She suggests that this is due to the lack of physical and psychological effects resulting from such attacks, when compared to more traditional terrorism acts such as bombings. As Stohl (2006) stated, "there have been no instances where cyber terrorism has mirrored a catastrophic loss of life or physical destruction associated with the most violent acts of "conventional" terrorism" (p. 224). He argues that terrorists are just using modern technologies such as the internet to accomplish the same goals they previously had – technology might enhance ease of operations, but it is not being used as an active method of attack.

Denning (2007a) suggests that there are varying indicators of cyberterrorism. These range from the most severe 'Execution of cyber attacks', through 'cyber weapons acquisition, development and training' (which could occur online or offline), 'Statements about cyberattacks' (including declarations of intent and discussions relating to the subject), 'Formal education in information technology' (particularly in network and information security) and finally the least severe 'General experience with cyberspace' (such as use of the Internet for general communications and propaganda). Denning (2007a) suggests that on this scale, a failed attack against power systems is more indicative of a threat than a successful website defacement. She indicates that no attack to date has caused enough damage to be considered an act of cyberterror, although some incidents have caused considerable disruption or have gained funds for the terrorist organization. If the Stuxnet worm, or similar malware, is found to be a product of terrorist activity, then it seems likely that Denning would classify this as an 'execution of cyber attack'. In addition, Denning (2007a) suggests that there is evidence for activity at the second most serious level, that of cyberweapons acquisition, development and training. She indicates that some terrorist

organizations are known to train their members in computer hacking techniques and are engaged in 'cyber reconnaissance' in order to gain information about infrastructure. Denning (2007a) also lists several examples of evidence for statements about cyberattacks. Denning (2007b) indicates that some terrorist groups have employed external hackers to aid in gathering information, or have attempted to buy illegally obtained software. However, it is also possible that terrorist organizations may recruit hackers into their own midst.

Rollins and Wilson (2007) suggest that as the United States puts in place tighter physical and border security, terrorists may attempt to use other methods to attack, perhaps developing new computer skills and considering a cyberattack against the critical infrastructure of the United States. They cite the Federal Bureau of Investigation (FBI) who report that cyberattacks by terrorists have been mostly limited to email bombings and website defacements, but that the FBI predicts that future large conventional attacks may be complimented with cyberattacks. Wilson (2005) considers the types of cyberattack which might be carried out by terrorists. He suggests that there are three potential methods of attack: physical attacks, electronic attacks and computer network attacks. A physical attack would involve the use of conventional weapons directed against a specific computer facility or communication lines. An electronic attack would use electromagnetic energy (possibly an electromagnetic pulse or EMP) to overload computer circuitry. Finally, a computer network attack would probably use malicious code to infect computers and exploit software weaknesses.

Yar (2006) indicates that there are four main advantages to virtual terror attacks. Firstly, the Internet permits terrorists to act remotely, even from other countries, thus reducing the impact of increased border controls since September 11th 2001, and allowing terrorist activity to take place within 'rogue states' which may protect the terrorist from foreign criminal justice agencies.

Secondly, Yar indicates that the Internet allows small terrorist organizations with limited resources to function as more serious threats. Thirdly, the anonymity provided by the internet poses a problem for counter-terrorist units. And finally the lack of regulation of the Internet results in many security holes, which can be exploited by terrorist organizations.

As previously noted, there has been no confirmed cyberterrorist attack to date, excluding cases such as Denial of Service attacks and website defacements. That is not to say that such an event will not occur in the future, although experts in the field are divided as to if critical infrastructures are vulnerable to such an attack, and whether there is sufficient redundancy in these systems to ensure that even if such an attack took place, there would be minimal disruption to the general public. The more recent events of the discovery of the Stuxnet worm and the software capable of shutting down the US power grid indicates that the risk is quite real. In addition, it seems likely that if terrorists did choose to launch a cyberattack, they would do so in combination with a more traditional form of attack. This possibility is considered in more depth later in the chapter.

Recruitment of New Members

Conway (2006) outlines how the internet enables potential recruits to become members of terrorist organizations in a number of ways. Firstly, it allows information gathering to be quicker and easier, with the information accessible in multiple formats, including video and audio files. For example, McDonald (2009) indicates that several propaganda videos for the Real IRA and Continuity IRA were easily available on the video sharing website YouTube. These videos included scenes of masked men in combat fatigues threatening Northern Ireland's deputy first minister while addressing a crowd in a bar. Other films showed masked gunmen firing weapons.

The Internet also allows a sense of anonymity in the searching for such information. It makes it easier for potential recruits to contact the terrorist group directly, and to assist the terrorist organization in a wider variety of methods. Active recruitment online is also possible, where the terrorist organization may search chat rooms or bulletin boards for individuals who may be receptive to the cause. Denning (2010) indicates that those who are recruited online may never formally join the terrorist organization, or travel to their physical centers. They may instead help the organization via donations of money, software or expertise.

Denning (2010) indicates that different websites offer different advice for potential recruits, and some have differing requirements from recruits. Some require oaths of loyalty to the terror leaders, while others indicate that all that is required is a wish to join. Perhaps most disturbing is the indication by Denning (2010) that there is evidence to suggest that online recruitment of children for terrorist causes uses a variety of techniques, including games, rap music videos and comic-book style readings.

Networking

Denning (2010) describes how the Internet permits members to be a highly organized, yet highly decentralized, network of cells, who may not even be recognized by the terrorist leadership. Similarly, Conway (2006) explains how the internet allows terrorist organizations to become decentralized, while still allowing members to communicate rapidly, cheaply and effectively. This enables the terrorist organization to avoid having a single headquarters, but allows responsibilities to be disseminated to many centers. Terrorist activities can also be organized in a less risky manner, as the internet reduces the need for face to face or telephone contact.

Funding

Conway (2006) describes how the advent of the internet allows for increased financial donations to terrorist organizations. She outlines how many terrorist websites have direct payment options that facilitate visitors in donating money to the organisation using credit cards. Websites may directly request donations, or may establish online stores selling various items which may or may not be related to their cause. But she also suggests that some terrorist organizations may use the internet to fund their activities through other illegal activities such as credit card fraud or advanced fee fraud, although solid evidence for this is not publicly available. Conway (2006) also describes how terrorist organizations, particularly those with Islamist roots, may use charities as fundraising vehicles.

Hacktivism vs. Cyberterrorism

There is some confusion in the literature as to the differences between hacktivism and cyberterrorism. In general, it is concluded that hacktivisists, despite using the internet as a method for political protest, are a different group to cyberterrorists. As Conway (2007) suggests, they are more interested in disrupting online activity, rather than causing destruction. Similarly, they do not seem interested in causing terror, but rather frustration and difficulty for administrators. Denning (2007a) indicates that, in order to be classified as cyberterrorism, the attack has to be destructive or disruptive to the extent that it generates fear similar to that which results from physical acts of terrorism. As such, most hacktivism attacks, including website defacements and some Denial of Service attacks, would not classify as cyberterrorism.

Gathering and Dissemination of Information

Conway (2006) indicates that terrorists use the internet to gather political and other information, but also as a tool for psychological warfare. By issuing threats online, releasing videos of terrorist leaders and terrorist activities (such as the beheadings of captives), and by spreading false information, terrorists can reach large numbers of people very quickly, very easily, and at little expense. Denning (2010) echoes this, indicating that, by using the Internet, terrorists can circumvent established media routes, such as newspapers and television, providing the information directly to users without censorship. The messages they circulate using the internet can also be presented in a more favourable light to the terrorist cause than would likely be available through traditional media.

Conway (2006) also describes how training materials are disseminated on the internet, including methods of creating homemade bombs and establishing underground organisations, which may be of use in terrorist and criminal acts. The information may not just be used by terrorist organizations, but also by aggrieved individuals who wish to seek revenge on some individual or organization. Denning (2010) indicates that while some of the instructional materials provided use out-of-date methods (sometimes by as much as 100 years), others are more modern, including information on computers and the Internet.

The terrorist dissemination of information is not limited to websites however, and Denning (2010) indicates that organizations have also been known to communicate with members using social networking websites (such as Orkut) and commercial networks, (such as Yahoo!). She also indicates that terrorist websites can use a variety of multimedia and interconnectivity tools, including video and audio files in a variety of formats, as well as boards, blogs and chatrooms. She also indicates that jihadists make use of news websites, such as Wikinews, to distribute information.

PSYCHOLOGY OF TERRORISM

Unfortunately there has been very little empirical study into the psychology of terrorism (Victoroff, 2005; Silke, 2008). Much of the research to date has been theoretical, or based on literature or anecdotal observations, rather than empirical investigations, although Silke (2008) suggests that there has been an increase in the use of statistical analysis in recent years and a general increase in research on terrorism related issues since the attacks on the United States of America on September 11ᵗʰ 2001. There are several reasons for this lack of terrorist empirical study. In the first instance, it can be difficult to find terrorists, particularly those who are willing to participate in a psychological study. Some researchers have studied incarcerated terrorists, but even this causes difficulties as it is necessary to get approval from the relevant authorities. In addition to this there are many practical issues, such as the expense of traveling, problems in gaining approval from ethical boards and language barriers. Finally, many researchers are understandably loathe to put their own personal safety at risk by directly contacting terrorists or by traveling to unstable regions.

Despite these issues, there are some interesting papers and studies relating to the psychology of terrorism which will be considered here. In particular, focus will be applied on the process of becoming a terrorist, motives for terrorism, and the personality traits of terrorists. In addition, the potential for psychological deviance in terrorists will also be considered, as will the possible similarities between traditional terrorists and cyberterrorists. Finally, the impact of cyberterrorism on victims and the public will also be discussed.

Becoming a Terrorist

There seems to be consensus that becoming a terrorist is a gradual process, involving several stages (Merari, 2007; Horgan & Taylor, 2001). McCauley and Moskalenko (2008) attempted to identify the methods of radicalization of individuals. They define political radicalization as "a dimension of increasing extremity of beliefs, feelings, and behaviours in support of intergroup conflict and violence" (p. 415). They distinguished between twelve mechanisms of radicalization, and identified that in ten of these, radicalization occurs in the context of a perceived threat to an identified in-group, such as an ethnic or religious group.

While it has been suggested that terrorists come from specific backgrounds, such as low socio-economic status, relative deprivation, education, occupation and specific religious faiths, Sageman (2004) suggests that there are difficulties in using these as predictors of terrorist tendencies, due to the high numbers of individuals who share the same background, but do not engage in terrorism. He agrees that relative deprivation is probably a necessary condition for terrorism, but it cannot explain terrorist tendencies in full.

Kruglanski and Fishman (2006) suggest that no single factor is either a sufficient or necessary cause of terrorist behaviour. They indicate that it requires certain conditions to occur in the right combination for an individual to support or become involved in a terrorist organization. Howitt (2009) suggests that some of the key motivations for becoming a terrorist include wanting to feel a sense of belonging and the development of personal identity. If a person is socially isolated, then it may eventually lead to terrorism. Perception of injustice is also a key factor.

Victoroff (2005) identifies social learning theory as a potential explanation of terrorist activity. It is possible that terrorism does not result from the individual's characteristics, but from a reconstruction of moral imperatives based on what is learned from others. This may occur in face to face settings, but it can also be derived from the dissemination of literature and audiovisual content by the terrorist organization, using the Internet and other means. However only a small percentage of those who are exposed to such material will go on to engage in terrorist activities.

Becoming a terrorist leader may be more difficult to explain. Locicero and Sinclair (2008) suggest that terrorist leaders combine "entrenched cognitive simplicity in one key ideological domain" (p. 227) with an ability for much greater complexity in other domains, such as planning and organizational skills. They explain that this type of leadership increases the likelihood of terrorist attacks, and specifically suicide attacks. They also indicate that the cognitive simplicity relating to a religious or political cause may make diplomacy more difficult to achieve.

Motives of Offenders

Horgan (2005) indicates that "very often, it seems that the goal of terrorism is simply to create widespread fear, arousal and uncertainty on a wider, more distant scale than that achieved by targeting the victim alone, thereby influencing the political process and how it might normally be expected to function" (pp. 1-2). He suggests that most terrorist movements seek to overthrow or destabilize a target regime or influence. He says that most are relatively small, and based on political or religious ideologies. Horgan also indicates that it is important to recognize the goal of inducing terror. He describes how the most important outcome for the terrorists of the 9/11 attacks was not the deaths of almost three thousand people at the time, but the "humiliation of the American government and the subsequent psychological arousal for the greater populace" (p. 2). Is it possible that a similar level of humiliation and psychological arousal could also be achieved using information technology?

With relation to cyberterrorism, Veerasamy (2010) suggests that terrorist activity online can best be understood by examining the motives

of traditional terrorist groups and determining how their intentions could be achieved using information technology. Colarik and Janczewski (2008) indicate that there are a number of potential motives for cyberattacks. Key amongst these motives is the same generation of fear in individuals, groups and societies as is evident for more traditional terrorism attacks. Second to this is the 'Spectacular factor' – "involving huge direct losses and/or resulting in a lot of negative publicity" (p. xv). Thirdly, cyberterror attacks may be carried out to emphasize the vulnerability of an organization, perhaps by causing a Denial of Service. These attacks may aim to demonstrate weaknesses in the system, to steal information, or to make political statements about the entity being attacked.

Rollins and Wilson (2007) cite Richard Clarke, the former Administration Counter Terrorism Advisor and National Security Advisor, who indicated that the probable target for a widespread cyberattack on the US would be the economy. Rollins and Wilson (2007) also suggest that the most effective use of a cyberattack would be to amplify a conventional attack. For example, a terrorist organization may use cyberterrorism to disable the communication networks of a country. This may be coupled with a traditional bombing or other violent attack. The disruption to communication networks may prevent bystanders and victims from making calls to the emergency services in order to gain assistance from police, ambulances or fire services, thus leading to a higher death toll.

Personality Characteristics of Offenders

There have been suggestions of some personality traits that might contribute to an individual engaging in terrorist acts, although there is little empirical evidence to support these claims. For example, Zuckerman (2002) has suggested that terrorism may be correlated with a sensation seeking personality type, who is attracted to the excitement that a terrorist lifestyle might offer. However, despite many efforts to demonstrate a personality type indicative of terrorists, Howitt (2009) indicates that there is now consensus in the research literature that a 'terrorist personality' does not exist. Similarly, Horgan (2008) states that "attempts to profile terrorists have failed resoundingly" (p. 80). Nevertheless, he suggests that psychology can still make a contribution to counter-terrorism measures, and particularly if greater attention is paid to the disengagement phase, which may or may not involve de-radicalisation.

Victoroff (2005) describes empirical research conducted on a number of terrorist organizations, including ETA and various Palestinian organizations. These studies did not reveal any striking psychological characteristics of members, with terrorists not differing from control groups substantially, and Victoroff concludes that much of the literature in the topic of terrorism does not take into account this heterogenity. Likewise, Silke (2003) indicates that the vast majority of terrorists cannot be described by a certain personality trait and Horgan (2003b) indicates that personality traits are useless as predictors of terrorist involvement.

However, Kruglanski and Fishman (2006) discuss how, while terrorists may not have unique personality traits, they may not be irrelevant to terrorism. They distinguished between terrorism as a 'syndrome' and terrorism as a 'tool'. If terrorism is a 'syndrome' it is a "psychologically meaningful construct with identifiable characteristics on individual and group levels of analysis" (p. 193) whereas if it is a 'tool' it "represents a strategic instrument that any party in a conflict with another may use" (p. 193). If terrorism is a syndrome, then there could be distinctive personality traits, motivations and socilisation histories associated with terrorists, and findings about one terrorist group could be generalized to other groups. If terrorism is a 'tool', then it assumes little about the psychological characteristics of the terrorist or organization, and assigns terrorism the role of an instrument that anyone could use to reach a desired goal. In this case, psychology can be insightful as to why a person might choose to use terrorism over other methods of obtaining that goal. Kruglanski and Fishman indicate that there has been little evidence to date for a 'syndrome' of terrorism, as there are little identifying psychological characteristics or traits that seem to characterize a terrorist personality. As such, Kruglanski and Fishman suggest that the 'tool' view is more appropriate, as it allows psychology to analyse the phenomenon in terms of mean-end analysis. This suggests that if an alternative method of obtaining the 'end' desired by the terrorist organization is available, and is preferable to terrorist activities, then it is likely that the terrorists will accept this 'means' instead, although this may not always occur. It also suggests that if terrorism is not envisioned as a potential successful means of reaching the end goal, then it will not be utilized, and alternative methods will be sought. As such, there is still a great deal of psychology within the 'tool' perspective, as it requires insight into the perceptions and decision making strategies of the terrorists involved.

Some researchers have considered the role of cognitive factors in terrorist activity. Taylor and Quayle (1994) suggest that it is possible that terrorists make fundamental attribution errors regarding the oppressors, which increases their likelihood of becoming actively engaged. However there is a lack of empirical support for this theory. Victoroff (2005) considers the decision making strategies of terrorists, considering how strategic/rational choice theory might explain the behaviour of terrorists. Nevertheless, it again does not explain why the vast majority of people who might have a desired objective, and who can see how terrorism may help to obtain that objective, do not engage in terrorism. While it may explain the decision making strategy of the terrorist, it does not help to differentiate them from the vast majority of others who do not engage in terrorist acts. Victoroff (2005) goes on to suggest that it is possible that terrorists may demonstrate cognitive factors such as inflexibility or other diminished executive functions, which may be important information for negotiators in attempting to determine how the terrorist may react under certain circumstances. Victoroff also suggests that other personality characteristics, such as novelty-seeking behaviour or subjective feelings of humiliation may also be linked with terrorist involvement, although again there is no evidence to support this apart from theoretical conjecture.

Social psychology may provide more insight into the behaviors of terrorists. Group dynamics are an important component of terrorist organizations. The organization provides support from others with similar goals, a well-defined personal role and sense of purpose, and the lifting of constraints on behaviours that might be considered unacceptable outside of the group (Victoroff, 2005). The group identity is important. Post, Sprinzak and Denny (2003) describe that "an overarching sense of the collective consumes the individual. This fusion with the group seems to provide the necessary justification for their actions, with an attendant loss of felt responsibility" (p. 176).

Victoroff (2005) concludes that in almost all cases, terrorism is determined by a combination of several factors, including development factors, innate and biological factors, cognitive capabilities, cognitive styles, environmental influence, temperament and group dynamics. He claims that the conclusion that there are no individual factors which identify those at risk of becoming terrorists is premature, as there are insufficient empirically valid studies to reach that conclusion. He suggests that there may be four traits which are characteristic of 'typical' terrorists. Initially, the person would have high affective opinion regarding an issue. However, as most individuals with this opinion would not go on to engage in terrorist activity, the potential terrorist will also have a personal stake that separates them from others holding the same opinion. This may be a sense of personal oppression, a strong need for vengeance, or a drive to express aggression, among other factors. In addition to this, the potential terrorist would need to have low cognitive flexibility, with an elevated tendency toward attribution error. Finally, the potential terrorist would need to be able to suppress moral constraints against harming innocent people. However, Victoroff does admit that this theory needs to be tested using further study.

Terrorism and Abnormal Psychology

As recently as 1981 psychopathy was the feature most commonly associated with terrorists (Horgan, 2003a). However, this is unlikely to be reflected in terrorist psychology. Silke (1998) supports the conclusion that terrorists are unlikely to hold any major psychopathology. He notes that despite significant interest in potentially describing terrorists as having psychopathic, narcissistic or paranoid personality disorders, there is little evidence to suggest that they actually do. He claims that those who suggest abnormality are mostly basing their theories on only anecdotal evidence or secondary sources. He claims that those who argue for the normality of terrorists are more likely to be those who have had direct contact and experience with actual terrorists. Post, Ali, Henderson, Shanfield, Victoroff and Weine (2009) extend the theory that terrorists are not clinically abnormal to suicide terrorists. They indicate that in order to comprehend suicide attacks, a multidisciplinary approach must be taken which considers psychological factors in conjunction with historical, economic, political and anthropological factors.

In a review of the literature of the field, Victoroff (2005) concludes that the evidence to date indicates that terrorists do not usually exhibit psychiatric disorders on Axis I or Axis II of the Diagnostic and Statistical Manual of the American Psychiatric Association. These Axes include most clinical disorders (such as schizophrenia, mood disorders, dissociative disorders and anxiety disorders) as well as the personality disorders (such as borderline, narcissistic, histrionic, and schizoid). Similarly, Victoroff (2005) suggests that the previously held belief that terrorists held similarities with psychopathic individuals is probably oversimplistic, particularly as many revolutionary terrorists may be risking their lives for the perceived benefits of others in their society. While Victoroff concedes that it is possible that some antisocial individuals may use the affiliation to the terrorist group to hide their aggressive tendencies, but it is expected that these are the minority of members.

Do Online Terrorists Differ From Offline Ones?

Theorizing as to the psychology of cyberterrorists is even more fraught with problems than considering the psychology of traditional terrorists. To date, it appears that there are no studies examining these individuals. However, some tentative conclusions may be drawn.

Firstly, it is possible that those who would engage in cyberterrorism are quite different to those who engage in other forms of terrorist attacks. Denning (2010) indicates that cyber-attacks provide the potential for non-violent individuals to add support to terrorist campaigns. This would expand the terrorist organization's potential for harm, even if it does not result in loss of life. The cyberterrorist may be a new type of individual within terrorist organizations, attracting those who would not previously have joined to become actively involved. In addition to this, Denning (2001) suggests that aspects of cyberterrorism which involve hacking are safer for the terrorists involved than engaging in physical methods. Opportunities in cyberterrorism may attract those who would not engage in other terrorist acts for fear of their own personal safety. Denning also indicates that the remote and anonymous nature of these attacks could gather extensive media coverage, which may encourage sensation-seeking individuals to engage in these activities.

With regard to those who are recruited using online terrorist methods, it seems that these individuals may be experiencing similar psychological processes to those recruited using traditional methods. Sageman (2008) suggests that online forums allow the development of the social identity which seems to be required by terrorists. He indicates that it is through these forums that the relationships are built, and the cognitions of the recruit are developed. This interactivity is key, and Sageman suggests that it is far more effective than passive perusal of websites.

Effects on Victims

As there has not been a successful cyberterrorism attack to date (at least, not according to researchers such as Denning, 2007a), we do not know what effect such an attack will have on victims. Nevertheless, we can consider the impacts of traditional terror attacks on victims and society. For traditional acts of terrorist violence, there can be considerable impact on those who are directly affected. DiMaggio and Galea (2006) completed a meta-analysis and found that the rate of Post Traumatic Stress Disorder in affected populations can reach as high as sixteen percent following terrorist incidents such as 9/11. Gabriel et al (2007) found that fifty-eight percent of commuters injured in the Madrid bombings in 2004 experienced mental health problems. Even amongst those who were not directly injured, but who lived in the local area and knew victims of the attack, over one in four showed some mental health disorders. Post Traumatic Stress Disorder was prominent, but was not the only mental health issue evident, and over half of the injured group showed at least two psychiatric disorders.

Traditional terrorist attacks have already had an impact on the cyberworld. Conway (2006) describes how, immediately after 9/11, the Nuclear Regulatory Commission (NRC) took down their entire website, for fear that the potentially sensitive information on it would fall into terrorist hands. When the website was restored, over one thousand documents had been removed from it. Other US government websites followed similar protocols, but much of the information on them may still be available from other sources, and so may still be very useful in planning potential terrorist attacks. Conway (2006) cites cases of terrorists and suspected terrorists who had sourced floorplans, photographs, maps and satellite images of potential targets from online resources.

It is possible that a cyberterrorist attack does not actually need to take place in order to have the desired effect on society. Stohl (2006) indicates that there has been a gap between the presumed threat of cyberterrorist attack, and the known online terrorist activities. He indicates that this may be partly explained by failure to distinguish between hacktivism and cyberterrorism. This may be supplemented by a failure to distinguish between using the internet for organizational purposes (such as communication and structure) and the use of the internet to actively commit terrorism. If the media reports issues relating to online terrorist activity irresponsibly, by failing to discriminate between these activities, it is possible that it may lead to increased fear of terrorist attack in the absence of any substantial risk. Media reporting of criminal events has been shown to impact on public perceptions of crime (see for example O'Connell, 2002), and it is likely that this could be extended to the role of the media in public perceptions of the threat of cyberterrorism.

If a successful cyberterror attack does take place it is unlikely to significantly increase fear in victims and the public unless it is combined with a more traditional terror attack. To refer back to the earlier example, in most cases disruption of communication would be considered an inconvenience and a frustration, but not sufficient to induce fear in most individuals. But if that loss of communication was coupled with a traditional terror attack, resulting in loss of life or serious injury, it may emphasise to individuals the weaknesses within the technological infrastructure and the potential harm

that can occur when these are targeted. Similar reactions might occur if cyberterrorists combine a traditional attack with disruption to water or power supplies, or to transportation networks, which may cause widespread confusion and panic. Thankfully, this is all speculative, and society has not yet had to face such an event. Nevertheless, it is important to consider the potential effect a cyberterror attack may have on victims and society, so that governments can respond appropriately if such a scenario occurred.

SOLUTIONS

There are several strategies that policymakers can employ in order to prevent cyberterrorist attacks. In the first instance, it is important that governments do not underestimate the potential impact of a cyberterrorist attack, and remain aware of the possible types of attack which may occur given current technologies. This may require increased emphasis on appropriate surveillance, a strategy which needs to be carefully implemented in light of public protest against excessive invasions of privacy. Wilson (2007) indicates that there needs to be increased awareness about the changing threats due to cyberterrorism, that appropriate responses to cyberattacks need to be developed, that commercial software products need to have improved security, and that private industry and government need to co-ordinate to protect against cyber-attack.

Legal systems have already attempted to specify how convicted cyberterrorists should be punished. Conway (2007) indicates how some laws have been introduced which could result in hacking offences being covered under terrorism laws; or cyberterrorist attacks treated as equivalent to bombings or violence which take human life. There are obvious problems with both of these outcomes, and it seems unlikely that this issue will be resolved unless a severe cyberterrorist threat unfolds.

It should be remembered that there are advantages for counter-terrorism agencies due to increased online terrorist activity. Conway (2006) indicates that although the internet may be a valuable tool for terrorist organizations online, it can also cause problems, as the data transferred by them may be tracked by law enforcement personnel. The terrorist organizations need to be extremely careful in order to ensure that they cover their tracks appropriately. Also, whatever information they do post publicly may contain useful information for counter-terrorism organizations about the groups' methods and personnel. However, problems in rapidly translating much of the material, as well as amalgamating and verifying the information, may result in important clues being missed. The sheer size of the Internet also makes systematic monitoring extremely difficult. Conway suggests that the FBI may also be using 'honeypots' – referring to fake websites designed to attract those individuals who they are hoping to monitor.

Similarly, Denning (2010) suggests that comparable benefits apply to counterterrorism agencies as apply to the terrorists themselves. She suggests that "counterterrorism activities can be performed remotely and from a safe location, avoiding the difficulties and risks associated with infiltrating terrorist's physical space" (p. 208). She indicates that counter-terrorism agencies have four main strategies at their disposal due to online terrorism activity. Firstly, they can monitor terrorist websites and forums for intelligence relating to terrorist activity and the location of resources. Secondly, they can prevent terrorist access to the Internet, shutting down their resources, and hence significantly hindering their ability to complete missions, although Denning acknowledges that the resources often appear in other online locations in short periods of time. Thirdly, the counter-terrorism agencies could use terrorist online resources to infiltrate the organization, potentially undermining terrorist objectives, creating discord amongst members and eroding trust in leaders.

Disadvantages associated with this strategy include the potential for unintended consequences of counter-terrorism actions, as well as the potential for confusion if this strategy is not properly coordinated with intelligence gathering strategies. Finally, counter-terrorism agencies could engage with potential recruits in online forums, hopefully persuading them of errors in terrorist beliefs and dissuading them from becoming involved in the organization. This strategy makes sense based on the terrorist need for socialization – it is possible that if the terrorist or potential recruit realizes that others hold opposing but valid viewpoints, and that they may develop social relations with these individuals, that it may fill their need for social belonging without engaging in terrorism.

While being cognizant of the threat of cyberterrorism, it is also important that authorities do not overemphasise its importance to the detriment of other counter-terrorist activity. It is possible that the threat of cyberterrorism, while remaining very real, has also been greatly exaggerated. Rollins and Wilson (2007) report that simulations have indicated that attempts to disable the US telecommunications infrastructure would not succeed. This is due to system redundancies that would prevent widespread damage. They also indicate that many observers believe that most critical infrastructure systems, such as air traffic control, power and water, would also probably recover quickly, based on evidence from natural disasters. However, Wilson (2007) indicates that as recently as 2002 major vulnerabilities detected in the infrastructure of the Internet could have enabled cyberterrorists to cripple telecommunications equipment worldwide, potentially disabling telephone networks and 'ground to air' flight control systems. Wilson also cites research at the Idaho National Laboratories (INL) in March 2007, where a simulated cyberattack on a power generator turbine was successful, resulting in the turbine overheating and shutting down. While the specific vulnerability is said to have been fixed, it raises the possibility that the Stuxnet worm was intended to work in a similar fashion. Regardless of the actual level of threat, Cohen (2010) indicates that despite the significant quantity of literature on the probability of cyberterrorist attacks, there was little reference as to how society could and should react to such an attack. Similarly, Lentz (2010) indicates that there is a lack of recognition in international law of the potential need for international collaboration following a cyberattack.

Governments, local authorities and private industry may also need to consider reducing the quantity of information available online which may be of use to terrorist organisations. There has already been evidence of terrorists accessing information such as maps online, and there may be other information useful to terrorists still available, including blueprints, information on anti-terrorism strategies and schedules of activities of important individuals. Bocij (2006) suggests that even an apparently innocuous application such as Google maps and Google Streetview might provide terrorists with information which would be useful in planning a terrorist attack.

FUTURE TRENDS AND RESEARCH

Without doubt, the topic of cyberterrorism, and indeed the topic of terrorism in general, requires more empirical research. However given that this has been the mantra of many academics in the area of terrorism for many years now, it seems unlikely that this will change anytime soon. The practical difficulties with completing empirical research on terrorism are extremely difficult to overcome. On the other hand, the need for substantial quantities of research on the specific topic of cyberterrorism needs to be carefully deliberated. Wall (2007) indicates that "the main weakness with the concept of cyber-terrorism is that its risk assessment is hard to disaggregate from its reality" (p. 57). Until now, the general consensus amongst experts in the field has been that the primary risk still comes from physical attacks and bombings, and that even if a

cyber-attack did occur, the effects would probably be minimal. In light of recent events, this position may need to change.

Given the consensus in the literature regarding the lack of pathology in terrorists, and the failure to identify any specific personality traits associated with them, it is likely that further research attempting to examine these topics is probably futile. The more useful information will probably come from studies examining the social identity of potential terrorists, and the methods by which they are socialised into terrorist organisations. This research could assist counter-terrorism agencies in operations regarding surveillance of terrorist websites and attempts to dissuade and de-radicalise terrorists and potential terrorist recruits. It may also be of use to consider the research on 'captology' (computers as persuasive technologies, see for example Fogg 2003, 2008) in relation to online terrorist recruitment and radicalisation. It is possible that captology could be employed to successfully deradicalise individuals, or to persuade them to find alternative methods to promote their perspective.

Ethical hacking should continue to be employed to determine potential weaknesses in critical infrastructure. Systems should be examined to ensure that failsafes are in place, should they become targeted, and the emphasis on security of online systems needs to be continued, in order to ensure that critical information and personal records of citizens do not fall into terrorist hands. Finally, research could be conducted with existing members of the hacking communities in order to determine if they have been approached by terrorist organisations for assistance, or asked to train recruits in hacking strategies.

CONCLUSION

While a growing concern, it seems unlikely that cyberterrorism will ever be as significant a risk as more traditional forms of attack. It is considerably easier to make a homemade bomb using instructions available online and substances found in most household cupboards, than to develop malware capable of shutting down critical infrastructure. Due to the visibility of the results from the homemade bomb, alongside the increased risk to human life, the bomb is also more likely to result in the desired reactions from government and society. Regardless of this, the conjunction of the two forms of terrorist activity in an amalgamated attack could substantially enhance the terror generated. Online activity is unlikely to cause the fear in societies and governments that other forms of terrorism can, but its role in spreading terrorist propaganda, raising funds and recruiting and organising personnel should not be underestimated either. There is much that governments and counter-terrorism agencies can do to reduce the risk of cyberterrorism, but this needs to be properly managed in order to ensure that it is not given undue emphasis, or that security is increased at the risk of public discontent with surveillance measures. Cyberterrorism is an important problem, but it is not one that should overshadow the threat of traditional terrorist activity.

REFERENCES

BBC News (2010a, September 24). *Stuxnet worm hits Iran nuclear plant staff computers.* Retrieved from http://www.bbc.co.uk/news/world-middle-east-11414483

BBC News (2010b, September 23). *Stuxnet worm 'targeted high-value Iranian assets.* Retrieved from http://www.bbc.co.uk/news/technology-11388018

Bocij, P. (2006). *The Dark Side of the Internet: Protecting Yourself and Your Family from Online Criminals.* Westport, CT: Praeger.

Cohen, A. (2010). Cyberterrorism: Are we Legally Ready? *Journal of International Business and Law, 9*, 1.

Colarik, A. M., & Janczewski, L. J. (2008). Introduction to Cyber Warfare and Cyber Terrorism. In Janczewski, L. J., & Colarik, A. M. (Eds.), *Cyber Warfare and Cyber Terrorism* (pp. xiii–xxx). Hershey, PA: Information Science Reference.

Conway, M. (2002). Reality Bytes: Cyberterrorism and Terrorist Use of the Internet. *First Monday, 7*, 11.

Conway, M. (2006). Terrorist 'use' of the Internet and fighting back. *Information and Security: An International Journal, 19*, 9–30.

Conway, M. (2007). Cyberterrorism: hype and reality. In Armistead, L. (Ed.), *Information warfare: separating hype from reality* (pp. 73–93). Potomac Books, Inc.

Denning, D. E. (2001). Activisim, Hacktivism and Cyberterrorism: The Internet as a Tool for Influencing Foreign Policy. In J. Arquilla and D.F. Ronfeldt's (eds.) *Networks and Netwars: The Future of Terror, Crime and Militancy, Issue 1382* (pp. 239-288). Santa Monica, CA: RAND.

Denning, D. E. (2007a). A View of cyberterrorism five years later. In Himma, K. E. (Ed.), *Internet Security: Hacking, Counterhacking and Society* (pp. 123–140). Sudbury, MA: Jones & Bartlett Publishers.

Denning, D. E. (2007b). Cyberterrorism – Testimony before the special oversight panel on terrorism committee on armed services US House of Representatives. In Linden, E. V. (Ed.), *Focus on Terrorism* (*Vol. 9*, pp. 71–76). New York: Nova Science Publishers Inc.

Denning, D. E. (2010). Terror's web: how the Internet is transforming terrorism. In Jewkes, Y., & Yar, M. (Eds.), *Handbook of Internet Crime* (pp. 194–213). Cullompton, England: Willan.

DiMaggio, C., & Galea, S. (2006). The behavioural consequences of terrorism: a meta-analysis. *Academic Emergency Medicine, 13,* 559–566. doi:10.1111/j.1553-2712.2006.tb01008.x

Fogg, B. J. (2003). *Persuasive Technology: Using computers to change what we think and do.* San Francisco, CA: Morgan Kaufmann.

Fogg, B. J. (2008). Mass interpersonal persuasion: An early view of a new phenomenon. In *Proc. Third International Conference on Persuasive Technology, Persuasive 2008.* Berlin: Springer.

Fottrell, M. (Producer) & Wiseman, L. (Director). (2007). *Live Free or Die Hard / Die Hard 4.0* [Motion picture]. United States of America: 20th Century Fox.

Gabriel, R., Ferrando, L., Sainz Corton, E., Mingote, C., Garcia-Camba, E., Fernandez-Liria, A. G., & Galea, S. (2007). Psychopathological consequences alter a terrorist attack: an epidemiological study among victims, police officers, and the general population. *European Psychiatry, 22,* 339–346. doi:10.1016/j.eurpsy.2006.10.007

Gordon, S., & Ford, R. (2003). *Cyberterrorism?* Retrieved from the Symantec Security Response White Papers website: http://www.symantec.com/avcenter/reference /cyberterrorism.pdf

Horgan, J. (2003a). The Search for the terrorist personality. In Silke, A. (Ed.), *Terrorists, Victims and Society: psychological perspectives on terrorism and its consequences.* John Wiley & Sons.

Horgan, J. (2003b). Leaving terrorism behind: An individual perspective. In Silke, A. (Ed.), *Terrorists, Victims and Society: psychological perspectives on terrorism and its consequences.* John Wiley & Sons.

Horgan, J. (2005). *The Psychology of Terrorism.* Abingdon, England: Routledge.

Horgan, J. (2008). From profiles to *pathways* and roots to *routes*: Perspectives from psychology on radicalization into terrorism. *The Annals of the American Academy of Political and Social Science, 618,* 80–94. doi:10.1177/0002716208317539

Horgan, J., & Taylor, M. (2001). The making of a terrorist. *Jane's Intelligence Review, 13,* 16–18.

Howitt, D. (2009). *Introduction to Forensic and Criminal Psychology* (3rd ed.). Harlow, England: Pearson Education.

Kruglanski, A. W., & Fishman, S. (2006). The psychology of terrorism: "Syndrome" versus "tool" perspectives. *Terrorism and Political Violence, 18,* 193–215. doi:10.1080/09546550600570119

Leman-Langlois, S. (2008). Introduction: technocrime. In Leman-Langlois, S. (Ed.), *Technocrime: Technology, crime and social control.* Cullompton, England: Willan.

Lentz, C. E. (2010). A State's Duty to Prevent and Respond to Cyberterrorist Acts. *Chicago Journal of International Law, 10,* 799.

Locicero, A., & Sinclair, S. J. (2008). Terrorism and Terrorist Leaders: Insights from Developmental and Ecological Psychology. *Studies in Conflict and Terrorism, 31,* 227–250. doi:10.1080/10576100701879638

Maghaireh, A. (2008). Shariah Law and Cyber-Sectarian Conflict: How can Islamic criminal law respond to cyber crime? *International Journal of Cyber-Criminology, 2,* 337–345.

McCauley, C., & Moskalenko, S. (2008). Mechanisms of Political Radicalisation: Pathways toward terrorism. *Terrorism and Political Violence, 20,* 415–433. doi:10.1080/09546550802073367

McDonald, H. (2009, August 2nd). MP calls on YouTube to remove Real IRA propaganda videos: 'Cyber-terrorism' films of dissident republicans could be banned from site. *The Observer Supplement. The Guardian Newspaper.* Retrieved on 10th October 2010 from http://www.guardian.co.uk/technology/2009/aug/02 /youtube-ira-facebook-cyber-terrorism

Merari, A. (2007). Psychological aspects of suicide terrorism. In Bongar, B., Brown, L. M., Beutler, L. E., Brecenridge, J. N., & Zimbardo, P. B. (Eds.), *Psychology of Terrorism* (pp. 101–115). New York: Oxford University Press.

Nelson, B., Choi, R., Iacobucci, M., Mitchell, M.& Gagnon, G. (1999, August) *Cyberterror: Prospects and Implications*, Center for the Study of Terrorism and Irregular Warfare, Naval Postgraduate School, Monterey, CA.

O'Connell, M. (2002). The portrayal of crime in the media: Does it matter? In O'Mahony, P. (Ed.), *Criminal Justice in Ireland* (pp. 245–267). Dublin: IPA.

Pollitt, M. M. (1997, October). Cyberterrorism: Fact or Fancy? *Proceedings of the 20th National Information Systems Security Conference*, pp. 285–289.

Post, J. M., Ali, F., Henderson, S. W., Shanfield, S., Victoroff, J., & Weine, S. (2009). The Psychology of Suicide Terrorism. *Psychiatry: Interpersonal and Biological Processes*, *72*, 13–31. doi:10.1521/psyc.2009.72.1.13

Post, J. M., Sprinzak, E., & Denny, L. M. (2003). The terrorists in their own words: Interviews with thirty-five incarcerated Middle Eastern terrorists. *Terrorism and Political Violence*, *15*, 171–184. doi:10.1080/09546550312331293007

Rollins, J., & Wilson, C. (2007). Terrorist capabilities for cyberattack: Overview and policy issues. In Linden, E. V. (Ed.), *Focus on Terrorism* (*Vol. 9*, pp. 43–63). New York: Nova Science Publishers Inc.

Sageman, M. (2004). *Understanding Terror Networks*. Philadelphia, PA: University of Pennsylvania Press.

Sageman, M. (2008). *Leaderless Jihad*. Philadelphia, PA: University of Pennsylvania Press.

Silke, A. (1998). Cheshire-cat logic: The recurring theme of terrorist abnormality in psychological research. *Psychology, Crime & Law*, *4*, 51–69. doi:10.1080/10683169808401747

Silke, A. (2003). Becoming a terrorist. In Silke, A. (Ed.), *Terrorists, Victims and Society: psychological perspectives on terrorism and its consequences*. John Wiley & Sons.

Silke, A. (2008). Research on Terrorism: A Review of the Impact of 9/11 and the Global War on Terrorism. *Terrorism Informatics*, *18*, 27–50. doi:10.1007/978-0-387-71613-8_2

Sterba, J. P. (Ed.). (2003). *Terrorism and International Justice*. New York, Oxford: Oxford University Press.

Stohl, M. (2006). Cyber terrorism: a clear and present danger, the sum of all fears, breaking point or patriot games? *Crime, Law, and Social Change*, *46*, 223–238. doi:10.1007/s10611-007-9061-9

Taylor, M., & Quayle, E. (1994). *Terrorist Lives*. London: Brassey's.

Veerasamy, N. (2010). Motivation for cyberterrorism. 9th Annual Information Security South Africa (ISSA) - Towards New Security Paradigms. Sandton Convention Centre, 2 - 4 August 2010, pp 6

Victoroff, J. (2005). The Mind of the Terrorist: A Review and Critique of Psychological Approaches. *The Journal of Conflict Resolution*, *49*, 3–42. doi:10.1177/0022002704272040

Wall, D. S. (2007). *Cybercrime: The Transformation of Crime in the Information Age*. Cambridge, England: Polity Press.

Weimann, G. (2004). WWW.terror.net: *How Modern Terrorism Uses the Internet* (Washington DC: United States Institute of Peace). http://www.usip.org/pubs/specialreports/ sr116.pdf, 5-11.

Whittaker, D. J. (2004). *Terrorists and Terrorism in the Contemporary World*. London: Routledge.

Wilson, C. (2005). *Computer Attack and Cyberterrorism: Vulnerabilities and Policy Issues for Congress*. Washington DC: Congressional Research Service: The Library of Congress. Retrieved 19th September 2010 from http://www.dtic.mil/cgi-bin/GetTRDoc?AD=ADA444799&Location=U2&doc=GetTRDoc.pdf

Wilson, C. (2007). *Botnets, Cybercrime and Cyberterrorism: Vulnerabilities and Policy Issues for Congress*. Washington DC: Congressional Research Service: The Library of Congress. Retrieved 23rd September 2010 from http://www.dtic.mil/cgi-bin/GetTRDoc?AD=ADA474929&Location=U2&doc=GetTRDoc.pdf

Wykes, M., & Harcus, D. (2010). Cyber-terror: construction, criminalization and control. In Jewkes, Y., & Yar, M. (Eds.), *Handbook of Internet Crime* (pp. 214–229). Cullompton, England: Willan.

Yar, M. (2006). *Cybercrime and Society*. London: Sage.

Zuckerman, M. (2002). Genetics of Sensation seeking. In Benjamin, J., Ebstein, R. P., & Belmaker, R. (Eds.), *Molecular Genetics and the Human Personality* (pp. 193–210). Washington, DC: American Psychiatric Publishing.

ADDITIONAL READING

Cohen, A. (2010). Cyberterrorism: Are we Legally Ready? *Journal of International Business and Law, 9*, 1.

Conway, M. (2002). Reality Bytes: Cyberterrorism and Terrorist Use of the Internet. *First Monday, 7*, 11.

Conway, M. (2006). Terrorist 'use' of the Internet and fighting back. *Information and Security: An International Journal, 19*, 9–30.

Conway, M. (2007). Cyberterrorism: hype and reality. In Armistead, L. (Ed.), *Information warfare: separating hype from reality* (pp. 73–93). Potomac Books, Inc.

Denning, D. E. (2001). Activisim, Hacktivism and Cyberterrorism: The Internet as a Tool for Influencing Foreign Policy. In J. Arquilla and D.F. Ronfeldt's (eds.) *Networks and Netwars: The Future of Terror, Crime and Militancy, Issue 1382* (pp. 239-288). Santa Monica, CA: RAND.

Denning, D. E. (2007a). A View of cyberterrorism five years later. In Himma, K. E. (Ed.), *Internet Security: Hacking, Counterhacking and Society* (pp. 123–140). Sudbury, MA: Jones & Bartlett Publishers.

Denning, D. E. (2010). Terror's web: how the Internet is transforming terrorism. In Jewkes, Y., & Yar, M. (Eds.), *Handbook of Internet Crime* (pp. 194–213). Cullompton, England: Willan.

Fogg, B. J. (2003). *Persuasive Technology: Using computers to change what we think and do*. San Francisco, CA: Morgan Kaufmann.

Horgan, J. (2005). *The Psychology of Terrorism*. Abingdon, England: Routledge.

Horgan, J. (2008). From profiles to *pathways* and roots to *routes*: Perspectives from psychology on radicalization into terrorism. *The Annals of the American Academy of Political and Social Science, 618*, 80–94. doi:10.1177/0002716208317539

Maghaireh, A. (2008). Shariah Law and Cyber-Sectarian Conflict: How can Islamic criminal law respond to cyber crime? *International Journal of Cyber-Criminology, 2*, 337–345.

Rollins, J., & Wilson, C. (2007). Terrorist capabilities for cyberattack: Overview and policy issues. In Linden, E. V. (Ed.), *Focus on Terrorism* (*Vol. 9*, pp. 43–63). New York: Nova Science Publishers Inc.

Silke, A. (2003). Becoming a terrorist. In Silke, A. (Ed.), *Terrorists, Victims and Society: psychological perspectives on terrorism and its consequences*. John Wiley & Sons.

Stohl, M. (2006). Cyber terrorism: a clear and present danger, the sum of all fears, breaking point or patriot games? *Crime, Law, and Social Change, 46*, 223–238. doi:10.1007/s10611-007-9061-9

Section 4
Crimes in Virtual Worlds

Chapter 12
Crime in Virtual Worlds:
Should Victims Feel Distressed?

ABSTRACT

The final type of cybercrime to be considered involves crimes that occur in online virtual worlds. While there is considerable literature available on other cybercrimes, as outlined in the previous chapters of this book, relatively little academic literature has been published concerning crime in online virtual worlds (Wall & Williams, 2007). Nevertheless, several cases have come to light concerning specific crimes in these environments, including both property offences (such as theft) and crimes against the person (such as sexual assault). It should be noted that while the term 'crime' will be used in this chapter to describe these events, they may not necessarily be illegal or criminal events, at least so far as the offline world would consider them to be. This chapter aims to describe these types of virtual crimes, and to determine if they could and should be considered criminal events. The effects of the crimes on the victims will also be considered, and the necessity for policing virtual worlds will be discussed. In addition, the online community needs to consider how to deal with virtual offenders – if their offence has real-world consequences, should they be punished offline, or only in the virtual world?

BACKGROUND

A virtual world, for the purposes of this chapter, refers to any computer generated representation of three-dimensional space. This does not necessarily mean that the world includes graphics – early vir-

tual worlds such as LambdaMoo were text-based, but the text used described a three-dimensional world. For example, upon entering LambdaMoo as a guest, you are greeted with the following description of your surroundings.

DOI: 10.4018/978-1-61350-350-8.ch012

The closet is a dark, cramped space. It appears to be very crowded in here; you keep bumping into what feels like coats, boots, and other people (apparently sleeping). One useful thing that you've discovered in your bumbling about is a metal doorknob set at waist level into what might be a door.

Most modern virtual worlds provide computer generated graphics in order for the user to more easily visualise their surroundings. Different virtual worlds have different functions. Some are socially based, such as 'Second Life' (www.secondlife.com, created by Linden Labs), where users are encouraged to interact with others and to develop their avatar and virtual property, but where there is no overall aim to the world. Second life has become so popular that there have been several published accounts of virtual lives within the world (see for example Guest, 2007 and Meadows, 2008). While Second Life targets adults, other social virtual worlds are aimed at children and adolescents, such as 'Habbo Hotel' (www.habbo.com) and Disney's 'Club Penguin' (www.clubpenguin.com).

Other virtual worlds are more goal-oriented, similar to traditional computer games. Probably the most famous of these is 'World of Warcraft' (or WoW, www.worldofwarcraft.com), a virtual world created by Blizzard Entertainment. World of Warcraft is a fantastical world, where users can choose to be either human, or one of many forms of mythological beings, each with various skills and weaknesses. There are various levels of gameplay in WoW, which players progress through, and new levels are added regularly to keep user interest high. Similarly, in 'The Legend of Mir 3' players can choose to be warriors, wizards, or other mythical beings, and gameplay is again largely directed by the completion of quests. The now defunct 'Matrix Online' was a mission oriented game based on the series of Matrix films, while 'EVE Online' (www.eveonline.com) is a science-fiction based virtual world. EVE Online is a particularly interesting world from the perspective of virtual crime, as it openly acknowledges the existence of criminal activities between players in the world (Verone, n.d.) and informs players that the games developer and publisher (CCP games) will not intervene in cases of virtual theft (Evelopedia, n.d.)

Many of these virtual worlds are also termed Massively Multiplayer Online Role Playing Games (or MMORPGs), referring to the fact that there can be hundreds or thousands of people playing these games online at a given time, and that each player takes on a 'role' or a character. In some games, such as World of Warcraft and EVE Online, players can form teams and collaborations in order to achieve goals. These collaborations can be fairly permanent in nature (such as the 'guilds' in World of Warcraft), or may be temporary in order to obtain a specific goal, after which the users disband.

Within this chapter, attention will be paid to two principal types of crime in virtual worlds – property crime and crimes against the person. Property crime refers to crimes such as larceny, burglary and theft, which normally do not involve violence or significant interaction between the offender and the victim. Crimes against the person, for the purposes of this chapter, involve any crime where there is significant interaction between the offender and victim, such as sexual assault, homicide and violence. Again, it should be noted that in this chapter these terms will be used where the event may be simply a simulation of an offline offence, without actually being a criminal event capable of prosecution in any offline court. As such while terms like 'offender' and 'criminal' will be used throughout, these are utilised in order to easily label the perpetuator of the virtual 'crime', rather than to indicate that they are offline offenders or have committed any actual infringements against offline laws of any country. Indeed, as outlined in the case of EVE Online above, in some cases these actions may be considered part of normal gameplay, and while not actively encouraged, they may not be subject to specific penalty either.

PROPERTY CRIMES

There have been several instances of property crimes in online communities (Hof, 2006; BBC News, 2005, 2007). One case involves CopyBot – software which enabled users of Second Life to copy objects and creations of other users (Hof, 2006), instead of paying for them. As this case involved objects with specific monetary value in Linden dollars, which can be exchanged for U.S. dollars, this is an example of a case which could be tried offline. A similar case occurred in Habbo Hotel in 2007, where Dutch teenagers allegedly stole €4,000 worth of virtual furniture by tricking other users into divulging their passwords (BBC News, 2007). In this case, at least one teenager was eventually arrested.

However, in some cases, offline authorities may not be able or willing to take action following a theft in a virtual world. One example of this occurred in 2005 when a Chinese 'The Legend of Mir' gamer, Zhu Caoyuan, sold a 'dragon sabre' which he had been loaned by Qiu Chengwei (BBC News, 2005). The sword had been earned through the investment of considerable time and effort playing the online game. Despite the sale value of the sword (approximately £460 GBP), the police claimed that it was not real property when Chengwei tried to make a complaint. Caoyuan offered to pay the money received from the sale to Chengwei, but despite this, Chengwei stabbed Caoyuan in the left chest and killed him. This case is interesting, both for the lack of action that the police took following the alleged crime, and the extreme reaction from Chengwei, despite the offer to repay the money. It demonstrates that the dragon sabre meant considerably more to Chengwei than its monetary value, and that he obviously experienced an extreme psychological reaction to the event.

CRIMES AGAINST THE PERSON

I was new and on the receiving end of disturbing sexual behavior. A male avatar teleported right in front of my character. He was so close that my avatar's body prevented me from seeing that he was nude. He stepped back, and then rammed my avatar so hard she was pushed back several steps. Before my character had come to a stand still he was coming at her again. After ramming her a second time he walked several steps passed her and to the right, and then turned so that he was in profile. By stepping further away and turning he ensured that I, a [sic] offline, flesh and blood person, was able to see that he was naked and had rammed my avatar with an erect penis. Although simulated, it was a deliberate, calculated, and practiced act of violence. It happened in seconds. I felt the person behind the avatar thought he had raped or simulated rape on my character, and wanted me to know that's what he had done.
- (Jay, 2007).

This event, described by a Second Life player on one of its mailing lists, was clearly disturbing for the human user behind the female avatar that was attacked. The victim goes on to express frustration at the inability to report her victimization, as the attacker had used an unusually long name for their character, which she had not had time to note before the attacking avatar disappeared, and also because there was insufficient space in the complaints form of the online community to describe the details of the event. She later found her thoughts returning to the incident, even though she tried to forget it and remind herself that she had not been physically harmed. Hers is not the only case of online sexual assault.

Probably the most famous example is the case of Mr. Bungle, as described by Julian Dibbell (1993) in which a series of sexual assaults occur in the online world LambdaMOO. A character called Mr. Bungle who is described as "a fat, oleaginous, Bisquick-faced clown" attacked several other players in the text-based online world using 'voodoo dolls', subprograms that attribute actions to other players' characters that they did not intend. Mr. Bungle was actually controlled by several university students acting as one to direct the attacks (as clarified by Dibbell in 1998). Bungle's rampage continued until he was eventually stopped by a more senior player. The Bungle case is particularly interesting because of the reported after-effects on the victims. One, 'legba', reported severe distress in the aftermath of the attack. Several other players reported their anger at the events, to the extent that many called for Mr. Bungle to be 'toaded' (banned from the virtual world, with the character deleted). Interestingly, Mr. Bungle himself indicated that the assault "…was purely a sequence of events with no consequence on my RL (real-life) existence", and as such the virtual attack seems to have had considerably less impact on him than it did on his victims.

The calls to toad Mr. Bungle led to debates amongst the community members, with some arguing that in the virtual world, rape had not been criminalised, and so it could not be considered punishable. It was also queried if the university students who had created the character of Mr. Bungle could be punished offline, perhaps under laws concerning obscene phone calls or punishment from the university authorities, although this course of action did not seem to be popular amongst the players involved. While no final decision was made by the players, eventually a 'wizard' (an administrator in the virtual world) acted alone and toaded (expelled) Mr. Bungle independently. As such, those who played Mr. Bungle were punished in the virtual world, where their 'crimes' took place, but not offline, where the effects were experienced by the victims. Eventually LambdaMOO developed a ballot system, where players could vote for the toading of a 'criminal' character, and if sufficient votes were received, then the wizards would complete the request. In-

terestingly, one of the players who controlled Mr. Bungle eventually returned to LambdaMOO with a new character, Dr. Jest, who also behaved in an unacceptable fashion, although he did not engage in sexual assaults. In spite of this, the residents of LambdaMOO did not vote in sufficient numbers to toad Dr. Jest. It appears that, at least in the minds of the residents of LambdaMOO, the character was the entity that needed to be punished, not the player who controlled that character.

More recently, in 2007, Belgian police commenced an investigation into an alleged rape in the online world Second Life (Lynn, 2007; Sipress, 2007). While publicly available details regarding that specific case are rare, to the extent that several online commentators queried as to whether the report was a hoax, it has provoked widespread discussion of online rape. Some online reports about the incident demonstrate mixed views about the seriousness of online rape. While it is generally considered to be a negative event, it is difficult to determine the severity of the attack. No writer suggests that it is as serious as offline sexual assault, and some suggest that the victims should just try to forget about it, and move on, but others see worrying trends. Some note that it is illegal to engage sexually with a minor online, and therefore wonder if adult rape should be treated similarly (Lynn, 2007).

One crime in virtual worlds which is considered illegal in several offline jurisdictions is virtual ageplay. This can be covered under child pornography laws in some countries. The most famous example of this type of offence is the Wonderland area of Second Life, where 'child' avatars engaged in sexual behaviour with other avatars, both child and adult (Adams, 2010). Although all the players controlling the avatars may be over the legal age of consent, laws regulate the depiction of even simulated images of child sexual abuse. There are therefore queries as to which crimes in virtual worlds should be considered offline crimes, and which should not.

ANALYSIS OF VIRTUAL CRIME

As so little is known about virtual crimes, much analysis regarding these offences is speculative in nature, and requires empirical investigation. Whitson and Doyle (2008) outline several reasons that may explain why so little research has been done examining crime in virtual worlds. These include a perception that the worlds are seen as too trivial for study, the speed of technological change, the need for researchers to participate in the virtual worlds, difficulties in verifying participant data and difficulties in achieving ethical approval (pp. 89-90).

For instance, it is impossible to predict how much virtual crime exists for several reasons. Firstly, it is likely that a significant number of victims of these offences do not report their victimization for a variety of reasons. This may be because they are unaware of their victimization (perhaps an item was stolen from their inventory and they had not noticed its absence), they may feel that it is unlikely that the authorities in the virtual world will do anything about the event (such as EVE Online's policy not to interfere in theft cases), or they may consider the event too trivial to report at all. Many may also feel that it is their own fault that they have been victimized, or that they will not be taken seriously if they report the incident (see the sections on self-blame and victim-blaming below). So it is to be expected that there is a relatively high 'dark figure' of crimes in virtual worlds (that is, crimes which have occurred but do not appear in any official statistics).

The motives of the offenders are also largely unknown. For some virtual property offenders, it is doubtless to help them to progress in the game faster. This is most likely the case for most thefts in EVE Online. In the case of the Legend of Mir 3 dragon sabre, the motive seems to have been real world financial gain, as Caoyuan sold the sword for an actual currency. The motives for offences against the person in virtual worlds are somewhat less clear. The actions of Mr. Bungle seem to have

been a prank by a group of college students, who may have experienced some elements of peer-pressure and coercion from within the group to carry out the virtual assault. Scully and Marolla (1993) indicate that part of the appeal of gang rape involves the sense of group cohesiveness "engendered by participating collectively in a dangerous activity" (p. 39), which suggests that there may be some overlap between the online and offline motives for this type of offence. The rape in Second Life described above appears to have been motivated by a desire for power, and so might be explained by Groth, Burgess and Holmstrom's (1977) taxonomy of rapists as either power-assurance or power-assertive. However, all this is speculation based on second and third-hand accounts of online events, and it would be dangerous to rely on these conclusions. Similarly, there is currently too little information available regarding offenders in virtual worlds to allow conclusions to be drawn regarding the psychological profile or personality characteristics of these individuals. Until more empirical work is done to examine the motives and psychology of these individuals, it is impossible to provide any more conclusive answers to this question.

EFFECTS ON VICTIMS

Victimization in online virtual worlds should not be considered as severe as if a similar offence occurred offline. There can be no doubt that a victim of an offline sexual assault is likely to experience post-victimization symptoms that are far more severe than those of an online victim. On the other hand, it would be an error to believe that an online victimization has no effect on the victim at all. In addition to this, it appears that crimes in virtual worlds appear have a more severe impact on some victims than others. Yet the effects of this 'virtual victimization' on the person, and the reasons why it is more severe for some than others, have not been considered in detail. It has been repeatedly demonstrated that victims of offline crimes can experience several negative consequences of their victimization – including Post Traumatic Stress Disorder (PTSD), self-blame and victim blaming by others (Scarpa, Haden & Hurley, 2006; Hoyle & Zedner, 2007]. It could be argued that the more the person feels immersed online (the greater the sense of *presence* in the online environment), the more likely it is that the victim experiences similar after-effects to offline victims. If this is the case, then greater care needs to be taken in online virtual worlds to ensure the safety and psychological well-being of their users, particularly after a crime in an online virtual world occurs.

Victim blaming appears to be particularly common for crime in online virtual worlds, with many arguing that victims of crime in online virtual worlds could easily escape. In Second Life, it is possible to engage in rape fantasies, where another player has control over the "victim's" avatar, but this is usually given with consent. It has been suggested that some individuals have been tricked into giving their consent, but even bearing this in mind, there has been widespread criticism by Second Life commentators of anyone who allows an attack to take place, as it is alleged that it is always possible to 'teleport' away from any situation. Even if teleportation fails, it is always possible for the victim to exit the game, disconnect from the network connection or turn off their computer and thus end the offence. It is clear that victims of crime in online virtual worlds do seem to experience some extent of victim blaming by others – they are in ways being blamed for not escaping their attacker. Those victims who experience the greatest degree of presence – those who are most immersed in the game - are probably those who are least likely to think of closing the application to escape. It should also be considered that a victim may experience discomfort at being victimized, even if they do escape relatively quickly. As in offline crime, the initial stages of the attack may be confusing or upsetting enough to cause significant distress, even if the victim

manages to escape quickly. There is also some evidence of self-blaming by various victims of crime in online virtual worlds. Some victims refer to their relative naivety in the online world prior to victimization (Jay, 2007), and indicate that if they had been more experienced they may have realized what was happening sooner. There are also suggestions that a victim who is inexperienced with the virtual world's user interface may inadvertently give control of their avatar to another user.

There is anecdotal evidence of limited symptoms of Acute Stress Disorder (ASD, see Chapter 2) in some victims of crime in online virtual worlds, including accounts of intrusive memories, emotional numbing and upset from victims of virtual sexual assault (Lynn, 2007; Sipress, 2007). Some explanation of this is provided by Williams (2006) who highlights the effects of 'speech acts' in computer mediated communication. He states that the "possibility for the abusive illocutionary act to simultaneously convey action in speech means that it does more than represent violence; it is violence" (p.101). Williams (2006) also indicates that "it is important to understand that events within online settings are not wholly separate from those in the offline world" (p. 99), and he goes on to analyse the case of Mr. Bungle with this in mind. Nevertheless, while it is impossible to make an accurate judgment without a full psychological evaluation, it seems very unlikely that these victims would receive a clinical diagnosis of either ASD or Post Traumatic Stress Disorder (PTSD). This is because there is no mention of either flashbacks or heightened autonomic arousal (possibly due to the lack of real danger to the victim's life), nor does it appear that the symptoms lasted for very long (in most cases the symptoms appear to reduce or dissipate within a few hours or days). There are also several accounts of individuals who have experienced online victimization, but who do not see it as a serious assault and do not appear to experience any severe negative reaction. Those most at risk appear to be those who have previously experienced victimization of offline sexual assault, where the online attack has served to remind the victim of the previous attack. As such, while not a major risk, the possibility of developing ASD or PTSD is a factor that should be monitored in future victims of serious online assaults, especially those who have been previously victimized offline.

Finally, there is substantial anecdotal evidence of a need for retribution in victims of crime in online virtual worlds. The victims of Mr. Bungle called for his toading, the Belgian victim of the rape in Second Life reported the incident to the police, and Chengwei stabbed the alleged thief when he failed to achieve a satisfactory response from the police after the sale of the virtual sabre. This is possibly the strongest evidence that victims of crimes in virtual worlds experience similar psychological reactions to victims of offline offences, although again, empirical evidence is lacking to date. This also raises the issue of determining suitable punishments for perpetrators of crime in online virtual worlds, which will be considered in more detail later in this chapter.

Probably the single most important risk factor for determining how severe the victim's reaction will be is *presence* – how immersed the user feels they are in the environment and Kirwan (2009) describes some of the literature that supports this. Jung (2008) found that presence can impact on member's intention to participate in Second Life, and also emphasized the importance of vividness of the environment in increasing presence, a point also noted by Bente, Rüggenberg, Krämer and Eschenburg (2008). Bente et al (2008) also noted that the use of an avatar also led to increased perceived intimateness, emotionally-based trust and visual attention, particularly in the early phase of interaction, and so it seems that when controlling avatars, users put themselves at greater emotional vulnerability. Pearce (2006) also notes that users of online virtual worlds demonstrate some significant dimensions of presence. Among these, she notes that some avatars' identities are partially constructed through a system of social feedback within the community, and so the online representation of the self is partially formed by how other avatars interact with it. It is conceivable therefore that a negative experience, such as an online victimization, may influence the development of the user's online identity. Pearce also notes that after a period of time in an online community, users feel that they are entitled to citizenship, and to have their rights protected, especially if they play a part in creating the virtual world, as residents of Second Life are encouraged to do. This has very obvious repercussions for virtual victimization – the cybercitizen has come to expect that they will be protected and cared for, because of their investment of time and energy into the online community.

It has previously been demonstrated that presence in virtual environments can induce specific emotional reactions in the user (Riva, Mantovani, Capideville, Preziosa, Morganti, Villani, Gaggioli Botella & Alcaniz, 2007), a phenomenon which is utilized by clinical psychology when virtual environments are used during therapy for phobias, post-traumatic stress disorder, and other psychological difficulties (Josman, Somer, Reisberg, Weiss, Garcia-Palacios & Hoffman, 2006; Wiederhold & Wiederhold, 2005). Virtual environments have also been demonstrated to elicit behaviors indicative of fear of crime (Park, Calvert, Brantingham & Brantingham, 2008) and to heighten the realism of sexually threatening role plays designed to help college women resist sexual attacks (Jouriles, McDonald, Kullowatz, Rosenfield, Gomez & Cuevas, 2009). Certain emotional states and personality traits can also increase the sense of presence in an immersive virtual world, including anxiety (Bouchard, St-Jacques, Robillard &Renaud, 2008). If the same applies to online virtual worlds, it could raise a query as to if the effects of an online crime, particularly a sexual or violent one, may be self-perpetuating.

It is likely that the more time that has been spent in the online community, the more likely it is that the victim will have a severe emotional reaction to the crime. If a person has invested heavily in their avatar, truly seeing it as an extension of themselves, instead of just a computer-generated image, then their reaction could be more severe. This may be particularly so if others have witnessed the offence, as happened in the case of Mr. Bungle – it may add a sense of shame and embarrassment, and a fear that their avatar will be permanently associated with the victimization. On the other hand, it is likely that those who are merely experimenting in the online community, who feel less immersed in the virtual world, and who have not built up an online life in that world, would emerge from an online victimization relatively unscathed, though perhaps a little more cautious in the future. Much of the shame, self-blame and secondary victimization could easily be removed by simply deleting the victimized avatar, and replacing it with a new one. However, this course of action is not always ideal – the user would be unlikely to feel a sense of retribution, as they may not feel that their 'attacker' had been adequately punished. It should also be remembered that this reaction would likely be considerably more difficult and less desirable for the dedicated user of the virtual world, who would have to start over with new online acquaintances and social groups in order to have a truly fresh start.

It would be of great interest to determine if there is a correlation between the victim's experience and the similarity of their avatar to their own physical appearance. Would a victim experience more severe after-effects if their avatar closely resembled their offline physical self? It is possible this realistic avatar would increase the sense of presence, and hence possibly the victim would feel the effects more acutely than if they had chosen an avatar which did not resemble them physically. A related factor which may impact on the effects felt by victims is the realism of the environment. LambdaMOO was a text-based virtual world, and the victims in that case read descriptions of

what Mr. Bungle was doing to their online selves. Second Life, and other graphical online worlds, are considerably more realistic, and as such probably increase the victim's sense of presence. It is possible that by seeing the graphical representation of the self attacked, the effects of victimization may be increased. This raises questions about the future of online virtual worlds – the more realistic they become, the more likely it is that the victim can be negatively affected. Related to that is a consideration of the behavioral mannerisms of the attacking avatar. Research indicates that the more realistic the behaviors of avatars, the greater the sense of presence experienced by the user (Garau, Slater, Vinayagamoorthy, Brogni, Steed & Sasse, 2003; Vinyagamoorthy, Brogni, Gillies, Slater & Steed, 2004). Therefore, as technology progresses and virtual worlds and avatars become more realistic, it is important that the reactions of victims of offences in virtual worlds are carefully considered.

It should also be considered that some personality traits such as locus of control and dissociation which have been shown to increase the sense of presence in immersive virtual environments (Murray, Fox & Pettifer, 2007) have also been linked with the development of post-traumatic stress disorder after crimes and traumatic events (Hood & Carter, 2008; Marmar, Metzler, Otte, McCaslin, Inslicht & Haase, 2007). As such, further research into the relationship between these potentially intervening variables could provide further insight into the effects of victimization of crime in virtual worlds. While considering personality variables, it is important to note that interactions have been noted between certain personality traits and increased levels of PTSD. These include low self-esteem (Adams & Boscarino, 2006), neuroticism (Lawrence & Fauerbach, 2003; Cox, MacPherson, Enns & McWilliams, 2004; Fauerbach, Lawrence, Schmidt, Munster & Costa, 2000), and low levels of extraversion (Fauerbach, Lawrence, Schmidt, Munster & Costa, 2000), openness to experience

(Kamphuis, Emmelkamp & Bartak, 2003) and agreeableness (Talbert, Braswell, Albrecht, Hyer & Boudewyns, 1993). However, it should be noted that some of these studies examined correlations rather than causality between the factors, and so remain inconclusive.

Victim Aid

These reactions by the victims of crime in online virtual worlds suggest that it may be useful if some form of victim aid was put in place to assist them with the process of dealing with their difficulties. This aid could take a number of different forms, including help with reporting the offence, emotional, financial and legal assistance, and the possible introduction of restorative justice.

Victims of offline offences normally have relatively straightforward procedures available to them for the reporting of criminal offences. Police helplines, patrols and stations are often the initial ports of call for a recent victim of offline crime. On the other hand, in online worlds, the reporting procedure may be less clear, and the user may need to invest time and energy to determine how to report their experience. Although many virtual worlds have procedures for reporting misconduct, these are not always found to be satisfactory by victims if they wish to report more serious offences (Jay, 2007). Similarly, reporting the occurrence to the administrators of the virtual world alone may not meet the victim's need for retribution, especially if they feel that they have experienced offline harm because of the crime in the online virtual world. In those cases, the victim may prefer to approach the offline authorities, as in the Belgian rape case and the theft of the dragon-sabre. To aid victims in this regard, many online worlds need to be clearer about their complaints procedures, and the possible outcomes of these. They may also need to be clearer about the possible repercussions of reporting crime in online virtual worlds to offline authorities.

Victims of offline crimes receive varying degrees of emotional, financial and legal aid, depending on the offence which occurred. In some cases, this aid is provided through charitable organizations, such as Victim Support, sometimes through government organizations, and also through informal supports such as family and friends. Financial aid is probably the least applicable to victims of crime in online virtual worlds, as although theft of property can occur, it is unlikely to result in severe poverty for the victim. Also, because items with a designated offline value are starting to be recognized by real-world authorities, there is some possibility of financial recompense. Legal aid, both in terms of the provision of a lawyer and in terms of help in understanding the court system, can also be provided to offline victims. The legal situation is somewhat less clear for victims of crime in online virtual worlds, particularly where the punishment is meted out in the virtual world, as in the Mr. Bungle case. In that event, the victims and other users were required to effectively set up a legal system themselves. But from the cases which have been publicized to date, it appears that the greatest need for assistance that online victims have is for emotional support. In some cases victims have sought this from other members of the online community, but the evidence of victim-blaming for crimes in online virtual worlds which has been apparent to date may result in increased upset for victims, instead of alleviating their distress.

One system which may help to alleviate any emotional anguish for the victim is restorative justice. This refers to processes involving mediation between the offender and the victim (Howitt, 2009). Rather than focusing on the criminal activity itself, it focuses on the harm caused by the crime, and more specifically, the victims of the crime. It often involves a mediated meeting between the victim and the offender, where both are allowed to express sentiments and explanations, and the offender is given the opportunity to apologize. The aims of restorative justice are a satisfied victim, an offender who feels that they have been fairly dealt with, and reintegration of the community, rather than financial compensation or specific punishment. If the mediation does not meet the satisfaction of all involved, alternative punishments can then be considered. It would appear that the restorative justice approach is ideally suited for many crimes in online virtual worlds as it allows the victim to feel that they have been heard, while allowing the community to remain cohesive. However, it should be noted that not all victims of offline crimes have felt satisfied by the process (Wemmers & Cyr, 2006), and so it is not suitable for all criminal events.

POLICING AND PREVENTION OF CRIMES IN VIRTUAL WORLDS

The Belgian police investigations into the alleged rape in Second Life, and their subsequent 'patrols' of the online world are one possible approach to policing crimes in virtual worlds. On the other hand, many individuals would be displeased that taxes and police resources were being spent patrolling and investigating crime in virtual worlds while offline crimes can often go unsolved. There is no doubt that online crimes with definite offline applications and risks should be under the remit of the appropriate police force. Yet in some cases the line is blurred – if a virtual attack is interpreted as an actual threat against the victim offline (where both the victim perceives it as a threat against their offline self, and the perpetrator intends it as an offline threat), it can be considered illegal in many jurisdictions.

As previously discussed, if an item is stolen in a virtual world, and the item can be judged to have an actual monetary value offline, then it may also be possible to prosecute the thief offline (Hof, 2006). However, the line between an offline crime, and an event which is purely virtual (and hence not necessarily a 'crime' in the legal sense), is less

coherent when the damages caused to the victim are emotional or psychological in nature, without any physical or monetary harm being caused. It is for these cases in particular that legal systems need to consider what the most appropriate course of action should be.

There are many ways in which this problem could be addressed. It is likely that each virtual world would need to be policed by separate law enforcement agencies, if only because different worlds have differing social norms and definitions of acceptable and unacceptable behaviors. For example, it would not be an acceptable solution if players in an online war game such as Battlefield begin to sue each other for 'avatar-slaughter' when they lose, especially as the avatars 'respawn' (are resurrected) after a short time. Similarly, the piracy and theft which is considered normal in EVE Online should probably not be policed. Conversely, if the same virtual murder or theft occurred in an online world aimed at young children, such as Club Penguin, it would obviously be unacceptable.

With this in mind, one solution might be that the creator of each virtual world is required to put in place a strict set of laws outlining what is and is not acceptable in the world, and to ensure that the virtual world is patrolled sufficiently well so that all wrongdoings are observed and punished appropriately. This solution is probably particularly appropriate if the creators of the virtual world are profiting financially from its users, although Linden Labs has shown reluctance to embrace this approach (Holahan, 2006). These actions would also condone a 'big brother' approach to life online, which could be strongly opposed by many cyber-citizens. It may be that the best alternative is to make cybersocieties mirrors of the offline world, where the police rely greatly on the citizens of the relevant society to report misconduct. As in real life, this approach may be open to abuse as one or more players could make unfounded allegations against another. In extreme cases, there may be a market for 'cyber-lawyers' who defend avatars against allegations by others or mount a case for cyber-prosecutions in virtual worlds. Finally, it needs to be considered what penalty should be imposed for committing a crime in a virtual world.

PUNISHMENT

If a person carries out a crime in a virtual world, but their offence has real-world consequences for the victim or society (be they emotional, financial or physical), should the offender be punished offline, in the virtual world, or both? Probably the best solution would involve the restorative justice approach outlined above, but there may be cases where this technique is considered inadequate or fails to satisfy those involved.

It has been argued that virtual punishment is the appropriate recourse for crimes which occur in an online community (McKinnon, 1997). As was seen in the Mr. Bungle case, banishment from an online community is often considered the most severe punishment possible in virtual worlds. This punishment is easily overcome however, simply by creating a new avatar. Even if the offender's IP address is blocked from using the virtual world, it is relatively easy to obtain a new IP address from which to access the world.

In theft cases where the item has a real-world value, then it may be possible in some jurisdictions to enforce an offline punishment also – perhaps a fine or a prison term. But to prosecute cases such as Mr. Bungle offline, it would require that laws are rewritten, perhaps to include malicious infliction of emotional distress using computer mediated communication (Brenner, 2001). It seems unlikely that these changes will be implemented unless victimisation in virtual worlds becomes a recurring complaint by users who feel that they have been persecuted in some way, to the extent that the criminal justice system finds it difficult to ignore.

FUTURE TRENDS AND RESEARCH

As is very evident in this chapter, there is exceptionally little empirical evidence examining the topic of crime in virtual worlds. It would seem particularly important to examine what aspects of such an offence lead to psychological distress in victims, so that attempts can be made to reduce this distress for others. Presence seems to be a key variable that needs to be examined, and particularly the effect of the realism of the avatar and the virtual world in which the crime takes place. This is a particularly important consideration given the improvement in three-dimensional graphics of recent years.

At some point in the future law enforcement agencies and criminal justice systems are likely to need to develop strategies to deal with criminal events in virtual worlds. While there are some suggested strategies outlined above, these would need to be tested in the field in order to determine their true effectiveness – as with many plans those that seem feasible and suitable in theory may not be appropriate when put into practice.

Adams (2010) raises the question as to the impact of the likely emergence of haptic interfaces for virtual worlds. Haptic interfaces allow users to experience technology through touch. For example, some virtual reality applications utilise haptic gloves that allow the user to touch certain stimuli within the world and feel their texture. Some haptic devices already exist for certain worlds, such as a gaming vest developed by the University of Pennsylvania which allows users to feel the physical effects of being shot in game (Mancheno, 2010). If use of these devices become more common, and are used in a wider variety of worlds, then users may feel an online virtual assault as well as seeing it occur, which would possibly lead to a greater psychological reaction on the part of the victim.

Finally, some consideration is required of what may happen if users eventually control a single avatar which is used in several online virtual worlds. Should the same penalties be applied across all virtual worlds, or only the one in which the crime took place? This is a complex question to answer, especially given the varying nature of acceptable behaviours in different virtual worlds.

CONCLUSION

Up to this time, cybersocieties have in many cases been forced to make the rules up as they go, trying to deal with individual cases of crime in online virtual worlds as and when they arise, often without the action being criminalized in the community beforehand. In some cases this has been relatively successful, but in others, victims of crimes in virtual worlds appear to experience quite serious emotional reactions to their victimization, with limited acceptance of their reaction from others. As online virtual worlds become more realistic, the associated increased sense of presence may also lead to increased victim suffering. It is clear that in the first instance, research needs to be conducted in order to determine how widespread crime in online virtual worlds actually is, and to establish how severely most victims react to it. The factors which lead to more severe reactions should then be identified, and presence is a logical place to start this investigation. If crime in online virtual worlds is determined to be a serious problem, with substantial effects on victims, then a greater focus needs to be placed on how online communities deal with this problem, and if legislation needs to be changed to reflect the psychological and emotional consequences of victimization. At this time, with increasing numbers of both children and adults joining multiple online communities, it is essential that this problem be addressed, so that adequate protection can be provided to the cybercitizen.

REFERENCES

Adams, A. A. (2010). Virtual Sex with Child Avatars. In Wankel, C., & Malleck, S. (Eds.), *Emerging Ethical Issues of Life in Virtual Worlds* (pp. 55–72). Charlotte, North Carolina: Information Age Publishing.

Adams, R. E., & Boscarino, J. A. (2006). Predictors of PTSD and Delayed PTSD After Disaster: The impact of exposure and psychosocial resources. *The Journal of Nervous and Mental Disease, 194*, 485–493. doi:10.1097/01.nmd.0000228503.95503.e9

BBC News (2005). *'Game theft' led to fatal attack.* Retrieved from http://news.bbc.co.uk/2/hi/technology/ 4397159.stm

BBC News (2007). *'Virtual theft' leads to arrest.* Retrieved from http://news.bbc.co.uk/2/hi/technology/ 7094764.stm

Bente, G., Rüggenberg, S., Krämer, N. C., & Eschenburg, F. (2008). Avatar-Mediated networking: Increasing social presence and interpersonal trust in net-based collaborations. *Human Communication Research, 34*, 287–318. doi:10.1111/j.1468-2958.2008.00322.x

Bouchard, S., St-Jacques, J., Robillard, G., & Renaud, P. (2008). Anxiety increases the feeling of presence in virtual reality. In *Presence Teleoperators and Virtual Environments,* 376-391. August.

Brenner, S. W. (2001). Is there such a thing as 'Virtual Crime'? *California Criminal Law Review, Volume 4.* Retrieved from http://www.boalt.org/bjcl/v4/v4brenner.pdf

Cox, B. J., MacPherson, P. S. R., Enns, M. W., & McWilliams, L. A. (2004). Neuroticisim and self-criticism associated with posttraumatic stress disorder in a nationally representative sample. *Behaviour Research and Therapy, 42*, 105–144. doi:10.1016/S0005-7967(03)00105-0

Dibbell, J. (1993). *A Rape in Cyberpspace*. Retrieved from http://loki.stockton.edu/~kinsellt/ stuff/ dibbelrapeincyberspace.html

Dibbell, J. (1998). *A Rape in Cyberspace*. Retrieved from http://www.juliandibbell.com/texts/ bungle.html

EVElopedia. (n.d.) *Corporation Management Guide*. Retrieved from http://wiki.eveonline.com/ en/wiki/ Corp_theft#Corp_Theft

Fauerbach, J. A., Lawrence, J. W., Schmidt, C. W., Munster, A. M., & Costa, P. T. (2000). Personality Predictors of Injury-Related Posttraumatic Stress Disorder. *The Journal of Nervous and Mental Disease*, *188*, 510–517. doi:10.1097/00005053-200008000-00006

Garau, M., Slater, M., Vinayagamoorthy, V., Brogni, A., Steed, A., & Sasse, M. A. (2003). *The Impact of Avatar Realism and Eye Gaze Control on the perceived Quality of Communication in a Shared Immersive Virtual Environment*. SIGCHI.

Groth, A. N., Burgess, A. W., & Holmstrom, L. L. (1977). Rape, power, anger and sexuality. *The American Journal of Psychiatry*, *134*, 1239–1248.

Guest, T. (2007). *Second Lives: A Journey Through Virtual Worlds*. London: Random House.

Hof, R. (2006). *Real Threat to Virtual Goods in Second Life*. Retrieved from http://www.businessweek.com/the_thread/techbeat/archives/2006/11/ real_threat_to.html

Holahan, C. (2006). *The Dark Side of Second Life*. Retrieved from http://www.businessweek.com/technology /content/nov2006/ tc20061121_727243.htm

Hood, S. K., & Carter, M. M. (2008). A Preliminary Examination of Trauma History, Locus of Control, and PTSD Symptom Severity in African American Women. *The Journal of Black Psychology*, *34*, 179–191. doi:10.1177/0095798407310541

Howitt, D. (2009). *Introduction to Forensic and Criminal Psychology* (3rd ed.). Pearson.

Hoyle, C., & Zedner, L. (2007). Victims, Victimization, and Criminal Justice. In Maguire, M., Morgan, R., & Reiner, R. (Eds.), *The Oxford Handbook of Criminology* (4th ed., pp. 461–495). Oxford University Press.

Jay, E. (2007). *Rape in Cyberspace. 2007*. Retrieved from https://lists.secondlife.com/pipermail/ educators/2007-May/009237.html

Josman, N., Somer, E., Reisberg, A., Weiss, P. L., Garcia-Palacios, A., & Hoffman, H. (2006). Busworld: Designing a Virtual Environment for Post-Traumatic Stress Disorder in Israel: A Protocol. *Cyberpsychology & Behavior*, *9*, 241–244. doi:10.1089/cpb.2006.9.241

Jouriles, E. N., McDonald, R., Kullowatz, A., Rosenfield, D., Gomez, G. S., & Cuevas, A. (2009). Can Virtual Reality Increase the Realism of Role Plays Used to Teach College Women Sexual Coercion and Rape-Resistance Skills? *Behavior Therapy*. doi:10.1016/j.beth.2008.09.002

Jung, Y. (2008). Influence of Sense of Presence on Intention to Participate in a Virtual Community. *Proceedings of the 41st Hawaii International Conference on System Sciences*.

Kamphuis, J. H., Emmelkamp, P. M. G., & Bartak, A. (2003). Individual differences in post-traumatic stress following post-intimate stalking: Stalking severity and psychosocial variables. *The British Journal of Clinical Psychology*, *42*, 145–156. doi:10.1348/014466503321903562

Kirwan, G. (2009, November). *Presence and the Victims of Crime in Online Virtual Worlds*. Proceedings of Presence 2009 – the 12th Annual International Workshop on Presence, International Society for Presence Research, November 11-13, Los Angeles, California. Retrieved from http:// astro.temple.edu/~tuc16417 /papers/Kirwan.pdf PROCEEDINGS ISBN: 978-0-9792217-3-6

Lawrence, J. W., & Fauerbach, J. A. (2003). Personality, Coping, Chronic Stress, Social Support and PTSD symptoms among adult burn survivors: A path analysis. *The Journal of Burn Care & Rehabilitation, 24*, 63–72. doi:10.1097/00004630-200301000-00016

Lynn, R. (2007). *Virtual Rape is Traumatic, but is it a Crime?* Retrieved from http://www.wired.com/culture/lifestyle/ commentary/sexdrive/2007/05/sexdrive_0504

Mancheno, C. (2010, April 11). With New Vest, Players feel the game. *The Daily Pennsylvanian.* Retrieved from http://www.dailypennsylvanian.com/article /new-vest-players-feel-game

Marmar, C. R., Metzler, T. J., Otte, C., McCaslin, S., Inslicht, S., & Haase, C. H. (2007). The Peritraumatic Dissociative Experiences Questionnaire: An International Perspective. In J.P. Wilson and C. So-kum Tang (Eds.) *Cross-Cultural Assessment of Psychological Trauma and PTSD* (pp. 197-217). Springer.

McKinnon, R. C. (1997). Punishing the persona: Correctional Strategies for the Virtual Offender. In Jones, S. (Ed.), *The Undernet: The Internet and the Other*. Sage.

Meadows, M. S. (2008). *I, Avatar: The Culture and Consequences of Having a Second Life*. Berkeley, CA: New Riders.

Murray, C. D., Fox, J., & Pettifer, S. (2007). Absorption, dissociation, locus of control and presence in virtual reality. *Computers in Human Behavior, 23*, 1347–1354. doi:10.1016/j.chb.2004.12.010

Park, A. J., Calvert, T. W., Brantingham, P. L., & Brantingham, P. J. (2008). The Use of Virtual and Mixed Reality Environments for Urban Behavioural Studies. *PsychNology Journal, 6*, 119–130.

Pearce, C. (2006). *Seeing and being seen: Presence & Play in Online Virtual Worlds. Online, offline and the concept of presence when games and VR collide*. USC Institute for Creative Technologies.

Riva, G., Mantovani, F., Capideville, C. S., Preziosa, A., Morganti, F., & Villani, D. (2007). Affective Interactions Using Virtual Reality: The Link between Presence and Emotions. *Cyberpsychology & Behavior, 10*, 45–56. doi:10.1089/cpb.2006.9993

Scarpa, A., Haden, S. C., & Hurley, J. (2006). Community Violence Victimization and Symptoms of Posttraumatic Stress Disorder. *Journal of Interpersonal Violence, 21*, 446–469. doi:10.1177/0886260505285726

Scully & Marolla. (1993). "Riding the bull at Gilley's": Convicted rapists describe the rewards of rape. (pp. 26-46). In P. Bart & E.G. Moran's (eds) *Violence against women: The bloody footprints*. Thousand Oaks, California: Sage.

Sipress, A. (2007). *Does Virtual Reality Need a Sheriff?* Retrieved from http://www.washingtonpost.com/wp-dyn/content/article/2007/06/01/AR2007060102671.html

Talbert, F. S., Braswell, L. C., Albrecht, I. W., Hyer, L. A., & Boudewyns, P. A. (1993). NEO-PI profiles in PTSD as a function of trauma level. *Journal of Clinical Psychology, 49*, 663–669. doi:10.1002/1097-4679(199309)49:5<663::AID-JCLP2270490508>3.0.CO;2-A

Verone (n.d.). Piracy Guide. *EVElopedia*. Retrieved from http://wiki.eveonline.com/en/wiki/Piracy_guide

Vinyagamoorthy, V., Brogni, A., Gillies, M., Slater, M., & Steed, A. (2004). An Investigation of Presence Response across Variations in Visual Realism. *Proceedings of Presence 2004: The 7th Annual International Workshop on Presence.*

Wall, D., & Williams, M. (2007). Policing diversity in the digital age: maintaining order in virtual communities. *Criminology & Criminal Justice, 7,* 391–415. doi:10.1177/1748895807082064

Wemmers, J. A., & Cyr, K. (2006). Victims' perspectives on restorative justice: how much involvement are victims looking for? *International Review of Victimology, 11,* 259–274.

Whitson, J., & Doyle, A. (2008). Second Life and governing deviance in virtual worlds. In Leman-Langlois, S. (Ed.), *Technocrime: Technology, crime and social control. Cullompton, Devon: Willan* (pp. 88–111).

Wiederhold, B. K., & Wiederhold, M. D. (2005). *Virtual Reality Therapy for Anxiety Disorders: Advances in Evaluation and Treatment.* American Psychological Association. doi:10.1037/10858-000

Williams, M. (2006). *Virtually Criminal: Crime, deviance and regulation online.* Oxon, England: Routledge.

ADDITIONAL READING

Adams, A. A. (2010). Virtual Sex with Child Avatars. In Wankel, C., & Malleck, S. (Eds.), *Emerging Ethical Issues of Life in Virtual Worlds* (pp. 55–72). Charlotte, North Carolina: Information Age Publishing.

Bouchard, S., St-Jacques, J., Robillard, G., & Renaud, P. (2008). Anxiety increases the feeling of presence in virtual reality. In *Presence Teleoperators and Virtual Environments,* 376-391. August.

Brenner, S. W. (2001). Is there such a thing as 'Virtual Crime'? *California Criminal Law Review, Volume 4.* Retrieved from http://www.boalt.org/bjcl/v4/v4brenner.pdf

Dibbell, J. (1998). *A Rape in Cyberspace.* Retrieved from http://www.juliandibbell.com/texts/bungle.html

McKinnon, R. C. (1997). Punishing the persona: Correctional Strategies for the Virtual Offender. In Jones, S. (Ed.), *The Undernet: The Internet and the Other.* Thousand Oaks, CA: Sage.

Murray, C. D., Fox, J., & Pettifer, S. (2007). Absorption, dissociation, locus of control and presence in virtual reality. *Computers in Human Behavior, 23,* 1347–1354. doi:10.1016/j.chb.2004.12.010

Riva, G., Mantovani, F., Capideville, C. S., Preziosa, A., Morganti, F., & Villani, D. (2007). Affective Interactions Using Virtual Reality: The Link between Presence and Emotions. *Cyberpsychology & Behavior, 10,* 45–56. doi:10.1089/cpb.2006.9993

Wall, D., & Williams, M. (2007). Policing diversity in the digital age: maintaining order in virtual communities. *Criminology & Criminal Justice, 7,* 391–415. doi:10.1177/1748895807082064

Whitson, J., & Doyle, A. (2008). Second Life and governing deviance in virtual worlds. In Leman-Langlois, S. (Ed.), *Technocrime: Technology, crime and social control. Cullompton, Devon: Willan* (pp. 88–111).

Chapter 13
On-Line Governance

ABSTRACT

Traditional government is being hollowed out as power dissipates upwards to supranational institutions and downwards to sub national agencies. Governments are also losing influence with their citizens as power is lost to interest groups, influential individuals and media organizations. Citizens are disengaging with the political process as they perceive their ability to effect change is diminishing. As individuals spend more time online, form relationships and interest groups in virtual worlds, the polis is becoming virtual. This chapter looks at how technology, which has already begun to transform service delivery in the public sector, can also transform consultation and participation. If power and influence has been dissipated from the government, can it be regained by finding new ways to engage online with the citizens on whose behalf it exists to serve?

BACKGROUND: GOVERNMENTS' LOSS OF POWER

Plato saw both the centrality of the citizen and justice as the natural state of man; 'justice is to the individual as sharpness is to a knife' (Plato, 400BC/2007, p.37). Others saw the state as a necessary evil, required to keep the peace in the face of man's desire for dominion or control. Thomas Moor imagined a utopia of city states with

power in the hands of the citizen, whilst Hobbs saw the destructive nature of man requiring a strong government to protect us from ourselves. The modern state has been defined as 'a legal and political organization with the power to require obedience and loyalty from its citizens' (Seton-Watson, 1977, p.1). The monopoly of this power and the maintenance of a territorial boundary are also seen as a defining feature (McCall, 1999). Hay (1996) sought to see the state in three distinct phases, or moments of 'stateness', the state as a nation, the state as a territory and the state

DOI: 10.4018/978-1-61350-350-8.ch013

as an institution. None of these models saw the citizen as a requirement at the centre of the state or its power. In recent years nation states have seen changes in the way they can exercise power. Power has gravitated to either the sub-national or supranational level. Morison (1998, p.517) has spoken about this as the 'hollowing out' of the State and discussed the 'fugitive nature of power'. This has led to predictions of the end of the nation State (Ohmae, 1996) but, Pierson (2004, p.176) argues that States are diversifying, and developing. In the case of virtual worlds, the idea of a government presence at all has been challenged for some time. In 1996, in a reaction to the Communications Decency Act in the US, John Perry Barlow, a Fellow at Harvard University's Berkman Center for Internet and Society, published 'A Declaration of the Independence of Cyberspace'. This document states, for example, *"Governments of the Industrial World.....I ask you of the past to leave us alone. You are not welcome among us. You have no sovereignty where we gather"* (quoted in Sustein, 2007, p153). As we will see later in this chapter, governments and state agencies have had a powerful role in the formulation and regulation of the internet and its virtual spaces since inception and this rather naive world view is inconsistent with the nature of our social development.

Vertical Dissipation of Power

Power has been seeded upwards at the supranational level to organizations like the European Union. Loughlin (2007, p.387) argues that the founders of European project sought to minimize the importance of the nation state by building a supranational European system as a foundation for a future federal Europe. States, if not losing sovereignty, are pooling sovereignty. Slaughter (2004, p.5), claimed that, *'states still exist but they are disaggregated'* and suggests that we stop thinking about states and focus instead on governments where the different elements of legislation,

adjudication and implementation interact with each other across borders.

Power has also been lost to, or diluted by, entities such as, The United Nations (UN), the International Monetary Fund (IMF), the World Bank, and the World Trade Organization (WTO). It might be assumed that governments would resist the transfer of power away from national parliaments but it has been argued elsewhere (Monbiot, 2001, p.305) that it has often been at the initiation of those in power, and against the wishes of those whom they represent, that these movements of power have occurred. This movement of power away from the citizen is one which is often either resisted by them, or done outside the national processes of scrutiny and accountability. According to Allain (2001, p.541),

The growth of internationalization qua globalization since the end of the Cold War, has meant that States have been willing to cooperate in new and expanding fields. This, in turn, has meant that increasingly States have moved to establish or reinvigorate inter-governmental institutions for the purpose of coordinated action. These institutions, to some extent, have escaped the scrutiny that ordinarily would be felt at the national level. With no true constituency to monitor their international activities and being one step removed from a general public to which they are accountable, States have sought and often achieved collectively what they could not accomplish individually.

In the absence of the scrutiny described above, improved standards of governance could be achieved by a form of peer review amongst nations. Boswell (2003, p.113) reviewed the proposition that international standards strengthen accountability and improve the performance of governance structures. The challenge was not in the creation of standards but how they are applied in practice and that peer review was the best way to ensure compliance. Governments must have the political will, the technical capacity, the resources, and there must be civil participation and oversight. It is also necessary for a trans-national framework, such as the EU to exist to facilitate the required trust and sense of common purpose that would be required. This concept of 'peer review' is consistent with the discussion of soft law in Chapter 1.

Power has also been devolved downwards through the growth of state agencies, regional assemblies, and the emergence of sub-national authorities. In many countries a process of agencifiation has occurred in the last twenty five years which has seen the number of state agencies grow significantly. In Ireland Quinn (2008) discusses how the number grew by more than four hundred. State agencies remain part of the system of government and the government is ultimately responsible for their performance (Dooney & O'Toole, 1998, p.189). Schmitter (1985, p.33) claims that *'the modern state is an amorphous complex of agencies with ill defined boundaries performing a great variety of not very distinctive functions.'*

The United Kingdom has seen the devolution of powers to the Scottish Parliament, the Welsh National Assembly and the Northern Ireland Assembly. Although in each case the transfer of power has occurred to a different degree, power has in each case been transferred away from the national government. Other sub-national bodies are increasingly taking on roles more traditionally associated with central government. Bomberg and Peterson (1998) argue that sub-national authorities (SNAs) working to pursue a local agenda on a European stage exert the most power by forming cross national coalitions and through informal policy networks. Jeffery (2000) maintains that rather than SNAs moving beyond the nation state and having an international role, they are representing their member state through their own domestic structures. This may move power closer to the citizen but in either case the power moves away from government.

The movement of power away from national governments has happened at a time when in-dividual citizens have seen their own ability to gather information, connect, and interact across national boundaries via the internet, increase exponentially. If a citizen is unhappy with a local situation and cannot seek resolution via local or national authorities, other routes are now available. The changing organizational structures combined with the ability to connect, means that a well informed individual can go direct to, for example, the EU or the European Courts of Justice. Alternatively, contacting national or world media has never been easier nor is the ability to publish one's own views directly via blogs, YouTube, or a dozen other social networking outlets.

The prospect of citizens populating virtual worlds, and using these to fulfill some of the activities associated with traditional governance, holds the possibility of an alternate existence running in parallel to the real world. However the real challenge is not that it becomes a parallel existence but rather that it is necessary to embrace our online existence as just a normal part of our every day experiences. This poses a different challenge to governments, law makers and other more traditional arms of society.

Horizontal Dissipation of Power

The transfer of power up or down in a vertical plane of influence has been accompanied by a horizontal seeping of power away from governments to organizations and individuals outside of the structures of state. This transfer of power is more undermining of the states influence, although potentially more empowering of the citizen. The distinction between vertical and horizontal transfer of power is that in the vertical plane the power moves from one form of established governance structure to another. In the case of horizontal transfer, the power moves out of the political or state sphere and into the hands of different actors.

Lukes (2005) sees power as much more than the ability to make decisions and enforce action. What he describes as a three dimensional view of power consists of; the power to influence the behavior of another, the power to define the agenda, and the power to mould perceptions and preferences. This third dimension is the most effective kind of power. It can be exercised *'through the control of information, through the mass media and through the process of socialization'* (Lukes, 2005, p.8). It is this third dimension of power that is seeping horizontally from governments. More than fifty years ago Lippmann (1952) was able to state that *'the significant revolution of modern times is not industrial or economic or political, but the revolution taking place in the art of creating consent among the governed'*. Morison (1998, p.518) also acknowledged that *'Government now is only one of many actors that may influence the course of events in society'*. Now more than ever there is a need for consultation and communication between the government and the governed.

If the government is no longer setting the agenda or creating consent, who is? Some studies have made a case for the media (McNair, 1999). A case can also be made for motivated individuals; either organized and well funded, or spontaneous and less organized. An example of the former would be the blog Instapundit run by Glenn Reynolds, a law professor at the University of Tennessee, whose blog receives more than 700,000 visitors each month. As Shirky (2009, p89) says *"There is no obvious point where a blog stops functioning like a diary for friends and starts functioning like a media outlet. Community now shades into audience; it's as if your phone could turn into a radio station at the turn of a knob."* An example of the latter, spontaneous and less organized example might be flickr.com. Originally conceived as a useful way of storing and sharing digital photographs it now has the capacity to provide images from breaking news stories anywhere in the world. Whatever happens, wherever in the world it happens, someone will have a camera or a phone and within seconds the world will have access to an image of the event via flickr. flickr dealt with the institutional or transaction cost of

managing photographs, *"not by increasing its managerial oversight over photographers but by abandoning any hope of such oversight in the first place, instead putting in place tools for the self-synchronization of otherwise latent groups"* (Shirky 2009, p39). As stated by Benz (2000, p.33) *'Independent actors, who formulate agendas and proposals, are often more important (and more powerful in governance) than those who have formal powers to participate in decisions'*.

REGAINING POWER BY RECONNECTING

How does the government respond? How does it begin to recapture this fugitive power, regain the trust of its citizens and the ability to set the agenda of public discourse? The notion of virtual worlds in which citizens are interacting virtually with each other and with the state is not as fanciful as it might seem and moves in that direction will be examined later in the chapter. First it is worth considering the major structural changes that have been occurring in the way governments and their bureaucracies have been reorganizing themselves in the last quarter century and the degree to which this has already been driven by, or facilitated by, advances in Information and Communications Technologies (ICT).

Loughlin (2004) argues that there was already one important shift, from the welfare state to the neo-liberal state, and that a further shift towards a third way is in progress. This third way envisages a form of networked governance where the state plays a facilitating role in partnership with civil society. Giddens (2008), who popularized the term 'the third way', wrote about *democratizing democracy*. It was not that the people had tired of the democratic state, but rather that they felt it not democratic enough. This *'reflexive citizenry'* called for more input into the process of government, driven in part by a growing distrust of politicians. An example of this greater input is described by Campbell (2008, p.11) who, writing about the Belfast/Good Friday agreement in Northern Ireland, saw it as an opportunity for *'refreshing citizenship'* as it required the state to be interventionist in the promotion of social movements and civic society. The inclusion of an equality agenda in the agreement promoted consultation and forced even high level issues such as the budget to be the subject of equality impact assessments (Campbell 2008, p.101). This new way of thinking about the states' relationship with the citizen coincided with the move from the *'Bureaucratic Century'* to the *'Information Age'* described by Kamarch (2007). This Foucauldian view sees power as localized. Power is not hierarchical, flowing from the top down, but everywhere, patters of power established in groups of individuals interact with patterns of power in institutions and throughout society.

This desire to improve, reconnect or 'modernize' government found expression in Clinton's *National Performance Review* and Bush's *Management Agenda*. In the UK there was the *Financial Management Initiative* and *New Public Management* program. In many cases the modernization agenda, with its focus on efficiency, led governments to information technology as a key enabler. Early attempts to use ICT in government focused on the citizen as consumer and various interactions between the citizen and the state were put on-line. In Ireland the Strategic Management Initiative (SMI) launched by Taoiseach [Prime Minister] Albert Reynolds in 1994 resulted in a coordinating group of secretaries general producing a report called *Delivering Better Government: A Program of Change for the Irish Civil Service*. Dealing as it did with quality customer service, regulatory reform, openness and transparency, HRM, financial management and ICT; it was very focused on the consumer view of the citizen.

Perhaps the most influential early work on NPM was *Reinventing Government* by Osborne and Gaebler (1992) who characterized NPM as entrepreneurial government and set out a clear road map for reform of government. Government needed to be close to its customers, performance driven, committed to continuous improvement, decentralized, have tight cost control, practice performance management and be target driven. A host of jargon entered the lexicon as governments needed to; delegate implementation (steer rather than row), contract out activities (outsource) and seek partnerships with the private and voluntary sectors (joined-up government). The purpose of implementing such changes was to produce specific results which are normally listed, for example by Pollitt (2002, p.279), as; savings, improved processes, improved efficiency, greater effectiveness, and increases in capacity. All of these results had to be specific and measurable and so were broken down into manageable, and more importantly, measurable units. Improved processes meant reduced waiting times or faster delivery. Improved efficiency measured changes in the ratio of inputs to outputs. Effectiveness meant less crime or more literacy, less homelessness or more jobs. All of these indicators could be measured, tracked and trended. Studies could be done quickly and improvements rewarded. All of this was facilitated by ICT and a move towards eGovernance.

By the late 1990s the limitations of NPM were becoming clear. Bevan and Hood (2006, cited in Lapsley 2008:85) analyzed the star system of evaluation of hospitals in the UK and found many examples of performance manipulation. The reasons given were mainly that the system was too narrow to measure a complex organization like a hospital. Modell (2004, cited in Lapsley, 2008, p.86) describes a reliance on quantification and performance measurement as a myth given its failure to achieve its purpose. In addition to the narrowness of the criteria of evaluation under NPM, a related issue is that of the reward structures put in place to incentivize performance. Writers such as Dunleavy et al (2005), make the case that implementation of NPM is at best stalled and in many counties being reversed. The focus of NPM on disaggregation and competition increases the number of autonomous units in the system of public administration and leads to more complex and dynamic interrelationships. As the weaknesses in some aspects of New Public Management were identified a number of alternative ways of thinking about governance emerged. These included network governance, Public Value Management (PVM) and Digital-Era Governance (DEG).

Governments were using ICT, but mainly to automate existing tasks, provide information online or improve service delivery options. Few were making use of the additional functionality of the technology to do new things. Hood (2007, p.2) takes the view that government is about social control and tries to shape our lives by applying administrative tools. This rather Orwellian view is countered by Pierson (2004, p.182) who asks how the state should more effectively be directed and controlled by its citizens and concludes that the solution is a challenge to our democratic imagination. ICT offers government new ways of engaging the public. Morison (2001, p178) argues that we need to develop the idea of an active, involved citizen as a participant in the process of government. Can ICT be used to develop some idea of e-democracy to widen and deepen the involvement of the citizen? Democracy should mean, after all, that power is ultimately invested in 'we the people'. As Zuboff (1988) asked in her book 'In the Age of the Smart Machine', will managers utilize ICT to support, and reinforce, existing political, social and organizational structures and processes or will they use ICT as a transformational agent to access its full potential?

Morison (2007) has discussed the broader use of ICT in the form of blogs, wikis, web chats and other participatory fora to increase participation of the citizen and feedback for the government. In Stanford University a considerable amount of work has been done in the Persuasive Technology Lab to determine what makes web sites credible and believable and a useful summary of the results of their annual surveys of perceptions of credibil-

ity is available in BJ Fogg's (2003, p.154) book on the subject. By these measures the information on many government web sites is far from persuasive or credible and does not fulfill their presumed intention of making a connection with the electorate. A good starting point on how blogs in particular might be better used by politicians to improve communications and increase civic engagement has been done by Wyld (2007) in his paper, 'The Blogging Revolution: Government in the Age of Web 2.0'.

Online Consultation

Greater participation of citizens has been attempted via differing forms of ICT. E-consultation, e-budgeting, electronic voting, provision of information and services have all been attempted with varying degrees of success. In the case of the Irish Republic public consultation has been sought online for proposed bills. In the United Kingdom greater use has been made of this methodology. Bristol city council, for example, has a website *askbristol.com* which allows consultation on various issues from the budget to the use of public spaces. In addition the web site of the British Prime Minister provides the facility to petition the government or take part in an existing petition. In the United States an organization called America Speaks has run e-consultation on topics as diverse as budgeting, climate change and disaster recovery. These 21st century town hall meetings have been held in states all over the US. In New York in 2002 a project called 'Listening to the City' brought 4,300 people together in a virtual space to give their thoughts about six preliminary concepts for the site of the World Trade Centre (www.listeningtothecity.org). Newman et al (2007) view e-consultation as part of the broader modernization agenda of government and lay particular importance on the co-design of consultation processes and technologies. In their work the objective of the consultation, as well as the stage in the process, is aligned to the most appropriate technology for that purpose. It is in the processes that involve the citizen that democracy is realized.

Democracy should be open, transparent, inclusive, accessible and responsive, all elements that can be built into an ICT strategy. However such systems need to be more than just responsive to external inputs. They should be preference forming and, as in a deliberative democratic structure, preference building. It is in this context that the recent electoral campaign by Barack Obama is instructive. Obama attempted to have a conversation with the American people. Those who wished to participate received almost daily texts, emails or video links from Obama, his wife, his running mate Joe Biden and various members of his campaign team. Of course these were mass communications sent centrally to thousands, or millions of subscribers. However the personalized nature of the opening 'Dear Andrew...........', the conversational style, and the named signature, created the illusion of a greater intimacy than was possible. Obama spoke, America listened (and donated) and trust was built. Obama was in a conversation with the citizen, information flowed in one direction, funds in the other. Obama was building social capital and doing it in a broad and inclusive way. His attempts to be inclusive gave him access to a wide section of his electorate.

Social capital makes its vital contribution to a new political economy through enabling us to focus on the crucial issue of the means by which the capacities of individuals to process information are distributed across an economy. - (Szreter, 2001)

Obama spoke of creating a transparent and connected democracy and using cutting-edge technologies to create a new level of transparency, accountability, and participation for America's citizens. On assuming office Obama appointed the first Federal Chief Technology Officer (CTO), Aneesh Chopra.

As technology becomes more prevalent in the lives of more of the electorate, barriers to entry will fall. The baby boomers are now retiring and the students of the dot.com explosion are taking their place in positions of influence. In their turn the children of the dot.com generation, the digital natives, are becoming the students of today. Prensky (2001) discussed the generational differences in the way we use and interact with technology and suggested that students today think differently and process information differently from previous students because of their interaction with technology. These students he calls Digital Natives. Digital natives are increasingly living in a dual world of virtual reality via environments like Second Life and World of Warfare. Second Life is discussed below as an example of an environment that governments have begun to use. Second Life, despite its rapid growth and its current population of thirteen million users it is still one of the smaller virtual worlds. It is dwarfed by the number of children using clubpenguin.com, webkinz.com, and barbiegirls.com amongst many others. In the August 2007 takeover of Club Penguin by Disney the number of activate users on the site was quoted as twelve million (Club Penguin, n.d.). According to Educational Games Research (n.d.). *"Club Penguin has almost 5 million unique monthly visitors, while Webkinz has around 6 million"*. Barbiegirls.com was the fastest growing of these sites reaching four million subscribers in the first three months of its launch (CNW, 2007). These children will have none of the reluctance of their parents about on-line interaction.

As citizens spend more time in virtual worlds or mediated environments their online activities are moving further from entertainment and towards social interaction, business, and occasionally crime. The growth of both virtual worlds and social networking are markers of the move from Web 1.0 to Web 2.0. This shift has less to do with technological change and more to do with the uses to which the web is being put and the increased capacity of the web to carry rich content inexpensively. This shift has moved the activities online from broadcasting to interaction. Web 1.0 was largely about pushing information in one direction; Web 2.0 is a two way system.

Online Community

The growth of online communities has dramatically increased the ability of individuals to communicate and come together for common purpose. Groups have always been important to the way we interact and achieve goals so anything that changes the way groups function has a profound effect on everything from commerce and government to media and religion. When we change the way we communicate we change society (Shirky, 2009, p17). We have already seen how some ICT tools have improved communication, e-mail for example enormously lowers the transaction cost of sending a message while creating the potential for massive distribution. The problem with the ease of forwarding a message is that e-mail is now too good a tool. For example, the cost of lobbying a politician is now so low that an e-mail message has become effectively meaningless (Shirky 2009, p287).

We saw earlier that one of the consequences of government's adoption of the New Public Management agenda of change and modernization was that citizens began to be viewed as consumers. Whilst this may have had some positive effects for driving service level objectives for the public service it is not a good outcome for the citizen's view of their role in a democracy. Each of us has rights and duties as citizens, not simply as consumers. According to Louis Brandis (quoted in Sunstein, 2007 p42) "the greatest threat to freedom is an inert people(and) public discussion is a political duty" (Whitney v. California, 274 U.S. 357,372(1927)(Brandeis, J., concurring)). Active engagement in politics, at least some of the time, is a responsibility, not just an entitlement.

Sunstein (2007) goes on to make the point that the Internet is dramatically increasing people's ability to hear echoes of their own voices and to wall themselves off from others. The technologies of Web 2.0 make it easier for people to surround themselves with the opinions of like-minded but otherwise isolated others, and to insulate themselves from competing views. For this reason he argues that social networks, and virtual worlds are a breeding ground for polarization, and potentially dangerous for both democracy and social peace. This potential for polarization has obvious consequences for democratic deliberation if true, or if not addressed through mediation of the environment.

Bridging the Technology Gap

Much has been written about the "digital divide" which is normally taken to mean the gap in access to new technologies which may occur between those who can afford expensive ICT equipment and those who cannot. A variation of this theme is that a divide has opened up, not on the basis of affordability but on the basis of age. It is further argued that, whatever the basis for this divide, the gap is growing with each advance in technology.

Whilst it is true, and has been highlighted earlier in this chapter, that each new generation is accepting as normal those technologies which their parents still see as novel, this has always been the case. It is also true that new technologies come at a cost and for early adopters the costs can be high. However, rather than any such economic or generational divide growing there is some evidence that it is in fact shrinking. According to Sunstein (2007, p17) *"....in both the domestic and in the international context, that problem (the digital divide) seems likely to diminish over time, as new technologies, above all the internet, are made increasingly available to people regardless of their income or wealth"* The issue is also well covered by Yochai Benkler in his 2006 book *The Wealth of Networks.*

The economic argument has been undermined by the emergence of the mobile phone as the preferred platform for much of the innovation in ICT. Penetration rates for mobile phones in even the poorest parts of the world are growing at enormous rates. With a world population of between six and seven billion people, it is forecasted by the International Telecommunication Union (ITU) that by the end of 2010, five billion will have cell phone subscriptions (Whitney, 2010). The explosion in cell phone use has been driven not only by developed countries, but by developing nations hungry for services like mobile banking and health care. The ITU also expects one billion mobile broadband subscriptions during 2010 (Whitney, 2010). The cell phone or mobile phone is fast becoming the device of choice for access to the internet leaving the laptop, PC or Mac behind. Hamadoun Touré the Secretary-General of the International Telecommunication Union (ITU), speaking in February 2010 said;

Even the simplest, low-end mobile phone can do so much to improve health care in the developing world, good examples include sending reminder messages to patients' phones when they have a medical appointment or need a pre-natal check-up, or using SMS messages to deliver instructions on when and how to take complex medication such as anti-retrovirals or vaccines. It's such a simple thing to do, and yet it saves millions of dollars and can help improve and even save the lives of millions of people (UN News Centre, 2010, paragraphs 6-7).

The argument that a digital divide exists and is growing based on age is also contestable. Technology once requiring advanced and specialized knowledge to understand and operate is becoming better and simpler to use. Advances in our understanding of human computer interaction and usability engineering, combined with the natural progression of technology from novel to normal is reducing this divide. In the 1920s one used to have to be a skilled mechanic to drive a car and in the 1970s be a programmer to use a computer. Today communication tools are becoming second nature to the most novice of user, young or old. As Shirky (2009, p105) has said;

Communications tools don't get socially interesting until they get technologically boring. [the tool] has to have been around long enough that most of society is using it. It's when a technology becomes normal, then ubiquitous, and finally so pervasive as to be invisible, that the really profound changes happen.

A VIRTUAL GOVERNMENT?

In recent years modernizing has meant doing the same things as before but better and faster using ICT. In the past reform of government has meant tinkering with the workings of parliament and consulting the citizens has meant more forms, more questions and less engagement. In a changing and increasingly virtual world, government needs to reconnect with the citizens where they are and move parliament on-line in a more meaningful way. The cybercitizen needs a cyber-parliament.

Early Innovators

One attempt at creating such a cyber-parliament has occurred in the social networking site Second Life. Second Life was created by Linden Labs of San Francisco. It is a virtual world which allows users to create their own world communities with images, sound, and video from the "real" world. The concept of such a "Metaverse" came from the Neal Stephenson 1992 novel Snow Crash. Second Life allows users to form communities for discussion, to buy online property, and develop businesses and other organizations. Business is done in 'Linden dollars' that can be converted to real U.S. currency. In the United States a virtual House of Representatives was created by George Miller, a California Democrat, and chairman of the House Education and Labor Committee (CNET, 2007). Miller worked with George Lucas and John Gage of SunMicrosystems who, together with Internet marketing company Clear Ink, built an entire virtual world for members of Congress and citizens to meet (Grove, 2007). In 2006 Democrat Mark Warner, a former Governor of Virginia conducted a Second Life interview and in January 2007 George Miller took questions at a Second Life 'press conference' (CNET, 2007). Miller is now running a project called 'Ask George', which allows voters to ask Miller questions about the Iraq war using videos, blogs, Facebook, text messages, Twitter, or email. If questions are marked 'Ask George' they are aggregated at the site, www. communitycounts.com.

This commitment to new forms of engagement has not been limited to the Democratic Party. Newt Gingrich, the former Speaker of the U.S. House of Representatives, spoke at Second Life's virtual Capitol building. On this occasion there was also the presence of virtual hecklers. Protesters were confined to an area behind the main seats, where they displayed banners like 'Conservatism Kills' and typed anti-Republican slogans. At the time Gingrich said; *Let me make a commitment right now, we will work out a time to have a Republican Party meeting in Second Life',* He also claimed a space to be called 'Legislative Life' was in development and would allow state legislatures to share ideas (Reuters, 2007).

Second Life has also been used to do informal polling of public opinion. In September 2008 Andrew Mallon from the Social Research Foundation in the United States, polled over 1,000 Second Life residents about the then upcoming presidential election (Reuters, 2008). Amongst both Ameri-

can and non-American citizens, Obama was the clear winner. During the presidential campaign in the United States supporters of Hillary Clinton, Barack Obama, and John Edwards set up de-facto headquarters and social organizations within Second Life. The communal aspect makes it a good place for politicians to connect with a new group of voters, and has the advantage over blogs and chat rooms of the physicality of the experience. By combining real-time communication and movement with physically embodied characters or avatars, the experience is more realistic or involving than other online interactions. Second Life gives a strong sense of place while participating and, according to Scola (2007, p.2), can be thought of as a physical internet.

In the French presidential election of 2007 all four major candidates opened virtual headquarters in Second Life, to engage in debates, hold political rallies and take part in protests. Le Pen was the first French presidential candidate to open a headquarters in Second Life, and was also the first to have it attacked by protesters. The campaigns attempted to create cyber-headquarters that reflected the personality and politics of the candidates. François Bayrou's headquarters included a farm with cows, a barn and a tractor, reflecting his roots in the farming community. The Second Life offices of Ségolène Royal, on 'Breton Island', were built of wood to reflect her concerns for the environment. Virtual headquarters built in cyberspace led to real people coming to visit. Interest in the French presidential campaigns was so high that France ended up with the second highest number of Second Life avatars (outside the US) of any country during the election. Second Life had estimated daily visit numbers of up to 20,000 for Ségolène Royal, 11,000 for Le Pen, 10,000 for Nicolas Sarkozy and 7,000 for François Bayrou. Second Life offers candidates an engaged international audience in a way that is more tangible than television, but still capable, reaching a large audience.

Moving forward to 2008, Ed Markey the democratic representative for the state of Massachusetts and chair of the House Energy and Commerce Subcommittee on Telecommunications and the Internet, held a congressional hearing simultaneously in congress and online. A number of government agencies in the United States are also using Second Life. The National Oceanic and Atmospheric Administration (NOAA) created a weather world to provide education on climate conditions and advice on preparation for climatic emergencies. The Center for Disease Control (CDC) provides an educational outreach service to children and adults, as does the National Library of Medicine and the National Aeronautics and Space Administration (NASA). As well as looking outwards, agencies are also using the sites to encourage collaboration between employees and have developed virtual 'water coolers', conference rooms and meeting halls. In the United Kingdom, Second Health was established on-line between the National Physics Laboratory and Imperial College London as an educational facility. It will be used both to provide health information to the public but also to allow doctors to train in a simulated 'hospital' environment.

In his comprehensive paper on the subject Wyld (2008) considers the issues faced by governments who wish to make use of these virtual environments and lists them as; the 'generation gap', identity, security, interoperability, accessibility, availability, staffing, virtual-world policies, and return on investment. Once these are considered it opens the way for governments to use virtual worlds to reconnect with citizens, collaborate between departments, conduct training and simulations, to recruit employees, and promote tourism and economic development. For example, a number of countries including Sweden and Serbia have established embassies in Second Life and some regions such as Tuscany in Italy have tourist centers. These examples, and many more, point to the possibilities for consultation and engagement between state and citizen. This is how the power described by Lukes, to mould perceptions and preferences, can be regained by governments, democracy democratized, and citizenship refreshed.

Rights and Responsibilities of the Cybercitizen

This chapter started with Plato's assertion that justice is the natural state of man and along the way considered the view of Justice Brandis that public discussion is a political duty. We have also discussed how the ability of the internet to facilitate group forming can have a polarizing effect on public discourse, and yet we see our political leaders beginning to make advances into the sphere.

What does it mean to be a citizen in a virtual world and does government have a role in it?

Citizenship is normally based on some fixed criteria, blood and soil in some countries, parentage and location in others. The rights of citizenship are universal in a given country but stop at the border of the next country. Your rights do not generally depend on your behavior (although some countries suspend the voting rights of prisoners) nor do they depend on your contribution to your community. Contrast this with the situation online where rights and privileges are determined by payment or skill level in a game or by status or by privilege (Mulgan 2007, p241). Membership of a community can be suspended or removed for bad behavior as we saw in the case of Mr. Bungle in Chapter 12. This gives rise to the various issues raised in Chapter 1 about the legal control or governance of life online. It does not tell us much about our attitude to the government of the real world 'intruding' into the virtual world.

The views expressed earlier in the 'Declaration of the Independence of Cyberspace' make it clear that for some the virtual world should be a 'no go' area for government. This view seems to be an extension of the view that there should be no regulation of the press and that is it an affront to free speech. However, newspapers and magazines, radio and television stations, and websites all benefit from government regulation every day. Broadcasters have their licenses as a result of government grants and they are legally conferred property rights, in the form of monopolies over frequencies. These property rights create power and they limit power. They determine who owns what, and they say who may do what to whom (Sunstein, 2007 p.155). The government also protects these rights, at taxpayers' expense, via civil and criminal law, both of which prohibit people from gaining access to what broadcasters "own".

In fact, a quick look back at the origin of the internet reveals that it was the US Department of Defense who developed the early version of the Arpanet or internet. It was the European government funded researchers at CERN in Geneva who developed the World Wide Web. Despite its origin as a series of government funded projects the internet is now largely free of ongoing federal supervision with the important exceptions of guaranteed property rights and various restrictions on unlawful speech (such as conspiracy and child pornography). As Sunstein (2007, p160) states *"the real question is what kind of regulation to have, not whether to have regulation. Even those who create open-source software rely heavily on property law, contract law (thought licenses) and at least some form of copyright law to control what happens to their software"*.

Chapter 1 showed how the governance of our online experiences is likely to be achieved by a mesh of private regulation, technical standards, and user preferences. Undoubtedly offline state laws will continue to play an important part. The threat of enforcement is still a powerful deterrent to unacceptable behavior which goes some way to explain why serious disruptions to service due to malicious attacks are still quite rare. A key reason is that site owners have a guarantee of entitlement to be free from trespass. This universal principle is protected in state, national and international law.

CONCLUSION

Morison (1998) states, *'there is now no possibility of returning power to the control of a single institution'*, but by embracing the possibilities of ICT in imaginative and innovative ways government can begin to regain some of the power which has seeped away. Government needs to reconnect with public spaces and public discourse and regain the ability to influence the agenda of the cybercitizen.

Plato argued, and it is emphasized above that governance rests with the citizen. It is by empowering civil society and giving voice to the citizen through consultation that we can achieve more meaningful self governance. In arguing that all classes be governed with equality, and that this should be a cornerstone of education he states,

And this is plainly the intention of the law, in the support it gives to all citizens……to establish some constitutional government in our children and educate the best of them to take over from the best of us: then we give them their freedom (Plato, ca. 400 BC/2007, p.333).

REFERENCES

Allain, J. (2001). The jus cogens nature of non-refoulement. *International Journal of Refugee Law*, *13*, 533–558. doi:10.1093/ijrl/13.4.533

Benkler, Y. (2006). *The Wealth of Networks*. New Haven, CT: Yale University Press.

Benz, A. (2000). Two types of multi-level governance: Intergovernmental relations in German and EU regional policy. *Regional & Federal Studies*, *10*, 21–44. doi:10.1080/13597560008421130

Bevan, G., & Hood, C. (2006). Have targets Improved Performance in the English NHS? *British Medical Journal*, *332*, 419–422. doi:10.1136/bmj.332.7538.419

Bomberg, E., & Peterson, J. (1998). European Decision Making: the Role of Sub-national Authorities. *Political Studies*, *46*, 219–235. doi:10.1111/1467-9248.00137

Boswell, N. (2003). International Law Standards for Domestic Governance: The Impact of International Law on Domestic Governance. *Proceedings of the 101ˢᵗ Annual Meeting of the American Society of International Law,* 133-137.

Campbell, B. (2008). *Agreement! The State, Conflict and Change in Northern Ireland*. London: Lawrence & Wishart.

Club Penguin. (n.d.). Retrieved from http://www.clubpenguin.com/ company/news/ 070801-the-walt-disney-company.htm

CNET. (2007, January 5). *Images: Virtual politics in 'Second Life'*. Retrieved from; http://news.cnet.com/2300-1028_3-6147452-1.html?tag=mncol

CNW. (2007, August 8). *BarbieGirls.com the first global virtual world designed for girls, celebrates 4 million registered users, making it the fastest growing virtual world online.* Retrieved from http://www.newswire.ca/en/releases/archive/August2007/08/c4844.html

Dooney, S., & O'Toole, J. (1998). *Irish Government Today*. Dublin: Gill and Macmillan.

Dunleavy, P., Margetts, H., Bastow, S., & Tinkler, J. (2005). New Public Management is Dead – Long Live Digital-Era Governance. *Journal of Public Administration: Research and Theory*, *16*, 467–494. doi:10.1093/jopart/mui057

Educational Games Research. (n.d.). Retrieved from http://edugamesresearch. com/ blog/ category/webkinz/

Fogg, B. J. (2003). *Persuasive Technology; Using computers to change what we think and do*. San Francisco: Morgan Kaufmann Publishers.

Giddens, A. (2008). *The Third Way: The Renewal of Social Democracy*. Cambridge: Polity.

Grove, S. (2007, January 19). *A Second Life in Politics*. Retrieved from; http://abcnews.go.com/Politics/Story?id=2809023&page=1

Hay, C. (1996). *Re-Stating Social and Political Change*. London: Open University Press.

Hood, C., & Margetts, H. (2007). *The Tools of Government in the Digital Age*. Palgrave Macmillan.

Jeffery, C. (2000). Sub-National Mobilization and European Integration: Does it Make Any Difference? *Journal of Common Market Studies*, *38*, 1–23. doi:10.1111/1468-5965.00206

Kamarch, E. (2007). *The End of Government as we know it: Making public policy work*. Lynne Rienner Publishers.

Lapsley, I. (2008). The NPM agenda: Back to the Future. *Financial Accountability and Management*, *24*, 77–96. doi:10.1111/j.1468-0408.2008.00444.x

Lippmann, W. (1952). *Public Opinion*. New York: Macmillan.

Loughlin, J. (2004). The "Transformation" of Governance: New Directions in Policy and Politics. *The Australian Journal of Politics and History*, *50*, 8–22. doi:10.1111/j.1467-8497.2004.00317.x

Loughlin, J. (2007). Reconfiguring the state: Trends in territorial governance in European states. *Regional & Federal Studies*, *17*, 385–403. doi:10.1080/13597560701691912

Lukes, S. (2005). *Power: a Radical View* (2nd ed.). Basingstoke, England: Palgrave Macmillan.

McCall, C. (1999). The Governance of Northern Ireland: From Modernity to Postmodernity? In McCall, C. (Ed.), *Identity in Northern Ireland: Communities, Politics and Change*. Basingstoke: Palgrave.

McNair, B. (1999). *An Introduction to Political Communication* (2nd ed.). London: Routledge.

Modell, S. (2004). Performance Measurement Myths in the Public Sector: A Research Note. *Finance Accountability & Management, 20,* 39-55.

Monbiot, G. (2001). Government in exile: the Corporate Bid for world Domination. In G. Monbiot *Captive State: The Corporate Takeover of Britain* (pp. 302-330). London: Pan.

Morison, J. (1998). The Case Against Constitutional Reform? *Journal of Law and Society, 25,* 510–535. doi:10.1111/1467-6478.00101

Morison, J. (2001). On-line Citizenship: Consultation and Participation in New Labour's Britain and Beyond. *International Review of Law Computers & Technology, 15,* 177–194. doi:10.1080/13600860120070501

Morison, J. (2007). Models of Democracy: From Representation to Participation? In Jowell, J., & Oliver, D. (Eds.), *The Changing Constitution* (6th ed., pp. 144–170). Oxford: Oxford University Press.

Mulgan, G. (2007). *Good and Bad Power*. London: Penguin.

Newman et al. (2007). *Technology Selection for E-Consultation*. Presented at EGOV07, Leeds Metropolitan University, 12th Sept.

Ohmae, K. (1996). *The End of the Nation State: The Rise of Regional Economies*. New York, NY: The Free Press.

Osborne, D., & Gaebler, T. (1992). *Reinventing Government: How the Entrepreneurial Spirit is Transforming the Public Sector*. New York, NY: Perseus Books.

Pierson, C. (2004). *The Modern State*. London: Routledge.

Plato. (2007). *The Republic*. London: Penguin (Original work published circa 400BC)

Pollitt, C. (2002). The New Public Management in international perspective: an analysis of impacts and effects. In McLaughlin, Osborne and Ferlie (Eds.) *New Public Management: Current Trends and Future Prospects* (pp. 274-293). London: Routledge.

Prensky, M. (2001). Digital Natives, Digital Immigrants. *MCB University Press, 9,* 1–6.

Quinn, O. (2008). *Advisers or Advocates? The Impact of State Agencies on Social Policy*. Dublin: IPA.

Reuters, E. (2007, September 27). *Second Life ready for primetime at Gingrich event*. Retrieved from http://secondlife.reuters.com/stories/2007/09/27/second-life-ready-for-primetime-at-gingrich-event

Reuters, E. (2008). Poll: Second Life residents prefer Obama to McCain by over 2 to 1. Retrieved from http://secondlife.reuters.com/stories/2008/09/23/poll-second-life-residents-prefer-obama-to-mccain-by-over-2-to-1

Schmitter, P. (1985). Neo-Corporatism and the State. In Grant, W. (Ed.), *The Political Economy of Corporatism*. New York: St. Martin.

Scola, N. (2007). Avatar Politics: The social applications of Second Life. *IPDI eNews*. Retrieved from http://www.ipdi.org/UploadedFiles/Avatar%20Politics.pdf

Seton-Watson, H. (1977). *Nations and States: An Enquiry Into the Origins of Nations and the Politics of Nationalism*. London: Methuen.

Shirky, C. (2009). *Here comes everybody*. London: Penguin.

Slaughter, A. (2004). *A New World Order*. Princeton, NJ: Princeton University Press.

Sunstein, C. R. (2007). *Republic.com 2.0*. Princeton, NJ: Princeton University Press.

Szreter, S. (2001). A New Political Economy: The Importance of Social Capital. In Giddens, A. (Ed.), *The Global Third Way Debate* (pp. 290–299). Oxford: Blackwell/Polity Press.

UN News Centre. (2010, February 15). *Robust demand for mobile phone services will continue, UN agency predicts*. Retrieved from http://www.un.org/ apps/news/ story.asp?NewsID =33770&Cr=Telecom&Cr1

Whitney, L. (2010, February 16). *Cell phone subscriptions to hit 5 billion globally*. Retrieved from http://reviews.cnet.com/8301-13970_7-10454065-78.html

Wyld, D. C. (2007). *The Blogging Revolution: Government in the Age of Web 2.0*. Washington: IBM Center for The Business of Government. Retrieved from http://www.businessofgovernment.org/pdfs/WyldReportBlog.pdf

Wyld, D. C. (2008). *Government in 3D: How Public Leaders Can Draw on Virtual Worlds*. Washington: IBM Center for The Business of Government. Retrieved from http://www.businessofgovernment.org/pdfs/Wyld3dReport.pdf

Zuboff, S. (1988). *In the age of the smart machine: The future of work and power*. New York: Basic Books.

ADDITIONAL READING

Benkler, Y. (2006). *The Wealth of Networks*. New Haven, CT: Yale University Press.

Campbell, B. (2008). *Agreement! The State, Conflict and Change in Northern Ireland*. London: Lawrence & Wishart.

Dunleavy, P., Margetts, H., Bastow, S., & Tinkler, J. (2006). *Digital Era Governance: IT Corporations, the State, and E-Government*. Oxford: Oxford University Press.

Fogg, B. J. (2003). *Persuasive Technology; Using computers to change what we think and do*. San Francisco: Morgan Kaufmann Publishers.

Giddens, A. (2001). *The Global Third Way Debate*. Oxford: Blackwell/Polity Press.

Giddens, A. (2008). *The Third Way: The Renewal of Social Democracy*. Cambridge: Polity.

Hood, C., & Margetts, H. (2007). *The Tools of Government in the Digital Age*. Palgrave Macmillan.

Kamarch, E. (2007). *The End of Government as we know it: Making public policy work*. Lynne Rienner Publishers.

Lukes, S. (2005). *Power: a Radical View* (2nd ed.). Palgrave Macmillan.

Monbiot, G. (2001). *Captive State: The Corporate Takeover of Britain*. London: Pan.

Mulgan, G. (2007). *Good and Bad Power*. London: Penguin.

Pierson, C. (2004). *The Modern State*. London: Routledge.

Prensky, M. (2001). Digital Natives, Digital Immigrants. *MCB University Press, 9*, 1–6.

Quinn, O. (2008). *Advisers or Advocates? The Impact of State Agencies on Social Policy*. Dublin: IPA.

Shirky, C. (2009). *Here comes everybody*. London: Penguin.

Slaughter, A. (2004). *A New World Order*. Princeton, NJ: Princeton University Press.

Sunstein, C. R. (2007). *Republic.com 2.0*. Princeton, NJ: Princeton University Press.

Compilation of References

Abbott, K. W., & Snidal, D. (2000). Hard and Soft Law in International Governance. *International Organization*, *54*, 421–456. doi:10.1162/002081800551280

Acre, R. (1998). Empirical studies on jury size. *Expert Evidence*, *6*, 227–241. doi:10.1023/A:1008886718211

Adams, R. E., & Boscarino, J. A. (2006). Predictors of PTSD and Delayed PTSD After Disaster: The impact of exposure and psychosocial resources. *The Journal of Nervous and Mental Disease*, *194*, 485–493..doi:10.1097/01.nmd.0000228503.95503.e9

Adams, A. A. (2010). Virtual Sex with Child Avatars. In Wankel, C., & Malleck, S. (Eds.), *Emerging Ethical Issues of Life in Virtual Worlds* (pp. 55–72). Charlotte, North Carolina: Information Age Publishing.

Ainsworth, P. B. (2002). *Psychology and Policing*. Cullompton, England: Willan Publishing.

Ainsworth, P.B. (2001). *Offender Profiling and Crime Analysis*. Cullompton, Devon: Willan Publishing.

Ajzen, I. (1985). *Action-control: from cognition to behaviour* (pp. 11–39). New York: Springer-Verlag.

Ajzen, I. (1988). *Attitudes, Personality and Behaviour*. Milton Keynes, UK: Open University Press.

Ajzen, I. (1991). The Theory of Planned Behaviour. *Organizational Behavior and Human Decision Processes*, *50*, 179–211. doi:10.1016/0749-5978(91)90020-T

Alexy, E. M., Burgess, A. W., Baker, T., & Smoyak, S. A. (2005). Perceptions of Cyberstalking Among College Students. *Brief Treatment and Crisis Intervention*, *5*, 279–289..doi:10.1093/brief-treatment/mhi020

Alison, L. J., Smith, M. D., Eastoman, O., & Rainbow, L. (2003). Toulmin's philosophy of argument and its relevance to offender profiling. *Journal of Psychology. Crime and Law*, *9*, 173–181. doi:10.1080/1068316031000116265

Alison, L. (2005). The Forensic Psychologist's Casebook: Psychological Profiling and Criminal Investigation. *Cullompton, Devon: Willan Publishing*.

Alison, L., & Kebbell, M. R. (2006). Offender Profiling: Limits and Potential. In Kebbell, M. R., & Davies, G. M. (Eds.), *Practical Psychology for Forensic Investigations and Prosecutions* (pp. 152–163). Chichester, West Sussex: John Wiley & Sons, Ltd.

Allain, J. (2004). Orientalism and International Law: The Middle East as the Underclass of the International Legal Order. *Leiden Journal of International Law*, *17*, 391–404. doi:10.1017/S0922156504001864

Allain, J. (2001). The jus cogens nature of non-refoulement. *International Journal of Refugee Law*, *13*, 533–558. doi:10.1093/ijrl/13.4.533

American Psychiatric Association. (2000). *Diagnostic and Statistical Manual of Mental Disorders* (*Fourth Edition, Text Revision*). Washington, DC: American Psychiatric Association.

Amir, M. (1971). *Patterns of Forcible Rape*. Chicago, IL: University of Chicago Press.

Anti-Phishing Working Group. (APWG, 2010, September 23). *Phishing Activity Trends Report, 1st Quarter, 2010*. Retrieved 11th October 2010 from http://www.antiphishing.org/reports/ apwg_report_Q1_2010.pdf

Ashcroft, J. (2001, May). *Stalking and Domestic Violence: Report to Congress*. Retrieved November 4, 2010 from http://www.ncjrs.gov/pdffiles1/ojp/186157.pdf

Associated Press. (2008, October 24). Japanese woman faces jail over online murder. *The Guardian.* Retrieved from http://www.guardian.co.uk/world/2008 /oct/24/ japan-games

Austin, J. (2000). *The Province of Jurisprudence Determined.* New York: Prometheus Books. (originally London 1832)

Babiak, P., & Hare, R. D. (2006). *Snakes in suits: When psychopaths go to work.* New York: Regan Books.

Bandura, A. (1965). Influence of models' reinforcement contingencies on the acquisition of imitative behaviours. *Journal of Personality and Social Psychology, 1,* 589–595. doi:10.1037/h0022070

Bandura, A. (1997). *Self-Efficacy: The exercise of control.* New York: WH Freeman and Company.

Baron, S. W. (2003). Self-control, social consequences and criminal behavior: Street youth and the general theory of crime. *Journal of Research in Crime and Delinquency, 40,* 403–425. doi:10.1177/0022427803256071

Bates, A., & Metcalf, C. (2007). A psychometric comparison of internet and non-internet sex offenders from a community treatment sample. *Journal of Sexual Aggression, 13,* 11–20. doi:10.1080/13552600701365654

BBC News Online. *(10th December 2009).* Hacker to appeal over extradition. *Retrieved 24th February 2010 from* http://news.bbc.co.uk/2/hi/uk_news/8406643.stm

BBC News Online. *(24th February 2010).* Robin Hood Hacker Exposes Bankers. *Retrieved 25th February 2010 from* http://news.bbc.co.uk/go/pr/fr/-/2/hi/technology/8533641.stm

BBC News Online. *(28th July 2009).* Hacker's 'moral crusade' over UFO. *Retrieved 24th February 2010 from* http://news.bbc.co.uk/go/pr/fr/-/2/hi/uk_news/8172842.stm

BBC News Online. *(31st July 2009).* Hacker loses extradition appeal. *Retrieved 24th February 2010 from* http://news.bbc.co.uk/go/pr/fr/-/2/hi/uk_news/8177561.stm

BBC News Online. *(9th June 2009).* Hacker 'too fragile' to extradite. *Retrieved 24th February 2010 from* http://news.bbc.co.uk/2/hi/uk_news/8090789.stm

BBC News (2005, March 31). Game theft led to fatal attack. *Technology.* Retrieved from http://news.bbc.co.uk/1/hi/technology /4397159.stm

BBC News (2007, November 14). 'Virtual theft' leads to arrest. *Technology.* Retrieved from http://news.bbc.co.uk/2/hi/technology /7094764.stm

BBC News (2010, October 18). *Identity fraud now costs £1.9 bn, says fraud authority.* Retrieved 21 October 2010 from http://www.bbc.co.uk/news/business-11553199

BBC News (2010, August 26). *Facebook child abuse images ringleader jailed.* Retrieved from http://www.bbc.co.uk/news/uk-england-11101149

BBC News (2010a, September 24). *Stuxnet worm hits Iran nuclear plant staff computers.* Retrieved from http://www.bbc.co.uk/news/world-middle-east-11414483

BBC News (2010a, October 27). *LimeWire file-sharing service shut down in US.* Retrieved October 30, 2010 from http://www.bbc.co.uk/news/technology-11635320

BBC News (2010a, September 24). *Stuxnet worm hits Iran nuclear plant staff computers.* Retrieved from http://www.bbc.co.uk/news/world-middle-east-11414483

BBC News (2010b, January 25). *$2m file-sharing fine slashed to $54,000.* Retrieved October 30, 2010 from http://news.bbc.co.uk/2/hi/technology/ 8478305.stm

BBC News (2010b, September 23). *Stuxnet worm 'targeted high-value Iranian assets.* Retrieved from http://www.bbc.co.uk/news/technology-11388018

BBC News (2010c, October 6). *Sick PCs should be banned from the net says Microsoft.* Retrieved from http://www.bbc.co.uk/news/technology-11483008

BBC News (2010c, October 12). *Irish court rules in favour of ISPs in piracy case.* Retrieved October 30, 2010 from http://www.bbc.co.uk/news/technology-11521949

BBC News (2010d, September 30). *Lawyers to continue piracy fight.* Retrieved October 30, 2010 from http://www.bbc.co.uk/news/technology-11443861

BBC News (25th January 2010). *$2 million file sharing fine slashed to $54,000.* Retrieved 20th August 2010 from http://news.bbc.co.uk/2/hi /technology/8478305.stm

243

Becker, J. U., & Clement, M. (2006). Dynamics of illegal participation in peer-to-peer networks: Why do people illegally share media files? *Journal of Media Economics, 19*, 7–32. doi:10.1207/s15327736me1901_2

Beech, A. R. (1998). A psychometric typology of child abusers. *International Journal of Therapy and Comparative Criminology, 42*, 319–339. doi:10.1177/0306624X9804200405

Beech, A. R., & Ward, T. (2004). The integration of etiology and risk in sex offenders: A theoretical model. *Aggression and Violent Behavior, 10*, 31–63. doi:10.1016/j.avb.2003.08.002

Belsey, B. (n.d.). *Cyber bullying: An emerging threat to the 'always on' generation.* Retrieved November 3, 2010 from http://www.cyberbullying.ca/pdf/ Cyberbullying_Article_by_Bill_Belsey.pdf

Benkler, Y. (2006). *The Wealth of Networks*. New Haven, CT: Yale University Press.

Bente, G., Rüggenberg, S., Krämer, N. C., & Eschenburg, F. (2008). Avatar-Mediated networking: Increasing social presence and interpersonal trust in net-based collaborations. *Human Communication Research, 34*, 287–318. doi:10.1111/j.1468-2958.2008.00322.x

Benz, A. (2000). Two types of multi-level governance: Intergovernmental relations in German and EU regional policy. *Regional & Federal Studies, 10*, 21–44. doi:10.1080/13597560008421130

Beran, T., & Li, Q. (2005). Cyber-Harassment: A study of a new method for an old behaviour. *Journal of Educational Computing Research, 32*, 265–277. doi:10.2190/8YQM-B04H-PG4D-BLLH

Bevan, G., & Hood, C. (2006). Have targets Improved Performance in the English NHS? *British Medical Journal, 332*, 419–422. doi:10.1136/bmj.332.7538.419

Beveran, J. V. (2001). A Conceptual Model of Hacker Development and Motivations. *The Journal of Business, 1*(Issue 2). Retrieved from http://www.dvara.net/HK/beveren.pdf.

Bhal, K. T., & Leekha, N. D. (2008). Exploring cognitive moral logics using grounded theory: The case of software piracy. *Journal of Business Ethics, 81*, 635–646. doi:10.1007/s10551-007-9537-7

Bhat, C. S. (2008). Cyber Bullying: Overview and Strategies for School Counsellors, Guidance Officers, and All School Personnel. *Australian Journal of Guidance & Counselling, 18*(1), 53–66. doi:10.1375/ajgc.18.1.53

Bickley, J. A., & Beech, A. R. (2001). Classifying child abusers: its relevance to theory and clinical practice. *International Journal of Offender Therapy and Comparative Criminology, 45*, 51–69. doi:10.1177/0306624X01451004

Bissett, A., & Shipton, G. (1999). Some human dimensions of computer virus creation and infection. *International Journal of Human-Computer Studies, 52*, 899–913. doi:10.1006/ijhc.1999.0361

Blackburn, R. (1996). What is forensic psychology? *Legal and Criminological Psychology, 1*, 3–16. doi:10.1111/j.2044-8333.1996.tb00304.x

Blackburn, R. (1993). *The Psychology of Criminal Conduct: Theory, Research and Practice*. Chichester, England: John Wiley & Sons.

Blackwell-Young, J. (2008). Witness evidence (pp. 209-233). In G. Davies, C. Hollin & R. Bull (eds) *Forensic Psychology.* Chichester, West Susex: Wiley.

Blanchard, R. (2009). The DSM Diagnostic Criteria for Pedophilia. *Archives of Sexual Behavior, 39*, 304–316.. doi:10.1007/s10508-009-9536-0

Blanchard, R., Lykins, A. D., Wherrett, D., Kuban, M. E., Cantor, J. M., & Black, T. (2008). Pedophilia, Hebephilia, and the DSM-V. *Archives of Sexual Behavior, 38*, 335–350..doi:10.1007/s10508-008-9399-9

Blickle, G., Schlegel, A., Fassbender, P., & Klein, U. (2006). Some personality correlates of business white-collar crime. *Applied Psychology: An International Review, 55*, 220–233. doi:10.1111/j.1464-0597.2006.00226.x

Blundell, B., Sherry, M., Burke, A., & Sowerbutts, S. (2002). Child Pornography and the Internet: Accessibility and Policing. *Australian Police Journal, 56*(1), 59–65.

Bocij, P. (2006). *The Dark Side of the Internet: Protecting yourself and your family from online criminals*. Westport, CT: Praeger Publishers.

Bomberg, E., & Peterson, J. (1998). European Decision Making: the Role of Sub-national Authorities. *Political Studies, 46*, 219–235. doi:10.1111/1467-9248.00137

Bonta, J. (1996). Risk-needs assessment and treatment. In Harland, A. T. (Ed.), *Choosing correctional options that work* (pp. 18–32). Thousand Oaks: Sage.

Boswell, N. (2003). International Law Standards for Domestic Governance: The Impact of International Law on Domestic Governance. *Proceedings of the 101st Annual Meeting of the American Society of International Law, 133-137.*

Bottoms, A. E. (2007). Place, space, crime, and disorder. In Maguire, M., Morgan, R., & Reiner, R. (Eds.), *The Oxford Handbook of Criminology* (4th ed., pp. 528–574). Oxford: Oxford University Press.

Bouchard, S., St-Jacques, J., Robillard, G., & Renaud, P. (2008). Anxiety increases the feeling of presence in virtual reality. In *Presence Teleoperators and Virtual Environments, 376-391.* August.

Bourke, M. L., & Hernandez, A. E. (2009). The 'Butner Study' Redux: A report of the incidence of hands-on child victimization by child pornography offenders. *Journal of Family Violence, 24,* 183–191. doi:10.1007/s10896-008-9219-y

Boyd, C. (2008). *Profile: Gary McKinnon.* On BBC News Online (30th July 2008). Retrieved 24th February 2010 from http://news.bbc.co.uk/2/hi/uk_news/7839338.stm

Boyle, J. (1997). Foucault in cyberspace: surveillance, sovereignty, and hardwired censors. *University of Cincinnati Law Review, 66,* 177–205.

Bremmer, L. A., Koehler, D. J., Liberman, V., & Tversky, A. (1996). Overconfidence in probability and frequency judgements: A critical examination. *Organizational Behavior and Human Decision Processes, 65,* 212–219. doi:10.1006/obhd.1996.0021

Brenner, S. W. (2006). Defining Cybercrime: A Review of State and Federal Law. In Clifford, R. D. (Ed.), *Cybercrime: The Investigation, Prosecution and Defense of a Computer Related Crime* (2nd ed., pp. 13–95). Durham, NC: Carolina Academic Press.

Brenner, S. W. (2001). Is there such a thing as 'Virtual Crime'? *California Criminal Law Review, Volume 4.* Retrieved from http://www.boalt.org/bjcl/v4/v4brenner.pdf

British Psychological Society. (2010). *Forensic Psychology.* Retrieved 18th August 2010 from http://www.bps.org.uk/careers/what-do-psychologists-do/areas/forensic.cfm

British Recorded Music Industry (nd). *Protecting UK music.* Retrieved October 31 2010 from http://www.bpi.co.uk/category/protecting-uk-music.aspx

British Software Alliance. (BSA, 2010). *Fifth Annual BSA and IDC Global Software Piracy Study.* Retrieved on October 31 2010 from http://portal.bsa.org/idcglobalstudy2007/ studies/2007_global_piracy_study.pdf

Britton, P. (1997). *The Jigsaw Man.* London: Corgi.

Britton, P. (2000). *Picking up the Pieces.* London: Corgi.

Broidy, L., Cauffman, E., Espelage, D. L., Mazerolle, P., & Piquero, A. (2003). Sex differences in empathy and its relation to juvenile offending. *Violence and Victims, 18,* 503–516. doi:10.1891/vivi.2003.18.5.503

Brown, S. (2005). *Treating sex offenders: An introduction to sex offender treatment programmes.* Oregon: Willan.

Brown, I., Edwards, L., & Marsden, C. (2009). Information Security and Cybercrime. In Edwards, L., & Waelde, C. (Eds.), *Law and the Internet* (pp. 671–692). Portland, OR: Hart Publishing.

Brown, K., Jackson, M., & Cassidy, W. (2006). Cyberbullying: Developing policy to direct responses that are equitable and effective in addressing this special form of bullying. *Canadian Journal of Educational Administration and Policy, 57.* Retrieved November 6, 2010 from http://www.umanitoba.ca/publications/ cjeap/articles/brown_jackson_cassidy.html

Bryant, R., & Marshall, A. (2008). Criminological and Motivational Perspectives. In *Robin Bryant & Sarah Bryant (2008). Investigating Digital Crime* (pp. 231–248). Chichester: Wiley.

Bryant, R. (2008). The Challenge of Digital Crime. In Bryant, R. (Ed.), *Investigating Digital Crime* (pp. 1–26). Chichester, England: John Wiley & Sons.

Bryce, J. (2008). *Bridging the Digital Divide: Executive Summary.* London: Orange and the Cyberspace Research Unit.

Bryce, J. (2010). Online sexual exploitation of children and young people. In Y. Jewkes and M. Yar (eds.) *Handbook of Internet Crime* (320-342). Cullompton, England: Willan Publishing

Bryce, J., & Rutter, J. (2005). *Fake Nation: A study into an everyday crime. Report for the Organized Crime Task Force – Northern Ireland Office.* Retrieved 30th October 2010 from http://digiplay.info/files/FakeNation.pdf

Burgess, A. W., & Hartman, C. (1987). Child abuse aspects of child pornography. *Psychiatric Annals*, 248–253.

Burgess-Proctor, A., Patchin, J. W., & Hinduja, S. (2009). Cyberbullying and online harassment: Reconceptualizing the victimization of adolescent girls. In Garcia, V., & Clifford, J. (Eds.), *Female Crime Victims: Reality Reconsidered* (pp. 162–176). Upper Saddle River, NJ: Prentice Hall.

Burke, A., Sowerbutts, S., Blundell, B., & Sherry, M. (2002). Child Pornography and the Internet: Policing and Treatment Issues. *Psychiatry, Psychology and Law, 9*, 79–84. doi:10.1375/pplt.2002.9.1.79

Buschman, J. (2007). *The position of child pornography in sex offending: First Dutch polygraph findings.* Poster presented at the 26th Annual Conference of the Association for the Treatment of Sexual Abusers, San Diego, CA.

Calcetas-Santos, O. (2001). Child pornography on the internet. In Arnaldo, C. A. (Ed.), *Child abuse on the internet* (pp. 57–60). Paris: UNESCO.

Calcutt, A. (1999). *White Noise: An A-Z of the Contradictions in Cyberculture.* London: MacMillan Press Ltd.

Calder, M. (2004). *Child Sexual Abuse and the Internet: Tackling the New Frontier. Lyme Regis.* United Kingdom: Russell House Publishing.

Campbell, J., Greenauer, N., Macaluso, K., & End, C. (2007). Unrealistic optimism in internet events. *Computers in Human Behavior, 23*, 1273–1284..doi:10.1016/j.chb.2004.12.005

Campbell, B. (2008). *Agreement! The State, Conflict and Change in Northern Ireland.* London: Lawrence & Wishart.

Cannataci, J., & Mifsud-Bonnici, J. (2007). Weaving the Mesh: Finding Remedies in Cyberspace. *International Review of Law Computers & Technology, 21*, 59–78. doi:10.1080/13600860701281705

Canter, D. (1994). *Criminal Shadows: Inside the Mind of the Serial Killer.* London: HarperCollins Publishers.

Canter, D. (2003). *Mapping Murder: Walking in Killers' Footsteps.* London: Virgin Books.

Canter, D., & Youngs, D. (2009). *Investigative Psychology: Offender Profiling and the Analysis of Criminal Action.* Chichester, England: Wiley.

Carey, L. (2009, July 29). Can PTSD affect victims of identity theft: Psychologists say yes. *Associated Content.* Retrieved on 21 October 2010 from http://www.associatedcontent.com/article/ 2002924/can_ptsd_affect_victims_of_identity.html

Carney, M., & Rogers, M. (2004). The Trojan Made Me Do It: A First Step in Statistical Based Computer Forensics Event Reconstruction. *International Journal of Digital Evidence, 2 (4).* Retrieved 28th April 2008 from http://cs.ua.edu/691Dixon/Forensics/trojan.pdf

Carrier, B., & Spafford, E. (2003). Getting physical with digital forensics investigation. *International Journal of Digital Evidence (Fall 2003).*

Casey, E. (2002). *Handbook of computer crime investigation: forensic tools and technology.* San Diego, Calif.: Academic Press.

Cawson, P., Wattam, C., Brooker, S., & Kelly, G. (2000). *Child Maltreatment in the UK: A Study of the Prevalence of Child Abuse and Neglect.* London: NSPCC.

Chesebro, J. W., & Bonsall, D. G. (1989). *Computer-Mediated Communication: Human Relationships in a Computerised World.* Tuscaloosa, AL: The University of Alabama Press.

Chiesa, R., Ducci, S., & Ciappi, S. (2009). *Profiling Hackers: The Science of Criminal Profiling as Applied to the World of Hacking.* Boca Raton, FL: CRC press.

Chiesa, R., Ducci, S., & Ciappi, S. (2009). *Profiling Hackers: The Science of Criminal Profiling as Applied to the World of Hacking.* Boca Raton, FL: Auerbach Publications.

Child Exploitation and Online Protection (CEOP) Centre. (2010). Annual Review 2009-2010. Retrieved from http://www.ceop.police.uk/Documents/ CEOP_Annual-Review_09-10.pdf

Clarke, R. V., & Felson, M. (1993). *Routine activity and rational choice*. New Brunswick, NJ: Transaction Publishers.

Club Penguin. (n.d.). Retrieved from http:// www.club-penguin.com/ company/news/ 070801-the-walt-disney-company.htm

CNET. (2007, January 5). *Images: Virtual politics in 'Second Life'*. Retrieved from; http://news.cnet.com/2300-1028_3-6147452-1.html?tag=mncol

CNW. (2007, August 8). *BarbieGirls.com the first global virtual world designed for girls, celebrates 4 million registered users, making it the fastest growing virtual world online*. Retrieved from http://www.newswire.ca/en/releases/archive/August2007/08/c4844.html

Cohen, L. E., & Felson, M. (1979). Social change and crime rate change: a routine activity approach. *American Sociological Review*, *4*, 588–609. doi:10.2307/2094589

Cohen, A. (2010). Cyberterrorism: Are we Legally Ready? *Journal of International Business and Law*, *9*, 1.

Colarik, A. M., & Janczewski, L. J. (2008). Introduction to Cyber Warfare and Cyber Terrorism. In Janczewski, L. J., & Colarik, A. M. (Eds.), *Cyber Warfare and Cyber Terrorism* (pp. xiii–xxx). Hershey, PA: Information Science Reference.

Coleman, J. (1994). *The criminal elite: The sociology of white collar crime*. New York: St. Martin's Press.

Collins, J. M. (2006). *Investigating Identity Theft: A Guide for Businesses, Law Enforcement, and Victims*. Hoboken, NJ: John Wiley & Sons.

Computer Security Institute. *(2009)*. CSI Computer crime and security survey 2009. *Retrieved 8th March 2010 from* http://gocsi.com/survey

Computer Security Institute (CSI). (December, 2009). *14th Annual CSI Computer Crime and Security Survey, Executive Summary*. Retrieved 7th October 2010 from http://pathmaker.biz/whitepapers /CSISurvey2009.pdf

Conner, B. T., Stein, J. A., & Longshore, D. (2008). Examining self-control as a multidimensional predictor of crime and drug use in adolescents with criminal histories. *The Journal of Behavioral Health Services & Research*, *36*, 137–149. doi:10.1007/s11414-008-9121-7

Conway, M. (2002). Reality Bytes: Cyberterrorism and Terrorist Use of the Internet. *First Monday*, *7*, 11.

Conway, M. (2006). Terrorist 'use' of the Internet and fighting back. *Information and Security: An International Journal*, *19*, 9–30.

Conway, M. (2007). Cyberterrorism: hype and reality. In Armistead, L. (Ed.), *Information warfare: separating hype from reality* (pp. 73–93). Potomac Books, Inc.

Cook, S. (2001). *The Real Cracker: Investigating the Criminal Mind*. London: Channel 4 books.

Cooney, R., & Lang, A. (2007). Taking Uncertainty Seriously: Adaptive Governance and International Trade. *European Journal of International Law*, *18*, 523. doi:10.1093/ejil/chm030

Cooper, A., Delmonico, D.L. & Burg, R. (2000). Cybersex users, abusers, and compulsives: New findings and implications. *Cybersex: The dark side of the force A special issue of the Journal of Sexual Addiction & Compulsivity*, *7*, 5-27.

Cortoni, F., & Marshall, W. L. (2001). Sex as a coping strategy and its relationship to juvenile sexual history and intimacy in Sexual Offenders. *Sexual Abuse*, *13*, 27–43. doi:10.1177/107906320101300104

Council of Europe. (2001). *Convention on Cybercrime*. Retrieved from http://conventions.coe.int/Treaty/ en/ Treaties/Html/185.htm

Cox, B. J., MacPherson, P. S. R., Enns, M. W., & McWilliams, L. A. (2004). Neuroticisim and self-criticism associated with posttraumatic stress disorder in a nationally representative sample. *Behaviour Research and Therapy*, *42*, 105–144..doi:10.1016/S0005-7967(03)00105-0

Cronan, T. P., Foltz, C. B., & Jones, T. W. (2006, June). Piracy, Computer Crime and IS Misuse at the University. *Communications of the ACM*, *49*, 85–89. doi:10.1145/1132469.1132472

Cushing, K. (2001, May10). Would you turn to the dark side? Computer Weekly, *p. 34.*

Cybercrime (n.d.) in *PC Magazine Encyclopedia*. Retrieved from http://www.pcmag.com/encyclopedia_term/0,2542,t=cybercrime&i=40628,00.asp

Cybercrime (n.d.) in *Princeton WordNet*. Retrieved from http://wordnetweb.princeton.edu/ perl/webwn?s=cybercrime

Cybercrime (n.d.). In *Macmillan Dictionary*. Retrieved from http://www.macmillandictionary.com /dictionary/british/cybercrime

Cybercrime (n.d.). In *New World Encyclopedia*. Retrieved from http://www.newworldencyclopedia.org /entry/Cyber_crime

D'Astous, A., Colbert, F., & Montpetit, D. (2005). Music piracy on the web – How effective are anti-piracy arguments? Evidence from the Theory of Planned Behavior. *Journal of Consumer Policy, 28,* 289–310. doi:10.1007/s10603-005-8489-5

Davey, G. (2008). *Psychopathology: Research, assessment and treatment in clinical psychology.* Chichester, England: John Wiley & Sons Ltd.

Davies, G., Hollin, C., & Bull, R. (2008). *Forensic Psychology.* Chichester, England: Wiley.

Dehue, F., Bolman, C., & Völlink, T. (2008). Cyberbullying: Youngers' Experiences and Parental Perception. *Cyberpsychology & Behavior, 11,* 217–223. doi:10.1089/cpb.2007.0008

DeMasi, F. (2007). The paedophile and his inner world: Theoretical and clinical considerations on the analysis of a patient. *The International Journal of Psycho-Analysis, 88,* 147–165. doi:10.1516/B5AJ-CG0B-E4HC-WB07

DeMore, S. W., Fisher, J. D., & Baron, R. M. (1988). The equity-control model as a predictor of vandalism among college students. *Journal of Applied Social Psychology, 18,* 80–91. doi:10.1111/j.1559-1816.1988.tb00007.x

Denning, D. E. (2007a). A View of cyberterrorism five years later. In Himma, K. E. (Ed.), *Internet Security: Hacking, Counterhacking and Society* (pp. 123–140). Sudbury, MA: Jones & Bartlett Publishers.

Denning, D. E. (2010). Terror's web: how the Internet is transforming terrorism. In Jewkes, Y., & Yar, M. (Eds.), *Handbook of Internet Crime* (pp. 194–213). Cullompton, England: Willan.

Denning, D. E. (2007b). Cyberterrorism – Testimony before the special oversight panel on terrorism committee on armed services US House of Representatives. In Linden, E. V. (Ed.), *Focus on Terrorism* (Vol. 9, pp. 71–76). New York: Nova Science Publishers Inc.

Denning, D. E. (2001). Activisim, Hacktivism and Cyberterrorism: The Internet as a Tool for Influencing Foreign Policy. In J. Arquilla and D.F. Ronfeldt's (eds.) *Networks and Netwars: The Future of Terror, Crime and Militancy, Issue 1382* (pp. 239–288). Santa Monica, CA: RAND.

Derezotes, D., & Snowden, L. (1990). Cultural factors in the intervention of child maltreatment. *Child and Adolescent Social Work, 7,* 161–175. doi:10.1007/BF00757652

Dhamija, R., Tygar, J. D., & Hearst, M. (2006). Why Phishing Works. [Montreal: CHI.]. *CHI, 2006*(April), 22–27.

Dibbell, J. (1993). *A Rape in Cyberspace*. Retrieved from http://loki.stockton.edu/~kinsellt/stuff/ dibbelrapeincyberspace.html

Dibbell, J. (1998). *A Rape in Cyberspace*. Retrieved from http://www.juliandibbell.com/texts/ bungle.html

DiMaggio, C., & Galea, S. (2006). The behavioural consequences of terrorism: a meta-analysis. *Academic Emergency Medicine, 13,* 559–566. doi:10.1111/j.1553-2712.2006.tb01008.x

Dobson, A. (2003). Caught in the Net. *Care and Health,* Feb. 13 pp. 6–9.

Dombrowski, S. C. (2003). Mandated reporting for mental health professionals: An overview. *Directions in Rehabilitation Counselling, 14,* 71–80.

Dombrowski, S. C., LeMasney, J. W., Ahia, C. E., & Dickson, S. A. (2004). Protecting children from online sexual predators: Technological, Psychoeducational and Legal Considerations. *Professional Psychology, Research and Practice, 35,* 65–73. doi:10.1037/0735-7028.35.1.65

Donato, L. (2009). An Introduction to How Criminal Profiling Could be used as a support for computer hacking investigations. *Journal of Digital Forensic Practice*, *2*, 183–195. doi:10.1080/15567280903140946

Dooney, S., & O'Toole, J. (1998). *Irish Government Today*. Dublin: Gill and Macmillan.

Douglas, J., & Olshaker, M. (1995). *Mind Hunter: Inside the FBI's Elite Serial Crime Unit*. New York: Pocket Books.

Douglas, J., & Olshaker, M. (1999). *The Anatomy of Motive*. London: Simon & Schuster.

Douglas, J., & Olshaker, M. (2000). *The Cases that Haunt Us*. London: Pocket Books.

Douglas, J. E., Ressler, R., Burgess, A., & Hartman, C. (1986). Criminal profiling from crime scene analysis. *Behavioral Sciences & the Law*, *4*, 401–421. doi:10.1002/bsl.2370040405

Douglas, K. S., & Dutton, D. G. (2001). Assessing the link between stalking and domestic violence. *Aggression and Violent Behavior*, *6*, 519–546. doi:10.1016/S1359-1789(00)00018-5

Duffield, G. & Grabosky, P. (2001, March). The Psychology of Fraud. *Australian Institute of Criminology: Trends & Issues in crime and criminal justice, No. 199.*

Dunleavy, P., Margetts, H., Bastow, S., & Tinkler, J. (2006). New Public Management is Dead – Long Live Digital-Era Governance. *Journal of Public Administration: Research and Theory*, *16*, 467–494. doi:10.1093/jopart/mui057

Dworkin, R. (1986). *Law's Empire*. Oregon: Hart Publishing.

Eckersley, R. (2007). Soft law, hard politics, and the Climate Change Treaty. In Reus-Smit, C. (Ed.), *The Politics of International Law* (pp. 80–105). Cambridge: Cambridge University Press.

Edelson, E. (2003). The 419 scam: Information warfare on the spam front and a proposal for local filtering. *Computers & Security*, *22*, 392–401. doi:10.1016/S0167-4048(03)00505-4

Edestein, R. S., Luten, T. L., & Ekman, P. (2006). Detecting lies in children and adults. *Law and Human Behavior*, *30*, 1–10..doi:10.1007/s10979-006-9031-2

Edgar-Nevill, D., & Stephens, P. (2008). Countering Cybercrime. In Bryant, R. (Ed.), *Investigating Digital Crime* (pp. 79–96). Chichester, England: Wiley.

Edgar-Nevill, D. (2008). Internet Grooming and Paedophile Crimes. In Bryant, R. (Ed.), *Investigating Digital Crime* (pp. 195–209). Chichester: Wiley.

Educational Games Research. (n.d.). Retrieved from http://edugamesresearch. com/ blog/ category/webkinz/

Edwards, A. (2002). The Moderator as an Emerging Democratic Intermediary: The Role of the Moderator in Internet Discussions about Public Issues. *Information Polity*, *7*, 3–20.

Einhorn, H. J., & Hogarth, R. M. (1978). Confidence in judgement: Persistence of the illusion of validity. *Psychological Review*, *85*, 395–416. doi:10.1037/0033-295X.85.5.395

Elliott, I. A., Beech, A. R., Mandeville-Norden, R., & Hayes, E. (2009). Psychological profiles of internet sexual offenders: Comparisons with contact sexual offenders. *Sexual Abuse*, *21*, 76–92. doi:10.1177/1079063208326929

Elliott, M., Browne, K., & Kilcoyne, J. (1995). Child sexual abuse prevention: What offenders tell us. *Child Abuse & Neglect*, *19*, 579–594. doi:10.1016/0145-2134(95)00017-3

Emigh, J. (2008, October 24). Online gamer arrested for 'virtual murder' in Japan. *Betanews.* Retrived from http://www.betanews.com/article/Online-gamer-arrested-for-virtual-murder-in-Japan/1224888499

Endrass, J., Urbaniok, F., Hammermeister, L. C., Benz, C., Elbert, T., Laubacher, A., & Rossegger, A. (2009). The consumption of Internet child pornography and violent and sex offending. *BMC Psychiatry*, *9*, 43.. doi:10.1186/1471-244X-9-43

Ess, C. (2009). *Digital Media Ethics*. Cambridge, England: Polity Press.

Evans, M. (2009). Gordon Brown and public management reform – a project in search of a 'big idea'? *Policy Studies*, *30*, 33–51. doi:10.1080/01442870802576181

EVElopedia. (n.d.) *Corporation Management Guide*. Retrieved from http://wiki.eveonline.com/en/wiki/Corp_theft#Corp_Theft

Eysenck, H. J. (1977). *Crime and Personality* (3rd ed.). London: Routledge.

Eysenck, S. B. G., & Eysenck, H. J. (1970). Crime and personality: an empirical study of the three-factor theory. *The British Journal of Criminology, 10*, 225–239.

Eysenck, S. B. G., & Eysenck, H. J. (1977). Personality differences between prisoners and controls. *Psychological Reports, 40*, 1023–1028. doi:10.2466/pr0.1977.40.3c.1023

Eysenck, H. J. (1996). Personality theory and the problem of criminality. In J. Muncie, E. McLaughlin & M. Langan (Eds.) *Criminological Perspectives: A reader* (pp. 81-98). London: Sage Publications Ltd. (Reprinted from *Applying psychology to Imprisonment*, pp. 30-46, by B. McGurk, D. Thornton and M. Williams, Eds., 1987, London: HMSO.

Farrell, G., & Pease, K. (2006). Preventing Repeat Residential Burglary Victimisation. In Welsh, B., & Farrington, D. (Eds.), *Preventing Crime: What works for children, offenders, victims and places* (pp. 161–177). Dordrecht, The Netherlands: Springer.

Farrington, D. P., Jolliffe, D., Loeber, R., Stouthamer-Loeber, M., & Kalb, L. M. (2001). The concentration of offenders in families, and family criminality in the prediction of boys' delinquency. *Journal of Adolescence, 24*, 579–596. doi:10.1006/jado.2001.0424

Farrington, D. P. (1990). Age, period, cohort and offending. In Gottfredson, D. M., & Clarke, R. V. (Eds.), *Policy and Theory in Criminal Justice: Contributions in Honour of Leslie T. Wilkins* (pp. 51–75). Aldershot: Avebury.

Fauerbach, J. A., Lawrence, J. W., Schmidt, C. W., Munster, A. M., & Costa, P. T. (2000). Personality Predictors of Injury-Related Posttraumatic Stress Disorder. *The Journal of Nervous and Mental Disease, 188*, 510–517. doi:10.1097/00005053-200008000-00006

Federal Trade Commission. (2006). *Identity theft survey report*. Retrieved 21 October 2010 from http://www.ftc.gov/os/2007/11/ SynovateFinalReportIDTheft2006.pdf.

Fergusson, D. M., Horwood, L. J., & Nagin, D. S. (2000). Offending trajectories in a New Zealand birth cohort. *Criminology, 38*, 525–552. doi:10.1111/j.1745-9125.2000.tb00898.x

Finch, E. (2003). What a tangled web we weave: identity theft and the internet. In Jewkes, Y. (Ed.), *Dot.cons: Crime, deviance and identity on the internet* (pp. 86–104). Cullompton, England: Willan Publishing.

Finch, E. (2007). The problem of stolen identity and the Internet. In Jewkes, Y. (Ed.), *Crime Online* (pp. 29–43). Cullompton, England: Willan Publishing.

Finkelhor, D. (1984). *Child Sexual Abuse. New Theory and Research*. New York: Free Press.

Finkelhor, D. (1986). *A Source Book on Child Sexual Abuse*. London: Sage.

Finkelhor, D. (2009). The Prevention of Childhood Sexual Abuse. *The Future of Children, 19*, 169–194. doi:10.1353/foc.0.0035

Finkelhor, D., & Lewis, I. A. (1988). An epidemiologic approach to the study of child molesters. In Quinsey, R. A., & Quinsey, V. L. (Eds.), *Human Sexual Aggression; Current Perspectives. Annals of the New York Academy of Sciences*. New York: Plenum.

Finn, J., & Atkinson, T. (2009). Promoting the safe and strategic use of technology for victims of intimate partner violence: Evaluation of the Technology Safety Project. *Journal of Family Violence, 24*, 53–59. doi:10.1007/s10896-008-9207-2

Finn, J., & Banach, M. (2000). Victimisation online: The down side of seeking human services for women on the Internet. *Cyberpsychology & Behavior, 3*, 243–254. doi:10.1089/109493100316102

Fisher, W., & Barak, A. (2001). Internet pornography: A social psychological perspective on internet sexuality. *Journal of Sex Research, 38*(4), 312–323. doi:10.1080/00224490109552102

Fogg, B. J. (2003). *Persuasive Technology; Using computers to change what we think and do*. San Francisco: Morgan Kaufmann Publishers.

Fogg, B. J. (2008). Mass interpersonal persuasion: An early view of a new phenomenon. In *Proc. Third International Conference on Persuasive Technology, Persuasive 2008*. Berlin: Springer.

Fötinger, C. S., & Ziegler, W. (2004). *Understanding a hacker's mind – a psychological insight into the hijacking of identities.* Danube-University Krems, Austria: RSA Security.

Fottrell, M. (Producer) & Wiseman, L. (Director). (2007). *Live Free or Die Hard / Die Hard 4.0* [Motion picture]. United States of America: 20th Century Fox.

Foucault, M. (1978). The history of sexuality: *Vol. 1. An introduction.* New York: Pantheon.

Frei, A., Erenay, N., Dittmann, V., & Graf, M. (2005). Paedophilia on the internet – a study of 33 convicted offenders in the Canton of Lucerne. *Swiss Medical Weekly, 135,* 488–494.

Frontline, P. B. S. (nd). *Studying the psychology of virus writers and hackers: an interview with researcher Sarah Gordon.* Retrieved 26th September 2010 from http://www.pbs.org/wgbh/pages/frontline/ shows/hackers/whoare/psycho.html

Furnell, S. (2010). Hackers, viruses and malicious software. In Jewkes, Y., & Yar, M. (Eds.), *Handbook of Internet Crime* (pp. 173–193). Cullompton, England: Willan.

Gabriel, R., Ferrando, L., Sainz Corton, E., Mingote, C., Garcia-Camba, E., Fernandez-Liria, A. G., & Galea, S. (2007). Psychopathological consequences alter a terrorist attack: an epidemiological study among victims, police officers, and the general population. *European Psychiatry, 22,* 339–346. doi:10.1016/j.eurpsy.2006.10.007

Garau, M., Slater, M., Vinayagamoorthy, V., Brogni, A., Steed, A., & Sasse, M. A. (2003). *The Impact of Avatar Realism and Eye Gaze Control on the perceived Quality of Communication in a Shared Immersive Virtual Environment.* SIGCHI.

Garlik (2009). UK Cybercrime Report 2009. Published September 2009. By Stefan Fafinski, *Neshan Minassian of Invenio Research.* Retrieved 8th March 2010 from http://www.garlik.com/cybercrime_report.php

Geiselman, R. E., Fisher, R. P., MacKinnon, D. P., & Holland, H. L. (1986). Enhancement of eyewitness memory with the cognitive interview. *The American Journal of Psychology, 99,* 385–401. doi:10.2307/1422492

Giddens, A. (2008). *The Third Way: The Renewal of Social Democracy.* Cambridge: Polity.

Gleeson, S. (2008, July 16). Freed hacker could work for police. *The New Zealand Herald.* p. A3

Glueck, B. C. Jr. (1955). *Final report: Research project for the study and treatment of persons convicted of crimes involving sexual aberrations, June 1952 to June 1955.* New York: New York State Department of Mental Hygiene.

Goldsmith, J. L. (1998). Against Cyberanarchy. *The University of Chicago Law Review. University of Chicago. Law School, 65,* 1199–1250. doi:10.2307/1600262

Goldstein, A. P. (1996). *The Psychology of Vandalism.* New York: Plenham Press.

Gopal, R., Sanders, G. L., Bhattacharjee, S., Agrawal, M., & Wagner, S. (2004). A behavioral model of digital music piracy. *Journal of Organizational Computing and Electronic Commerce, 14,* 89–105. doi:10.1207/s15327744joce1402_01

Gordon, S. (1993). Inside the Mind of the Dark Avenger. *Virus News International, January 1993.* Abridged version retrieved on 7th October 2010 from http://www.research.ibm.com/antivirus/ SciPapers/Gordon/Avenger.html

Gordon, S. (1994). *The Generic Virus Writer. Presented at the 4th International Virus Bulletin Conference.* Jersey. 8-9th September. Retrieved on 7th October 2010 from http://vx.netlux.org/lib/asg03.html

Gordon, S. (1996). The generic virus writer II. In *Proceedings of the 6th International Virus Bulletin Conference,* Brighton, UK, 19th-20th September. Retrieved on 7th October 2010 from http://vx.netlux.org/lib/static/vdat/epgenvr2.htm

Gordon, S. (2000). Virus writers: The End of the Innocence? In *Proceedings of the 10th International Virus Bulletin Conference.* Orlando, FL, 28-29th September. Retrieved on 7th October 2010 from http://www.research.ibm.com/antivirus/ SciPapers/VB2000SG.htm

Gordon, S., & Ford, R. (2003). *Cyberterrorism?* Retrieved from the Symantec Security Response White Papers website: http://www.symantec.com/avcenter/reference / cyberterrorism.pdf

Gottfredson, M. R., & Hirschi, T. (1990). *A general theory of crime.* Stanford, CA: Stanford University Press.

Greenberg, A. (2007, July 16). The top countries for cybercrime: China overtakes U.S. in hosting web pages that install malicious programs. *MSNBC.* Retrieved November 20, 2010 from http://www.msnbc.msn.com/id/19789995/ns/technology_and_science-security

Greenhouse, L. (2007, February 27). Justices decline case on 200-year sentence for man who possessed child pornography. *The New York Times*, p. A13.

Griffin, D., & Tversky, A. (1992). The weighting of evidence and the determinants of confidence. *Cognitive Psychology*, *24*, 411–435. doi:10.1016/0010-0285(92)90013-R

Groth, A. N., & Birnbaum, H. J. (1978). Adult sexual orientation and attraction to underage persons. *Archives of Sexual Behavior*, *7*, 175–181. doi:10.1007/BF01542377

Groth, A. N., Burgess, A. W., & Holmstrom, L. L. (1977). Rape, power, anger and sexuality. *The American Journal of Psychiatry*, *134*, 1239–1248.

Grove, S. (2007, January 19). *A Second Life in Politics*. Retrieved from; http://abcnews.go.com/Politics/Story?id=2809023&page=1

Grubb, A., & Harrower, J. (2008). Attribution of blame in cases of rape: An analysis of participant gender, type of rape and perceived similarity to the victim. *Aggression and Violent Behavior*, *13*, 396–405. doi:10.1016/j.avb.2008.06.006

Gudaitis, T. M. (1998). The missing link in information security: Three dimensional profiling. *Cyberpsychology & Behavior*, *1*, 321–340..doi:10.1089/cpb.1998.1.321

Gudjonsson, G. H. (2003). *The psychology of interrogations and confessions: A handbook*. Chichester, West Sussex: Wiley.

Gudjonsson, G. H., & Haward, L. R. C. (1998). *Forensic Psychology: A guide to practice*. New York: Routledge.

Guest, T. (2007). *Second Lives: A Journey Through Virtual Worlds*. London: Random House.

Gunkel, D. J. (2005). Editorial: Introduction to hacking and hacktivism. *New Media & Society*, *7*, 595–597. doi:10.1177/1461444805056007

Haines, H. H. (1996). *Against Capital Punishment: The Anti-Death Penalty Movement in America 1972-1994*. Oxford University Press.

Hall, G. C. (1996). *Theory-Based Assessment, Treatment and Prevention of Sexual Aggression*. Oxford: Oxford University Press.

Hall, G. C., & Hirschman, R. (1991). Towards a theory of sexual aggression: a quadripartite model. *Journal of Consulting and Clinical Psychology*, *59*, 662–669. doi:10.1037/0022-006X.59.5.662

Halsey, M., & Young, A. (2002). The Meanings of Graffiti and Municipal Administration. *Australian and New Zealand Journal of Criminology*, *35*, 165–186. doi:10.1375/acri.35.2.165

Haney, C., Banks, C., & Zimbardo, P. (1973). Interpersonal dynamics in a simulated prison. *International Journal of Criminology and Penology*, *1*, 69–97.

Hanson, R. K., & Bussiere, M. T. (1998). Predicting relapse: a meta-analysis of sexual offender recidivism studies. *Journal of Consulting and Clinical Psychology*, *66*, 348–362. doi:10.1037/0022-006X.66.2.348

Hanson, R. K., & Harris, A. J. R. (2000). Where should we intervene? Dynamic predictors of sexual offence recidivism. *Criminal Justice and Behavior*, *27*, 6–35. doi:10.1177/0093854800027001002

Hart, H. L. A. (1994). *The Concept of Law* (2nd ed.). Oxford, UK: Oxford University Press.

Hastie, R. (1993). Introduction. In R. Hastie (ed.) *Inside the Juror: The Psychology of Juror Decision Making* (3-41). Cambridge: Cambridge University Press.

Hay, C. (1996). *Re-Stating Social and Political Change*. London: Open University Press.

Hayes, D. (1989). *Behind the Silicon Curtain: The Seductions of Work in a Lonely Era*. London: Free Association Books.

Hazler, R. J. (1996). *Breaking the cycle of violence: Interventions for bullying and victimization*. Bristol, PA: Accelerated Development.

Hessing, D. J., Elffers, H., Robben, H. S. J., & Webley, P. (1993). Needy or Greedy? The social psychology of individuals who fraudulently claim unemployment benefits. *Journal of Applied Social Psychology, 23*, 226–243. doi:10.1111/j.1559-1816.1993.tb01084.x

Higgins, G. E. (2007). Digital piracy: An examination of low self-control and motivation using short-term longitudinal data. *Cyberpsychology & Behavior, 10*, 523–529. doi:10.1089/cpb.2007.9995

Higgins, G. E., Fell, B. D., & Wilson, A. L. (2006). Digital piracy: Assessing the contributions of an integrated self-control theory and social learning theory. *Criminal Justice Studies: A Critical Journal of Crime. Law and Society, 19*, 3–22.

Higgins, G. E., Wolfe, S. E., & Marcum, C. D. (2008). Music piracy and neutralization: A preliminary trajectory analysis from short-term longitudinal data. *International Journal of Cyber Criminology, 2*, 324–336.

Hill, C. W. (2007). Digital piracy: causes consequences and strategic responses. *Asia Pacific Journal of Management, 24*, 9–25. doi:10.1007/s10490-006-9025-0

Hinduja, S., & Patchin, J. W. (2008). Cyberbullying: An exploratory analysis of factors related to offending and victimisation. *Deviant Behavior, 29*, 129–156.. doi:10.1080/01639620701457816

Hinduja, S., & Patchin, J. W. (2010). Bullying, cyberbullying and suicide. *Archives of Suicide Research, 14*, 206–221..doi:10.1080/13811118.2010.494133

Hinduja, S. (2007). Neutralization theory and online software piracy: An empirical analysis. *Ethics and Information Technology, 9*, 187–204. doi:10.1007/s10676-007-9143-5

Hinduja, S., & Patchin, J. (2010b). Cyberbullying *fact sheet: Identification, Prevention, and Response*. Cyberbullying Research Center. Retrieved November 6, 2010, from http://www.cyberbullying.us/Cyberbullying_Identification_Prevention_Response_Fact_Sheet.pdf

Hinduja, S., & Patchin, J. W. (2009). *Bullying Beyond the Schoolyard: Preventing and Responding to Cyberbullying.* Thousand Oaks, CA: Sage Publications (Corwin Press).

Hines, D., & Finkelhor, D. (2007). Statutory sex crime relationships between juveniles and adults: A review of social scientific research. *Aggression and Violent Behavior, 12*, 300–314. doi:10.1016/j.avb.2006.10.001

Hof, R. (2006). *Real Threat to Virtual Goods in Second Life*. Retrieved from http://www.businessweek.com/the_thread/techbeat/archives/2006/11/real_threat_to.html

Holahan, C. (2006). *The Dark Side of Second Life*. Retrieved from http://www.businessweek.com/technology/content/nov2006/tc20061121_727243.htm

Holt, T. J., & Graves, D. C. (2007). A Qualitative analysis of advance fee fraud e-mail schemes. *International Journal of Cyber Criminology, 1 (1)*. Retrieved 21 October 2010 from http://www.cybercrimejournal.com/thomas&danielleijcc.htm

Holtfreter, K., Reisig, M. D., Piquero, N. L., & Piquero, A. R. (2010). Low self-control and fraud: Offending, victimization and their overlap. *Criminal Justice and Behavior, 37*, 188–203. doi:10.1177/0093854809354977

Home Office. *(2005)*. Fraud and Technology Crimes: findings from the 2002/03 British Crime Survey and 2003 Offending, Crime and Justice Survey. *(Home Office Online Report 34/05). Retrieved on 26th July 2005 from*www.homeoffice.gov.uk/rds/pdfs05/rdsolr3405.pdf

Hood, C. (1983). *The Tools of Government*. Basingstoke, UK: Macmillan.

Hood, S. K., & Carter, M. M. (2008). A Preliminary Examination of Trauma History, Locus of Control, and PTSD Symptom Severity in African American Women. *The Journal of Black Psychology, 34*, 179–191. doi:10.1177/0095798407310541

Hood, C., & Margetts, H. (2007). *The Tools of Government in the Digital Age*. Palgrave Macmillan.

Horgan, J. (2005). *The Psychology of Terrorism*. Abingdon, England: Routledge.

Horgan, J. (2008). From profiles to *pathways* and roots to *routes*: Perspectives from psychology on radicalization into terrorism. *The Annals of the American Academy of Political and Social Science, 618*, 80–94. doi:10.1177/0002716208317539

Horgan, J., & Taylor, M. (2001). The making of a terrorist. *Jane's Intelligence Review*, *13*, 16–18.

Horgan, J. (2003a). The Search for the terrorist personality. In Silke, A. (Ed.), *Terrorists, Victims and Society: psychological perspectives on terrorism and its consequences*. John Wiley & Sons.

Horgan, J. (2003b). Leaving terrorism behind: An individual perspective. In Silke, A. (Ed.), *Terrorists, Victims and Society: psychological perspectives on terrorism and its consequences*. John Wiley & Sons.

Howitt, D. (1999). *Introduction to Forensic & Criminal Psychology* (3rd ed.). Harlow, England: Pearson Education Ltd.

Howitt, D. (1995). Pornography and the paedophile: Is it criminogenic? *The British Journal of Medical Psychology*, *68*, 15–27. doi:10.1111/j.2044-8341.1995.tb01810.x

Howitt, D., & Cumberbatch, G. (1990). *Pornography: Impacts and Influences. A Review of Available Research Evidence on the Effects of Pornography*. London: Home Office Research and Planning Unit.

Howitt, D., & Sheldon, K. (2007). The role of cognitive distortions in paedophilic offending: Internet and contact offenders compared. *Psychology, Crime & Law*, *13*, 469–486. doi:10.1080/10683160601060564

Howitt, D. (2009). *Introduction to Forensic and Criminal Psychology* (3rd ed.). Pearson.

Howitt, D. (2006). Paedophilia prevention and the Law. In Moss, K., & Stephens, M. (Eds.), *Crime Reduction and the Law. Abington*. Routledge.

Hoyle, C., & Zedner, L. (2007). Victims, Victimization, and Criminal Justice. In Maguire, M., Morgan, R., & Reiner, R. (Eds.), *The Oxford Handbook of Criminology* (4th ed., pp. 461–495). Oxford University Press.

Hsu, J., & Shiue, C. (2008). Consumers' willingness to pay for non-pirated software. *Journal of Business Ethics*, *81*, 715–732. doi:10.1007/s10551-007-9543-9

Huang, D., Rau, P. P., & Salvendy, G. (2010). Perception of information security. *Behaviour & Information Technology*, *29*, 221–232. doi:10.1080/01449290701679361

Hughes, D., Rayson, P., Walkerdine, J., Lee, K., Greenwood, P., Rashid, A., et al. (2008). *Supporting law enforcement in digital communities through natural language analysis*. In Proceedings of IWCF'08 Washington, DC, USA, August, 2008

Hunter, A. (2009). High-Tech Rascality: Asperger's Syndrome, Hackers, Geeks, and Personality Types in the ICT Industry. *New Zealand Sociology*, *24*, 39–61.

Huss, M. T. (2009). *Forensic Psychology: Research, clinical practice, and applications*. Chichester, England: Wiley-Blackwell.

Ingram, J., & Hinduja, S. (2008). Neutralizing music piracy: an empirical examination. *Deviant Behavior*, *29*, 334–366. doi:10.1080/01639620701588131

International Federation of Phonographic Industries. (IFPI, 2010). *IFPI Digital Music Report: Music how, when, where you want it*. Retrieved October 31 2010 from http://www.ifpi.org/content/library /DMR2010.pdf

Jahankhani, H., & Al-Nemrat, A. (2010). Examination of Cyber-criminal Behaviour. *International Journal of Information Science and Management, Special Issue*. January/June 2010. Retrieved 18th August 2010 from http://www.srlst.com/ijist/special%20issue/ijism-special-issue2010_files/Special-Issue201041.pdf

Jaishkankar, K. (2008). Identity related crime in cyberspace: Examining phishing and its impact. *International Journal of Cyber Criminology*, *2*, 10–15.

Jamel, J. (2008). Crime and its causes. In Davies, G., Hollin, C., & Bull, R. (Eds.), *Forensic Psychology* (pp. 3–28). Chichester, England: John Wiley & Sons Ltd.

Jay, E. (2007). *Rape in Cyberspace. 2007*. Retrieved from https://lists.secondlife.com/pipermail/ educators/2007-May/009237.html

Jeffery, C. (2000). Sub-National Mobilization and European Integration: Does it Make Any Difference? *Journal of Common Market Studies*, *38*, 1–23. doi:10.1111/1468-5965.00206

Jewkes, Y., & Yar, M. (2010). Introduction: the Internet, cybercrime and the challenges of the twenty-first century. In Jewkes, Y., & Yar, M. (Eds.), *Handbook of Internet Crime* (pp. 1–15). Cullompton, England: Willan Publishing.

Jewkes, Y. (2010). Public policing and Internet crime. In Jewkes & M. Yar (eds.) *Handbook of Internet Crime* (pp. 525-545). Cullompton, England: Willan Publishing.

Johnson, D., & Post, D. (1996). Law and Borders – The Rise of Law in Cyberspace. *Stanford Law Review, 48*, 1367–1402. doi:10.2307/1229390

Jolliffe, D., & Farrington, D. P. (2004). Empathy and offending: A systematic review and meta-analysis. *Aggression and Violent Behavior, 9*, 441–476. doi:10.1016/j. avb.2003.03.001

Jones, T. (2003). Child abuse or computer crime? The proactive approach. In MacVean, A., & Spindler, P. (Eds.), *Policing paedophiles on the Internet. John Grieve Centre for policing and Community Safety*. Bristol: The New Police Bookshop.

Joseph, J. (2003). Cyberstalking: an international perspective. In Jewkes, Y. (Ed.), *Dot.cons: Crime, deviance and identity on the Internet* (pp. 105–125). Cullompton, England: Willan Publishing.

Josman, N., Somer, E., Reisberg, A., Weiss, P. L., Garcia-Palacios, A., & Hoffman, H. (2006). Busworld: Designing a Virtual Environment for Post-Traumatic Stress Disorder in Israel: A Protocol. *Cyberpsychology & Behavior, 9*, 241–244. doi:10.1089/cpb.2006.9.241

Jouriles, E. N., McDonald, R., Kullowatz, A., Rosenfield, D., Gomez, G. S., & Cuevas, A. (2009). Can Virtual Reality Increase the Realism of Role Plays Used to Teach College Women Sexual Coercion and Rape-Resistance Skills? *Behavior Therapy*..doi:10.1016/j.beth.2008.09.002

Jung, Y. (2008). Influence of Sense of Presence on Intention to Participate in a Virtual Community. *Proceedings of the 41st Hawaii International Conference on System Sciences.*

Kabay, M. E. *(1998)*. ICSA White Paper on Computer Crime Statistics. *Retrieved on 29th April 2005 from* www.icsa.net/html/library/whitepapers/crime.pdf

Kamarch, E. (2007). *The End of Government as we know it: Making public policy work*. Lynne Rienner Publishers.

Kamphuis, J. H., Emmelkamp, P. M. G., & Bartak, A. (2003). Individual differences in post-traumatic stress following post-intimate stalking: Stalking severity and psychosocial variables. *The British Journal of Clinical Psychology, 42*, 145–156. doi:10.1348/014466503321903562

Kapardis, A. (2003). *Psychology and Law: A Critical Introduction (2nd Edition)*. Port Melbourne: Cambridge University Press.

Kassin, S. M., & Wrightsman, L. S. (1985). Confession evidence. In Kassin, S. M., & Wrightsman, L. S. (Eds.), *The Psychology of evidence and trial procedures* (pp. 67–94). London: Sage.

Katsh, E. (2007). Online Dispute Resolution: Some Implications for the Emergence of Law in Cyberspace. *International Review of Law Computers & Technology, 21*, 97–107. doi:10.1080/13600860701492096

Kebbell, M. R., & Hurren, E. (2006). Improving the Interviewing of Suspected Offenders. In Kebbell, M. R., & Davies, G. M. (Eds.), *Practical Psychology for Forensic Investigations and Prosecutions* (pp. 101–119). Chichester, West Sussex: John Wiley & Sons, Ltd. doi:10.1002/9780470713389

Kenny, M. C., & McEachern, A. G. (2000). Racial, ethnic and cultural factors of childhood sexual abuse: A selected review of the literature. *Clinical Psychology Review, 20*, 905–922. doi:10.1016/S0272-7358(99)00022-7

Kickert, W. J. M., Klijn, E. H., & Koppenjan, J. F. M. (1997). *Managing Networks in the Public Sector. Managing Complex Networks*. London: Sage.

Killias, M., Scheidegger, D., & Nordenson, P. (2009). Effects of Increasing the Certainty of Punishment: A Field Experiment on Public Transportation. *European Journal of Criminology, 6*, 387–400. doi:10.1177/1477370809337881

Kilpatrick, R. (1997). Joy-riding: an addictive behavior. In Hodge, J. E., McMurran, M., & Hollin, C. R. (Eds.), *Addicted to Crime?* (pp. 165–190). Chichester, England: Wiley.

Kingston, D. A., Fedoroff, P., Firestone, P., Curry, S., & Bradford, J. M. (2008). Pornography use and sexual aggression: the impact of frequency and type of pornography use on recidivism among sexual offenders. *Aggressive Behavior, 34*, 341–351. doi:10.1002/ab.20250

Kirwan, G. (2009, November). *Presence and the Victims of Crime in Online Virtual Worlds.* Proceedings of Presence 2009 – the 12th Annual International Workshop on Presence, International Society for Presence Research, November 11-13, Los Angeles, California. Retrieved from http://astro.temple.edu/~tuc16417/papers/Kirwan.pdf PROCEEDINGS ISBN: 978-0-9792217-3-6

Kirwan, G. H. *(2006).* An Identification of Demographic and Psychological Characteristics of Computer Hackers Using Triangulation. *PhD Thesis, Institute of criminology, College of business and law, School of law. University College Dublin. June 2006*

Kirwan, G.H. (2009). *Victim facilitation and blaming in cybercrime cases.* Proceedings of Cyberspace 2009. Brno, Czech Republic. November 20-21.

Klain, E., Davies, H., & Hicks, M. (2001). *Child Pornography: The Criminal-Justice-System Response.* Washington, D.C.: National Center for Missing & Exploited Children. www.missingkids.com/en_US/publications/NC81.pdf.

Kline, P. (1987). Psychoanalysis and crime. In McGurk, B. J., Thornton, D. M., & Williams, M. (Eds.), *Applying Psychology to Imprisonment: Theory and practice.* London: HMSO.

Klinger, D. A. (2001). Suicidal intent in victim-precipitated homicide: Insights from the study of "suicide-by-cop.". *Homicide Studies, 5*(3), 206–226. doi:10.1177/1088767901005003002

Knight, W. (2005, August 18). Computer characters mugged in virtual crime spree. *New Scientist.* Retrieved from http://www.newscientist.com/article/dn7865

Kohlberg, L. (1969). State and sequence: the cognitive-developmental approach to socialization. In Goslin, D. A. (Ed.), *Handbook of Socialization Theory and Research.* Chicago: Rand McNally.

Kowalski, R. M., & Limber, S. P. (2007). Electronic Bullying Among Middle School Students. *The Journal of Adolescent Health, 41,* S22–S30. doi:10.1016/j.jadohealth.2007.08.017

Kramer, S., & Bradfield, J. C. (2010). A general definition of malware. *Journal in Computer Virology, 6,* 105–114. doi:10.1007/s11416-009-0137-1

Krause, M. (2009). Identifying and Managing stress in child pornography and child exploitation investigators. *Journal of Police and Criminal Psychology, 24,* 22–29.. doi:10.1007/s11896-008-9033-8

Krone, T. (2004). *A Typology of Online Child Pornography Offending.* Trends & Issues in Crime and Criminal Justice, No. 279. Canberra: Australian Institute of Criminology. www.aic.gov.au/publications/tandi2/tandi279.pdf.

Kruglanski, A. W., & Fishman, S. (2006). The psychology of terrorism: "Syndrome" versus "tool" perspectives. *Terrorism and Political Violence, 18,* 193–215. doi:10.1080/09546550600570119

Lafrance, Y. *(2004).* Psychology: A Previous Security Tool. *Retrieved on29thApril2005 from*http://cnscentre.future.co.kr/resource/security/hacking/1409.pdf

Lam, A., Mitchell, J., & Seto, M. C. (2010). Lay Perceptions of Child Pornography Offenders. *Canadian Journal of Criminology and Criminal Justice, 52,* 173–201. doi:10.3138/cjccj.52.2.173

Lamb, M. E., Orlbach, Y., Hershkowitz, I., Esplin, P. W., & Horowitz, D. (2007). Structured forensic interview protocols improve the quality and informativeness of investigative interviews with children: A review of research using the NICHD Investigative Interview Protocol. *Child Abuse & Neglect, 31,* 1201–1231..doi:10.1016/j.chiabu.2007.03.021

Langevin, R., & Curnoe, S. (2008). Are the mentally retarded and learning disordered overrepresented among sex offenders and paraphilics? *International Journal of Offender Therapy and Comparative Criminology, 52,* 401–415. doi:10.1177/0306624X07305826

Langleben, D. D. (2008). Detection of deception with fMRI: Are we there yet? *Legal and Criminological Psychology, 13,* 1–9..doi:10.1348/135532507X251641

Lanning, K. V. (2001). Child molesters and cyber paedophiles: A behavioural perspective. In Hazelwood, R., & Burgess, A. W. (Eds.), *Practical aspects of rape investigation: A multidisciplinary approach* (3rd ed., pp. 199–220). Boca Raton, FL: CRC Press. doi:10.1201/9781420042375.ch11

Lanning, K., & Burgess, A. (1989). Child Pornography and Sex Rings. In Zillmann, D., & Bryant, J. (Eds.), *Pornography: Research Advances & Policy Considerations*. Hillsdale, New Jersey: Lawrence Erlbaum.

Lanning, K. (2001). *Child Molesters: A Behavioral Analysis* (4th ed.), Washington, DC: National Center for Missing and Exploited Children. Retrieved June 23, 2010 from http://www.ncmec.org/en_US/publications/ NC70.pdf

Lapsley, I. (2008). The NPM agenda: Back to the Future. *Financial Accountability and Management, 24*, 77–96. doi:10.1111/j.1468-0408.2008.00444.x

LaRose, R., & Kim, J. (2007). Share, steal or buy? A social cognitive perspective of music downloading. *Cyberpsychology & Behavior, 10*, 267–277. doi:10.1089/cpb.2006.9959

LaRose, R., Lai, Y. J., Lange, R., Love, B., & Wu, Y. (2005). Sharing or piracy? An exploration of downloading behaviour. *Journal of Computer-Mediated Communication, 11*, 1–21. doi:10.1111/j.1083-6101.2006.tb00301.x

LaRose. (2008, March). Rifon & Enbody, (2008). Promoting Personal Responsibility for Internet Safety. *Communications of the ACM, 51*(3), 71–76.. doi:10.1145/1325555.1325569

Laulik, S., Allam, J., & Sheridan, L. (2007). An investigation into maladaptive personality functioning in Internet sex offenders. *Psychology, Crime & Law, 13*, 523–535. doi:10.1080/10683160701340577

Lawrence, J. W., & Fauerbach, J. A. (2003). Personality, Coping, Chronic Stress, Social Support and PTSD symptoms among adult burn survivors: A path analysis. *The Journal of Burn Care & Rehabilitation, 24*, 63–72. doi:10.1097/00004630-200301000-00016

Lee, D., Larose, R., & Rifon, N. (2008). Keeping our network safe: a model of online protection behaviour. *Behaviour & Information Technology, 27*, 445–454. doi:10.1080/01449290600879344

Lee, Y., & Larson, K. R. (2009). Threat or coping appraisal: determinants of SMB executives' decision to adopt anti-malware software. *European Journal of Information Systems, 18*, 177–187. doi:10.1057/ejis.2009.11

Leman-Langlois, S. (2008). Introduction: technocrime. In Leman-Langlois, S. (Ed.), *Technocrime: Technology, crime and social control*. Cullompton, England: Willan.

Lenhart (2007). *Pew Internet and American Life Project: Cyberbullying and Online Teens*. Retrieved November 6, 2010 from http://www.pewinternet.org/~/media//Files / Reports/2007/PIP%20Cyberbullying%20Memo.pdf.pdf

Lentz, C. E. (2010). A State's Duty to Prevent and Respond to Cyberterrorist Acts. *Chicago Journal of International Law, 10*, 799.

Lessig, L. (2000). *Code and Other Laws of Cyberspace*. Princeton, NJ: Princeton University Press.

Levi, M. (2001). "Between the risk and the reality falls the shadow": Evidence and urban legends in computer fraud (with apologies to T.S. Eliot). In Wall, D. (Ed.), *Crime and the Internet* (pp. 44–58). London, New York: Routledge.

Levine, S. Z. (2008). Using intelligence to predict subsequent contacts with the criminal justice system for sex offences. *Personality and Individual Differences, 44*, 453–463. doi:10.1016/j.paid.2007.09.010

Levy, S. (1984). *Hackers: Heroes of the Computer Revolution*. London: Penguin Books.

Li, Q. (2006). Cyber bullying in schools: A research of gender differences. *School Psychology International, 27*(2), 157–170. doi:10.1177/0143034306064547

Li, Q. (2007). New bottle but old wine: A research of cyberbullying in schools. *Computers in Human Behavior, 23*, 1777–1791. doi:10.1016/j.chb.2005.10.005

Liao, C., Lin, H.-N., & Liu, Y.-P. (2009). Predicting the Use of Pirated Software: A Contingency Model Integrating Perceived Risk with the Theory of Planned Behavior. *Journal of Business Ethics, 91*, 237–252. doi:10.1007/s10551-009-0081-5

Liebowitz, S. J. (2006). File Sharing: Creative destruction or just plain destruction? *The Journal of Law & Economics, 49*, 1–28. doi:10.1086/503518

Lininger, R., & Vines, R. D. (2005). *Phishing: Cutting the Identity Theft Line*. Indianapolis, IN: Wiley Publishing Inc.

Lippmann, W. (1952). *Public Opinion*. New York: Macmillan.

Livingstone. S. (2009). *Children and the Internet: Great Expectations, Challenging Realities.* Cambridge, England: Polity.

Locicero, A., & Sinclair, S. J. (2008). Terrorism and Terrorist Leaders: Insights from Developmental and Ecological Psychology. *Studies in Conflict and Terrorism, 31,* 227–250. doi:10.1080/10576100701879638

Loftus, E., Miller, D. G., & Burns, H. J. (1978). Semantic integration of verbal information into a visual memory. *Journal of Experimental Psychology. Human Learning and Memory, 4,* 19–31. doi:10.1037/0278-7393.4.1.19

Loftus, E., & Palmer, J. C. (1974). Reconstructions of automobile destruction: an example of the interaction between language and memory. *Journal of Verbal Learning and Verbal Behavior, 13,* 585–589. doi:10.1016/S0022-5371(74)80011-3

Lombroso, C., & Ferrero, W. (1895). *The Female Offender.* London: Fisher Unwin.

Loper, D. K. (2000, November). *Profiling Hackers: Beyond Psychology.* Paper presented at the Annual Meeting of the American Society of Criminology, San Francisco, CA. Retrieved on 29th April 2005 from http://webpages.csus.edu/~doc/ASC2000_ProfilingHackers.pdf

Lopez-Leon, M., & Rosner, R. (2010). Intellectual quotient of juveniles evaluated in a forensic psychiatry clinic after committing a violent crime. *Journal of Forensic Sciences, 55,* 229–231. doi:10.1111/j.1556-4029.2009.01225.x

Loughlin, J. (2004). The "Transformation" of Governance: New Directions in Policy and Politics. *The Australian Journal of Politics and History, 50,* 8–22. doi:10.1111/j.1467-8497.2004.00317.x

Loughlin, J. (2007). Reconfiguring the state: Trends in territorial governance in European states. *Regional & Federal Studies, 17,* 385–403. doi:10.1080/13597560701691912

Lukes, S. (2005). *Power: a Radical View* (2nd ed.). Basingstoke, England: Palgrave Macmillan.

Lynn, R. (2007). *Virtual Rape is Traumatic, but is it a Crime?* Retrieved from http://www.wired.com/culture/lifestyle/ commentary/sexdrive/2007/05/sexdrive_0504

MacKinnon, R. C. (1997). Punishing the Persona: Correctional Strategies for the Virtual Offender. In Jones, S. (Ed.), *Virtual Culture: Identity and communication in cybersociety* (pp. 206–235). London: Sage.

MacSíthigh, D. (2008). The mass age of internet law. *Information & Communications Technology Law, 17,* 79–94. doi:10.1080/13600830802204187

Maghaireh, A. (2008). Shariah Law and Cyber-Sectarian Conflict: How can Islamic criminal law respond to cyber crime? *International Journal of Cyber-Criminology, 2,* 337–345.

Maguire, M., Morgan, R., & Reiner, R. (2007). *The Oxford Handbook of Criminology* (4th ed.). Oxford: Oxford University Press.

Malesky, L. A. Jr. (2007). Predatory Online Behaviour: modus operandi of convicted sex offenders in identifying potential victims and contacting minors over the internet. *Journal of Child Sexual Abuse, 16,* 23–32. doi:10.1300/J070v16n02_02

Malin, J., & Fowers, B. (2009). Adolescent self-control and music and movie piracy. *Computers in Human Behavior, 25,* 718–722. doi:10.1016/j.chb.2008.12.029

Mancheno, C. (2010, April 11). With New Vest, Players feel the game. *The Daily Pennsylvanian.* Retrieved from http://www.dailypennsylvanian.com/article /new-vest-players-feel-game

Marmar, C. R., Metzler, T. J., Otte, C., McCaslin, S., Inslicht, S., & Haase, C. H. (2007). The Peritraumatic Dissociative Experiences Questionnaire: An International Perspective. In J.P. Wilson and C. So-kum Tang (Eds.) *Cross-Cultural Assessment of Psychological Trauma and PTSD* (pp. 197-217). Springer.

Marshall, A., & Stephens, P. (2008). Identity and Identity Theft. In Bryant, R. (Ed.), *Investigating Digital Crime* (pp. 179–193). Chichester, England: John Wiley & Sons.

Marshall, W. L. (1997). Pedophilia: Psychopathology and theory. In Laws, D. R., & O'Donohue, W. (Eds.), *Sexual deviance: Theory, assessment, and treatment* (pp. 152–174). New York: Guilford Press.

Marshall, W. L., & Barbaree, H. E. (1990). An integrated theory of the etiology of sexual offending. In Marshall, W. L., Laws, D. R., & Barbaree, H. E. (Eds.), *Handbook of Sexual Assault: Issues, Theories and Treatment of the Offender* (pp. 257–275). London: Plenum Press.

Martin, G., Richardson, A., Bergen, H., Roeger, L., & Allison, S. (2003). Family and Individual characteristics of a community sample of adolescents who graffiti. Presented at the *Graffiti and Disorder Conference,* Brisbane, Australia. 18-19 August. Retrieved 8th October 2010 from http://www.nograffiti.com/martinstudy.pdf

Maruna, S., & Mann, R. E. (2006). A fundamental attribution error? Rethinking cognitive distortions. *Legal and Criminological Psychology, 11,* 155–177.. doi:10.1348/135532506X114608

Marziano, V., Ward, T., Beech, A. R., & Pattison, P. (2006). Identification of five fundamental implicit theories underlying cognitive distortions in child abusers: A preliminary study. *Psychology, Crime & Law, 12,* 97–105.. doi:10.1080/10683160500056887

Maslow, A. H. (1970). *Motivation and Personality* (2nd ed.). New York: Harper & Row.

McAfee-NCSA. (2007). *McAfee-NCSA Online Safety Study – Newsworthy Analysis,* October 2007. http://download.mcafee.com/products/ manuals/en-us/McAfeeNCSA_Analysis09-25-07.pdf

McCall, C. (1999). The Governance of Northern Ireland: From Modernity to Postmodernity? In McCall, C. (Ed.), *Identity in Northern Ireland: Communities, Politics and Change.* Basingstoke: Palgrave.

McCauley, M. R., & Fisher, R. P. (1995). Facilitating children's eyewitness recall with the revised cognitive interview. *The Journal of Applied Psychology, 80,* 510–516. doi:10.1037/0021-9010.80.4.510

McCauley, C., & Moskalenko, S. (2008). Mechanisms of Political Radicalisation: Pathways toward terrorism. *Terrorism and Political Violence, 20,* 415–433. doi:10.1080/09546550802073367

McDonald, H. (2009, August 2nd). MP calls on YouTube to remove Real IRA propaganda videos: 'Cyber-terrorism' films of dissident republicans could be banned from site. *The Observer Supplement. The Guardian Newspaper.* Retrieved on 10th October 2010 from http://www.guardian.co.uk/technology/2009/aug/02 /youtube-ira-facebook-cyber-terrorism

McGuire, J. (2004). *Understanding psychology and crime: perspectives on theory and action.* Maidenhead, England: Open University Press.

McGuire, J. (1997). 'Irrational' shoplifting and models of addiction. In Hodge, J. E., McMurran, M., & Hollin, C. R. (Eds.), *Addicted to Crime?* (pp. 207–231). Chichester, England: Wiley.

McKinnon, R. C. (1997). Punishing the persona: Correctional Strategies for the Virtual Offender. In Jones, S. (Ed.), *The Undernet: The Internet and the Other.* Sage.

McNair, B. (1999). *An Introduction to Political Communication* (2nd ed.). London: Routledge.

McQuade, S. C. (2006). *Understanding and managing cybercrime.* Boston, MA: Allyn & Bacon.

Meadows, M. S. (2008). *I, Avatar: The Culture and Consequences of Having a Second Life.* Berkeley, CA: New Riders.

Mears, D. P., Mancini, C., Gertz, M., & Bratton, J. (2008). Sex Crimes, Children and Pornography: Public Views and Public Policy. *Crime and Delinquency, 54,* 532–559. doi:10.1177/0011128707308160

Mehta, M. D. (2001). Pornography in Usenet: a study of 9,800 randomly selected images. *Cyberpsychology & Behavior, 4,* 695–703. doi:10.1089/109493101753376641

Meier, M. H., Slutske, W. S., Arndt, S., & Cadoret, R. J. (2008). Impulsive and callous traits are more strongly associated with delinquent behavior in higher risk neighborhoods among boys and girls. *Journal of Abnormal Psychology, 117,* 377–385. doi:10.1037/0021-843X.117.2.377

Meinel, C. P. (1998). How hackers break in... and how they are caught. *Scientific American, 279,* 98–105. doi:10.1038/scientificamerican1098-98

Meloy, J. R. (1998). The psychology of stalking. In Meloy, J. R. (Ed.), *The psychology of stalking: Clinical and Forensic Perspectives* (pp. 1–23). London: Academic Press.

Meloy, J. R. (2000). Stalking (obsessional following). In Meloy, J. R. (Ed.), *Violence, risk and threat assessment* (pp. 167–191). San Diego, CA: Specialised Training Services.

Mendelsohn, B. (1956). A New Branch of Bio-Psychological Science: La Victimology. *Revue Internationale de Criminologie et de Police Technique, 10*, 782–789.

Merari, A. (2007). Psychological aspects of suicide terrorism. In Bongar, B., Brown, L. M., Beutler, L. E., Brecenridge, J. N., & Zimbardo, P. B. (Eds.), *Psychology of Terrorism* (pp. 101–115). New York: Oxford University Press.

Mesch, G. S. (2009). Parental mediation, online activities and cyberbullying. *Cyberpsychology & Behavior, 12*, 387–393. doi:10.1089/cpb.2009.0068

Microsoft. (2009, February 10). *29% of European teenagers are victims of online bullying*. Retrieved November 6, 2010 from http://www.microsoft.com/emea/presscentre/pressreleases/OnlinebullyingPR_100209.mspx

Middleton, D. (2008). From Research to practice: The development of the internet sex offender treatment programme (i-SOTP). *Irish Probation Journal, 5*, 49–64.

Middleton, D., Elliott, I. A., Mandeville-Norden, R., & Beech, A. R. (2006). An investigation into the application of the Ward and Siegert pathways model of child sexual abuse with Internet offenders. *Psychology, Crime & Law, 12*, 589–603. doi:10.1080/10683160600558352

Middleton, D., Mandeville-Norden, R., & Hayes, E. (2009). Does treatment work with internet sex offenders? Emerging findings from the internet sex offender treatment programme (i-SOTP). *Journal of Sexual Aggression, 15*, 5–19. doi:10.1080/13552600802673444

Middleton, D., Elliott, I. A., Mandeville-Norden, R., & Beech, A. R. (2006). An investigation into the applicability of the Ward and Siegert Pathways Model of child sexual abuse with Internet offenders. *Psychology, Crime & Law, 12*, 589–603. doi:10.1080/10683160600558352

Middleton, D. (2009). Internet Sex Offenders. In Beech, A. R., Craig, L., & Browne, K. D. (Eds.), *Assessment and treatment of sex offenders: A handbook* (pp. 199–215). Chichester: Wiley.

Middleton, D. (2004). Current treatment approaches. In Calder, M. (Ed.), *Child sexual abuse and the Internet: Tackling the new frontier* (pp. 99–112). Lyme Regis, UK: Russell House Publishing.

Miller, A. K., Markman, K. D., & Handley, I. M. (2007). Self-blame among sexual assault victims prospectively predicts revictimisation: A perceived sociolegal context model of risk. *Basic and Applied Social Psychology, 29*, 129–136. doi:10.1080/01973530701331585

Mishra, A., & Mishra, D. (2008). Cyber Stalking: A challenge for web security. In Janczewski, L. J., & Colarik, A. M. (Eds.), *Cyber Warfare and Cyber Terrorism* (pp. 216–225). Hershey, PA: Information Science Reference.

Mitchell, K. J., Finkelhor, D., Jones, L. M., & Wolak, J. (2010). Use of Social Networking Sites in Online Sex Crimes Against Minors: An Examination of National Incidence and Means of Utilization. *The Journal of Adolescent Health.*.doi:10.1016/j.jadohealth.2010.01.007

Mitchell, K. J., Finkelhor, D., & Wolak, J. (2007). Youth internet users at risk for the most serious online sexual solicitations. *American Journal of Preventive Medicine, 32*, 532–537. doi:10.1016/j.amepre.2007.02.001

Mitchell, K. J., Wolak, J., & Finkelhor, D. (2005). Police posing as juveniles online to catch sex offenders: Is it working? *Sexual Abuse, 17*, 241–267. doi:10.1177/107906320501700302

Mitchell, K. J., Wolak, J., & Finkelhor, D. (2008). Are blogs putting youth at risk for online sexual solicitation or harassment? *Child Abuse & Neglect, 32*, 277–294. doi:10.1016/j.chiabu.2007.04.015

Mitnick, K. D., & Simon, W. L. (2002). *The Art of Deception: Controlling the Human Element of Security*. Indianapolis, IN: Wiley Publishing Inc.

Mitnick, K. D., & Simon, W. L. (2005). *The Art of Intrusion: The Real Stories Behind the Exploits of Hackers, Intruders and Deceivers*. Indianapolis, IN: Wiley Publishing Inc.

Mizrach, S. *(n.d.)*. Is there a Hacker Ethic for 90s Hackers? *Retrieved on16ᵗʰJune2010 from*http://www.fiu. edu/~mizrachs/hackethic.html

Modell, S. (2004). Performance Measurement Myths in the Public Sector: A Research Note. *Finance Accountability & Management, 20,* 39-55.

Monbiot, G. (2001). Government in exile: the Corporate Bid for world Domination. In G. Monbiot *Captive State: The Corporate Takeover of Britain* (pp. 302-330). London: Pan.

Montada, L. (2003). Justice, Equality and Fairness in Human Relations. In Millan, T., Lerner, M. J., & Weiner, I. B. (Eds.), *Handbook of Psychology: Personality and Social Psychology* (pp. 537–568). Wiley.

Moore, R., & McMullan, E. C. (2009). Neutralizations and Rationalizations of Digital Piracy: A qualitative analysis of university students. *International Journal of Cyber Criminology, 3,* 441–451.

Morison, J., & Livingstone, S. (1995). *Reshaping Public Power*. London: Sweet & Maxwell.

Morison, J., & Newman, D. (2001). On-line Citizenship: Consultation and Participation in New Labour's Britain and Beyond. *International Review of Law Computers & Technology, 15,* 171–194. doi:10.1080/13600860120070501

Morison, J. (1998). The Case Against Constitutional Reform? *Journal of Law and Society, 25,* 510–535. doi:10.1111/1467-6478.00101

Morison, J. (2007). Models of Democracy: From Representation to Participation? In Jowell, J., & Oliver, D. (Eds.), *The Changing Constitution* (6th ed., pp. 144–170). Oxford: Oxford University Press.

Morris, R., & Higgins, G. (2009). Neutralizing potential and self-reported digital piracy: A multitheoretical exploration among college undergraduates. *Criminal Justice Review, 34,* 173–195. doi:10.1177/0734016808325034

Morris, R. G., & Higgins, G. E. (2010). Criminological theory in the digital age: The case of social learning theory and digital piracy. *Journal of Criminal Justice*. Retrieved from http://dx.doi.org/10.1016/ j.jcrimjus.2010.04.016

Morris, S. (2008, November 14). Internet affair leads to couple's real life divorce. *The Guardian*. Retrieved from http://www.guardian.co.uk/technology/2008 /nov/14/ second-life-virtual-worlds-divorce

Motion Picture Association of America. (MPAA, 2006). *Worldwide study of losses to the film industry and international economies due to piracy: Pirate profiles*. Retrieved October 31, 2010 from http://www.fact-uk.org.uk/site/ media_centre/documents/2006_05_03leksumm.pdf

Mulgan, G. (2007). *Good and Bad Power*. London: Penguin.

Muncie, J., McLaughlin, E., & Langan, M. (1996). *Criminological Perspectives: A Reader*. London: Sage Publications Ltd.

Murphy, C. (2004, June). Inside the Mind of the Hacker. *Accountancy Ireland, 36,* 12.

Murray, C. D., Fox, J., & Pettifer, S. (2007). Absorption, dissociation, locus of control and presence in virtual reality. *Computers in Human Behavior, 23,* 1347–1354. doi:10.1016/j.chb.2004.12.010

Nathanson, H. S. (1995). Strengthening the criminal jury: long overdue. *Criminal Law Quarterly, 38,* 217–248.

National Centre for Missing and Exploited Children. (2007, February 28). *Press Release: National Centre for Missing and Exploited Children Creates New Unit to help find 100,000 missing sex offenders and calls for states to do their part*. Retrieved from http://www.missingkids. com/missingkids/ servlet/NewsEventServlet?LanguageC ountry =en_US&PageId=3081

Nayar, P. K. (2010). *An Introduction to New Media and Cybercultures*. Chichester, England: Wiley Blackwell.

Nelken, D. (2007). White-collar and corporate crime. In Maguire, M., Morgan, R., & Reiner, R. (Eds.), *The Oxford Handbook of Criminology* (4th ed., pp. 733–770). Oxford: Oxford University Press.

Nelson, B., Choi, R., Iacobucci, M., Mitchell, M.& Gagnon, G. (1999, August) *Cyberterror: Prospects and Implications*, Center for the Study of Terrorism and Irregular Warfare, Naval Postgraduate School, Monterey, CA.

Newman et al. (2007). *Technology Selection for E-Consultation*. Presented at EGOV07, Leeds Metropolitan University, 12th Sept.

Ng, B. Y., Kankanhalli, A., & Xu, Y. C. (2009). Studying users' computer security behaviour: A health belief perspective. *Decision Support Systems, 46*, 815–825. doi:10.1016/j.dss.2008.11.010

Ng, B. Y., & Rahim, M. A. (2005). *A Socio-Behavioral Study of Home Computer Users' Intention to Practice Security*. The Ninth Pacific Asia Conference on Information Systems, 7 - 10 July, Bangkok, Thailand.

Nhan, J., Kinkade, P., & Burns, R. (2009). Finding a pot of gold at the end of an internet rainbow: Further examination of fraudulent email solicitation. *International Journal of Cyber Criminology, 3*, 452–475.

Nuñez, J. (2003). Outpatient treatment of the sexually compulsive ephebophile. *Sexual Addiction & Compulsivity, 10*, 23–51. doi:10.1080/10720160309047

Nykodym, N., Taylor, R., & Vilela, J. (2005). Criminal profiling and insider cybercrime. *Computer Law & Security Report, 21*, 408–414. doi:10.1016/j.clsr.2005.07.001

O'Ciardhuain, S. (2004). An Extended model of cybercrime investigations. *International Journal of Digital Evidence, 3 (1)*. Retrieved on 28th April 2008 from http://www.utica.edu/academic/institutes /ecii/publications/articles/A0B70121-FD6C-3DBA-0EA5C3E93CC575FA.pdf

O'Connell, R. (2003). *A Typology of Child Cyberexploitation and Online Grooming Practices. Lancashire: Cyberspace Research Unit*. University of Central Lancashire.

O'Donnell, I. & Milner, C. (2007). *Child Pornography: Crime, Computers and Society*. Cullompton, Devon: Willan Publishing.

Oberholzer-Gee, F., & Strumpf, K. S. (2007). The effect of file sharing on record sales: An empirical analysis. *The Journal of Political Economy, 115*, 1–42. doi:10.1086/511995

O'Brien, M. D., & Webster, S. D. (2007). The construction and preliminary validation of the Internet Behaviours and Attitudes Questionnaire (IBAQ). *Sexual Abuse, 19*, 237–256. doi:10.1177/107906320701900305

O'Connell, M. (2002). The portrayal of crime in the media: Does it matter? In O'Mahony, P. (Ed.), *Criminal Justice in Ireland* (pp. 245–267). Dublin: IPA.

Ogan, J., & Allison, L. (2005). Jack the Ripper and the Whitechapel murders: a very Victorian critical incident. In Allison, L. (Ed.), *The Forensic Psychologist's Casebook: Psychological Profiling and criminal investigation* (pp. 23–46). Cullompton, England: Willan Publishing.

Ohmae, K. (1996). *The End of the Nation State: The Rise of Regional Economies*. New York, NY: The Free Press.

Ollmann, G. (2008). The evolution of commercial malware development kits and colour-by-numbers custom malware. *Computer Fraud & Security, 9*, 4–7. doi:10.1016/S1361-3723(08)70135-0

Osborne, D., & Gaebler, T. (1992). *Reinventing Government: How the Entrepreneurial Spirit is Transforming the Public Sector*. New York, NY: Perseus Books.

Palmer, E. J., & Hollin, C. R. (1998). Comparison of patterns of moral development in young offenders and non-offenders. *Legal and Criminological Psychology, 3*, 225–235. doi:10.1111/j.2044-8333.1998.tb00363.x

Park, A. J., Calvert, T. W., Brantingham, P. L., & Brantingham, P. J. (2008). The Use of Virtual and Mixed Reality Environments for Urban Behavioural Studies. *PsychNology Journal, 6*, 119–130.

Patchin, J. W., & Hinduja, S. (2006). Bullies move beyond the schoolyard: A preliminary look at cyberbullying. *Youth Violence and Juvenile Justice, 4*, 148–169.. doi:10.1177/1541204006286288

Patchin, J. W., & Hinduja, S. (2010). Traditional and nontraditional bullying among youth: A test of general strain theory. [published online ahead of print]. *Youth & Society*, (May): 7. doi:.doi:10.1177/0044118X10366951

Paulsen, D. J. (2006). Connecting the dots: assessing the accuracy of geographic profiling software. *Policing: An International Journal of Police Strategies and Management, 29*, 306–334..doi:10.1108/13639510610667682

Pavlov, I. (1965). On conditioned reflexes. In Hernstein, R. J., & Boring, E. G. (Eds.), *A source book in the history of psychology*. Cambridge, MA: Harvard University Press. (Original work published 1904)

Payne, J. W. (1980). Information processing theory: Some concepts and methods applied to decision research. In Wallsten, T. S. (Ed.), *Cognitive processes in choice and decision behaviour*. Hillsdale, NJ: Erlbaum.

Pearce, C. (2006). *Seeing and being seen: Presence & Play in Online Virtual Worlds. Online, offline and the concept of presence when games and VR collide*. USC Institute for Creative Technologies.

Peitz, M., & Waelbroeck, P. (2006). Why the music industry may gain from free downloading – The role of sampling. *International Journal of Industrial Organization, 24*, 907–913. doi:10.1016/j.ijindorg.2005.10.006

Perez, L. M., Jones, J., Englert, D. R., & Sachau, D. (2010). Secondary Traumatic Stress and Burnout among law enforcement investigators exposed to disturbing media images. *Journal of Police and Criminal Psychology, 25*, 113–124..doi:10.1007/s11896-010-9066-7

Philips, F., & Morrissey, G. (2004). Cyberstalking and Cyberpredators: A threat to safe sexuality on the Internet. *Convergence, 10*, 66–79.

Pierson, C. (2004). *The Modern State*. London: Routledge.

Piquero, A. R., Moffitt, T. E., & Wright, B. E. (2007). Self control and criminal career dimensions. *Journal of Contemporary Criminal Justice, 23*, 72–89. doi:10.1177/1043986206298949

Piquero, N. L. (2005). Causes and prevention of intellectual property crime. *Trends in Organised Crime, 8*, 40–61. doi:10.1007/s12117-005-1013-0

Plato. (2007). *The Republic*. London: Penguin (Original work published circa 400BC)

Platt, C. (1994, November Issue 2.11). Hackers: Threat or Menace? *Wired*, 82-8. Retrieved from http://www.wired.com/wired/archive/2.11/hack.cong.html

Pollitt, C. (2002). The New Public Management in international perspective: an analysis of impacts and effects. In McLaughlin, Osborne and Ferlie (Eds.) *New Public Management: Current Trends and Future Prospects* (pp. 274-293). London: Routledge.

Pollitt, M. M. (1997, October). Cyberterrorism: Fact or Fancy? *Proceedings of the 20th National Information Systems Security Conference*, pp. 285–289.

Porter, S., & ten Brinke, L. (2008). Reading between the Lies: Identifying concealed and falsified emotions in universal facial expressions. *Psychological Science, 19*, 508–514..doi:10.1111/j.1467-9280.2008.02116.x

Post, D. (1996). Governing Cyberspace. *Wayne Law Review, 43*, 155–171.

Post, J. M., Ali, F., Henderson, S. W., Shanfield, S., Victoroff, J., & Weine, S. (2009). The Psychology of Suicide Terrorism. *Psychiatry: Interpersonal and Biological Processes, 72*, 13–31. doi:10.1521/psyc.2009.72.1.13

Post, J. M., Sprinzak, E., & Denny, L. M. (2003). The terrorists in their own words: Interviews with thirty-five incarcerated Middle Eastern terrorists. *Terrorism and Political Violence, 15*, 171–184. doi:10.1080/0954655 0312331293007

Prensky, M. (2001). Digital Natives, Digital Immigrants. *MCB University Press, 9*, 1–6.

Preuß, J., Furnell, S. M., & Papadaki, M. (2007). Considering the potential of criminal profiling to combat hacking. *Journal in Computer Virology, 3*, 135–141..doi:10.1007/s11416-007-0042-4

Privitera, C., & Campbell, M. A. (2009). Cyberbullying: The new face of workplace bullying? *Cyberpsychology & Behavior, 12*, 395–400. doi:10.1089/cpb.2009.0025

Quayle, E., & Taylor, M. (2001). Child Seduction and Self-Representation on the Internet. *Cyberpsychology & Behavior, 4*(5), 597–608. doi:10.1089/109493101753235197

Quayle, E., & Taylor, M. (2002). Child pornography and the Internet: perpetuating a cycle of abuse. *Deviant Behaviour: An Interdisciplinary Journal, 23*, 365–395.

Quayle, E., Vaughan, M., & Taylor, M. (2006). Sex offenders, internet child abuse images and emotional avoidance: The importance of values. *Aggression and Violent Behavior, 11*, 1–11. doi:10.1016/j.avb.2005.02.005

Quayle, E., Erooga, M., Wright, L., Taylor, M., & Harbinson, D. (2006). Abuse Images and the Internet. In *Only Pictures? Therapeutic work with Internet sex offenders*. Edited by: Quayle E, Erooga M, Wright L, Taylor M, Harbinson D. Lyme Regis: Russell House Publishing Ltd; 2006:1-11.

Quinn, O. (2008). *Advisers or Advocates? The Impact of State Agencies on Social Policy.* Dublin: IPA.

Rabinow, P. (1984). *The Foucault Reader.* London: Penguin.

Rantala, R. R. (for the US Dept of Justice, Bureau of Justice Statistics; 2008). *Cybercrime against Businesses, 2005.* Published Sept 2008; NCJ 221943. Retrieved 8th March 2010 from http://bjs.ojp.usdoj.gov/content/pub/pdf/cb05.pdf

Raskauskas, J., & Stoltz, A. D. (2007). Involvement in traditional and electronic bullying among adolescents. *Developmental Psychology, 43,* 564–575. doi:10.1037/0012-1649.43.3.564

Reijnen, L., Bulten, E., & Nijman, H. (2009). Demographic and Personality Characteristics of Internet Child Pornography Downloaders in Comparison to Other offenders. *Journal of Child Sexual Abuse, 18,* 611–622. doi:10.1080/10538710903317232

Rennie, L., & Shore, M. (2007). An Advanced model of hacking. *Security Journal, 20,* 236–251. doi:10.1057/palgrave.sj.8350019

Renold, E., Creighton, S. J., Atkinson, C., & Carr, J. (2003). *Images of Abuse: A Review of the Evidence on Child Pornography.* London: The National Society for the Prevention of Cruelty to Children.

Reuters (2005, March 30). Gamer gets life for murder over virtual sword. *CNET.* Retrieved from http://news.cnet.co.uk/gamesgear/ 0,39029682,39189904,00.htm

Reuters, E. (2007, September 27). *Second Life ready for primetime at Gingrich event.* Retrieved from http://secondlife.reuters.com/stories/2007/09/27/second-life-ready-for-primetime-at-gingrich-event

Reuters, E. (2008). Poll: Second Life residents prefer Obama to McCain by over 2 to 1. Retrieved from http://secondlife.reuters.com/stories/2008/09/23/poll-second-life-residents-prefer-obama-to-mccain-by-over-2-to-1

Riegel, D. L. (2004). Effects on boy-attracted pedosexual males of viewing boy erotica. *Archives of Sexual Behavior, 33,* 321–323. doi:10.1023/B:ASEB.0000029071.89455.53

Riva, G., Mantovani, F., Capideville, C. S., Preziosa, A., Morganti, F., & Villani, D. (2007). Affective Interactions Using Virtual Reality: The Link between Presence and Emotions. *Cyberpsychology & Behavior, 10,* 45–56. doi:10.1089/cpb.2006.9993

Robins, L. N., West, P. A., & Herjanic, B. L. (1975). Arrests and delinquency in two generations: a study of black urban families and their children. *Journal of Child Psychology and Psychiatry, and Allied Disciplines, 16,* 125–140. doi:10.1111/j.1469-7610.1975.tb01262.x

Rock, P. *(2007). Sociological Theories of Crime (pp. 3-42). In Mike Maguire, Rod Morgan and Robert Reiner's (eds)* The Oxford Handbook of Criminology (4th edition). *Oxford: Oxford University Press.*

Rogers, M. (2003). The role of criminal profiling in the computer forensic process. *Computers & Security, 22,* 292–298..doi:10.1016/S0167-4048(03)00405-X

Rogers, M. K., Siegfried, K., & Tidke, K. (2006). Self-reported computer criminal behaviour: A psychological analysis. *Digital Investigation, 3S,* S116–S120. doi:10.1016/j.diin.2006.06.002

Rogers, M. K., Smoak, N., & Liu, J. (2006). Self-reported criminal computer behaviour: a big-5, moral choice and manipulative exploitive behaviour analysis. *Deviant Behavior, 27,* 1–24. doi:10.1080/01639620600605333

Rogers, R. W. (1975). A protection motivation theory of fear appeals and attitude change. *The Journal of Psychology, 91,* 93–114. doi:10.1080/00223980.1975.9915803

Rogers, R. W. (1983). Cognitive and physiological processes in fear appeals and attitude change: a revised theory of protection motivation. In Cacioppo, J., & Petty, R. (Eds.), *Social Psychophysiology* (pp. 153–176). New York: Guildford Press.

Rogers, M. *(2000).* A New Hacker Taxonomy. University of Manitoba, [Online]. *Retrieved on6thMarch2010 from*http://homes.cerias.purdue.edu/~mkr/hacker.doc

Rollins, J., & Wilson, C. (2007). Terrorist capabilities for cyberattack: Overview and policy issues. In Linden, E. V. (Ed.), *Focus on Terrorism (Vol. 9,* pp. 43–63). New York: Nova Science Publishers Inc.

Ropelato, J. (2006). *Internet Pornography Statistics.* Retrieved June 23, 2010, from Internet Filter Review Web Site: http://internet-filter-review.toptenreviews.com/internet-pornography-statistics.html

Rosenstock, I. M. (1966). Why people use health services. *The Milbank Memorial Fund Quarterly, 44,* 94–124. doi:10.2307/3348967

Rusch, J. J. (2002, June 21). *The social psychology of computer viruses and worms.* Paper presented at INET 2002, Crystal City, Virginia. Retrieved 8ᵗʰ October 2010 from http://m4dch4t.effraie.org/vxdevl/papers/ avers/g10-c.pdf

Sageman, M. (2004). *Understanding Terror Networks.* Philadelphia, PA: University of Pennsylvania Press.

Sageman, M. (2008). *Leaderless Jihad.* Philadelphia, PA: University of Pennsylvania Press.

Sanders-Reach, C. (2005, May16). Beware Pharming and Other New Hacker Scams. New Jersey Law Journal.

Scarpa, A., Haden, S. C., & Hurley, J. (2006). Community Violence Victimization and Symptoms of Posttraumatic Stress Disorder. *Journal of Interpersonal Violence, 21,* 446–469. doi:10.1177/0886260505285726

Schäfer, A. (2006). Resolving Deadlock: Why International Organisations Introduce Soft Law. *European Law Journal, 12,* 194–208. doi:10.1111/j.1468-0386.2006.00315.x

Schmitter, P. (1985). Neo-Corporatism and the State. In Grant, W. (Ed.), *The Political Economy of Corporatism.* New York: St. Martin.

Schmucker, M., & Lösel, F. (2008). Does sexual offender treatment work? A systematic review of outcome evaluations. *Psicothema, 20,* 10–19.

Schneider, J. P. (2000). Effects of Cybersex Addiction on the Family: Results of a Survey. In Cooper, A. (Ed.), *Cybersex: The Dark Side of the Force.* New York: Brunner/Mazel.

Schneier, B. (2003, November/December)... *IEEE Security and Privacy, 1,* 6.

Scola, N. (2007). Avatar Politics: The social applications of Second Life. *IPDI eNews.* Retrieved from http://www.ipdi.org/UploadedFiles/Avatar%20Politics.pdf

Scott, S. (2001). *The Politics and Experience of Ritual Abuse. Beyond Disbelief.* Buckingham: Open University Press.

Scully & Marolla. (1993). "Riding the bull at Gilley's": Convicted rapists describe the rewards of rape. (pp. 26-46). In P. Bart & E.G. Moran's (eds) *Violence against women: The bloody footprints.* Thousand Oaks, California: Sage.

Sears, S., & Kraus, S. (2009). I think therefore I am: cognitive distortions and coping style as mediators for the effects of mindfulness meditation on anxiety, positive and negative affect, and hope. *Journal of Clinical Psychology, 65,* 561–573..doi:10.1002/jclp.20543

Senden, L. (2004). *Soft Law in European Community Law.* Portland, OR: Hart Publishing.

Sentencing Guidelines Council. (2007). *Sexual Offences Act 2003: Definitive Guideline.* April 2007. Retrieved 5ᵗʰ July 2010 from http://www.sentencing-guidelines.gov.uk/docs/0000_SexualOffencesAct1.pdf

Seto, M., Maric, A., & Barbaree, H. (2001). The role of pornography in the etiology of sexual aggression. *Aggression and Violent Behavior, 6,* 35–53. doi:10.1016/S1359-1789(99)00007-5

Seto, M. C., Cantor, J. M., & Blanchard, R. (2006). Child pornography offenses are a valid diagnostic indicator of pedophilia. *Journal of Abnormal Psychology, 115,* 610–615. doi:10.1037/0021-843X.115.3.610

Seto, M. C., & Eke, A. W. (2005). The criminal histories and later offending of child pornography offenders. *Sexual Abuse, 17,* 201–210. doi:10.1177/107906320501700209

Seton-Watson, H. (1977). *Nations and States: An Enquiry Into the Origins of Nations and the Politics of Nationalism.* London: Methuen.

Shariff, S. (2005). Cyber-dilemmas in the new millennium: School obligations to provide student safety in a virtual school environment. *McGill Journal of Education, 40*(3).

Shariff, S., & Gouin, R. (2005). *Cyber-Dilemmas: Gendered Hierarchies, Free Expression and Cyber-Safety In Schools.* Paper presented at the Oxford Internet Institute (OII), Oxford University Conference on September 8, 2005. Retrieved November 4 2010 from http://www.oii.ox.ac.uk/microsites/ cybersafety/extensions/pdfs/papers/shaheen_shariff.pdf

Sharp, T., Shreve-Neiger, A., Fremouw, W., Kane, J., & Hutton, S. (2004). Exploring the psychological and somatic impact of identity theft. *Journal of Forensic Sciences*, *49*, 131–136.

Sheldon, K., & Howitt, D. (2007). *Sex Offenders and the Internet*. Chichester, England: Wiley.

Sheridan, L. P., & Grant, T. (2007). Is cyberstalking different? *Psychology, Crime & Law*, *13*, 627–640. doi:10.1080/10683160701340528

Sheridan, L., & Davies, G. (2004). Stalking. In Adler, J. R. (Ed.), *Forensic Psychology: Concepts, debates and practice* (pp. 197–215). Cullompton, England: Willan Publishing.

Shernoff, D. J., Csikszentmihalyi, M., Schneider, B., & Shernoff, E. S. (2003). Student engagement in high school classrooms from the perspective of Flow Theory. *School Psychology Quarterly*, *18*, 158–176. doi:10.1521/scpq.18.2.158.21860

Shirky, C. (2009). *Here Comes Everybody*. London: Penguin.

Siegfried, K. C., Lovely, R. W., & Rogers, M. K. (2008). Self-Reported Online Child Pornography Behaviour: A Psychological Analysis. *International Journal of Cyber Criminology*, *2*, 286–297.

Silbert, M. (1989). The Effects on Juveniles of Being Used for Pornography and Prostitution. In Zillmann, D., & Bryant, J. (Eds.), *Pornography: Research Advances & Policy Considerations*. Hillsdale, New Jersey: Lawrence Erlbaum.

Silke, A. (1998). Cheshire-cat logic: The recurring theme of terrorist abnormality in psychological research. *Psychology, Crime & Law*, *4*, 51–69. doi:10.1080/10683169808401747

Silke, A. (2008). Research on Terrorism: A Review of the Impact of 9/11 and the Global War on Terrorism. *Terrorism Informatics*, *18*, 27–50. doi:10.1007/978-0-387-71613-8_2

Silke, A. (2003). Becoming a terrorist. In Silke, A. (Ed.), *Terrorists, Victims and Society: psychological perspectives on terrorism and its consequences*. John Wiley & Sons.

Simon, L. (2000). An Examination of the Assumptions of Specialization, Mental Disorder, and Dangerousness in Sex Offenders. *Behavioral Sciences & the Law*, *18*, 275–308. doi:10.1002/1099-0798(200003/06)18:2/3<275::AID-BSL393>3.0.CO;2-G

Sindico, F. (2006). Soft Law and the Elusive Quest for Sustainable Global Governance. *Leiden Journal of International Law*, *19*, 829–846. doi:10.1017/S0922156506003608

Sipress, A. (2007). *Does Virtual Reality Need a Sheriff?* Retrieved from http://www.washingtonpost.com/wp-dyn/content/article/2007/06/01/AR2007060102671.html

Sky News. (October 31, 2007). *Paedophiles target Virtual World*. Retrieved 6th July 2010 from http://news.sky.com/skynews/Home/Sky-News-Archive/Article/20080641290719

Slaughter, A. (2004). *A New World Order*. Princeton, NJ: Princeton University Press.

Smallbone, S., & Wortley, R. (2000). *Child Sexual Abuse in Queensland: Offender Characteristics and Modus Operandi*. Brisbane: Queensland Crime Commission.

Smith, F., & Bace, R. (2003). *A guide to forensic testimony: The art and practice of presenting testimony as an expert technical witness*. Boston, MA: Addison Wesley.

Smith, C. (2005). Gender and crime. In Hale, C., Hayward, K., Wahidin, A., & Wincup, E. (Eds.), *Criminology* (pp. 345–365). Oxford: Oxford University Press.

Smith, R. G. (2007). Biometric solutions to identity-related cybercrime. In Jewkes, Y. (Ed.), *Crime Online* (pp. 44–59). Cullompton, England: Willan Publishing.

Smith, R. G. (2010). Identity theft and fraud. In Jewkes, Y., & Yar, M. (Eds.), *Handbook of Internet Crime* (pp. 173–301). Cullompton, England: Willan Publishing.

Smith, P., Mahdavi, J., Carvalho, M., & Tippet, N. (2006, July). *An investigation into cyberbullying, its forms, awareness and impact, and the relationship between age and gender in cyberbullying*. Retrieved November 4 2010 from http://www.plymouthcurriculum.swgfl.org.uk/resources/ict/cyberbullying/Cyberbullying.pdf

Smith, R. G. (2004). Cyber Crime Sentencing. The Effectiveness of Criminal Justice Responses. *Crime in Australia: International Connections.* Australian Institute of Criminology International Conference, Hilton on the Park, Melbourne, Australia. 29-30 November 2004.

Snook, B., Zito, M., Bennell, C., & Taylor, P. J. (2005). On the complexity and accuracy of geographic profiling strategies. *Journal of Quantitative Criminology, 21*(1).. doi:10.1007/s10940-004-1785-4

Socarides, C. W. (2004). *The mind of the paedophile: psychoanalytic perspectives.* London: H. Karnac Ltd.

Sommer, P. (1997). Computer forensics: An introduction. Retrieved June 3, 2003, from http://www.virtualcity.co.uk/ vcaforensics.htm

Spinello, R. (2000). Information Integrity. In Langford, D. (Ed.), *Internet Ethics* (pp. 158–180). London: MacMillan Press.

Spitzberg, B., & Hoobler, G. (2002). Cyberstalking and the technologies of interpersonal terrorism. *New Media & Society, 4,* 71–92. doi:10.1177/14614440222226271

Spitzner, L. (2003). *Honeypots: Tracking Hackers.* Boston, MA: Addison-Wesley Inc.

Steel, C. M. S. (2009). Child pornography in peer-to-peer networks. *Child Abuse & Neglect, 33,* 560–568. doi:10.1016/j.chiabu.2008.12.011

Stephens, P. (2008). IPR and Technological Protection Measures. In Bryant, R. (Ed.), *Investigating Digital Crime* (pp. 121–131). Chichester, England: Wiley.

Sterba, J. P. (Ed.). (2003). *Terrorism and International Justice.* New York, Oxford: Oxford University Press.

Sterling, B. (1992). *The Hacker Crackdown: Law and Disorder on the Electronic Frontier.* New York: Penguin.

Stohl, M. (2006). Cyber terrorism: a clear and present danger, the sum of all fears, breaking point or patriot games? *Crime, Law, and Social Change, 46,* 223–238.. doi:10.1007/s10611-007-9061-9

Strom, P. S., & Strom, R. D. (2005). When teens turn cyberbullies. *Education Digest, 71,* 35–41.

Sue, D., Sue, D. W., & Sue, S. (2005). *Essentials of Understanding Abnormal Behaviour.* Boston: Houghton Mifflin.

Sunstein, C. R. (2007). *Republic.com 2.0.* Princeton, NJ: Princeton University Press.

Svenson, S., & Maule, A. (1993). *Time pressure and stress in human judgement and decision making.* New York: Plenum.

Swire, P. (2005). Elephants and mice revisited: law and choice of law on the Internet. *University of Pennsylvania Law Review, 153,* 1975–2001. doi:10.2307/4150654

Sykes, G., & Matza, D. (1957). Techniques of neutralization; a theory of delinquency. *American Sociological Review, 22,* 664–670. doi:10.2307/2089195

Symantec (2010). Symantec Intelligence Quarterly: July-September 2010. Retrieved November 20, 2010 from http://www.symantec.com/content/en/us/ enterprise/ white_papers/b-symc_intelligence_qtrly_july_to_sept_ WP_21157366.en-us.pdf

Symantec (2010, April). *Symantec Global Internet Security Threat Report (Volume XV).* Retrieved 7th October 2010 from http://eval.symantec.com/mktginfo/enterprise /white_papers/b-whitepaper_internet_security_threat_re-port_xv_04-2010.en-us.pdf

Symantec (n.d.) *What is Cybercrime?* Retrieved from http://www.symantec.com/norton/ cybercrime/definition.jsp

Szreter, S. (2001). A New Political Economy: The Importance of Social Capital. In Giddens, A. (Ed.), *The Global Third Way Debate* (pp. 290–299). Oxford: Blackwell/ Polity Press.

Talbert, F. S., Braswell, L. C., Albrecht, I. W., Hyer, L. A., & Boudewyns, P. A. (1993). NEO-PI profiles in PTSD as a function of trauma level. *Journal of Clinical Psychology, 49,* 663–669. doi:10.1002/1097-4679(199309)49:5<663::AID-JCLP2270490508>3.0.CO;2-A

Tam, L., Glassman, M., & Vandenwauver, M. (2009). The psychology of password management: a tradeoff between security and convenience. *Behaviour & Information Technology, 29,* 233–244..doi:10.1080/01449290903121386

Tate, T. (1990). *Child Pornography: An Investigation.* London: Methuen.

Tavani, H. T. (2007). *Ethics and Technology: Ethical Issues in an Age of Information and Communication Technology* (2nd ed.). Hoboken, NJ: John Wiley & Sons.

Taylor, P. (1999). *Hackers*. London: Routledge. doi:10.4324/9780203201503

Taylor, M., Holland, G., & Quayle, E. (2001). Typology of paedophile picture collections. *The Police Journal, 74*, 97–107.

Taylor, M., & Quayle, E. (2003). *Child Pornography: An Internet Crime*. Hove: Brunner-Routledge.

Taylor, M., Quayle, E., & Holland, G. (2001). Child pornography, the Internet and offending, ISUMA. *The Canadian Journal of Policy Research, 2*, 94–100.

Taylor, M., & Quayle, E. (1994). *Terrorist Lives*. London: Brassey's.

Taylor, P. (2001). Hacktivism: in search of lost ethics? In Wall, D. S. (Ed.), *Crime and the Internet* (pp. 59–73). London: Routledge.

Taylor, P. A. (2003). Maestros or misogynists? Gender and the social construction of hacking (pp. 126-146). In Yvonne Jewkes (2003) *Dot.cons: Crime, deviance and identity on the Internet*. Cullompton, Devon (UK): Willan Publishing.

Thakker, J., Ward, T., & Navathe, S. (2007). The Cognitive Distortions and Implicit Theories of Child Sexual Abusers. In Gannon, T. A., Ward, T., Beech, A. R., & Fisher, D. (Eds.), *Aggressive Offenders' Cognition: Theory, Research and Practice* (pp. 11–29). Chichester, West Sussex: John Wiley & Sons Ltd.doi:10.1002/9780470746295.ch1

Thompson, R. (2005). Why spyware poses multiple threats to society. *Communications of the ACM, 48*, 41–43. doi:10.1145/1076211.1076237

Thompson, C. (2004, February 8). The Virus Underground. *The New York Times Magazine, pp 30-33, 72, 79-81.*

Thornton, D. (2002). Constructing and testing a framework for dynamic risk assessment. *Sexual Abuse, 14*, 139–154. doi:10.1177/107906320201400205

Torres, A. N., Boccaccini, M. T., & Miller, H. A. (2006). Perceptions of the validity and utility of criminal profiling among forensic psychologists and psychiatrists. *Professional Psychology, Research and Practice, 37*, 51–58. doi:10.1037/0735-7028.37.1.51

Toth, K., & King, B. H. (2008). Asperger's Syndrome: Diagnosis and Treatment. *The American Journal of Psychiatry, 165*, 958–963. doi:10.1176/appi.ajp.2008.08020272

Trevethan, S. D., & Walker, L. J. (1989). Hypothetical versus real-life moral reasoning among psychopathic and delinquent youth. *Development and Psychopathology, 1*, 91–103. doi:10.1017/S0954579400000286

Truta, F. (2008, January 18). Russia - Gamer Kills Gamer over Gamer Killing Gamer... Er, In-Game! *Softpedia*. Retrieved from http://news.softpedia.com/news/Russia-Gamer-Kills-Gamer-over-Gamer-Killing-Gamer-Er-In-Game-76619.shtml

Tversky, A., & Kahneman, D. (1974). Judgement under uncertainty: Heuristics and biases. *Science, 211*, 453–458. doi:10.1126/science.7455683

Twyman, K., Saylor, C., Taylor, L. A., & Comeaux, C. (2009). Comparing children and adolescents engaged in cyberbullying to matched peers. *Cyberpsychology & Behavior, 12*, 1–5.

Tynes, B. M. (2007). Internet Safety Gone Wild? Sacrificing the Educational and Psychosocial benefits of online social environments. *Journal of Adolescent Research, 22*, 575–584. doi:10.1177/0743558407303979

U.S. Department of Health and Human Services. (2007). *Child Maltreatment. Administration for Children and Families*. Retrieved from http://www.acf.hhs.gov/programs/cb/pubs/cm07/cm07.pdf

U.S. Department of Homeland Security. (2003). *National Strategy to Secure Cyberspace*. Retrieved from http://www.dhs.gov/files/publications /editorial_0329.shtm

UN News Centre. (2010, February 15). *Robust demand for mobile phone services will continue, UN agency predicts*. Retrieved from http://www.un.org/ apps/news/story.asp?NewsID =33770&Cr=Telecom&Cr1

United Press International. (2008, April 9). *Survey: Cyber-bullying affects US teens.* Retrieved November 3, 2010 from http://www.upi.com/NewsTrack/Health/ 2008/04/09/survey_cyberbullying_affects_us_teens/3823/

Veerasamy, N. (2010). Motivation for cyberterrorism. 9th Annual Information Security South Africa (ISSA) - Towards New Security Paradigms. Sandton Convention Centre, 2 - 4 August 2010, pp 6

Verone (n.d.). Piracy Guide. *EVElopedia.* Retrieved from http://wiki.eveonline.com/en/wiki/Piracy_guide

Victoroff, J. (2005). The Mind of the Terrorist: A Review and Critique of Psychological Approaches. *The Journal of Conflict Resolution, 49,* 3–42. doi:10.1177/0022002704272040

Vinyagamoorthy, V., Brogni, A., Gillies, M., Slater, M., & Steed, A. (2004). An Investigation of Presence Response across Variations in Visual Realism. *Proceedings of Presence 2004: The 7th Annual International Workshop on Presence.*

Voiskounsky, A. E., & Smyslova, O. V. (2003). Flow-based model of computer hacker's motivation. *CyberPsychology and Behaviour, 6,* 171–180. doi:10.1089/109493103321640365

Von Hirsch, A., Bottoms, A. E., Burney, E., & Wickstrom, P. O. (1999). *Criminal deterrence and sentence severity.* Oxford: Hart.

Vrij, A. (2006). Detecting Deception. In Kebbell, M. R., & Davies, G. M. (Eds.), *Practical Psychology for Forensic Investigations and Prosecutions* (pp. 89–102). Chichester, West Sussex: John Wiley & Sons, Ltd.

Walker, C. (2001). The Criminal Courts Online. In Wall, D. S. (Ed.), *Crime and the Internet* (pp. 195–214). London: Routledge.

Walklate, S. (2006). *Imagining the Victim of Crime.* Open University Press. 2006.

Wall, D. S. (2007). *Cybercrime: The Transformation of Crime in the Information Age.* Cambridge, England: Polity Press.

Wall, D., & Williams, M. (2007). Policing diversity in the digital age: maintaining order in virtual communities. *Criminology & Criminal Justice, 7,* 391–415. doi:10.1177/1748895807082064

Wall, D. S., & Yar, M. (2010). Intellectual property crime and the Internet: cyber-piracy and 'stealing' information intangibles. In Jewkes, Y., & Yar, M. (Eds.), *Handbook of Internet Crime* (pp. 255–272). Cullompton, England: Willan Publishing.

Wang, W., Yuan, Y., & Archer, N. (2006). A contextual framework for combating identity theft. *IEEE Security & Privacy, 4,* 30–38. doi:10.1109/MSP.2006.31

Ward, T., & Casey, A. (2009). Extending the mind into the world: A new theory of cognitive distortions in sex offenders. *Aggression and Violent Behavior, 15,* 49–58. doi:10.1016/j.avb.2009.08.002

Ward, T., & Siegert, R. J. (2002). Toward a comprehensive theory of child sexual abuse: A theory knitting perspective. *Psychology, Crime & Law, 8,* 319–351. doi:10.1080/10683160208401823

Ward, T. (2001). Hall and Hirschman's quadripartite model of child sexual abuse: a critique. *Psychology, Crime & Law, 7,* 363–374.

Ward, T., Polaschek, D., & Beech, A. R. (2006). *Theories of Sexual Offending.* Chichester, England: Wiley.

Ward, T., & Siegert, R. (2002). Toward a comprehensive theory of child sexual abuse: a theory of knitting perspective. *Psychology, Crime & Law, 8,* 319–351. doi:10.1080/10683160208401823

Warren, G., Schertler, E., & Bull, P. (2009). Detecting Deception from Emotional and Unemotional Cues. *Journal of Nonverbal Behavior, 33,* 59–69. doi:10.1007/s10919-008-0057-7

Warren, M., & Leitch, S. (2009). Hacker Taggers: A new type of hackers. *Information Systems Frontiers.* doi:. doi:10.1007/s10796-009-9203-y

Webb, L., Craissati, J., & Keen, S. (2007). Characteristics of Internet Child Pornography Offenders: A Comparison with Child Molesters. *Sexual Abuse, 19,* 449–465.

Weimann, G. (2004). WWW.terror.net: *How Modern Terrorism Uses the Internet* (Washington DC: United States Institute of Peace). http://www.usip.org/pubs/specialreports/ sr116.pdf, 5-11.

Wellard, S.S. (2001). Cause and Effect. *Community Care,* March 15–21, pp. 26–27.

Welsh, B., & Farrington, D. (2006). *Preventing Crime: What works for children, offenders, victims and places.* Dordrecht, The Netherlands: Springer.

Welsh, B. C., & Farrington, D. P. (2004). Effective programmes to prevent delinquency. In Adler, J. (Ed.), *Forensic Psychology: Concepts, debates and practice. Cullompton, Devon: Willan Publishing* (pp. 245–265).

Wemmers, J. A., & Cyr, K. (2006). Victims' perspectives on restorative justice: how much involvement are victims looking for? *International Review of Victimology, 11,* 259–274.

West, D. J., & Farrington, D. P. (1977). *The delinquent way of life.* London: Heinemann.

West, D. (1996) Sexual Molesters. In: N. Walker *Dangerous People,* London: Blackstone Press.

Whitney, L. (2010, February 16). *Cell phone subscriptions to hit 5 billion globally.* Retrieved from http://reviews.cnet.com/8301-13970_7-10454065-78.html

Whitney, L. (2010, March 26). Symantec finds China top source of malware. *CNET Security.* Retrieved November 20, 2010 from http://news.cnet.com/8301-1009_3-20001234-83.html

Whitson, J., & Doyle, A. (2008). Second Life and governing deviance in virtual worlds. In Leman-Langlois, S. (Ed.), *Technocrime: Technology, crime and social control. Cullompton, Devon: Willan* (pp. 88–111).

Whittaker, D. J. (2004). *Terrorists and Terrorism in the Contemporary World.* London: Routledge.

Wiederhold, B. K., & Wiederhold, M. D. (2005). *Virtual Reality Therapy for Anxiety Disorders: Advances in Evaluation and Treatment.* American Psychological Association. doi:10.1037/10858-000

Willard, N. E. (2007). *Cyberbullying and Cyberthreats: Responding to the challenge of online social aggression, threats, and distress.* Research Press.

Williams, M. (2006). *Virtually Criminal: Crime, deviance and regulation online.* Oxon, England: Routledge.

Wilson, C. (2005). *Computer Attack and Cyberterrorism: Vulnerabilities and Policy Issues for Congress.* Washington DC: Congressional Research Service: The Library of Congress. Retrieved 19th September 2010 from http://www.dtic.mil/cgi-bin/GetTRDoc?AD=ADA444799&Location=U2&doc=GetTRDoc.pdf

Wilson, C. (2007). *Botnets, Cybercrime and Cyberterrorism: Vulnerabilities and Policy Issues for Congress.* Washington DC: Congressional Research Service: The Library of Congress. Retrieved 23rd September 2010 from http://www.dtic.mil/cgi-bin/GetTRDoc?AD=ADA474929&Location=U2&doc=GetTRDoc.pdf

Winterdyk, J., & Thompson, N. (2008). Student and non-student perceptions and awareness of identity theft. *Canadian Journal of Criminology and Criminal Justice, 50,* 153–186. doi:10.3138/cjccj.50.2.153

Wolak, J., Finkelhor, D., & Mitchell, K. J. (2005). *Child-Pornography Possessors Arrested in Internet-Related Crimes: Findings From the National Juvenile Online Victimization Study.* Alexandria: National Center for Missing & Exploited Children.

Wolak, J., Finkelhor, D., & Mitchell, K. (2008). Is talking online to unknown people always risky? Distinguishing online interaction styles in a national sample of youth internet users. *Cyberpsychology & Behavior, 11,* 340–343.. doi:10.1089/cpb.2007.0044

Wolak, J., Finkelhor, D., Mitchell, K., & Ybarra, M. (2008). Online "Predators" and Their Victims: Myths, Realities, and Implications for Prevention and Treatment. *The American Psychologist, 63,* 111–128. doi:10.1037/0003-066X.63.2.111

Wolak, J., Mitchell, K. J., & Finkelhor, D. (2007). Does online harassment constitute bullying? An exploration of online harassment by known peers and online-only contacts. *The Journal of Adolescent Health, 41,* S51–S58. doi:10.1016/j.jadohealth.2007.08.019

Wolak, J., Finkelhor, D., & Mitchell, K. (2004). Internet-initiated sex crimes against minors: Implications for prevention based on findings from a national study. *Journal of Adolescent Health, 35,* 424.e11–424.e20.

Wolak, J., Finkelhor, D., & Mitchell, K. (2009). Law Enforcement Responses to Online Child Sexual Exploitation Crimes: The *National Juvenile Online Victimization Study,* 2000 & 2006. Retrieved from http://www.unh.edu/ccrc/pdf/LE_Bulletin_final_Dec_09.pdf

Wolak, J., Mitchell, K., & Finkelhor, D. (2006). Online victimization of youth: Five years later. *National Center for Missing & Exploited Children Bulletin -* #07-06-025. Alexandria, VA. Retrieved from http://www.unh.edu/ccrc/pdf/CV138.pdf

Wolfe, S. E., Higgins, G. E., & Marcum, C. D. (2008). Deterrence and Digital Piracy: A Preliminary Examination of the Role of Viruses. *Social Science Computer Review, 26,* 317–333. doi:10.1177/0894439307309465

Woman faces jail for hacking her virtual husband to death (2008, October 10). *The Irish Times.* Retrieved from http://www.irishtimes.com/newspaper/ front-page/2008/1025/1224838828960.html

Woo, J. J., Kim, Y., & Dominick, J. (2004). Hackers: Militants or merry pranksters? A content analysis of defaced web pages. *Media Psychology, 6,* 63–82. doi:10.1207/s1532785xmep0601_3

Woo, H. J. *(2003). The hacker mentality: Exploring the relationship between psychological variables and hacking activities.* Dissertation Abstracts International, 64, 2A, *325.*

Working Group on Internet Governance. (2005) *Report of the Working Group on Internet Governance.* Retrieved from http://www.wgig.org/docs/WGIGREPORT.doc

Working to Halt Online Abuse. (WHOA, 2010b). *2009Cyberstalking Statistics.* Retrieved November 5, 2010 from http://www.haltabuse.org/resources/stats/2009Statistics.pdf

Working to Halt Online Abuse. (WHOA, 2010a). *Online Harassment/Cyberstalking Statistics.* Retrieved November 5, 2010 from http://www.haltabuse.org/resources/stats /index.shtml

World Summit on the Information Society. (2010). *Home.* Retrieved from http://www.itu.int/wsis/index.html

Wortley, R., & Smallbone, S. (2006). *Child pornography on the internet.* Retrieved June 23 2010, from http://www.cops.usdoj.gov/files/ric/ Publications/e04062000.pdf

Wright, S. (2006). Government-run Online Discussion Forums: Moderation, Censorship and the Shadow of Control. *British Journal of Politics and International Relations, 8,* 550–568. doi:10.1111/j.1467-856X.2006.00247.x

Wrightsman, L. S. (2001). *Forensic Psychology.* Stanford, CT: Wadsworth.

Wykes, M. (2007). Constructing crime: stalking, celebrity, 'cyber' and media. In Jewkes, Y. (Ed.), *Crime Online* (pp. 128–143). Cullompton, England: Willan Publishing.

Wykes, M., & Harcus, D. (2010). Cyber-terror: construction, criminalization and control. In Jewkes, Y., & Yar, M. (Eds.), *Handbook of Internet Crime* (pp. 214–229). Cullompton, England: Willan.

Wyld, D. C. (2007). *The Blogging Revolution: Government in the Age of Web 2.0.* Washington: IBM Center for The Business of Government. Retrieved from http://www.businessofgovernment.org/pdfs/WyldReportBlog.pdf

Wyld, D. C. (2008). *Government in 3D: How Public Leaders Can Draw on Virtual Worlds.* Washington: IBM Center for The Business of Government. Retrieved from http://www.businessofgovernment.org/pdfs/Wyld3dReport.pdf

Yar, M. (2006). *Cybercrime and Society.* London: Sage Publications Ltd.

Yar, M. (2007). Teenage kicks or virtual villainy? Internet piracy, moral entrepreneurship and the social construction of a crime problem. In Jewkes, Y. (Ed.), *Crime Online* (pp. 95–108). Cullompton, England: Willan Publishing.

Yar, M. (2010). Public perceptions and public opinion about internet crime. In Jewkes, Y., & Yar, M. (Eds.), *Handbook of Internet Crime* (pp. 104–119). Cullompton, England: Willan Publishing.

Yates, H. (2005). *A review of evidence-based practice in the assessment and treatment of sex offenders: Pennsylvania Department of Corrections: Office of Planning.* Research, Statistics and Grants.

Ybarra, M. L., Mitchell, K. J., Finkelhor, D., & Wolak, J. (2007). Internet Prevention Messages: Targeting the Right Online Behaviours. *Archives of Pediatrics & Adolescent Medicine*, *161*, 138–145. doi:10.1001/archpedi.161.2.138

Ybarra, M. L. (2004). Linkages between depressive symptomatology and internet harassment among young regular internet users. *Cyberpsychology & Behavior*, *7*, 247–257. doi:10.1089/109493104323024500

Ybarra, M. L., & Mitchell, K. J. (2004). Online aggressor/targets, aggressors, and targets: A comparison of associated youth characteristics. *Journal of Child Psychology and Psychiatry, and Allied Disciplines*, *45*(7), 1308–1316. doi:10.1111/j.1469-7610.2004.00328.x

Young, R., Zhang, L., & Prybutok, V. R. (2007). Hacking into the Minds of Hackers. *Information Systems Management*, *24*, 281–287. doi:10.1080/10580530701585823

Zentner, A. (2004). *Measuring the effect of online music piracy on music sales.* Retrieved from http://economics.uchicago.edu/download/ musicindustryoct12.pdf

Zuboff, S. (1988). *In the age of the smart machine: The future of work and power*. New York: Basic Books.

Zuckerman, M. (2002). Genetics of Sensation seeking. In Benjamin, J., Ebstein, R. P., & Belmaker, R. (Eds.), *Molecular Genetics and the Human Personality* (pp. 193–210). Washington, DC: American Psychiatric Publishing.

Zuckoff, M. (2006). The Perfect Mark: How a Massachusetts psychotherapist fell for a Nigerian e-mail scam. *The New Yorker, May 15,* pp. 36-42.

About the Authors

Gráinne Kirwan is a lecturer in psychology in the Institute of Art, Design and Technology (IADT), Ireland. She led the development of the MSc in Cyberpsychology programme in IADT, and co-ordinated the programme during its initial years. She has been teaching in higher education for twelve years and her primary areas of research are forensic psychology, virtual reality and cyberpsychology. Her doctoral research examined the motives and psychological characteristics of hackers. Her current research examines the use of virtual reality as an aid to police investigations and public attitudes towards cybercriminals and their victims. She has been quoted by several major publications regarding her expertise in the field of cyberpsychology, and she has also been interviewed by both regional and national radio and television stations. She regularly presents work at international psychological conferences and reviews articles for 'Cyberpsychology, Behaviour and Social Networking' and 'Computers in Human Behaviour'.

Andrew Power is the Head of School of Creative Technologies at the Institute of Art, Design and Technology, Ireland. Prior to his academic career Andrew worked for sixteen years in industry, initially working for multinationals such as Digital Equipment Corporation and Intel, later for the Irish eLearning company SmartForce. Andrew also serves on the board of directors of a number of not-for-profit organizations in Ireland. Andrew has written in the fields of eGovernance, cyberlaw, online democracy, and is currently researching social networking and active citizenship at the Institute of Governance, Queens University Belfast.

Index